JOHN C.
CALHOUN

JOHN C.
CALHOUN

★ ★ ★ ★ ★ ★ ★ ★

A Biography

IRVING H. BARTLETT

W·W·NORTON & COMPANY·*NEW YORK·LONDON*

FRONTISPIECE PHOTOGRAPH: *Portrait of John C. Calhoun, 1845 by George P. A. Healy.* © *Greenville County Museum of Art*

FIRST EDITION

The text of this book is composed in Avanta with the display set in Trump Medieval and Caslon #471. Composition and manufacturing by The Haddon Craftsmen. Book design by Marjorie J. Flock.

Library of Congress Cataloging-in-Publication Data
Bartlett, Irving H.
    Calhoun: a biography / Irving H. Bartlett.
        p.   cm.
    Includes index.
        1. Calhoun, John C. (John Caldwell), 1782–1850.   2. Legislators—
—United States—Biography.   3. United States. Congress. Senate—
—Biography.   4. United States—Politics and government—1815–1861.
5. South Carolina—Politics and government—1775–1865.   I. Title.
E340.C15B27   1993
973.5′092—dc20
    [B]   92-46242
                            ISBN 0-393-03476-3

W.W. Norton & Company, Inc., 500 Fifth Avenue, New York, N.Y. 10110
    W.W. Norton & Company Ltd., 10 Coptic Street, London WC1A1PU

                        1 2 3 4 5 6 7 8 9 0

*Dedicated to librarians, archivists,
and scholarly editors everywhere
who make it possible
for books like this to be written*

Contents

Illustrations

Acknowledgments

THIS BOOK was begun several years ago at the suggestion of my editor, James Mairs, who, among his many other virtues, has shown enormous patience in waiting for the manuscript. The study on Calhoun is part of a continuing attempt to understand how the political culture of this country has been expressed and shaped by leaders conventionally designated as liberal, conservative, radical, or reactionary. It represents my first serious scholarly excursion into the Old South, and I have profited from the assistance of many people both north and south of Mason and Dixon's line. John Sproat, then chair of history at the University of South Carolina, introduced me to the wealth of Calhoun materials available in Columbia, and Walter Edgar welcomed me to the University's Institute for Southern Studies over a period of several summers. Clyde N. Wilson has been unfailingly generous in sharing his knowledge and insights on Calhoun with me and in providing access to unpublished materials in the archives of the Papers of John C. Calhoun Project. His associates Shirley Bright Cook and Alexander Moore were equally considerate and helpful. Alan Stokes and his entire staff have done their best to help me, as they have countless other scholars, explore the rich holdings of the South Carolinian Library.

Back in Boston I have been assisted by several generations of graduate students, including Mark Primack, Jayne Triber, and Lawrence Houghteling. At an early stage of research my conversations with Kenneth Greenberg, who allowed me to read the manuscript version of his book on the political culture of slavery, played a significant role in shaping the approach I took to Calhoun. My colleague Lou Ferleger directed me to materials which I hope have helped me clarify some of the economic realities underlying the ferocious rhetoric of the tariff controversy. The manuscript for this book was read in part or in whole by Clyde Wilson, John Sproat, my colleagues Lou Ferleger and Martin Quitt, and my wife, Virginia K. Bartlett. Although I may not always have followed their advice, I have benefited from their insight.

J O H N C.
CALHOUN

Prologue

WHILE WAITING for the stage in Columbia, South Carolina, about two years after the nullification crisis, the British geologist and traveler G. W. Featherstonhaugh was instructed by a professor from South Carolina College on the way slavery contributed to republicanism in the United States. Maintaining that slavery was not understood outside the South, his companion argued that in the North almost every young man had to scramble to make his fortune, and this created a "rapacious spirit" incompatible with political virtue and the character of a gentleman. In the South, however, where plantations and slaves descended from fathers to sons, a kind of gentleman had been bred who put honor above profit and was always "jealous of his own and the natural friend of public liberty." It followed, therefore, that "the dignity which had belonged to southern gentlemen from Washington down to the present time" was relatively rare in the North. The professor "adduced Mr. Calhoun, the leader of the Nullifying party, as an eminent instance of the justice of what he said. This gentleman, he remarked, was a planter and a slaveholder, who in private life never had been known to be guilty of a mean action, and in public life never omitted an opportunity of vindicating the Constitution from the attempts of sordid persons to pervert its intentions. For these reasons, he said, Mr. Calhoun, independent of his great intellectual powers, was universally honored in his native state and was justly looked up to as the vigilant guardian of its rights."

While pondering this homage to John C. Calhoun, who had twice been elected Vice President of the United States and now served as Senator from South Carolina, Featherstonhaugh observed his approaching coach, which carried on its roof, chained down with the rest of the baggage, a runaway black man. Upon bidding farewell to his friend from the college and boarding the coach, he found himself joined by a white man in irons, several other poor whites equally disreputable who appeared to be cronies of the prisoner, and a deputy sheriff. Once under way the sheriff handed a bottle around, and it soon came out that the man in custody had been sentenced to hang for killing a slave in a card game dispute and that he had been condemned not for homicide but for breaking the law against gambling with slaves. As the bottle circulated and everyone, except Featherstonhaugh (and the black man staked out on top), including the prisoner, drank his fill, "the deputy and other fellows laughed and joked and told their stories *exactly as if they were his equals.*" Finally the liquor did its job, and the party fell asleep, leaving the gentlemanly Englishman "shut up as I was in a vehicle with such a horrid combination of beings" to reflect on the cultural paradoxes of the Old South.

In reporting his southern travels to readers at home, Featherstonhaugh pointed out that the great cotton estates in the South had been created by "grinding to the earth helpless beings who had no appeal from the cruel greediness of their oppressors." But as a convinced Tory he insisted that slavery was probably working its greatest damage by encouraging the "sovereign people" in the new American democracy to think better of themselves than they had any right. "The white animal," he wrote, no matter how "degraded, dirty and illiterate, will always think himself a superior being where the black one is a slave."

Some months after his traumatic journey from Columbia, Featherstonehaugh saw another side of southern culture when he visited Calhoun at his Fort Hill plantation in the South Carolina backcountry. The two men had met earlier in Georgia, where Calhoun kept a slave gang busy working a gold mine. Frontier conditions prevailed in Georgia, and the talk then had turned on the technical problems of mineral extraction. At Fort Hill, a stately white-pillared mansion which dominated the adjoining landscape much like an English gentleman's country estate, Featherstonhaugh was treated to the kind of southern hospitality which one day was to become the stuff of popular fiction and film. Closely attended by Calhoun's house servants, he was wined and dined in memorable style and afterward even serenaded on the broad piazzas of the Calhoun mansion by the soft strumming of a slave's guitar. Being received at Fort Hill, Featherstonhaugh later recalled, was a little like spending an evening in a gracious Tuscany villa with a host of noble blood.

Fort Hill could hardly bear comparison to any of the great country houses in England, and Calhoun, born of an Irish immigrant Indian fighter, was certainly no English lord, but the English guest could begin to see what the South Carolina professor has been trying to tell him back in Columbia. "Of all the men I have ever known in the United States," he wrote, "Mr. C. is the most remarkable for his genius; his intellect is so active and comprehensive that he is able to grasp the most intricate subjects without an effort. He is also one of the most perfect gentlemen I have ever known." Calhoun's great misfortune, Featherstonhaugh decided, and the reason he would never become President, was not that he defended slavery, but that he refused to play the democratic game in a country where political demagoguery was the only sure road to success. Otherwise he might have been "almost as great a man and certainly a more brilliant one than Washington."[1]

1

Casting the Iron, 1782–1800

WHEN JOHN C. CALHOUN died in 1850, he had become identified with southern sectionalism, and some of his supporters tended to blame his earlier nationalism on the "errors of youth." But James Henry Hammond, soon to replace Calhoun in the Senate, contended that "Mr. Calhoun had no youth to our knowledge. He sprang into the arena like Minerva from the head of Jove, fully grown and clothed in armor: a man every inch himself, and able to contend with any other man."[1]

Hammond was referring somewhat obliquely to the same qualities in Calhoun that inspired Harriet Martineau to label him the "cast-iron man": his gravity, implacable determination, incredible industry, and apparent immunity to the lighter moments in human experience. Daniel Webster spoke to the same point on the floor of the Senate when he said he had never known a man more interested in work and less in recreation.[2]

Hammond was also referring to the fact that as a young man Calhoun seemed to come from nowhere. In Jefferson's inaugural year he was an eighteen-year-old farmer on the South Carolina frontier with almost no formal education. Ten years later he was a Yale graduate, a lawyer, a former state representative in South Carolina, and a Congressman-elect prepared to help James Madison lead the country into the War of 1812.

It is hard to know how much Calhoun was aware of the image he projected and how much he consciously contributed to his own mythology. Although he frequently recalled his political past in congressional speeches and elsewhere, there is little in the printed or manuscript record about his childhood. The closest he ever came to writing an autobiography was in 1843, when he collaborated with political supporters in a seventy-six-page pamphlet written to bolster his chances for a presidential nomination. The pamphlet (hereafter referred to as the autobiography) is more political than a personal biography, but the first half dozen pages provide us with the fullest account Calhoun ever wrote (or authorized) of his early years and suggest the dominant cultural influences that shaped his mind and character in his most formative years.[3]

John Caldwell Calhoun was born near Abbeville in the Appalachian foothills of South Carolina's backcountry on March 18, 1782. Although he was to know fame as a conservative statesman and political thinker, he was really a child of the Revolution. Most of the killing had stopped in the colonies in 1782, but South Carolina had been bloodied far beyond most colonies, and the boy's earliest memories were associated with the war. He learned that his namesake and maternal uncle, John Caldwell, had been murdered by Tories in cold blood and in his own yard, while another uncle had been butchered at Cowpens with thirty saber wounds, and a third "immured for nine months in the dungeons of St. Augustine." Caldwell blood meant patriotic blood. John's mother, "remarkable for intelligence and energy of character and a strong will and high temper," never let him forget that. As a vigorous man of sixty-one Calhoun attributed his strong physical constitution to his mother, but he might also have added his ardent youthful nationalism and an entrenched hostility to anything British.[4]

Calhoun always kept his family life completely separate from his public life. In his autobiography there are no pious reminiscences of reciting the golden rule or learning to read the Bible at his mother's knee, but he could hardly hide the debt he owed to his extraordinary father. Patrick Calhoun was born in County Donegal, Ireland, in 1727 and came to Virginia with his parents as a young boy to settle the rich lands of Augusta County. We know little about the first generation of Calhoun's family except that they were yeoman farmers and part of an extended kinship settlement near what is now Wytheville, Virginia. We also know that John Calhoun maintained a keen interest in his family's history throughout his life, making a special trip to Wytheville at the age of sixty-four "to visit the ancient residence of our family in Reed Creek, a few miles from that place. They made a noble location of several miles up and down the creek including 3,000 acres of fertile low grounds and a large body of rich high lands."[5]

John Calhoun was never one to waste time in fantasy or idle speculation, but one cannot help wondering if on gazing at the site of his
grandfather's cabin, he might not have thought about what could have
happened if the Calhouns had remained in Virginia, where President
making was to become a state tradition, instead of moving to South
Carolina, where defending the minority was to become a way of life.

Calhoun has little to say about his family's move to Long Canes in
South Carolina except that it took place in 1756, when his father,
Patrick, and his grandmother Catherine Calhoun, and his uncles John,
William, and Ezekiel Calhoun, were driven out of southwestern Virginia "after Braddock's defeat," but we know that the Calhouns did not
travel alone. They were part of a steady stream of Scotch-Irish settlers
moving south through the Appalachian foothills. Like most of the settlers, the Calhouns tended to be a clannish lot, sticking close to kin and
neighbors they had known in Virginia, like the Pickenses, Nobles, and
Andersons. Most families traveled light: a small wagon of household
goods, a few farm tools, a pair of horses or oxen, and some livestock and
poultry. To judge from the size of their Virginia holdings, Patrick Calhoun and his brothers may have started out better equipped, may even
have had servants or slaves, but whatever more they carried with them
in material goods was less important than a common culture which
would decisively shape their way of life in the Carolina backcountry.
This was a culture based on faith in family farms and family Bibles, in
the dignity of individuals and the indignity of class distinction, in close-
knit communities, militant morality, and uninhibited free enterprise.
In South Carolina, unlike other parts of the country settled by Scotch-
Irish, it was a culture that would embrace black slavery with alacrity and
great success.[6]

When Patrick Calhoun first moved to the Long Canes region in the
Abbeville district of South Carolina, the wealth and fame of that colony were associated with Charleston and the rich rice, indigo, and
long-staple cotton plantations in the tidewater or low-country counties.
Colonists living there led all other Americans in per capita wealth and
enjoyed an economic growth rate that was perhaps the highest in the
Western world. In 1756 Pat Calhoun may never have heard of Henry
Middleton and his fifty thousand acres and eight hundred slaves, but he
knew that land was fertile, abundant, and cheap in the Carolina back-

country, and he was willing to bet that he and his kin could make a good living there.[7]

There were probably only about seven thousand whites and three hundred slaves in the entire South Carolina backcountry when Calhoun's father put up his first lean-to or cabin. It was spectacular, wild country, "one vast brake of canes" head high or higher, abounding with game of all kinds. The buffalo were probably all gone when John was born, but the last panther was not killed on Long Cane Creek until 1797, and the man who was often accused of an obsession with abstract speculation grew up in a neighborhood where the state still paid a bounty for the pelts of very real panthers, wolves, and wildcats. The boy also learned from his parents about the many times the neighboring Oconees and Cherokees had acted as if there were a bounty on white scalps, about how Isaac Cloud and his two children had been murdered in their beds on a nearby branch of the Little Saluda, and about that fatal day in 1760 when his father and a party of thirteen other settlers, including his grandmother and his father's sister, were overwhelmed in an Indian ambush a few miles from their cabin. John would have heard this story about his murdered grandmother and kidnapped aunt a hundred times and how his father had lived to tell not only that tale but others like it—for example, the time he outdueled an Indian chief in the forest by putting his hat on a stick and drawing the Indian's fire. Surely young John Calhoun would have been taken to that fateful massacre site to read the inscription which his father had carved on a stone.

> Pat[k] Calhoun Esq
> In Memory of Mrs
> Catherine Calhoun
> Aged 76 years who
> With 22 others was
> Here Murdered by
> The Indians. The
>
> First of Feb 1760

That monument and perhaps his father's hat, perforated by four musket balls, were the most important family artifacts when he was growing up.[8]

Indian fighting skills were enough to make a man stand out on the Carolina frontier in the 1750s and 1760s, but Pat Calhoun had a lot more to offer than that. In 1758, after an arduous two-week journey on horseback, he visited Charleston for the first time and was made a deputy surveyor. Returning to Long Canes as the only surveyor in the region for several years, he carried out surveys for hundreds of other settlers and in the process built up his own landholdings to almost twelve hundred acres. By 1764 Patrick Calhoun's leadership role in his part of the colony was so well recognized that the royal governor asked him to aid in the settlement of a company of Huguenot immigrants and assured him that his help in building up the "Populous" of the back-country would "promote the value of all the neighboring lands" by encouraging other immigrants searching for "civil and religious liberty here." Patrick Calhoun laid out the survey for the Huguenot settlement in Hillsboro township and for other towns as well. Only eight years after building his own cabin in the wilderness he had become known as a leader in what was often perceived of as a losing game: the attempt to promote orderly growth in the Carolina backcountry.[9]

Three major obstacles lay in the way of civilizing the country in which the Calhouns had settled. First, there were the Indians, and Patrick Calhoun's ability to cope with the Indian threat resulted in 1764 in his commission as captain of a troop of twenty rangers assigned to patrol the Long Canes settlement, which remained subject to occasional Indian attacks until a few years before John was born. It is noteworthy, however, that although Patrick Calhoun was an Indian fighter, he was not an Indian hater, and a year after his commission he protested vigorously when a rumor spread that he was harassing the Indians by asking to see their papers as they approached white settlements. There is no record of the actual incident or incidents involved, but Patrick was probably reassured to hear from a friend: "I have never heard the Indians accuse you of any ill treatment to them." This historical fragment is of more than passing interest because John Calhoun, who would have naturally absorbed his father's attitude toward Indians, would one day as Secretary of War be in charge of the United States Indian Bureau.[10]

It would not have taken Patrick Calhoun very long after settling in Long Canes to realize that the Indians were not the only savages on the

Carolina frontier. There were no towns, schools, or courts in the back-country in the mid-eighteenth century, and the isolated living encour-aged the development of a rootless, lawless population addicted to idle-ness, fornication, bastardy, robbery, drunkenness, and brawling. An Anglican clergyman who attempted to bring the blessings of the Gos-pel to the backcountry about ten years after the Calhouns had settled there provides us with vivid descriptions of these people who supported themselves mostly from hunting. Reverend Charles Woodmason was struck by the way their cabins swarmed with children but "in many places have naught but a gourd to drink out of, not a plate, knife or spoon, a glass cup or anything," and in summer men and women (par-ticularly the young women) went around practically naked. At a meet-ing in Flatt Creek Woodmason preached to "a vast body" most of which "had never before seen a minister or heard the Lord's Prayer, service or sermon in their days." After staying in place long enough to see about twenty children baptized and four couples married, the min-ister's woodsy congregation "went to Revelling, Drunken singing, Dancing, and Whoring—and most of the company were drunk before I quitted the spot." At another meeting "a Band of rude fellows" let loose "57 Dogs (for I counted them)" during the sermon, and on still another occasion a reveler entered the cabin where Woodmason was staying, stole his clerical gown, "putting it on—and then visiting a women in Bed, and getting to Bed with her, and making her give out the next day that the Parson came to bed with her."[11]

These stories of the censorious preacher confounded by the uproari-ous amorality of high-spirited frontier folk may seem amusing to mod-ern Americans, but Patrick Calhoun and the other serious-minded, ambitious Scotch-Irish farmers who had come down to Carolina from Pennsylvania and Virginia found the slovenliness and lawlessness they discovered on the frontier intolerable. In addition to tales about the rigors of the early frontier and about Indians and revolutionary heroes, John Calhoun grew up hearing stories about how shiftless pioneers sheltered gangs of bandits that roamed the backcountry before he was born, terrorizing peaceful, hardworking citizens—how they had used hot irons on a neighbor named Davis in nearby Pinetree Hill, for exam-ple, to get his money, then burned down his house and left him tied to watch it.[12]

Eventually settlers in the backcountry like Patrick Calhoun routed the bandits with a vigilante violence of their own, but their first reaction was to institutionalize self-discipline among themselves by organizing churches and empowering local justices to keep the peace. Patrick Calhoun was founder of the Presbyterian church in Long Canes, and he and his brothers regularly served as justices of the peace after 1764 with authority to issue warrants, take depositions, and arrest, jail, and fine disorderly persons. They were the local law administrators, and their diligence in monitoring the behavior of their neighbors is suggested by the fact that on January 8, 1772, John Calhoun's uncle William convicted one Charles Boyles "twice in ye same day for swearing one profane oath viz by God."[13]

As a grown man Calhoun became known for his iron self-discipline. As a father he warned his children that life was a struggle against evil and that the great purpose of education was "to learn to control our dispositions; to restrain those that are too strong, and to strengthen those that are too weak." This was the stern credo of the Calhouns passed on through the generations.[14]

A final obstacle in the way of local leaders who sought to bring order to the backcountry was the colonial government, or what passed for government, in Charleston. The most striking political fact about South Carolina in the mid-eighteenth century was that political power rested almost exclusively in the hands of wealthy planters in the vicinity of Charleston while the dynamic growth in the colony was taking place in the backcountry, where there were no towns, no courts or judges, no formal institutions of local political control, and no representation in the legislature. If a man wanted anything from the government, he had to make the long, expensive, and dangerous ride to Charleston to get it and once there suffer the condescension and contempt which most stylish low-country planters and bureaucrats reserved for their rustic western brethren.[15]

By the late 1760s, as more and more of the small farmers filling up the backcountry came to see that their stake in society was threatened by the anarchy endemic to the region, they organized to do for themselves what the government in Charleston would not. The regulator movement, which played an important role in South Carolina history before the Revolution, was a sustained vigilante action that worked not only to apprehend and punish bandits and other criminals but also to enforce the kind of moral discipline that hardworking Scotch-Irish settlers took seriously. Just as Patrick Calhoun and his troop of rangers patrolled the frontier to control the Indian menace, troops of regulators scoured the backcountry, hanging murderers and thieves, whipping vagrants and men who neglected their families, ducking immoral women, and setting idle hands to work in the fields. Backcountry yeomen took the law into their own hands and in so doing finally got the attention of the government in Charleston. Patrick Calhoun had friends among the regulators, and John would have learned from them about their exploits in cleaning up the frontier. His parents probably told him how the regulators in their zeal sometimes aped the savagery of the bandits themselves. As one of the leading men in the backcountry the elder Calhoun sympathized with the regulators but did not join the movement. He had too much to lose by becoming embroiled with that kind of extralegality, but he had lived on the frontier long enough to know that a man sometimes had to take direct action to secure his rights. As his son proudly recalled, the effect of this mode of life "upon a mind naturally strong and inquisitive was to create a certain degree of contempt for the forms of civilized life, and for all that was merely conventional in society. He claimed all the rights which nature and reason seemed to establish, and he acknowledged no obligation which was not supported by the like sanctions."

In remembering his father this way, John Calhoun was describing qualities of mind and personality that he had internalized himself, qualities that typified the ordinary backcountry planter who lived in a simple cabin, worked his one or two hundred acres with his own hands and the help of a large family, attended the small local dissenting church, lived simply, worked hard, and was quick to resent anyone who did not work as hard as he did or who tried to limit his freedom.

When he looked for leadership, the backcountry yeoman tended to look for one of his own, a man who shared his values and understood the way he behaved, someone who stood out not because he was different but because he had accomplished more in the sense that he tilled more acres, perhaps with the help of servants, lived in a house rather than a cabin, and possessed a few books or a feather bed. Patrick Calhoun became known as one of the leading men in the backcountry for his special skills as a surveyor, his courage as an Indian fighter, his success in carving a substantial and productive farm out of the long canes, and his willingness to take on larger responsibilities for the community. Thus, when the regulators began to turn their attention to the need for backcountry representation in the government at Charleston, they naturally turned to him. The colony at that time was divided into parishes, but every parish except Prince William focused solely on coastal interests and denied the vote to backcountry residents. Abbeville was in Prince William Parish. In 1768 Patrick Calhoun signed a petition to the South Carolina General Assembly requesting courts and roads for the backcountry, and in the following year his son recalled "he and his neighbors went down within twenty-three miles of Charleston, armed with rifles, to exercise a right of suffrage which had been disputed: a contest which ended in electing him to the Legislature of the state, in which body he served for thirty years."[16]

When John Calhoun was born, Patrick Calhoun had been heavily involved in the political life of the colony for more than thirteen years. The boy's earliest memories of his father were of a man nearly always in the public eye and always in charge. In church the boy saw Elder Calhoun. Out in the fields he watched and helped the Deputy Surveyor at work. At home he watched the Justice of the Peace, taking depositions, issuing warrants, resolving disputes, the Legislator regularly going off to Charleston to counsel with the high and mighty, and the Patriarch presiding over a family that included John's mother, his three brothers and one sister, and a dozen or more slaves.

Patrick Calhoun liked to refer to his "family black and white." When he died, he owned thirty-one slaves, making him one of the largest slaveholders in the backcountry. Years later his son John found it necessary to rely on theoretical arguments to justify slavery, but these arguments are less important in understanding how he really felt than the fact that he was brought up by a father who was deferred to not only for his illustrious public achievements but also because he owned a substantial number of black slaves. Young John Calhoun played with the slave children and later worked in the fields with them. He accepted their deference to him because it seemed as natural as the deference he was expected to show his father.[17]

Patrick Calhoun was a significant actor in South Carolina politics for more than a quarter century. Serving first for one term in the House, he later represented the backcountry district called Ninety-Six in the First and Second Provincial Congresses and served in the General Assembly from 1777 to 1788. He was elected in 1791 to the State Senate and served there until his death. In addition, he frequently held local office as judge and tax collector, supervised elections, erected a school, and generally supported measures toward the development of the backcountry.[18]

As he rode down the rough road from Abbeville to Charleston, Pat Calhoun would have passed a number of wagons loaded with hemp, tobacco, indigo, or salable farm products like butter. One day in 1771 an observer counted 113 such wagons en route to the city.[19] The men who owned the wagons were on their way to market, hoping to get enough for what they had to manage the purchase of one or more slaves. They were playing their part in the key economic and demographic development in the backcountry: the rise of commercial agriculture and the growing demand for slaves. No single individual had been more important than Calhoun in promoting the development of the region. He had laid out the first plots and defended them from the Indians, and as a legislator he was repeatedly called upon to use his detailed knowledge of western topography to recommend sites for bridges, ferries, and mills.[20] Patrick Calhoun also knew that development in the backcountry went hand in hand with the spread of slavery—not only because slaves made land more valuable but because owning slaves made backcountry planters more respectable in the eyes of low-country planters close to the center of power in the colony. While coastal legislators had been mobilizing against the alleged tyranny of the Stamp Act, backcountry planters had tried in vain to get some attention paid to their own grievances, and they were not about to be stampeded into a dangerous alliance with men who could ignore their petitions for relief in order to debate such measures as a sixty-thousand-dollar appropriation "for an exchange for the merchants and a ballroom for the ladies of Charleston."[21] Thus, when the fighting started in the backcountry, it was both civil war and revolution as patriot and Tory battled each other, especially from 1778 to 1780, when the colony fell under British control. Patrick Calhoun had too many kin at risk in the war to support the Tories, but he seems to have

Patrick Calhoun.

Copy from the Collection of Fort Hill, Department of Historic Houses, Clemson University.
Original in possession of Creighton Lee Calhoun, Jr.

taken a tolerant attitude toward neighbors who identified their problems less with England than with the abuse of power by South Carolinians in Charleston.

Everything that we know about Patrick Calhoun's political convictions and behavior must be pieced together from scattered newspaper reports of legislative debates, one or two manuscript letters, and a few paragraphs written by his son. Although the record is thin, the story is consistent and shows that he was a vigorous representative of the ideology which sustained the Revolution and was to become the ideological foundation for his son's career as a major political thinker and actor. Scores, perhaps hundreds of scholarly articles and monographs have been written about republicanism. It was less a systematic body of thought than a political temperament and consensus about people, power, and politics. A good republican believed that human beings had basic rights to liberty and property that could be secured only through government, but because every person was driven to a large extent by self-interest, the great danger in government was always corruption of power. People too weak and wicked to live peacefully together without government constantly had to guard against being enslaved by the political power civilized life required. This had been tolerably accomplished in English history through the constitution, but republicans constantly admonished one another to beware the attempts of current wielders of power to subvert the constitution for their own purposes.

Republicanism in America followed to some extent the "country ideology" popularized by Whig writers like Viscount Bolingbroke, John Trenchard, and Thomas Gordon in the early eighteenth century, but it was also rooted in the experience of colonists who too often had seen corruption in the appointment of royal governors, councillors, judges, tax collectors, etc., and it was particularly relevant to politically conscious backcountry planters in South Carolina who found it easy to believe that their government in Charleston was little more than a money machine designed and run to keep coastal politicians rich and powerful. Although republicans believed that corrupt and tyrannical governments had no legitimacy, they thought of revolution only as a last desperate resort and shared none of Thomas Paine's glee at the prospect of overthrowing established institutions. People who could not be trusted to sustain legitimate government without constant vigilance could hardly be trusted with revolution. Instead republicans tended to see politics as a moral struggle in which they must constantly strive for a government that was led by talented, virtuous men (it was assumed that this usually meant men of property) committed to the public good. Political success, understood in this sense, would never create utopia, but it would bring men as close to the virtuous republic as they could expect to get in this world.[22]

John Calhoun's father was a model of republican virtue. He had raised himself to a prominent position in the backcountry through talent, industry, and character and was sent to the colonial legislature after having demonstrated solid leadership abilities to his neighbors. Although he may have presented a rustic spectacle sitting next to some of the bewigged and powdered legislators in Charleston, they knew who he was, and he soon became recognized as an authority on land use, land grants, and Indian relations in the West. No political leader in South Carolina had been closer to these matters than he had. "Mr. P. Calhoun gave a clear account of the situation in this country before and after the Indian War," a Charleston newspaper wrote in March 1786. "He mentioned a case where Lt. Governor Bull granted land 20 miles beyond the boundary line, which was afterwards annulled. He thought our territorial right terminated at the Oconees mountains."[23]

Although he was something of a legislative specialist, Patrick Calhoun involved himself in all kinds of legislative matters, and the committees he served on touched most of the problems South Carolina faced in the 1770s and 1780s. As a legislator Patrick studied long-term problems like the future of manufacturers in South Carolina and short-term problems like raising taxes to support the revolutionary government and finding ways to restore property and citizenship to Tories. He served on the Ways and Means Committee and the committee charged with the delicate task of proportioning representation. He studied the possibility of endowing colleges near Charleston and Abbeville, helped revise the city charter of Charleston, and examined the "principles of an Act for regulating marriages."[24]

In his public demeanor Patrick Calhoun seems to have been plain-spoken, spirited, and sometimes humorous. On February 17, 1786, for example, the *Charleston Morning Post and Daily Advertizer* carried the following report of a debate over the proposal to provide a bounty for killing predators and vermin:

Mr. P. Calhoun was of opinion that a reward being given for killing noxious animals might have a good effect by inducing such persons as were employed in fire hunting to turn themselves to killing wild beasts; if this should happen he entertained great hopes because it was always best to let a thief catch a thief; as to what has been urged about a premium being offered for destroying rats, he would rather recommend to give a premium to encouraging the breed of cats.

There is a certain sardonic quality to these remarks, a kind of implicit admission that the shiftless backwoodsmen who destroyed game and timber by hunting with fire at night would never mend their ways. He was to pass on to his son this recognition of human depravity—but not his ability to joke about it.

Republicans believed in fiscal integrity and distrusted speculators. On this score Patrick Calhoun was sound. In the winter of 1786 the state was drained of cash, and Charleston merchants owed twenty thousand dollars in back duties on imported goods. When a move was made in the legislature to force the merchants to pay and thus replenish the state treasury, some representatives sympathized with the merchants, many of whom were British and traded in slaves. This drew an angry response from Calhoun, who accused the merchants of encouraging backcountry planters to invest in slaves far beyond their means, thus sending the money abroad and making it impossible to pay taxes and support the ordinary expenses of government. "Pray whose voice was it," Patrick Calhoun asked, "that called for the negro merchants or importers of dry goods?—nobody. These good natured gentlemen had the goodness to come amongst us of their own choice. We received them in kindness and they in turn exerted their endeavors to carry every shilling out of the country." When he went on to say he "sincerely wished no more negroes might be imported into this or any other state," Calhoun's father was attacking not slavery but the kind of reckless speculation, the boom-and-bust psychology his son was to find so distasteful in Jacksonian America. "What sort of character should we establish in our sister states and in foreign countries," he asked, "if it went abroad that we were unable to pay our state officers? A very bad one undoubtedly, which we might find difficult to get rid of."[25]

Patrick Calhoun wanted officeholders to be paid—but not too much. When the low-country senators balked at reducing the governor's salary to eight hundred pounds, he insisted it was "a handsome salary; at least it was as much as the times could bear; for such murmurings prevailed amongst the back country people on account of our expensive civil list, that if it was not reduced, considerably reduced, the taxes would not be paid." Stung by this threat, low-country lawmakers sought to retaliate by reducing legislators' reimbursement to seven shillings a day. This brought on a clash between Calhoun and Edward Rutledge, the brother and mouthpiece of the illustrious former war governor John Rutledge. After Rutledge ostentatiously announced that he had never taken a shilling as a legislator, Calhoun pointed out that "country gentlemen" were paid not for attendance but for their expenses. Since Charleston members had no expenses, they deserved no compensation, and he "would willingly agree when the legislature met at Columbia to give up any allowance."[26]

John C. Calhoun's renowned conservatism and independent-mindedness seem to have been foreshadowed in his father. When a bill was proposed to change the tax law to include cattle, the elder Calhoun opposed it on the ground that "We had passed three tax bills and the people are becoming so familiarized to them that to introduce innovations might be very disagreeable." He sought more efficient tax collectors, not more laws. On this, as on most issues, Patrick was speaking for the "country people" who were his constituents. He was prepared to defend their interest against anyone—as long as it coincided with his own convictions. In supporting the movement of the state capital from Charleston to Columbia, for example, he followed his constituents' wishes, but he opposed them when he cast what could have been the deciding vote to make Charleston the site of the convention to ratify the Constitution.[27]

John Calhoun was only thirteen when his father died, and it is difficult to know how much he ever learned in detail about his father's political career. He remembered his father's telling him that a good government protected society while preserving maximum liberty for the individual, and he accounted for his father's refusal to support the ratification of the Constitution on this basis. Patrick Calhoun's only recorded observation on the Constitution came during a debate on the floor of the House of Representatives when he "made some observations on the too great latitude in religion." In view of his earlier position when he signed a petition asserting that all Protestant denominations are "equally entitled to religious as well as civil Freedom and Liberties," it is difficult to understand this objection unless it expressed the desire of backcountry planters to keep themselves free of troublesome, dissenting sects that elsewhere had begun to emphasize the sinfulness of slaveholding. Calhoun's fuller objections to the Constitution were probably expressed by his fellow countryman James Lincoln, who attacked the proposed Constitution for giving too much power to the executive, for not having a bill of rights, and for putting power "into the hands of a set of men who live one thousands miles from you." Years later John recalled his father's reaction upon learning that the Constitution gave the power of taxation to the federal government. A delegate returning from the state convention had stopped in Abbeville to pass on the news, and although he had been only "a small boy standing between his father's knees," Calhoun remembered distinctly that his father had said, "That was wrong, we ought never to give others the power to tax us."[28]

John Calhoun had internalized his father's independent spirit and basic political convictions long before he entered public life. His father's principles in opposing the Constitution would be his own as he sought to reshape the Constitution a half century later, but the resemblance does not stop here. In February 1786, when the South Carolina legislature was about to agree to a change in the Articles of Confederation giving the Continental Congress power to regulate commerce with a majority of nine votes, "Mr. Calhoun made a modest declaration of the diffidence with which he stood up to oppose what appeared so heartily concurred in by all parts of the house. He could not, however, agree with permitting so much power to rest with nine states, but would move that eleven be the number necessary for so important a measure. Mr. Calhoun's amendment was then put and lost."[29]

Whether he knew it or not, John was not the first Calhoun to think of the concurrent majority—or to see the idea rejected.

It is much easier to identify the cultural and parental forces that shaped John Calhoun's life in the beginning than it is to reconstruct his boyhood. In his eulogy of Calhoun, James Henry Hammond asked, "How was it that this young man, coming but a few years from the wilderness . . . without knowledge of books, unknown to himself and destitute of powerful friends, should, in so short a time, become a national leader?" Hammond answered the question by emphasizing Calhoun's early years as a child of nature who learned to think on his own. "Having acquired this mighty power . . . he strode onward like a conqueror. . . . His course was a stream of light."[30]

Nineteenth-century Americans liked to believe that their great men were nurtured in the field and forest. More often than not the idea was a fiction, but it helped make Andrew Jackson President, and even Daniel Webster, who found his most loyal constituents among great urban industrialists and merchants, was presented to the voters as a man of the soil. Although Calhoun's youth in the relatively isolated and undeveloped Carolina hinterland gave him a lifelong attachment to rural life, his rapid political advancement was perfectly consistent with the circumstances of his birth.

There were about nine thousand people in the Abbeville district of South Carolina when John C. Calhoun was born, including seventeen hundred slaves and a handful of free blacks. Backcountry society had become quite structured; slaves and free blacks were at the bottom of the hierarchy, followed in ascending order by subsistence farmers, artisans, storekeepers, and larger farmers. Two-thirds of the households had no slaves, and the average farmer owned about three hundred acres, a little livestock, and a simple one- or two-room house with a few pieces of plain pine furniture. A feather bed was a symbol of prosperity.

The backcountry elite was composed of wealthy landowners. Some of the heads of households in this class, like John Gervais and William Rapley, had come from Charleston and had kinship ties with the tidewater aristocracy. Others, like the Presbyterian minister John Harris, a college graduate, were distinguished by their education. And still others, like Patrick Calhoun, claimed their high status on the basis of personal accomplishments and public service.

John Calhoun did not grow up in the wealthiest household in Abbeville. A neighboring physician, who lived on a plantation by the Savannah River, was able to furnish his house with carpets, mahogany furniture, a piano, and fine crystal and porcelain and adorn his barnyard with ornamental poultry. Another neighbor, Richard Rapley, emulated his Charleston connections with three plantations, eighty-eight slaves, dozens of Thoroughbred horses, and a splendid library.[31]

Although Patrick Calhoun was not a man to spend his money on crystal or ornamental poultry, he had built the first framed house in the district. Colonel W. Pinkney Starke, who claimed to have slept at the Calhoun place several times when he was a boy, remembered that it was "two stories high" and "had four rooms on each story." An inventory taken after Patrick's death lists eleven horses, seventy hogs, forty-five cattle, twenty sheep, and twenty-eight slaves. Personal furnishings included a rifle, two shotguns, a case of pistols, a loom, eleven chairs, one mahogany desk, a still, and seven feather beds. The estate was later appraised at over nine thousand dollars.[32]

Everything we know about John Calhoun's youth suggests that he grew up in a family that enjoyed unusual economic and emotional security. His parents were strong-minded and competent. As the fourth youngest in a family of five children he received affectionate support from his older brothers and sister as well as from his parents, and he had the honor of the Calhoun name, one of the most illustrious in his part of the state.

Judgments pronounced on Calhoun after he had become famous— that he seemed to have missed out on youth and lacked all interest in recreation—make one wonder if he ever learned to play as a boy. His autobiography mentions an early "fondness for hunting, fishing and other country sports," but as a grown man he once chided his son and a group of friends for wasting their shot. When he was a boy, Calhoun said, he had always come home with at least a squirrel in his bag. This anecdote, reported by one of his young listeners many years later, conjures up an image of the youthful Calhoun tramping the woods and fields with the same purposefulness that was to characterize the mature statesman.[33]

Knowing what we do about his later personality, we can assume that John took to work at an early age. Like his older brothers before him, he learned how to plow and sow, how to harvest wheat and barley, and how to cultivate the valuable cotton plants that backcountry planters everywhere were beginning to grow as a cash crop. Learning how to farm meant working with and learning how to direct slaves. Colonel Starke, a dubious source on some of the details of Calhoun's early life, claimed to have talked to a Calhoun slave named Sawney who had fished and hunted and worked in the field with the young master. "Many's the times in the boilin' sun," Sawney is supposed to have said, "me and Marse John has plowed together." The credibility of the anecdote is strengthened by the fact that many years later Calhoun gave special privileges to Sawney, who remained on the plantation and lived to an old age.[34]

We do not know much about John's earliest education. He was probably taught to read by his parents and may have attended one of the simple country schools in which "reading, writing and arithmetic were imperfectly taught." Considering how rapidly he advanced once he encountered good teaching, it is reasonable to assume that he read whatever he could find at home. The inventory after Patrick Calhoun's death lists a bookcase valued at thirty-five pounds, and although there is no list of the books which stood on the shelves, one of them must have been the weighty volume of John Tillotson's sermons that now resides in the South Carolina State Archives with Patrick Calhoun's signature on the top of the third page. Tillotson, the archbishop of Canterbury in the late seventeenth century, was celebrated for sermons which brought dissenters and believers into the fold through rational persuasion. His most famous sermon, "The Wisdom of Being Religious," is a masterful argument, laid out with syllogistic precision, to show that religious belief is both logical and true to human experience. The appeal throughout is to the head rather than to the heart, and it is highly probable that John encountered this sermon at an early age, either from his own reading or from hearing his father read it to the family. "He that is careful to avoid all sin will sincerely endeavor to perform his duty," Tillotson warned. *"The whole of our duty* may be expressed . . . most fitting by departing from evil." Such preaching could only reinforce the stern injunctions John had already learned from his father about the importance of duty and the necessity to regard life as a struggle against evil. Repeated exposure to Tillotson's sermons may also have given the boy a respect for the power of deductive reasoning long before he ever heard of Aristotle.[35]

Patrick Calhoun was fifty-five when his fourth son was born, and when the boy grew old enough to understand his father's double role as head of the family and the community, it was natural to think of him more as a kind of patriarch than as a confidant and friend. Patriarchal families were the rule among South Carolina planters. Fathers were expected to exemplify personal and social standards of excellence and to extract absolute loyalty from sons who would bear the family name, sustain the family fortune, and defend the family honor. Patrick had four sons, and he had built an estate large enough to leave each of them a modest patrimony, but he seems to have sensed that John was the one most likely to succeed him as a public man as well as a planter and that the boy needed more education than he himself had received if he were to do full justice to the family name. The problem was not in finding the money but in finding the school, but once Moses Waddel came into the family, that problem took care of itself.[36]

Waddel, a heavyset, austere young North Carolinian and graduate of Hampden-Sydney College, had created a sensation on a preaching assignment in Long Canes and in the process had wooed and won John Calhoun's older sister, Catherine. Waddel combined his clerical duties with keeping a small school on the other side of the Savannah River, and it was here that John was sent in the winter of 1795. A half century later Calhoun authorized an account of the sequence of events that followed:

At the age of thirteen he was placed under the charge of his brother-in-law to receive his education. Shortly after, his father died; this was followed by the death of his sister, Mrs. Waddel, within a few weeks, and the academy was then discontinued, which suspended his education before it had fairly commenced. His brother-in-law, with whom he was still left, was absent the greater part of the time, attending to his clerical duties, and his pupil thus found himself on a secluded plantation, without any white companion during the greater portion of the time. A situation apparently so unfavourable to improvement turned out, in his case, to be the reverse. Fortunately for him, there was a small circulating library in the house, of which his brother-in-law was librarian, and, in the absence of all company and amusements, that attracted his attention. His taste, although undirected, led him to history, to the neglect of novels and other lighter reading; and so deeply was he interested, that in a short time he read the whole of the small stock of historical works contained in the library, consisting of Rollin's Ancient History, Robertson's Charles V., his South America, and Voltaire's Charles XII. After dispatching these, he turned with like eagerness to Cook's Voyages (the large edition), a small volume of Essays by Brown, and Locke on the Understanding, which he read as far as the chapter on Infinity. All this was the work of but fourteen weeks. So intense was his application that his eyes became seriously affected, his countenance pallid, and his frame emaciated. His mother, alarmed at the intelligence of his health, sent for him home, where exercise and amusement soon restored his strength. . . .[37]

Calhoun's laconic recollection of what surely was the most traumatic experience in his life deserves careful attention. He had become the chosen son, singled out from his older brothers, with a mandate to go beyond them, to learn things even his father did not know. We do not know what visions danced before his youthful eyes or what anxieties tugged at his heart as he left home for the first time. Perhaps John did not notice that his aging father was increasingly beset by fever and other ailments. He had always been old, always indestructible; his father would live forever. And then, almost before it had begun, his bright new way of life was shattered. The father who had survived the sudden butchery of savages and for more than sixty years had overcome the rigors of a frontier that could kill a man a hundred different ways, the towering figure who had been a father to the community as well as to the son, suddenly died, followed, almost immediately, by an only sister, whom John loved dearly. The thirteen-year-old boy was forced to cope with this double disaster alone. There were no kin to mourn with him; his brother-in-law, Waddel, was swallowed up in his own grief, and the rest of the family was fifty long miles away in Abbeville. For more than three months he "found himself on a secluded plantation without any white companion the greater part of the time." In his recollection Calhoun discussed the incident with characteristic coolness and would have us believe that by absorbing himself in the books in Waddel's small library, he transformed this period of mournful solitude into a situation favorable to "improvement." This was the sixty-one-year-old Calhoun speaking, the cast-iron man who had encountered repeated adversity in his political career without ever admitting defeat. A half century earlier, as a thirteen-year-old boy, bereaved, isolated, and in despair, he had thrown himself at those volumes with such a vengeance that his eyes failed; he became emaciated, and his mother had to take him home. The experience remained so vivid in his mind that Calhoun remembered the titles of the five volumes he had read then, including the point at which he had stopped in Locke.

Once back home again and in good health, the boy found himself thrust into his father's role. His older brothers, William and James, had been sent off to town to learn how to be merchants, and with his mother's help and that of his twelve-year-old brother, Patrick, John assumed the direction of a twelve-hundred-acre plantation with about thirty slaves. According to the autobiography, he spent the next four years "in attention to the business of the farm" and "to the entire neglect of his education." As a famous political leader and candidate for President Calhoun was apparently content to have his readers think that this crucial period in his development was significant because it improved his health and solidified his ties to rural life. What actually seems to have happened is that as a boy on the verge of adolescence he was suddenly called to assume the responsibilities of manhood.

Patrick Calhoun had been no ordinary man, and his mantle surely would have weighed more heavily upon the son's shoulders than Calhoun chose to remember fifty years later. A few months before, he had worked in the fields alongside his father's slaves and, accompanied by the black-skinned Sawney, had carelessly tramped the woods and fished the adjoining creeks. Now he was Sawney's master. Now he had to wrestle with decisions that his father had seemed to make effortlessly: how many acres to plant in grain, how many in cotton; when to plant, harvest, and sell; when to be the kind master and when to threaten the lash.

In the beginning Calhoun relied on his mother, an exceptually strong-minded woman from every account we have, and on his older brothers, only a day or two away by horseback for advice. Once he had grown accustomed to the responsibilities of running the plantation, he became less dependent on them and more conscious of the need to prepare himself for the future. In sending him off to study with Waddel, Patrick had announced that he would be the chosen son. John had shown that he could take over the plantation, but did he have the formal education necessary to build on his father's example in politics?

Although there is no hard evidence to show that John Calhoun's political ambition had begun to burn while he was still in his teens, an intriguing family artifact in the form of a well-marked copy of the *South Carolina Gazette* reporting the proceedings of Congress for April 11 and 13, 1798, suggests that the father's interest in politics had already left its mark upon the son.

In the autobiography Calhoun stated that his education was completely neglected during the four years after his father's death. The implication is that he had neither the time nor the books to continue on the path he had begun at Waddel's, but it is clear that as abortive as that experience had been, it made a lasting impact by introducing him to the world of ideas and to the possibilities of a professional education. Without books at hand, he now had books in his head, and as he turned over the possibilities for his future, he might well have been reminded of Voltaire's *History of Charles XII,* which was one of the volumes he had devoured at Waddel's. There was reason for Calhoun to have been fascinated by the audacious Swedish monarch who was killed at thirty-six "after having experienced all the grandeur of prosperity, and all the hardships of adversity, without being either softened by the one, or the least disturbed by the other . . . the only king that ever lived without failings." Charles had been born a century earlier, but there were certain parallels to Calhoun's own temperament and situation. A precocious child, the young Swedish king, orphaned at fifteen, "betrayed an inflexible obstinacy. The only way to influence him was to awaken his sense of honor." Supposedly under the care of a guardian until his eighteenth year, Charles had insisted on ruling himself while still a boy.[38]

Calhoun was in his eighteenth year, with memories of Voltaire's book fresh in his mind, when he took charge of his own life. When his brother James asked him if he would consider returning to school to prepare for one of the professions, John coolly replied that he would "far rather be a planter than a half-informed physician or lawyer." He would consider a professional career only if his brothers would commit themselves to run the family plantation and subsidize his education. He wanted the best he could get and expected it to take seven years.[39]

The hidden message in Calhoun's response was that if his brothers expected him to carry on the illustrious tradition established by their father, it would have to be on his terms. Calhoun was correct when he recalled that with the deaths of his father and sister "a situation apparently so unfavorable to improvement turned out, in his case, to be the reverse," but it was not Moses Waddel's library but his own rapid maturity, which began with his father's death, that made the difference. When he went off to Waddel's academy at eighteen, he left his schoolboy days behind. There would be no identity conflicts in his future; he already knew who he was and where he was going. Thereafter he would always insist on setting his own course. The iron in his personality had been cast, and he would spring into the arena not, as Hammond contended, "like Minerva from the head of Jove," but as the son of Patrick and the product of the culture of the postrevolutionary South Carolina frontier, "fully grown and clothed in armor: a man every inch himself, and able to contend with any other man."[40]

2

Education, Marriage, and Career,
1800–1810

JOHN CALHOUN began to prepare for college on the first of July 1801, when he returned to Waddel's school, which had been reorganized in Vienna, South Carolina, only a few miles from Abbeville. He was fortunate in having his brother-in-law for a teacher. Waddel soon established an academy in nearby Willington that was to become famous throughout the South as a kind of backwoods Eton or Rugby under the "Carolina Dr. Arnold." Although no record survives of Calhoun's experience in the Vienna school, we can assume that it was similar in style and substance to the education students later received at the more famous Willington academy. William Grayson likened that school to a "rural republic with a perpetual dictator," and one well-known alumnus recalled that Waddel built his reputation for educating "hardy, rustic youth, most of whom probably never had a broadcloth coat a linen shirt or a pair of stockings on in their lives." Over the years this rustic student body included Calhoun's Georgia adversary William H. Crawford, the talented South Carolina unionist J. L. Petigru, and Calhoun's protégé George McDuffie as well as the writer A. B. Longstreet.[1]

Waddel taught his students at Willington in a large two-room log cabin shaded by huge oak trees and flanked by log cabin study buildings. Students were called each morning by a horn, fed corn bread and bacon, and herded into the classroom, where every Monday morning they recited hundreds of lines of Virgil and Horace. Waddel was an austere but amiable master, always in a pleasant mood at flogging time. He never whipped for a bad lesson but used hickory saplings, "beautifully trimmed," to punish the lazy and mischievous. It is unlikely that Calhoun ever felt the hickory's sting. He came to school already disciplined and eager to build the foundation in mathematics and classical languages necessary for college. He and Waddel were close. They had suffered together, and John looked up to his older brother-in-law as a second father. Later, as a famous public figure he went out of his way to honor Waddel by participating in commencement exercises at the University of Georgia when Waddel became its president, and when the old schoolmaster lay dying, he sent young John C. Calhoun, Jr., to visit him and get his final benediction.[2]

On May 14, 1801, Catherine Caldwell Calhoun died unexpectedly, and John told a cousin that he had "never experienced so sever [sic] and unexpected a shock" as he did upon hearing the news. His mother's death completed the process of rapid maturation which had begun to shape John five years earlier. He was free now to pursue a college education wherever he chose, and on September 6, 1801, while still with Waddel, he wrote asking his cousin Andrew Pickens, Jr., for advice. Calhoun wanted to prepare for the junior class in "a college in the highest repute northerly" and was "at a stand to know what study to presue [sic], as every college has its particular routine of study for each class." Even before writing Pickens, Calhoun had been attracted to Yale, and he enrolled there as a junior in October 1802.[3]

The documentary record of Calhoun's experience at Yale is scanty. Having passed through Charleston and New York on his way, he must have found the villagelike atmosphere of New Haven's sandy streets and the cows grazing on the common comfortably bucolic, but as he stood on College Street in front of Connecticut Hall for the first time, he must have thought he was coming to study in a palace. Old Connecticut with its ninety-six rooms and long hallways was a far cry from the rusticity of Waddel's academy. Fortunately, however, South Carolina students were no novelty at Yale, and rooming with Christopher Edwards Gadsden from Charleston would have helped John adjust to his new surroundings. At six feet two inches, with stiff black hair standing straight up from his head to make him look taller, Calhoun made a striking appearance, but he was too reserved to make friends quickly and could not overcome a "repugnance to addressing perfect strangers." Once in the classroom, however, when he discovered that Waddel's preparation allowed him to compete successfully with graduates from the fashionable New England academies and that he was actually ahead of his classmates in mathematics, the social reticence began to disappear. He became treasurer of the socially active Phi Beta Kappa chapter and developed lifelong friendships with Gadsden, James Mac-bride, and John Felder, fellow Carolinians who were to make their marks in religion, medicine, and politics, and with Micah Sterling, who was to represent New York in Congress and name one of his sons after Calhoun.

Although he was developing social graces that stood him in good stead the rest of his life, Calhoun had arrived too late on the college scene ever to be "one of the boys." The careless dissipations and frivolous rituals that add zest to the college experience for many students left him cold. When his cousin Andrew Pickens wrote to deplore the fact that his college days were over, Calhoun replied by caricaturing the rigors and monotonous routine of student life: the morning bell before daybreak; required attendance in the frozen chapel; the dreary and repeated recitations; the midnight candle burning over "Books, books, books," before the poor student, "pale and meager with a shattered constitution," could retire to his bed. "Keep those things in view and tell me, dear Andrew, where is the pleasure in collegiate life? Will you place it in the approbation of his teachers and the applause of his competitors? They are vain and unsatisfying. Will you in the gratification of his ambition? That ambition must be small indeed which can be gratified in college. Rather, then, rejoice that you have passed through college and that you are now engaged in the busy scenes of the 'Scrambling World.' " Here Calhoun was trying to exercise a talent he would never possess; he was trying to banter with his friend, but anyone who knew him well would have known he was more than half serious. If Calhoun acted like a man among boys at Yale, it was because that was what he was, and his classmates respected him for it, especially after his confrontation with President Timothy Dwight.[4]

In a letter written shortly after reaching New Haven, Calhoun described Dwight as "a very amiable man and well calculated to perform the duties of his office. I trust that I shall like him as an instructor." An intellectual prodigy who had graduated from Yale at seventeen, Dwight had been named president of Yale in 1795 after having built a reputation as a preacher, theologian, and man of letters. When Calhoun matriculated, Timothy Dwight *was* Yale. Under his direction Yale students had improved in character and grown in numbers. Deists were routed, unbelievers converted, sluggish intellects wakened. Dwight was energetic and dogmatic, his powerful mind firmly enclosed by the doctrines of Calvinism and New England federalism. With Thomas Jefferson about to be elected President for a second term, Dwight's political juices were always on the boil, ready to scald any student who might express sympathy with the Jacobin world view President Dwight associated with the party in power.

Calhoun first discovered what it was like to be scalded by President Dwight on November 2, 1803. The class was debating the question "Would it not be politic to encourage the importation of foreigners in the U. States?" The first two speakers took the negative case, arguing that immigrants usually came from the "vicious" classes. Calhoun demurred, claiming that most immigrants would come from the middle class and citing South Carolina as an example. At this point Dwight interrupted and "completely refuted" Calhoun by announcing the well-known fact that immigrants were far more inclined than native-born Americans to insurrection and disorder. After the interruption Calhoun attempted to conclude by showing the beneficial effects of immigration on manufacturing, agriculture, and population growth, but the session terminated with the president declaring himself "decidedly against the importation of foreigners" because "No men leave their country (with a very moderate exception) except worthless characters!"[5]

The only source of this encounter is a classmate's diary, which does not tell us how Calhoun reacted to Dwight's dogmatic challenges, but he could not have accepted the assertion that his father and grandfather had been worthless characters. For his part, Dwight was testing Calhoun, knowing that he was a top student, a southerner, probably a follower of Jefferson, and one of the relatively few students who had remained unmoved by the preaching and praying that had been so successful in converting other students. Under the circumstances it was almost inevitable that he would test the young man again, and sometime the following year the mind and character of Timothy Dwight collided with the mind and character of John Calhoun.

The confrontation took place in a moral philosophy class when Dwight asked, "What's the legitimate source of power?" Everyone knew that the right answer was to say something about God and the constituted authorities, but Calhoun responded, "The people," and in the ensuing dialogue he not only held his ground but drew on Jefferson for support. Not surprisingly the students instantly raised Calhoun's reputation to heroic proportions. Meanwhile, the college president, at first indignant at being crossed ideologically and intellectually, is supposed to have relented on sober second thought and to have admitted that his young adversary had ability enough "to be President of the United States" and one day might "occupy that office."[6]

That Dwight actually did predict that Calhoun would be a presidential candidate is probably true. Professor Silliman remembered the incident, and Calhoun had the statement included in the autobiography of 1843. No doubt Dwight, like most pugnacious thinkers, admired strength of character and conviction in others, but he may also have known that Calhoun was an essentially conservative Jeffersonian who was actually contemplating a career in politics. Certainly Calhoun's friends at Yale would have known that he admired his cousin Senator John Ewing Colhoun of South Carolina, who had broken with Jefferson's administration by voting against dismantling the federal courts in 1802. Senator Colhoun had died in October 1802, and the following January John Calhoun had written to his cousin "By his death our country has lost one of its most sincere friends and our family one of its brightest ornaments. Mr. Calhoun by his spirited behavior in the last Congress gained himself much honor in N. England. . . . It is probable dear Andrew, that we shall follow the same pursuits of life, that he did, let us therefore be ambitious to emulate his virtues and knowledge." At Yale John Calhoun followed his own advice by defending his own principles without alienating the Federalists around him, and when he was rewarded for his academic achievements with a top place in the commencement exercises, he chose to give his oration on "The Qualifications Necessary to Make a Statesman."

It is interesting to speculate about that oration. Would it have been of sound republican doctrine, informed by the example of his father, emphasizing devotion to liberty and public virtue along with the necessity for personal independence? We will never know because Calhoun fell gravely ill of dysentery in August 1804 and did not participate in the September commencement exercises. Although he was disappointed at missing the culminating experience of his college career, he had a right to be proud of what he had accomplished in just two years at Yale. Having mastered as good as the country could offer in undergraduate liberal education, he was already looking forward to the challenges of professional training. Four months before graduation he had written to Pickens about the necessity for undertaking the "dry and laborious" study of law. "Upon what does greater honour attend," he asked, "than upon accurate and comprehensive knowledge of law? But why is this honour attendant on legal knowledge? Surely because it demands a strong and comprehensive mind. . . . Were the law so simple and concise as to be attainable by every one, with moderate application and abilities, where would be the honour of its acquisition?"[7]

Yale had taught Calhoun to equate honor with the triumphs of the mind. He had been an intellectual leader in a class which included not only his able South Carolina friends but John Hampton (Chief Justice of the Massachusetts Superior Court, 1820–1829), David Plant (Member of Congress, Connecticut, 1827–1829), Henry Storrs (Member of Congress, Connecticut, 1817–1821, 1823 to 1831), Bennet Tyler (president of Dartmouth), and John Pierpont (Unitarian minister and poet). Patrick Calhoun had been one of the "leading men" in South Carolina. In becoming one of the leading young men at Yale, John Calhoun had joined a tiny national elite and was well on his way toward achieving the distinction his family expected.

Sometime in the summer of 1804 Calhoun was invited to Newport, Rhode Island, by the widow of his cousin John Ewing Calhoun, who was summering there with her children. He arrived in late September, pale and drawn from a prolonged bout with dysentery but overjoyed to be with kin again. Floride Bonneau Colhoun came from a wealthy Huguenot family. She had brought a handsome property with her when she married and had inherited enough as a widow to travel from South Carolina to Rhode Island in a four-horse coach with a British coachman in full livery. She was Calhoun's wealthiest relative, and he had been sufficiently impressed by her invitation to write a formal letter of acceptance which did not contain a single misspelled word. We know from the rest of his correspondence that this could not have been accidental. Finding the fresh Newport breezes and the affectionate hospitality of Floride and her children marvelously convalescent, Calhoun readily agreed to return with them to South Carolina in November.

The agreement which the Calhoun brothers had reached in 1800 stipulated that John would be supported for seven years of study. Four years had gone by, and John planned to divide his time over the next three reading law in South Carolina and studying at the nation's first law school in Litchfield, Connecticut. On December 24, 1804, he launched the final phase of his carefully planned preparation by paying "100 Guineas" to enter the Charleston law firm of De Saussure and Ford as a student. Henry William De Saussure, known as the Chesterfield of South Carolina, was one of the state's most learned jurists and lawyers. Having served as an officer under Washington in the Revolution and as superintendent of the mint, De Saussure was a committed Federalist who had strongly opposed extending representation in the South Carolina legislature to the backcountry, which he suspected for having too much democracy and not enough slavery. By choosing to read law in De Saussure's office, Calhoun was once again showing his intellectual independence by seeking the best minds he could find, Republican or Federalist. De Saussure, for his part, seems to have been pleased by the qualities he found in his student, and when Calhoun was ready to go back to Connecticut in the spring of 1805, he wrote to the Federalist Robert Goodloe Harper that the "son of old Patrick Calhoun . . . has been educated in New Haven and has acquired more knowledge than is usual at his age—and there are indications of a superior mind." In the same letter De Saussure gloated over the way the Senate had routed Jefferson and the "wild measures of democracy" by acquitting Supreme Court Justice Samuel Chase, who had been impeached by Republican votes in the House of Representatives.[8]

When Calhoun visited Newport, he had been impressed by the salubrious environment and physical beauty of the place but had thought "its manners, customs and moral and religious character" seemed "much inferior" to the rest of New England. Some months later, back in South Carolina, he deplored the moral behavior of Charlestonians "so extremely corrupt and particularly so inattentive to every call of religion. . . . Surely no people ever so much needed a reform as those in the parishes near Charleston." What he objected to in both places was the self-indulgence, idleness, and unnecessary luxury of the rich. This was the Presbyterianism of the frontier passing judgment on the frivolous and dissipated East. Newport was too much like the Carolina low country to suit Calhoun.[9]

At the same time Calhoun appears to have enjoyed sharing the elegant life-style of his cousin Floride, and he readily agreed to accompany her and her children on their way north in May 1805. It was a comfortable, leisurely trip with frequent layovers when the day grew too warm, and his cousin's four-horse carriage was a far cry from the tortures of travel by stage. In Washington the party paused while Calhoun visited President Jefferson. Presumably the interview could have been arranged by Floride, who may already have seen John Calhoun as a worthy successor to her late husband the Senator. Whatever the circumstances, and even accounting for the easy access to high public officers in the early days of the Republic, Calhoun reported the event to young Andrew Pickens in an astonishingly matter-of-fact letter. After commenting that he had little to communicate that was new or interesting, he went on to describe the attention given by the press to the war between France and England and the movement of the French fleet.

Newspaper readers and scribblers have formed various opinions as to its destination and success. I heard the President (I got acquainted with him at Washington) express his opinion. The destination was not Jamaica as originally believed but Trinidad. However this may be, it is certainly a lesson to the English that her foreign possessions are not so secure as she imagined, and has given the war a much more distracting character than it had at its commencement. Remember me to Mrs. Pickens. . . .[10]

Calhoun left Floride and her family at Newport in July 1805 and departed for Litchfield. In Hartford he was joined on the stage by Tapping Reeve, one of the two masters of the Litchfield Law School. Reeve was seventy-one, a tall, bowed man, dressed in the old-fashioned style, complete with the buckled breeches and powdered queues that New England Federalists favored. Although gentle in demeanor and frequently lost in a cloud of legal abstractions, Reeve was an even more passionately partisan Federalist than Timothy Dwight. He was to be indicted for libel against the President while Calhoun was at Litchfield, and his relationship to his brother-in-law Aaron Burr, the man who had almost defeated Jefferson for the presidency in 1800 and had killed

Alexander Hamilton, gave Reeve an unmistakable aura that made Litchfield students wary. Calhoun reported that he found Reeve "open and agreeable" on the stage, but it is unlikely that he would have turned the conversation to a discussion of his late visit with the President.

Although Litchfield was definitely enemy country as far as Jeffersonians were concerned, Calhoun seems to have approached the experience without qualms. For one thing he knew he would have his college friend and countryman Felder to keep him company. For another he knew that Tapping Reeve and his young Federalist partner, James Gould, were the two most celebrated lecturers on law in the country—Reeve for his brilliant, meandering discourse loaded with intuitive insights, Gould for his tightly organized, systematic lectures which covered everything a young lawyer needed to know under forty-eight subjects. Like Timothy Dwight and William Henry De Saussure, Reeve and Gould had something Calhoun wanted; he would take that and leave the rest alone.

The school provided the kind of structured Spartan learning environment in which Calhoun had prospered with Waddel. Muffled and mittened in winter months, students sat in a single classroom, listened to lectures for one and a half hours a day, and spent the rest of the time reading the authorities cited and formally writing up notes, which were eventually compiled in five thick volumes.[11]

What amazed Calhoun's fellow students was not so much the ease with which he absorbed details of the law as the effortless way he appeared to use his knowledge in the debates presided over by Judge Gould. As his Maryland friend Virgil Maxcy recalled, Calhoun rarely argued from an outline or took notes of opponents' arguments. "He relied on his tenacious memory for preserving the order established in his own mind."[12]

Although the Litchfield experience reinforced the confidence Calhoun had gained at Yale in his own ability to compete with the best minds anywhere, it did not lead to a love affair with the law. Admitting to Floride that he had embarked on a "dry and solitary journey," he went on to say, "I always feel myself in the best health when studying closely." Another time he put the matter more pointedly: "I confess, from my aversion to law, I draw a motive to industry. It must be done, and the sooner the better is often my logic." John Calhoun may never have seen the inside of many New England churches, but the Puritan within him would have made any of Jonathan Edwards's descendants proud.[13]

Calhoun was as circumspect outside the classroom in Litchfield as he was assiduous within. "This place is so much agitated by party feelings," he wrote Floride, "that both Mr. Felder and myself find it prudent to form few connections in town." Sometimes he was homesick, and his affectionate family connections in Rhode Island seemed almost as far away as South Carolina. Thus, when another John Calhoun, a physician in Cornwall, Connecticut, invited him to visit, he accepted with enthusiasm and was soon walking thirty miles a week to spend the weekends with a distant kinsman; kin was kin even in Yankee country.

Calhoun seems to have gone out of his way to keep a low political profile in Litchfield. Perceiving on an almost daily basis a political dogmatism in Reeve and Gould even more intense than that which he had encountered in Timothy Dwight, he avoided confrontation. But everyone knew where Calhoun stood, and when a local newspaper editor was jailed for criticizing the local Federalists, he joined a tiny protest march to salute him in his cell.

The larger part of Calhoun's correspondence which has been preserved for this period consists of letters to and from his cousin Floride, and these letters reveal a growing intimacy. Sharing a carriage with the Colhouns for the long journey seems to have made John Calhoun feel like an immediate member of the family, and he confessed to being lonesome after first setting up quarters in Litchfield. When Floride responded in a particularly warm and caring way, Calhoun thanked her for her "affectionate" letter, claiming, "Your whole actions in kindness and affection have been to me like a mother's tenderness." There is a tradition passed down in the Calhoun family that John wanted more than a mother's tenderness, and it is easy to believe that the young man may well have felt something stronger than kinship ties tugging at his heart. Floride was handsome, wealthy, widowed, and still in her thirties. Marriage between cousins was commonplace in South Carolina, and Calhoun was at an age when even Puritans had to come to terms with the imperatives of sexual energy. He was the more diligent correspondent (writing once in the midst of a lecture), and he confessed that he hounded the Litchfield post office "on every Eastern mail" only to "have uniformly had the mortification of disappointment." This suggestion of dependency is out of character with the self-assurance that seems to characterize the rest of his life at this time. Floride Colhoun was the most important woman in Calhoun's life then. She was an affectionate mother figure, filling much the same role as Moses Waddel's after Patrick died. Floride supplied a secure and loving haven for John away from home, encouraged him to think more about religion, and lent him money. For his part, John helped fill the masculine void left by her deceased husband. She tried to get him to pursue his studies at Newport, put him in charge of arrangements when they traveled together, and sought his advice about educating her children. "I only wish I could have your advice verbally," she wrote on one occasion, "but must be content to have it by letter."[14]

Calhoun made his last visit to Newport in August 1806, returned to finish his course of lectures at Litchfield, and set off for South Carolina probably sometime in late October or early November, making the greater part of the long journey on horseback. After spending a few days in Abbeville, he went to Charleston to resume study in De Saussure's office.

Most young bachelors would have found the prospect of living in Charleston exhilarating, but not Calhoun. He had probably been warned about the city by his father. When Patrick attended legislative sessions in Charleston, the men of the Revolution had still dominated Charleston society. As William Grayson remembered, it was an intensely masculine society, hard-drinking, hard-swearing, jovial, and rough. The women sought refuge in their churches while the men raced, drank, fought, and went to parties where it was a breach of etiquette to leave sober. The place of a Charleston gentleman was considered to be under the table, and it was not unheard of for one of the more abstemious sort to jump out a window in order to get home on his own feet. Anyone like Patrick Calhoun, who had helped bring order out of the social anarchy on the Carolina frontier, would have been dismayed by the upper-class licentiousness in Charleston, especially when it extended to legislators, who sometimes paraded uproariously with drum and fiddle through the streets at night, "smashing the doors of those who did not rise to join them."

Of course, one did not have to be drunk to appreciate Charleston, which one historian has aptly called the "sensuous city." Its streets lined with some of the most stately mansions in the country, its markets thronged with a cosmopolitan population so that a person might hear French, German, Portuguese, and Gullah spoken within the space of one city block, Charleston was tropical, inviting pleasure, with an exotic smell of decay like Venice. John Calhoun, however, had not been brought up to appreciate the exotic. He had been schooled early to avoid self-indulgence of any kind, and he spent his time in the sensuous city poring over the law books in De Saussure's office and living with a French Protestant minister on Church Street. "It is a quiet place," he wrote Floride, "and answers my purpose well."[15]

At Litchfield Calhoun had studied the great authorities like Coke and Blackstone. In Charleston he also studied the laws of South Carolina. In both Connecticut and South Carolina the great body of the law was concerned with the ownership and disposition of property, but the similarity stopped there because the most valuable property in South Carolina was its slaves. The logic of slavery had been built into the colony with the first settlements. The British wanted the colonists to plant and export staples, but they could plant little without imported labor. When rice became the big crop, the case for African slavery, which was already flourishing in the West Indies and Virginia, became overwhelming, and Charleston became the slave capital of the Western world. It is estimated that about 40 percent of all Africans brought to North America in the eighteenth century came through Charleston, "the Ellis Island of black Americans."

Blacks outnumbered whites in South Carolina by a good margin especially in Charleston, where their presence was vivid and indispensable. Most of the slaves had been brought directly from the west coast of Africa. More than forty thousand had been transported from 1740 to 1764, and the result was a more powerful African presence than in most other slave states. In Charleston slaves were everywhere, charged with the most menial tasks, running errands for their masters and mistresses, and performing most of the skilled labor which white artisans did in the North. They seemed to live on close terms with the white population and obviously were essential to the functioning of the city. No Charlestonian could conceive of the city without slaves. Northerners were usually impressed by the picturesque dimension of the system, carefree black children playing in the streets, the women in colorful bandannas, the men working to the rhythms of African songs and talking to each other in a strange new dialect which seemed to be part African, part English, and part everything else.[16]

The large black underclass which made life charming and comfortable for most white people also made thoughtful citizens uneasy and may have contributed to Calhoun's discomfort in Charleston. He had grown up with slaves and owned a substantial number, but the black population had always been a relatively small minority in Abbeville, while Charleston for all its blackness was a white oasis, surrounded by rice-growing parishes in which Africans outnumbered whites by as much as ten to one. Calhoun, like every other slaveowner, knew that slaves were not always happy, carefree, and docile. He had heard about the rebellion in St. Paul's Parish, fifteen miles from Charleston in which more than twenty whites had been butchered. That had happened more than seventy-five years earlier, and although there had been no comparable insurrection since that time, Calhoun knew that resistance to slavery on the plantation was not uncommon and that a slave had once tried to poison his cousin Floride's husband. Like every other planter, he had heard of the plot uncovered in 1804 at Major Hazzard's plantation on the Eutaw River. William Grayson, sixteen years old at the time, remembered how the suspected ringleaders were seized, "tried without delay and ten or a dozen condemned to be hanged. Their heads were cut off, stuck on poles and set up along the highway" as a warning to others. Calhoun was not shocked by these examples, believing, as he did, that life was a struggle against evil and that men everywhere had always plotted against and murdered one another. He might well have worried, however, about the future of slavery in a city like Charleston, where so many in the white population seemed oblivious of the high demands slavery was supposed to place on the character of the masters. To own and work slaves was a high calling, and the large proportion of slaves together with the slack morality of the masters in Charleston made for a dangerous mix and underscored the necessity for controlling the black population while trying to improve the morals of the whites. Eventually the town fathers came to grips with the problem by building a well-maintained workhouse and treadmill and a scientifically designed flogging apparatus to keep unruly slaves in line. That was one way of shoring up the system, and Calhoun himself made use of it in later years. Meanwhile, he studied the laws of a slave society and bemoaned the moral dissolution around him. When an epidemic swept through Charleston, he blamed it on "the misconduct of the inhabitants" and told Floride it might "be considered as a curse for their intemperance and debaucheries."[17]

He did not despair of South Carolina, however. "Providence has given us a fine country," he wrote to Floride; "all that is lacking is our own exertions." Calhoun wrote this on October 1, 1807. He would not have believed it possible then, but there would come a time when the "fine country" in which he was born would discover that it was threatened not from within but without, when the continued existence of slavery and all the institutions that went along with it would have to be rationalized before an increasingly hostile world, and when he would be called upon to defend not only South Carolina but slavery and the South.[18]

Sometime in June 1807 Calhoun left Charleston in order to escape the sickly season and to finish his law training with George Bowie in Abbeville. His return could not have gone unnoticed. Patrick Calhoun's memory was still green around Abbeville, and although another Calhoun, John's sixty-year-old cousin Joseph, had taken Patrick's place in the legislature, his retirement would make it possible for John to take up the leadership role his father held for so many years. As John mulled over these possibilities, he must have been struck by the changes that had taken place in his home district since he was a boy. In the first place, people living there referred to themselves now as living in the "upper" country rather than the backcountry, and indeed, the dynamic growth in the region made the earlier designation sound archaic. There were four times as many people now in the upper than in the lower country. Many of the farmers Calhoun had known as a boy now owned slaves and planted cotton, and as more and more slaves had come into the region, many of the poorer whites had begun to move out. Although the old sectional differences were beginning to disappear, the rough, egalitarian spirit of the frontier lingered, and just two years earlier the coachman of an English aristocrat had been severely beaten by up-country wagoners for trying to get them to turn aside for "his lordship." Knowing the leveling tendencies of his home district, Calhoun was careful not to flaunt his fancy northern education, and the evening foot races he competed in against other young lawyers in front of George Bowie's office must have helped reassure some of his old Abbeville friends that John had not let the Yankees cut him off from his roots.[19]

However open and unassuming he seemed, John Calhoun was no more one of the boys back in Abbeville than he had been at Yale; the officer of the British frigate *Leopard* who fired on the American *Chesapeake* without provocation just outside the Virginia coast on June 22, 1807, saw to that. This affront to American sovereignty grew out of a long-standing dispute between Britain and the United States over the right of the former to stop and search American vessels for deserters from the British navy. Outraged Americans everywhere organized protest meetings in cities, towns, and villages. Calhoun attended the meeting at Abbeville Courthouse and was immediately named to the committee to draft and present protest resolutions. At a Charleston meeting called for the same purpose the conservative town fathers urged the large crowd to act with "coolness and dignity," remembering that in large, democratic meetings "measures were agreed upon and carried out too hastily." In Abbeville Calhoun prepared a series of resolutions which accused the British of "murderous conduct," recommended that the militia be prepared for war, and applauded "our Fellow-citizens" in Virginia for having rioted to protest the attack. Exactly what Calhoun said that day (August 3, 1807) in Abbeville has not been recorded, but one observer remembered that he "astonished everybody" and laid the foundation for his enduring political popularity in the district. From now on he would be recognized not only as Patrick Calhoun's son but as a presence in his own right.[20]

Calhoun was admitted to the South Carolina bar in December 1807, and his success in attracting clients undoubtedly was influenced by his celebrated performance in the *Chesapeake* affair. His own reaction, however, and what we know about his practice, suggests that it was long on quantity but short on quality. Calhoun apparently never contemplated practicing in Charleston, where a good man could concentrate on insurance and admiralty cases and earn twenty thousand dollars or more a year. Instead he worked the up-country courts, searching titles and litigating claims involving land, slaves, and horses. In February 1809 he successfully defended Robert Elgin and his wife against a suit brought by the children of Elgin's wife to obtain owner-ship of the "natural increase" of the slaves Phebe and Daniel. Later in the year he convinced a jury that John Gilbert should pay Benjamin Houston seven hundred dollars for selling him the slave Charley, "a most intolerable rogue and runaway," under false pretenses. Such cases were hardly momentous, but Calhoun put his whole energy and intel-lectual power into them. The brief for *Hick Barksdale v. J. Nelson Newby* survives in his hand as a good example. Calhoun's client Newby was appealing a judgment to pay for a horse traded with Barksdale on the ground that Barksdale's horse had "the string halt" and gave out on him on a trip to North Carolina. Calhoun carefully outlined the argu-ment:

1st that from all the circumstances of the case it is presumable that the plain-tiff had knowledge of the defect; and of course practiced a fraud on Defendant by concealing it

2dly that the object for which the horse was purchased failed and of course destroyed the contract

3dly that the horse got by plaintiff in exchange was worth much more than the string halt one and the plaintiff on that account not entitled to recover

4th Verdict contrary to law and evidence

We do not know whether the judge was impressed by Calhoun's reasoning or not, because he refused the appeal ("Let the verdict sleep"), apparently believing that the law should steer clear of horse traders. It would not be the first time that Calhoun discovered to his sorrow that logic does not always win the day.[21]

It did not take Calhoun long to decide against a law career. He had been practicing less than a year when he wrote Floride that he felt "almost as a slave chained down to a particular place and course in life. . . . I feel a strong aversion to the law; and am determined to forsake it as soon as I can make a decent independence." It was about this time, also, that Calhoun launched the political career he had predicted for himself at Yale. In October 1808 he was elected to the South Carolina House of Representatives, where he was to serve for two sessions. The brief nine-week sessions of the legislature at this time may account for the paucity of information we have about him as a state legislator, but it is clear that the formal entrance of Patrick Calhoun's son on the South Carolina political stage made an impression. In December he was made "aide-de-camp to Governor Drayton" and the following year appointed a trustee of South Carolina College. Such high recognition for a young newcomer still in his twenties and not particularly inclined to defer to his elders made some veteran lawmakers uneasy. Joe Alston, also from the upper country and a political manipulator of some experience, spoke for them when he said, "I am afraid I shall find this long, awkward fellow from Abbeville hard to manage."[22]

During the 1808 session of the General Assembly Calhoun participated in the final legislative vote needed to amend the state constitution so as to provide reasonable parity in representation between the low and upper country. As Calhoun cast his vote supporting a compromise which provided that half the members of the General Assembly be chosen on the basis of population and half on the basis of taxable property, he remembered the many times his father complained about the unfair political domination of wealthy tidewater planters. Now the necessary agreement had been reached allowing each section to balance the power of the other. It never occurred to Calhoun that his own section with the larger population should have been given more power. He saw the compromise as a victory for republican principles. Later he pointed to it as a model for the Republic.

If a consensus over republican values helped hold Carolinians together, so did the expansion of slavery, and as chairman of the legislature's Committee on Claims Calhoun was brought face-to-face with some of the less appealing aspects of South Carolina's most distinctive institution. In 1740 the General Assembly, in order "that owners of slaves may not be tempted to conceal the crimes of their slaves to the prejudice of the public," had provided that the owners of executed slaves could be compensated by a sum not to exceed $200. The Committee on Claims was charged with reviewing these and other claims against the state. Records in the South Carolina Archives show that in one eight-day period in December 1809 Calhoun recommended that the state pay $665 to a former prisoner of war during the Revolution, $80 to William Knox for a mare lost in the attack on Fort Congaree, and $120.40 each for eight executed slaves belonging to different masters. There was nothing particularly unusual about Calhoun's role; he was performing a routine committee assignment involving personal property rights in the same way that he performed routine legal business involving the purchase and inheritance of slaves. Like other Carolinians, he had become part of a culture in which what was considered routine in South Carolina in 1809 would be considered increasingly bizarre and barbaric in other parts of the country in the years ahead.[23]

We do not know much about the circumstances attending the particular cases Calhoun reported, but we know what happened in similar cases. For example, the slaves Jim and Summers were convicted of burglary in Abbeville Court and sentenced to death. Before the verdict was carried out, Jim was appraised at $300 and Summers at $150. After Jim and Summers had been executed, two justices directed the state treasurer to reimburse their owners. William Ware of Abbeville petitioned the General Assembly for $500 for his slave Jim, who was stabbed to death trying to apprehend a runaway. "My fellow," he wrote, "was among the first class of Negroes." On another occasion the black Primus murdered his owner John Bonnet. Primus was executed, and Bonnet's estate petitioned the General Assembly for $600. The Committee on Claims rejected the petition because the law did not cover slaves executed for murder. Finally, James Delaire's slave Figaro had been confined at length in the Charleston workhouse in connection with an insurrection investigation. The court ordered Delaire to transport Figaro out of the state and sell him. Delaire transported Figaro and sent the following petition to the General Assembly: "[I]t appears that from the intense cold the said Figaro had suffered in the Work House at Charleston & the long pressure of the leg irons on his legs, very few days after the sailing he was taken with a swelling about the ankles which turned into a sore & that a mortification of the flesh ensuing, his toes rotted & one of his feet dropped off entirely so that being totally disabled Mr. Duncan Hill who had charge of said Figaro could not get more than about twenty dollars, whereas had he been sound the said Figaro would have fetched between 350 and 400 dollars." The petition concluded with an endorsement by Judge De Saussure and two surgeons certifying that the amputation operation Figaro required "would come to more than the worth of him."[24]

Calhoun would have been familiar with cases like these because disposing of them took a significant part of a man's time whether he was a planter, lawyer, or legislator. If there was some flaw in a system which held that a slave was both an economic object and a person responsible for obeying the law, Calhoun did not see it. He could own slaves, think of them fondly, and still believe that the Primuses and Jims and Figaros whose primitive energy fueled the success of South Carolina's economy and polity were necessarily subject to a lower order of justice than their masters. He could not question the morality of slavery because he had grown up with it in the new nation and watched its expansion bring honor to his father and prosperity and republican civility to the upper country and unity to the entire state.

As a young and ambitious lawyer-legislator Calhoun started off each day with a three-mile walk designed to cultivate "the power of attention" by focusing his mind on a single subject. As a prominent public figure he became famous for his ability to stick with an argument until he had exhausted all its possibilities, and his friend Alexander Bowie believed that he owed his celebrated powers of concentration to this habit. We do not know what he thought about in his solitary pacing: perhaps about politics, perhaps about his career, perhaps about such mundane matters as the legal status of a stringhalt horse—and almost certainly about women.[25]

All his life Calhoun enjoyed the company and conversation of intelligent, attractive women, but we know practically nothing about his early relationships with them except those revealed in his correspondence with Floride Colhoun and her daughter. At Yale he was studious but not reclusive, enjoying himself on sleigh rides and as a frequent visitor in the house of Sarah Sherman, who lived across the street from the campus. The Sherman house was well known to students because Roger Sherman, Sarah's father, had helped write the Constitution, and George Washington had once stopped there for tea. Apparently it was more than Sarah's celebrity status which attracted Calhoun, for her son George Frisbie Hoar recalled that "Mr. Calhoun was very intimate in my grandmother's household when he was in college and always inquired with great interest after the young ladies of the family when he met anyone who knew them. He had a special liking for my mother who was about his own age and always inquired for her."[26]

Let us allow for an occasional memory of Sarah Sherman to break Calhoun's determined concentration as he trudged the rutted country roads near Abbeville, and let us allow for a good many warm thoughts about Floride and her family. The more fascinating question is, did he also allow his concentration to be shattered by the image of Slab Town barmaid Nancy Hanks?

This question, which will startle anyone unfamiliar with South Carolina folklore, is forced upon us by the myth still told there that John C. Calhoun fathered Abraham Lincoln. The story, which appears to have grown out of the conflicting accounts Lincoln's law partner William Herndon gave of Lincoln's parentage, holds that young lawyer Calhoun, while traveling to court, fell into the habit of staying over at a stagecoach tavern in Slab Town, near Anderson, where the attraction was "a fine handsome young girl" named Nancy Hanks. The ardent young couple became lovers, and "in the course of time Mr. Calhoun hired a man, bought two horses to take Nancy to her relatives in Kentucky, where Abraham was born, Nancy riding all the way on horseback. It is said Mr. Calhoun often remembered Nancy and the boy, went once to see them." This particular account was written down by an elderly Abbeville resident in 1909 and sent to the *Charleston News and Courier,* but the oral tradition goes back much earlier to descendants of the Hanks family that had run the tavern. The tavern existed, and so did Nancy Hanks, but the story is false because the Nancy Hanks who became Lincoln's mother had already married Thomas Lincoln and borne a daughter to him in Kentucky at the time of Calhoun's alleged indiscretion.[27]

Calhoun was not the only famous political figure said to have sired Lincoln, an honor given to John Marshall, among others. The obvious irony involved in thinking of the Defender of the South as the father of the Great Emancipator obviously contributed to the popularity of the story, but there is more to it than that. Later in his life and after his death Calhoun's eulogists repeatedly pointed to what Robert Rhett called the "crowning glory of Mr. Calhoun's character—his private life." Despite the fierce political battles in which he engaged, Calhoun's reputation has been singularly free of the scandalous disclosures and salacious innuendo that at some point touch the lives of most public figures. That is probably one reason the Nancy Hanks story has persisted; sin is never more attractive than when it appears to stain slightly the memory of a noble leader. But quite apart from the tendency of Americans to cut their heroes down to size, it is possible to believe that the Calhoun–Nancy Hanks legend could have some basis in fact without being inconsistent with Calhoun's character. Calhoun would have been in his mid-twenties when his alleged affair with the barmaid took place. In the culture of the South Carolina upper country at the turn of the century young bachelor lawyers were expected to drink, gamble, and frolic—and let nature take its course. Although Calhoun was never given to self-indulgence, he was not monastic and certainly not a prude. Nor was he squeamish about sex. When his cousin Wentworth Boiusseau was accused of a sexual crime (probably sodomy), which was a capital offense in South Carolina, Calhoun was able to explain the incident in a matter-of-fact manner to Floride (Boiusseau's aunt) and to give his cousin enough money to get him out of the country. Years later, when one of his own sons came down with venereal disease, Calhoun counseled him with a sorrowful but compassionate firmness that did great credit to him as a father. Perhaps Calhoun was able to understand the waywardness of others because like most people who magnify the importance of self-control, he felt the dangerous pull of passion within himself. Although he would certainly have understood what St. Paul meant when he said it was better to marry than burn, Calhoun would also have seen the wisdom in Benjamin Franklin's advice to young men: "Rarely use venery except for procreation and health."[28]

We will probably never know for certain about Calhoun's legendary relationship with the barmaid at Slab Town, but we can be sure that during the three years from 1808 to 1811, as he launched his legal and political career, his thoughts increasingly turned toward marriage. Sometime early in 1808 he visited Floride Colhoun at Bonneau's Ferry, at her Cooper River plantation, where he apparently saw her namesake and daughter as a woman for the first time. The younger Floride was then sixteen, petite, pretty, socially accomplished, and ideally prepared through her mother's example to assume the responsibilities of the plantation lady. Only a few years earlier Calhoun had looked upon her as a little girl; now he saw her as a desirable woman and perhaps a bride. It took a year of separation for Calhoun to convince himself that he was

in love. After explaining his plight to the elder Floride, he confessed
that he was heartsick at the possibility that her daughter might not
accept him. "It will be useless for me to conceal from you my increased
anxiety on that subject," he wrote; "if I should finally be disappointed
by any adverse circumstance, which heaven forbid, it will be by far the
most unlucky accident of my life."

Whatever misgivings the mother may have had about letting her
daughter receive a suitor's attentions at such an early age must have
been counteracted when she found that the marriage was already being
talked about in Charleston in the summer of 1809. She soon broached
the matter to her daughter and found her receptive. "I can scarcely
describe my emotions," Calhoun wrote upon receiving the news. "I
formerly thought that it would be impossible for me to be strongly
agitated in an affair of this kind, but that opinion now seems to me
wholly unfounded." For perhaps the only time in his adult life John
Calhoun was overwhelmed.[29]

He did not actually see the young woman who was challenging his
self-control until early January 1810. Upon returning home from a visit
to Bonneau's Ferry, he found himself transported but anxious to maintain propriety, and he continued to address Floride not in letters directly but through her mother to avoid gossip. That restraint dissolved,
however, when the elder Floride took her young charge off once more
to Newport for the summer. "I have only received one letter from you
and not one from Floride since you left Carolina," he wrote in near
panic on August 24. "I on my part have written eight or nine."[30]

In the one letter to "Miss Floride" which has survived, Calhoun
assured her that his love glowed "with no less ardour than at the moment of parting," a happy omen which showed that he loved her as
much for her "character," "innocence," and "cheerfulness" as for her
physical beauty. "Such, my dear Floride, are the charms by which you
have conquered over your subject whom you hold in willing servitude."
It was a love letter with a little moral lecture included, but by the time
he reached the end Calhoun had forgotten all about character. "Adieu
my love; my heart's delight," he wrote. "I am your true lover."[31]

The wedding took place at Bonneau's Ferry in January 1811 and
attracted guests from among the better families all over South Carolina. John was twenty-eight; Floride eighteen. They were second cous-

Floride Bonneau Calhoun.

Copy from the Collection of Fort Hill.
Original monotone is at the High Museum of Art in Atlanta, Georgia

ins, but marriages between cousins were commonplace within the state, and Calhoun kin celebrated the latest strengthening of family ties. Meanwhile, many other Carolinians could not help noticing how appropriate it was that a low-country heiress should be marrying a leader from the upper country at a time when the state was becoming more politically unified than ever before.

Just three months before his marriage Calhoun had been elected to replace his cousin Joseph in the United States House of Representatives. Although obviously a love match for Calhoun, marriage brought him the necessary financial independence he needed to support a career in politics and public service. By now his two older brothers, William and James, had begun plantations of their own while his younger brother, Patrick, attended the Abbeville property. All the brothers were on their way to becoming substantial slaveholders, William and Patrick with the help of marriages to wealthy heiresses from the upper country and James with profits from a cotton brokerage in Augusta. Floride's dowry together with John's share of his father's estate would make it possible for the newlyweds to build their own plantation on the banks of the Savannah not far from Waddel's school.

Because their future plantation, which was called Bath, had no suitable house, John and Floride spent the spring months after their marriage at her mother's Bonneau's Ferry plantation and summered at another property owned by the elder Floride in the hill village of Pendleton. To be in love in Charleston in the spring is irresistible, and John's pride in showing off his petite and lovely bride in the parlors and ballrooms of the tidewater elite overcame his inbred disdain for Charleston's decadent ways. Although the prejudices of frontier Presbyterianism prevented him from accompanying Floride to the theater, he was happy to be able to report to her mother that she had returned from that visit with "no inclination" to return. "I was pleased to see," he wrote, "that her good sense prevented her from being dazzled by the glare of novelty." By this time Floride was already carrying their first child, Andrew Pickens Calhoun, who was born at Bonneau's Ferry on October 15, 1811, just nine months to the week after their marriage.[32]

Calhoun had a bare fortnight with Floride and their new son before setting off to claim his seat in Congress. It was the first in what was to be a long history of painful separations, but as Calhoun headed toward

John C. Calhoun upon entering the Congress in 1811.
One of the earliest likenesses.

From the Frontispiece Volume Ten of the Calhoun papers. National Portrait Gallery

Washington, his heart was full. His new family was healthy, his politics were right, his connections impeccable, his training was outstanding, and there was little chance that life in the distant capital city would change him in any meaningful way; he was far too rooted for that.

3

The War Hawk, 1810–1817

CALHOUN took his seat in the United States House of Representatives on November 6, 1811. He was twenty-nine years old, only
five years out of law school with minimal experience in law and
politics. He had sat in the South Carolina legislature for no more than a
few weeks; now as a young Congressman he would be called upon
almost instantly to help steer the country into war, and he would have
to hold his own against some of the most illustrious and eloquent political leaders in the country. Calhoun had found his place; Washington
would be a second home to him for almost forty years.

The capital city was not entirely strange to him since he had passed
through it on his way to Connecticut. Many visitors to Washington for
the first time commented on the dreary aspects of the place. Unfinished government buildings surrounded by scattered shacks inter-
spersed with gullies, thickets, and swamps in which a Congressman
would get lost within a mile of the Capitol did not invite comparison
with the splendors of London or Paris. Daniel Webster, who had never
seen London, but was familiar with the Georgian elegance of Ports-
mouth, New Hampshire, and Boston, thought that Washington looked
"more like Hampstead heath than a city."[1]

Calhoun was not a person to worry much about appearances. It was
not the unfinished architecture in Washington but the unsettled confrontation between republican virtue and imperial tyranny that caught
his attention. Part of the the animus Calhoun harbored for Great Britain came from his father, and part from the fact that British warships
were not permitting South Carolina cotton to be shipped to Europe.
One of the first letters Calhoun wrote after reaching Washington was
to advise his brother "to sell as soon as possible" if he could get a decent
price for his crops. Nothing done in Washington would change the
commercial future in the short run, but the new Congressman ex-

pected that "strong measures will be resorted to." Calhoun did not need to remind his brother that these measures would be directed against the British. The real cause of the disruption of American commerce was the war between Britain and France, but most Americans outside Federalist New England blamed the British navy for forcing American ships to sit quietly rotting in port, for attacking American vessels within sight of the American shore, and for impressing freeborn American seamen into the Royal Navy. When Calhoun combined these outrages with what appeared to be an unholy alliance between British agents and Indian savages on the American frontier (the famous Battle of Tippecanoe was being fought when Calhoun took his seat in Congress), he concluded that the new Republic was being systematically dishonored by its old enemy. American rights, American liberties were at stake, and the only sure remedy was a return to the militance of 1776.[2]

Although Calhoun had been forced to leave Floride and their infant son, Andrew Pickens Calhoun, at home, he did not find himself among strangers in Washington. Most Congressmen at that time lived in boardinghouses grouped according to regional and political interest, and Calhoun was quickly welcomed into what was soon called the War Mess with South Carolina colleagues Langdon Cheves and William Lowndes, Felix Grundy of Tennessee, and Henry Clay. Cheves was an old friend who, after a childhood similar to Calhoun's in the Carolina backcountry, had become a successful commercial lawyer in Charleston and had served as attorney general of South Carolina. Lowndes, a towering scarecrow of a man, with courtly manners and an exceptional mind, had also been active in the South Carolina legislature and soon became one of Calhoun's closest friends. Grundy, who had married one of Calhoun's second cousins, was a product of the Kentucky frontier and, like Calhoun, had lost close family members to the Indians and had begun his formal education in a simple frontier academy. Stocky, red-faced, and blunt-spoken, Grundy was a successful criminal lawyer with the "idiom and manner of the unadulterated West." Calhoun, Cheves, and Lowndes were twenty-nine. Grundy was thirty-seven, and Clay thirty-four. The acknowledged leader of the War Mess, Clay had already served twice in the United States Senate and once as speaker of the house in Kentucky. Coming from an obscure poor to middling-class family in Virginia and almost without formal education, Clay had had the good fortune to be taken in hand by Jefferson's friend George Wythe, and his political career had skyrocketed after he moved to Kentucky, culminating in his recent elevation to Speaker of the U.S. House of Representatives. Lanky, careless in dress, with a long, narrow face and a wide mouth that could move instantly to expressions of mirth, rage, and scorn, Clay was noted for his ability to control others. He had already begun to develop a domestic legislative program emphasizing tariffs and internal improvements, and the calculated poise and apparent indifference that he assumed on the floor of the House belied his fierce ambition and deadly determination. In Kentucky a man was expected to put his honor where his mouth was, and Clay had already fought one duel growing out of an encounter in the Kentucky legislature.[3]

With Clay clearly in command of the House, important committee assignments were distributed to the newly elected young War Hawks. Calhoun was given the number two position on the Foreign Relations Committee, which would, he assured his brother, "in a great measure determine the course that will be pursued." The first business of the committee was to respond to President Madison's message to Congress which complained of continued violations of American neutral rights by the warring powers and asked for measures to strengthen the national defense. Working with his chairman, Peter Porter, from upstate New York, whom he had known at Yale and Litchfield, and with his mess mate Grundy, Calhoun wrote most of the report castigating Britain for refusing to follow Napoleon's example and curtail its attacks on American commerce. Recalling "that proud spirit of liberty and independence which sustained our fathers," the report included resolutions asking Madison to add ten thousand troops to the authorized strength of the regular army and giving him the power to recruit fifty thousand volunteers, muster the militia, prepare the navy, and arm the merchant marine.[4]

Although Calhoun was shortly forced to defend his report in spirited debate with John Randolph and other members of the opposition, his maiden speech in the Congress was appropriately not on foreign policy but on a matter of constitutional interpretation. The House had reported an apportionment bill fixing representation under the census of 1810 at a ratio of thirty-seven thousand. When the Senate amended the bill, Calhoun contended that the action was contrary to the principle "that liberty can only exist in a division of the sovereign power . . . where each of the parts had within itself the means of protection." He was worried not about the ratio but about the principle, and if the Constitution allowed the Senate to restrict the power of the House in such a vital matter, it was "a case of omission" by the founders. "Let it not be said, the Senate will always exercise this power with discretion," Calhoun warned. "Faith is an article of religion but not of politics." In a version of this speech reported by a Baltimore paper, he likened the Senate to "a diplomatic corps" designed to protect "state rights" while members of the House were "the guardians of the national principle incorporated, and wisely incorporated into this government."[5]

Calhoun's initial effort in congressional debate, passed over for the most part by colleagues and historians, is important not just because it shows his early nationalism, which has long been recognized, but because it demonstrates his fascination from the beginning with fundamental constitutional principles and his insistence that the separate interests making up the American federal system be allowed to protect themselves. His argument to protect the national interest could just as easily have been used to support the concept of states' rights and a concurrent majority.

Although Calhoun's friends in the Twelfth Congress paid little heed to their colleague's concern for constitutionality, they could not help being impressed by the way he handled John Randolph. One of the legendary figures in the Congress, Randolph had once been Jefferson's floor manager before falling out with the Republicans and becoming a party of one. Randolph looked and acted more like an eccentric member of the House of Lords than an American Congressman. A Virginia planter with more than four hundred slaves, he stalked the House imperiously, booted and spurred, swathed in voluminous overcoats, and attended by a pack of hounds. Nervous, shrill-voiced, and emaciated, he had a comic look about him, but he was no laughing matter and would challenge an opponent at the drop of a pin.

When the report of the Committee on Foreign Relations was issued, Randolph, a vociferous minority member in the committee, attacked it with typical severity. Ridiculing the flimsiness of American charges against Britain, he predicted that Americans would be too absorbed in advancing personal interest to go to war or pay for it. Calhoun replied on December 12 and immediately lifted the level of debate from a discussion of national interest to a defense of national honor. Since American rights were at stake, he urged that "when we contend let us contend for all our rights. The doubtful and the certain, the unimportant and the essential." Scorning Randolph's assertion that Americans would not pay taxes to defend their rights, Calhoun called it "[o]nly fit for shops and counting houses" which "ought not to disgrace the seat of sovereignty by its squalid and vile appearance." The country could never be safe "but under the shield of honor"; every citizen must be protected in the lawful pursuit of business because "protection and patriotism are reciprocal." Others could worry about calculating costs if they chose; Calhoun would not pretend "to estimate in dollars and cents the value of national independence or national affection."[6]

About a week after his encounter with Randolph, Calhoun, desperate for news about his wife and baby son, received separate letters from Floride and her mother telling him that all was well back at Bonneau's Ferry. He had discovered that communication between Washington and South Carolina was difficult and slow. It took several days to make the trip between his home and the capital, whether he chose to rely on horsepower and go overland through North Carolina and Virginia or travel partway along the coast by boat. A letter sometimes took a month to get from Bonneau's Ferry to Washington. He had every reason to be worried about Floride. He had left her, still almost a girl at nineteen and not yet recovered from the birth of their first child, and would not return for eight months. "I feared that her anxiety of mind at my leaving her might injure her health," he wrote his mother-in-law, and "I am sure I have great cause to be thankful that she has entirely recovered." During the six years he served in the House long absences from home and labored communications with his wife were the rule. She would be mother and father to their son, would learn how to manage their new plantation in his absence, and would bear and lose two daughters. It was the beginning of a process which in the end made her as self-sufficient as her husband was.

Calhoun could bear the separation from his family stoically because he believed that he was making history. John Randolph might rail about the indignity of being scourged "by the unfledged politicians of the day," but the real message, which Randolph and other members of the old guard did not want to hear, was that a new generation was taking over in Washington. Calhoun put the matter nicely when he wrote to a friend in South Carolina: "It is the commence[ment] of a new era in our politics. Heretofore the conductors of our affairs have attempted to remove difficulties by a sort of political management. They thought that national honor and interest could both be maintained and respected, not by war, or a preparation for it, but by commercial arrangement and negotiations." This policy reaped "distrust at home and contempt abroad. We have said we will change, we will defend ourselves by force."[7]

During much of his later career Calhoun vainly tried to stem the national tide in America; now he savored the opportunity to run with it. "Were I a single man I would certainly take a commission," he wrote to his cousin. "The war will be a favourite one with the country. Much honor awaits those who may distinguish themselves." Patriotic ardor mixed with personal ambition is the powerful engine that drove Calhoun during the winter of 1812. He stayed out of society, concentrating all his efforts as chair of the Committee on Foreign Relations to maintain the prowar majority in the House, where it was understood that the President would ask for a declaration of war by June 1812 if England did not change its policies.[8]

Meanwhile, Calhoun continued to fend off Randolph, who by May had become desperate enough to claim a recent eclipse and passing comet as signs that the heavens were displeased with the country's warlike leaders. A less zealous politician might have smiled at Randolph's foolishness and let it pass, but as other members of the House were beginning to realize, Calhoun did not smile easily, and almost never over matters of serious political difference. Even if the outcome was absolutely sure one way or the other, he rarely missed a chance to score a point. After replying to his older adversary with a careful, reasoned defense of the embargo policy, which Randolph was criticizing, Calhoun proceeded to dismiss him as a voice out of the past: "The gentleman from Virginia has told us much of the signs of the times. I did hope that the age of superstition was past. . . . Are we to renounce our reason. . . . If so, the times are bad indeed. . . . Sir, if we must examine the auspices; if we must inspect the entrails of the times, I would pronounce the omens good . . . and what more favorable could we desire than that the nation is, at last roused from its lethargy, and that it has determined to vindicate its interest and honor."[9]

On May 29 Randolph made one last attempt to talk down the war effort. He was interrupted on a point of order by Calhoun and ruled out of order by Henry Clay. The perpetual talking machine was silenced in the House for the first time in more than twelve years. Four days later, June 3, 1812, John Calhoun, acting on the recommendations of President Madison and the House Committee on Foreign Relations, presented a bill declaring war on Great Britain. It passed by a vote of 79 to 49. New York, New Jersey, Delaware, and all the New England states voted for peace. Calhoun wrote his cousin that he hoped the "courage and patriotism of the people" would make the war "as fortunate as just."[10]

Less than a month after declaring war Congress adjourned, and Calhoun hurried home for a long-overdue reunion with his wife and son. During his first year in Washington he had not ventured out much socially, preferring work in his room or the company of familiar boardinghouse friends to the elegant levees over which James and Dolley Madison presided in the handsome oval room of the presidential mansion. As a leading War Hawk he was naturally accused of partiality to France and stayed away as a matter of principle from the Christmas ball at that embassy. Curiously enough, however, Calhoun, Clay, and other members of the War Mess entertained the British ambassador, Augustus John Foster, for dinner on July 11. This gathering, following so closely on the formal declaration of war, has a certain nostalgic quality about it. Warmaking in 1812 was far different from warmaking today. Calhoun does not tell us what he thought of the dinner, but Henry Clay seems clearly to have been in charge. Foster, alternately bemused and baffled by these young American leaders so obsessed with national honor, reported simply that "the speaker was very warlike."[11]

By the summer of 1812 home for Calhoun had come to mean several places in South Carolina. Floride and the baby were staying with her mother in Charleston and at Bonneau's Ferry. The Calhoun plantation at Long Canes was being attended by John's brothers, who also kept an eye on the newly acquired plantation at Bath on the hills overlooking the Savannah River, where the Calhouns planned to build. Calhoun probably visited all these places in the summer in 1812, and his constituents in Abbeville must have been gratified to meet their new Congressman, whose father had served them in Charleston and Columbia decades earlier.

However attentive Calhoun may have been to old friends and constituents, most of his attention would have been given to Floride. During their courtship he had made a distinction between sexual attraction, which "requires the perpetual presence of the object to keep it alive," and the attraction of character, which "bids defiance to time." In Washington this distinction had blurred. He was successful in converting pent-up sexual energy into patriotic passion, but the pangs of separation remained severe, and he once "dreamed all night" of being with Floride "nursing our dear son, and regretted when I awoke to find it was a dream. I was in hopes that this morning's mail would bring me a letter from you, but was disappointed. It is near a month since I had one." All dreams came true that summer, and the following February Floride was to bear their second child.[12]

Back in Washington again as a bachelor in October 1812, Calhoun discovered that it was one thing for a brash new nation to declare war against the most powerful empire in the world and something else to win it. When he left Washington in July, he had predicted that Canada would quickly fall to American troops and that a wave of patriotism would overwhelm the antiwar sentiment in the northeastern states. When he returned in October, the Canada campaign had turned into an American disaster from Niagara to Fort Dearborn (site of Chicago), and New England was in a practical state of revolt over the war. For the next two years Calhoun worked as hard as any man in the country to turn the tide. In the process he began to exhibit some of those traits of mind and personality that later made him one of the most controversial public figures in the country.

Calhoun's fierce partisanship put off some Congressmen. He seemed determined to stifle all resistance to the war. After Randolph and others had tried to block the raising of additional troops, Calhoun reminded them that war had been declared "by a law of the land" and "till our opponents can prove that they have a right which is paramount to the public interest, we must persist in denying the right to thwart the success of the war." When Randolph argued that warring against England meant fighting for Catholicism, Calhoun simply jeered at him. "Because Bonaparte is not a Protestant you must surrender your rights!" And he accused him of wanting to tie politics to religion, "the unnatural union that has engendered the foulest progeny of human woes."[13]

If putting down John Randolph had become almost a matter of routine, the same could not be said for the new Representative from New Hampshire, Daniel Webster. Just Calhoun's age and, like him, the product of a simple frontier background and a fine college and professional education, Webster was not a man to be taken lightly. Heavy-browed and dark-complexioned with blazing eyes and a voice that could make the chamber ring, he combined the charismatic qualities of the great actor with an extraordinary mind. Webster could glance at a page once and remember it forever, and like Calhoun, he would not be intimidated by anyone. Clay may have assigned Webster to Calhoun's committee in order to contain him. If so, the strategy failed because Webster's first significant action in Congress was to introduce a resolution which in effect accused President Madison of having concealed information from France that might have encouraged England to revoke its sanctions against American trade, thus making a declaration of war unnecessary. The result was a furious debate over "Mr. Madison's war" and a flurry of publicity for Daniel Webster. Madison ultimately set the matter right, but the credibility of the war managers was so damaged that Calhoun could only remark darkly about Webster's motives and protest the futility of letting "ourselves to be beaten to death" while worrying whether France was as great a villain as England. Later, when Webster reminded the House that the abortive invasion of Canada was "not that entertainment to which we were invited . . . not that harvest of greatness and glory" that Calhoun and others had promised, the Carolinian accused Webster of talking as if he had "possessed all of the talent and confidence of the country" and sneered at his "miserable stale and absurd objections against offensive operations in Canada."[14]

When the war went badly, as it did most of the time, the administration needed to be able to count on Calhoun's tenacity in debate and his unwillingness to surrender a single point, but he was hardly a slavish disciple. In private he did not hesitate to belittle the President or, for that matter, the entire administration. "Our executive officers are most incompetent men," he wrote his friend James Macbride in December 1812, "and will let the best of causes I fear perish in their hands. We are literally borne down under the effects of error and mismanagement. I am sorry to say that many of them lie deep and are coeval with the existence of Mr. Jefferson's administration."[15]

Reviewing this period twenty years later, Calhoun was careful to emphasize his independence on party measures, citing as an example a speech delivered shortly after war had been declared in which he opposed the nonimportation acts for stifling the commercial genius of the American people and blunting patriotic enthusiasm for the war by making government "odious." It was this speech that Henry Adams later celebrated by writing: "With a single gesture this young statesman of the new school swept away the statesmanship of Jefferson and Adams, and waved aside the strongest convictions of his party."

Although Calhoun was willing enough to oppose traditional Republican party policies, his own political philosophy was classically republican. Like the revolutionary fathers, Calhoun believed that England's arbitrary rule over the sea was an example of unchecked power. "It originated in power, has grown just in proportion as opposing power has been removed, and can only be restrained by power." In some of his speeches Calhoun appeared to be lecturing his colleagues on the need for constancy, warning them especially against the dangers of a "factious opposition" in which "the attachment *to a party* becomes stronger than that to *our country.*" This, of course, was the kind of old-fashioned republican doctrine that could help Calhoun and the prowar majority put a leash on their antiwar colleagues.

Calhoun believed that in addition to the dangers from "factious opposition," the Republic was weakened from within by the tendency of Americans to put market values above national honor. New England was disaffected because the war hurt trade. Referring to "some pecuniary difficulties in Massachusetts and in other places," Calhoun asked scornfully, "Must we for them renounce our lasting prosperity and greatness? Have we no fortitude, no self-command? Must we, like children, yield to the impulse of present pleasure, however fatal?" The remedy for this and every other public vice would only be found in "the good sense and virtue of the people."[16]

Calhoun's message and style were not calculated to please everyone, and he had already begun to make enemies, even back in South Carolina. Before leaving Abbeville to take up his congressional seat in the fall of 1811, he admitted to a friend that his unwillingness to distribute favors had turned some local politicians against him, and he dismissed one of them, William Smith, as a "weak political intriguer." Smith later served eleven years in the United States Senate. He was an older man of considerable wealth, influence, and power in the state. He may or may not have expected favors from the twenty-nine-year-old Calhoun, but surely it was the young Representative's arrogance, his tendency to dismiss opponents with a condescension bordering on contempt, that turned Smith into a lifelong enemy and was already alienating some of Calhoun's colleagues in the House. Richard Stockton of New Jersey grumbled about being forced to endure Calhoun's "lectures" on the danger of factions, and Zebulon Shipherd from New York complained about his manner "bespeaking the authority of an apostle." Calhoun might lose his share of votes, but like an oracle, he would never admit that he was wrong; that may have been what the Maryland Representative had in mind when he called him an "ignis-fatuus."[17]

In December 1813 the House met in secret session to debate an embargo. Calhoun was on record as opposing any restriction on trade, but in the final roll call he switched his vote to support the administration. After subsequently voting against making the embargo debates public, he was accused by Thomas Grosvenor of New York of wanting to conceal his inconsistency on the issue. The exchange which immediately flared up between the Carolinian and the New Yorker grew heated. "Calhoun keeps back and so far has borne patiently Grosvenor's philippic of yesterday," one member reported. That patience was soon exhausted. Grosvenor issued a challenge; seconds were chosen, and the duel was to be fought on the Virginia side of the Potomac at one o'clock on December 27. The Speaker, never one to refuse a challenge himself, contemplated the affair with "infinite regret" but confessed that the House was powerless to intervene. Along with others in his party Clay was gratified to read in the *National Intelligencer* on December 28 that the dispute had been "arranged in a manner entirely honorable to both parties." We do not know exactly how Calhoun behaved in this matter. Duels were almost commonplace in South Carolina among men of his class, and he could not have refused a challenge without serious political damage at home. Of course, the entire shape of American history could have been radically changed had the encounter taken place, but it is idle to speculate about that. The point is that there was always a fire burning underneath the controlled "cast-iron" exterior of John Calhoun. The man was made for confrontation, and this inflexibility was to cost him dearly in the future.[18]

The lowest point in the war came on August 24, 1814, when the British captured and burned Washington. Calhoun had been home since May, and his joy in greeting a new baby daughter was cut short by news of the disaster. How did he react? Did he despair? Did he realize that the taunting of men like Webster and Randolph which he had so scornfully repelled may have been on the mark after all? The record does not tell us, but we do know that at this time of extreme vulnerability Calhoun was felled by fever and was a month late in returning to Congress that October. It is hard to imagine a more demoralizing situation. The House met in Blodgett's Hotel to hear the President's message. The Capitol lay in ashes, the government was practically bankrupt, and the New England states were about to meet in Hartford to discuss the probability of going their own way.

Confronted with disaster at every turn, the administration gave top priority to restoring national credit, and Calhoun was asked to steer a new national bank bill through Congress. Even at this critical moment he found it difficult to follow party discipline. Refusing to support the fiscally irresponsible "contrivance" reported by Secretary of the Treasury Alexander Dallas, Calhoun added so many amendments that it was essentially his own bill when it was rejected by the House. After helping defeat a second administration bill originating in the Senate, Calhoun, with some help from Webster and others, put together a bank bill that passed Congress only to be vetoed by the President.

In his autobiography Calhoun points to this episode as an example of personal independence, his willingness to bear "patiently the denunciation daily levelled against him" by angry party members, and his ability to maintain a leadership position without sacrificing his own convictions. The truth is that he was lucky. Had the war lasted much longer, Calhoun would have been placed in the impossible position of having sabotaged his own cause. Ultimately he presented a bank bill Madison could accept, which was to last for twenty years. Finally, in the midst of the congressional deadlock in the winter of 1815, news came that the war was over.[19]

On February 11, 1815, Calhoun sent his cousin in Abbeville the "glorious news that the British have evacuated the Island of Orleans." Two days later, while the House was still arguing about a bank, news arrived that American commissioners in Ghent had signed a peace treaty. The treaty, which had been concluded before Jackson routed the British at New Orleans, did little to resolve the issues over which the war had presumably been fought, but Calhoun, like the rest of the country, was willing to overlook that and proclaim victory. "To all practical purposes," he exulted to his colleagues, "we have achieved complete success."[20]

Three days after Calhoun proclaimed military victory Congress adjourned, and the exhilarated wartime legislator returned to his Savannah River plantation to suffer the first great domestic loss in his married life. His fifteen-month-old daughter, named after her mother, was just beginning to talk and walk when Calhoun arrived on March 20. Within days, to the delight of her parents, the little girl was scampering all over the house "in the bloom of life," only to be struck down by "fever and vomiting" on the night of April 6 and carried away in a matter of hours. Reporting "the heaviest calamity that ever occured [*sic*] to us," Calhoun wrote to his mother-in-law that Floride had isolated herself in grief beyond his reach. He reminded her that life was uncertain, that "almost all parents have sufferred [*sic*] equal calamity," and that "Providence" would assure that their daughter would be "far more happy than she could be here with us," but every word of consolation seemed to make Floride more miserable. "She thinks only of her dear child; and recalls to her mind every thing that made her interesting, thus furnishing food for her grief."[21]

Calhoun experienced many losses in his life but never despair. During his courtship he had come as close as he ever would to losing control of his emotions, but temperament and conviction combined to prevent him from joining Floride in the depths of her suffering. Calhoun's remarks about that unhappy event are revealing for what they say about his religious belief. Immune to evangelical appeals, he never joined a church, never made a formal profession of Christian faith, and never expressed the slightest doubt that a higher Providence directed the affairs of human beings.

Even as they mourned, the young couple conceived another child. As Floride's body thickened during the summer and fall of 1815 so did their hopes that Providence would send them another daughter. Calhoun had to leave for Washington before the baby was due, but he was careful to make arrangements for Floride to be confined in Charleston under the care of his college friend Dr. James Macbride.[22] Floride gave birth sometime in January, and the new baby was christened Jane Calhoun. But once again Providence proved unkind, and Jane probably died before Calhoun could see her. There is no mention of the event in the Calhoun papers, but it could only have intensified Floride's agony.

Meanwhile, back in Washington history seemed to be taking a more positive turn as Calhoun found himself cast in a central role leading a legislative program that expressed the nationalist consensus dominating the country in wake of the war. Calhoun seemed to glory in the change in public sentiment. "We see everywhere a nationality of feeling," he informed the House on January 2, 1816. "We hear sentiments from every part of the House in favor of union and against sectional spirit— Let us direct our attention, then . . . to the objects calculated to accomplish the prosperity and greatness of the nation, and we shall certainly create a national spirit."[23]

Calhoun's vision of a strong national future assumed that Americans would persist in the moral and military strength that had brought them victory. He saw Europe emboldened by the banishment of Napoleon, poised as one nation to keep the liberties of citizens in the New World from infecting the institutions of the Old, and he was sure that future wars with England were not only possible but highly probable. "Future wars, long and bloody, will exist between this country and Great Britain. . . . You will have to encounter British jealousy and hostility in every shape." Thus Calhoun pleaded against too rapid demobilization of the armed forces and argued for the establishment of military academies in different parts of the country accessible not just to the sons of the wealthy but to those from the middle and lower ranks of society, where there are "stronger stimulants" to upward mobility.

Calhoun paired military with moral strength. He hoped that war had taught Americans how to get along without British goods and that it would also teach them "to throw off the thralldom of thought." Although he was speaking primarily in terms of political institutions and legal precedents, the sentiment is very close to the position Emerson took years later when he called for a new American scholar.[24]

Like many other thoughtful Americans in his generation, Calhoun was highly conscious of the stern moral legacy passed on by men like his father who had launched the Republic. He had lived long enough to believe that nineteenth-century Americans seemed to belong to a softer breed, and in a speech supposedly devoted to a bill on tax policy, he lectured the House on the importance of national character. History showed that nations tended to fall into decline by succumbing, like Rome and France, to the lure of perpetual war and conquest or by "sinking into nothingness through imbecility and apathy." He thought the second extreme more likely for Americans blessed with almost too much of the good things in life. The ease of American life worked "on the dispositions and habits of this people, with something like the effects attributed to southern climates—they dispose them to pleasure and inactivity, except in pursuit of wealth." The American nation, Calhoun concluded, was in the position of young Hercules, who could have chosen a life of "ease and pleasure" or one of "labor and virtue. The hero adopted the latter and his fame and glory are known to the world. May this nation, the youthful Hercules, possessing his form and muscles, be inspired with similar sentiments and follow his example."

One of the reasons that Calhoun became a nationally visible leader so quickly is that he instinctively seemed to understand what it meant to be a new nation not only politically but culturally and economically. It was appropriate, for example, that he should have chaired the joint committee which commissioned John Trumbull's monumental Revolutionary War paintings for the Capitol rotunda. "We too have now our heroes," Calhoun said. "It is impossible that we can now be denigrated by comparisons."[25]

When Calhoun told the House more than ten years before Webster became famous for the words that he believed "the *liberty* and the *union* of this country were inseparably united," he was saying that despite the divisiveness of the war, it was the unity within the nation that brought victory. He believed that unity would persist as the nation developed with essential, evenhanded assistance from the federal government. Looking back on his part in the legislation of the period from the vantage point of 1843, Calhoun tried to diminish his role in supporting the Tariff of 1816, but his speech in its favor is a strong, clear endorsement that a healthy American manufacturing interest will "bind together more closely one widely spread Republic."[26]

No man in Congress had been more constant in supporting the war. He naturally thought that it had been carried on in a way that was fair to all the states, and it was just as natural for him to expect that the government which presided over the developing nation at peace would put the common welfare ahead of special interests. Thus his support for internal improvements. Remembering that a barrel of flour shipped to Detroit during the war cost fifty dollars and that it had cost the army fifty cents a pound to transport cannon and ball, he knew how important roads, bridges, and navigable waterways were to national security. But it was more a concern for union than for national defense that lay behind his often quoted speech of February 4, 1817, in which he warned against the divisive tendencies in a great, rapidly, almost "fearfully growing" nation, "our pride and danger—our weakness and strength. . . . We are under the most imperious obligation to counteract every tendency to disunion." Madison had argued that federalism would overcome the difficulties involved in governing a large republic, but Calhoun knew it would take more than that: It would be necessary to "conquer space." Then, as now, the conquest of space required vision. Calhoun called for a citizenry with "enlarged views," a kind of civic imagination not required of citizens in a small republic.[27]

It was partly in the interest of conquering space that Calhoun voted to raise the compensation of members of the House from six dollars a day to fifteen hundred dollars a session. "We ought," he said later, "to attract suitable talents from the most distant part of our Republic by a full and generous allowance." Here Calhoun misjudged the popular sentiment. Constituents all over the country were outraged at what they saw as a pay grab. Sentiment in South Carolina followed the national pattern. Two former Congressmen in Calhoun's district came out against him, one of them, General William Butler, offering himself as an opposing candidate. Calhoun's friends advised him to go to the people and apologize. He refused, but he did address public meetings at Edgefield and Abbeville to explain his position, and unlike most Congressmen who had supported the bill (two-thirds of the members were not returned), he was "triumphantly re-elected."[28]

Back in Washington in the winter of 1817 Calhoun found himself surrounded by new faces belonging to Congressmen who claimed they were "instructed" to repeal the compensation law. Calhoun was appalled. By conviction and temperament he found it difficult to retreat, compromise, or apologize, and the idea of carrying instructions from the electorate like a common messenger repelled him. "Are we bound in all cases to do what is popular?" he asked his new colleagues. "If so, how are political errors once prevalent ever to be corrected?" Calling the notion "an innovation on the principles of our government," Calhoun assured the newcomers, *"I am not instructed.* The Constitution is my letter of instruction."[29]

As Madison's second term came to an end, it was clear that Calhoun's role as a national political player was secure and there seemed no limit to what he might legitimately aspire to. Without becoming a national hero like Andrew Jackson he had reaped honor for his role in the war. He had been willing to lead in time of crisis, and he had led confidently and intelligently. The inflexibility in his character had served him well in the causes he supported. He was a man for the times—a new leader in a new nation, riding a new wave of patriotism into what could be a magnificent future. If he dreamed on occasion of a greater role as the authentic American Hercules, he had reason.

4

Secretary of War, 1817–1824

CALHOUN returned home as a United States Congressman for the last time in March 1817. He was excited by the prospect of meeting his new daughter, Anna Maria, born the previous month, who was to grow up to be closer to him than any of his children. He was also pleased at the state of the country and his own political future. James Monroe, Madison's Secretary of State, was the new President, and the Federalists were paying the price for having opposed what was now popularly believed to have been a glorious war. Calhoun had worked closely with Monroe as chair of the House Committee on Foreign Relations and had supported him in the party caucus in which he had narrowly defeated William Crawford. Whether in Congress or in some other capacity he was bound to play a significant role in the new administration. Calhoun could hardly have been surprised, therefore, when Monroe wrote him in October asking him to be Secretary of War.

Accepting the President's invitation meant that Calhoun had to establish himself as a social as well as a political presence in Washington. James and Dolley Madison had presided over the lively Washington social scene with energy and grace, but because the Monroes were relatively antisocial, Cabinet officers and their wives would be expected to take up the social slack in a city known for its constant round of receptions, banquets, and balls. As a Congressman Calhoun had been able to live a frugal, bachelorlike existence in a Capitol Hill boardinghouse. Now he set off with his wife, his young son, and his infant daughter in a four-horse carriage driven by one of his own slaves. The trip from Charleston to Washington took about two weeks, and they were soon established in a large house on the corner of Sixth and E streets near the present National Gallery of Art. The house cost nine thousand dollars and, together with a much larger establishment the elder Floride was to purchase for them as a summer home in George-town, put the Calhouns at the center of Washington society. Mean-while, he had work to do.

In accepting a position in Monroe's Cabinet, Calhoun brushed aside the advice of friends who thought his intellectual and verbal powers made him more suited for parliamentary than executive duties. This assumption did not square with his own supreme self-confidence. He accepted the assignment to prove that he could lead in action as well as argument, because he believed that the political agenda in the immediate future would focus on the administration of the national legislative program recently passed, and because he knew that the route to the presidency had traditionally led through the Cabinet.

Calhoun had supported Monroe in 1816 over Secretary of the Trea-sury William Crawford because he saw Monroe as the legitimate heir to a tradition of principle and policy going back to Jefferson and before that to the patriots of his father's generation. The major way in which John Calhoun in 1817 differed from Patrick Calhoun in thinking about the government lay in the use of power. When Patrick Calhoun ap-proached the seat of power in London, Charleston, or Philadelphia, he invariably sniffed a potential for tyranny. His son, however, had gone to school in the politics of a Congress at war, when the key problem had been to mobilize power for a victory which preserved republican virtue and honor. During the war disunion had been the great danger; power employed for the common good had saved the Union, and John Cal-houn had come to believe that power justly administered could keep the Republic free and make it great.

Except for his brief maiden speech on apportionment Representa-tive Calhoun had paid little attention to constitutional issues. In his last major speech proposing the establishment of a permanent fund to sup-port internal improvements, he had admitted, "He was no advocate for refined arguements [*sic*] on the Constitution. The instrument was not intended as a thesis for the logician to exercise his ingenuity on. It ought to be construed with plain good sense." Although he later changed his mind, Calhoun thought then that clauses empowering the Congress to levy taxes and provide for the general welfare provided a constitutional basis for his proposal, and he was shocked when Madison vetoed the bill. He had not given up, however, on the plan to conquer space, and he knew that the Secretary of War, the largest disbursing officer in the government, was the only Cabinet officer with the resources to accomplish that.[1]

In accepting Monroe's offer, Calhoun joined an extremely able and experienced group of political leaders. At the head of the Cabinet was Secretary of State John Quincy Adams, son of the second President. The fifty-year-old Adams had been educated abroad, had completed diplomatic assignments in Russia, Germany, and the Netherlands, and had negotiated the Treaty of Ghent with Henry Clay and Albert Gallatin. An accomplished scholar and serious political thinker, Adams was enormously gifted for public life in every way except his personality. Socially clumsy, blunt to the point of rudeness, and almost pathologically jealous of colleagues and competitors, Adams had broken with the Federalists some years earlier but had never really been accepted by the Republicans. On the basis of intelligence, experience, and position in the Cabinet, Adams was a logical candidate for the succession, but he would come to any presidential contest with heavy liabilities.

William Crawford was a planter from Georgia and a native of Virginia who, like Calhoun, had taken his early schooling under Waddel. Ten years older than Calhoun, Crawford had entered political life as a reformer by helping expose the massive Yazoo land frauds. A Jeffersonian of the states' rights school, he had served in the Senate, as ambassador to France, and as Secretary of War before becoming Madison's Secretary of the Treasury. Crawford had been the Republicans' second choice for President in 1816 and, as Monroe's Secretary of the Treasury, had good reason to think of himself as the heir apparent. A big, roughhewn man who never backed away from a fight (he had killed one man in a duel and wounded another), Crawford seemed to understand instinctively that a new kind of politics based on party connections and patronage was emerging in America. He soon became Calhoun's *bête noire*.

William Wirt, Attorney General, was the least political but one of the most engaging of the Cabinet members. A Virginia lawyer who had made his reputation by prosecuting Aaron Burr and was one of the country's leading literary mythmakers, Wirt had just finished an ambitious biography of Patrick Henry. He cared little for politics, everything for law and literature.

Smith Thompson, fifty-one, well connected in New York politics through a marriage into the Livingston family, had been chief justice in that state. He was known to be a favorite of the powerful young Martin Van Buren, and his term as Secretary of the Navy of the Monroe Cabinet would prove to be a way station on the road to the United States Supreme Court.

The President who took counsel from this talented assemblage has been compared unfavorably with his more distinguished predecessors, but he was unquestionably the most experienced American still active in public life. A revolutionary veteran wounded at Trenton, Monroe had studied law with his friend Jefferson and had been active in Congress during the Confederation and in making and ratifying the Constitution. He had served as governor and Senator for Virginia, ambassador to France, and Madison's Secretary of War and Secretary of State. Monroe may have lacked Washington's ability to command, Jefferson's creativity, and the mind of an Adams or a Madison, but he was obviously prepared to be President, and Calhoun, never overly impressed with competitors or superiors, regarded him with the respect he deserved.

There had been several names ahead of Calhoun's on Monroe's list for Secretary of War. Andrew Jackson, an obvious choice, was not interested, Henry Clay, angry at being passed over for Secretary of State, refused, as did Kentucky Governor Isaac Shelby and Calhoun's friend William Lowndes. To have been invited into the Cabinet almost by default does not seem to have bothered Calhoun. He knew that he was still relatively junior in the national political hierarchy, and he could recognize a great opportunity when he saw one.

Calhoun took over his duties on December 14, 1817, replacing Acting Secretary George Graham. Six days later he wrote a former colleague in the House that he was impressed by two things: the magnitude of his job and the lack of "exactness, economy and dispatch" in the way the department did its business. The reasons why Monroe had had so much difficulty finding a Secretary of War were becoming obvious. The department had become a fiscal and administrative nightmare. Calhoun was expected to cope with an enormous paper backlog (forty-five million dollars in unsettled accounts, twenty thousand pension claims) and bring order to bear over an army in the throes of a pell-mell demobilization, with all the chaos that implied, and without a rational organizational structure. This army, about eight thousand men, had no chief of staff, no chain of command, and an impossible mission. It was divided into a Northern and Southern Division and charged with the task of spreading its resources thinly enough to defend a land area of almost two million square miles. Calhoun soon learned what this meant in practice when he heard from T. Joseph Prince, assigned to garrison three forts and defend Charleston Harbor. The beleaguered lieutenant had just fourteen men at his disposal, hardly enough to man a lifeboat.[2]

The new Secretary presided over his shaky empire in a building flanking the executive mansion. The Treasury Department had a building of its own on the other side of the mansion; Calhoun shared his with the departments of State and Navy. He directed a staff of about twenty clerks under the chief clerk, Christopher Vandeventer, a former major who acted more or less as an undersecretary. Calhoun served as Secretary of War for eight years, and his papers for this period have been published in eight weighty volumes. A great deal of this material was prepared by clerks and signed by Calhoun, who was one of the least likely people in Washington to put his signature to any document he did not understand. Reading these volumes, one has to be impressed with his detailed involvement in the day-to-day operation of the army. In addition to advising the President, maintaining a constructive relationship with Congress, supervising the deployment of troops and the maintenance and construction of military installations, the Secretary had to decide such mundane matters as: whether a general had the authority to cut off an ear or put a brand on a deserter; whether the army should pay for a horse used by a soldier who in pursuing a deserter had also deserted, taking the horse with him; whether the unauthorized purchases of an assistant apothecary in New Orleans were fraudulent; whether a resigning chaplain living at home was entitled to collect for housing and forage; whether the government should continue to lend gunpowder to the du Ponts.[3]

Calhoun was determined to reverse a long tradition of mediocre leadership in the War Department. No one had been able to do for that department what Hamilton had been able to do for the Treasury because of the long-standing prejudice of Americans against a standing army. The idea of a citizen army sat better in the mind of republicans imbued with the myth that their untrained militia troops had twice defeated the professional British army. Actually, Washington's regular Continental Army had been a key element in keeping resistance alive in the 1770s, and militia troops had failed miserably in the first two years of the War of 1812. From his vantage point on the Foreign Relations Committee Calhoun had seen the debacle of 1812–1814, and when he complained that the war effort had broken down "under the effects of error and mismanagement," he was pointing directly at leadership and disorganization in the War Department and overreliance on militia troops.[4]

Secretary Calhoun moved quickly to tighten army organization. He strengthened a recently created general staff by ordering the chief of engineers to move from West Point to Washington and adding professionally trained officers as surgeon general and commissary general of subsistence. He was the first War Secretary to stress systematically the importance to the army of diet, clothing, health, and sanitation. He attacked the problem of accountability, reducing unsettled accounts from forty-five to three million dollars and imposing tighter controls on the way disbursing officers handled public money. Such efficiencies spoke well for Calhoun's administrative skill but did not address the anxiety of critics who opposed the policy of a strong standing army for ideological or economic reasons. In the spring of 1820 Congress directed Calhoun to submit a plan for reducing the army by about a third. He submitted a plan for reduction on December 12 in a report which a recent historian of the army calls "one of the pivotal documents in the history of American military thought."

Turning his back once again on the conventional wisdom of his party, Calhoun insisted that "a standing army in peace, in the present improved state of the military science, is an indispensable preparation." Untrained militia might be relied upon to garrison forts and "act in the field as light troops," but "to rely on them beyond this, to suppose our militia capable of meeting in the open field the regular troops of Europe, would be to resist the most obvious truth, and the whole of our experience as a nation. War is an art, to attain perfection in which much time and experience, particularly for the officers, are necessary." The Secretary went on to argue that the object of a military establishment in peace should be to "perpetuate military skill and experience" so that the peacetime army could be raised to wartime capability as quickly and efficiently as possible. To this end Calhoun borrowed from Alexander Hamilton the idea of an expandable army with a high proportion of professional officers. In time of crisis such a skeleton force could double in size almost immediately without organizing new regiments.

Congress ignored Calhoun's recommendations and proceeded with its own haphazard reduction scheme, slashing the number of authorized regiments and cutting the fortifications appropriations from $800,000 to $202,000. Secretary Calhoun was defeated in his immediate goal, but his argument for a permanent expandable army lived on to challenge military thinkers and planners after the Civil War and on into the twentieth century.[5]

Calhoun's unwillingness to rely on civilian soldiers was matched by his suspicion of civilian businessmen doing army work, a suspicion confirmed by his experience as Secretary of War. Not long after he took office the department awarded a major contract to Elijah Mix, a New York businessman of shady reputation and no capital, for providing stone for two forts at the mouth of Chesapeake Bay. It later transpired that Mix was brother-in-law to Calhoun's chief clerk, Vandeventer, and the latter, despite Calhoun's advice to the contrary, had helped finance Mix and had bought part of the contract, which he later sold at a profit. Eventually Mix got into a wrangle with others who bought into his enterprise, and the President received an anonymous letter claiming collusion within the War Department. Calhoun reprimanded his chief clerk, launched an internal investigation which led nowhere, and the issue died temporarily, to be revived a few years later when Calhoun became a presidential candidate.[6]

In the early nineteenth century, as in the later twentieth century, War Department expenditures far exceeded those of any other arm of government, and opportunities to fashion personal profit out of patriotic duty were legion. After Calhoun's chief of engineers, Joseph Swift, left the service, for example, he became surveyor for the Port of New York and a lobbyist for government contractors. In January 1821, Swift received a letter from General Alexander Macomb, headquartered near Detroit. The general had purchased more than six hundred acres of land on the American side of the Detroit River overlooking a British fort. It would be in the national interest for the army to build a site there, Macomb said, and he wondered if the Secretary of War might find it in his own interest to make that decision. "It has often been recommended as the most proper place for a fortification and military depot for the frontier," Macomb wrote. "If Mr. Calhoun could with pressing enter into the speculation he might serve his country and make his fortune too." Presumably the matter went no farther than that. The Secretary who a few years earlier had paid a London bookseller "8½ years interest" on an overlooked bill was about as immune to that kind of temptation as any man alive. But Calhoun was the exception; Vandeventer, Mix, Swift, and Macomb were the rule, and the latter was ultimately promoted to chief of engineers.[7]

It was not fortune but public esteem and political advancement that Calhoun sought. At this stage of his career he wanted to demonstrate that he was one of those rare leaders who could be fastidious about detail without loosening their grasp of the grand design. Many of the fourteen hours a day he spent in his office were concerned with matters that would seem extraordinarily petty to a Cabinet officer today. He never lost sight of the big goal, however: an army with a core of professionally trained, well-paid officers that in peacetime could plan and man a set of coastal and frontier fortifications for national defense and help construct the network of roads and waterways needed for defense and national growth. To this end Calhoun became aggressively interested in the improvement of West Point, appointed Sylvanus Thayer, an engineer who had studied abroad, its superintendent, and supported him during a long, undignified squabble with his predecessor. Under Thayer's leadership the Point was transformed from a bedraggled army outpost into a national ornament and center for engineering education.[8]

Like other enthusiastic nationalists of the period, Calhoun believed that westward expansion was inevitable, and he believed the army could play an essential role in making it safe and orderly. By 1818 American fur traders, pioneers, and settlers had begun to push well beyond the thin line of military outposts on the northwestern frontier. Calhoun proposed to extend this to the north by putting a garrison at the junction of the Mississippi and Minnesota rivers and to the west by sending an expedition from St. Louis eighteen hundred miles up the Missouri to establish a post near what is now Bismarck, North Dakota. It was the second proposal, known as the Yellowstone Expedition, that caught the public and the President's eye. Anglophobic Americans applauded this thrust at British control of the Northwest Frontier while businessmen counted on an additional million dollars a year from the fur trade. Calhoun apparently had all this in mind and more. He arranged for a small scientific group to accompany the Yellowstone Expedition, and in directing General Thomas A. Smith to begin organizing the effort, in March 1818, he predicted that soldiers would endure the hardships involved in such an unprecedented undertaking because of "the glory in planting the American flag at a point so distant in so noble a river. . . . The world will behold in it the mighty growth of our republic, which but a few years since was limited by the Allegheny, but now is ready to push its civilization and laws to the western confines of the continent."

Here again was a grand design, and here again, as with the proposal for an expandable army, Calhoun was to encounter failure. To move a detachment of several hundred men eighteen hundred miles through country where few Americans (except Lewis and Clark) had ventured involved transportation and logistical problems of great magnitude. It was a job for professionals, but it was given to James Johnson, a civilian contractor from Kentucky, brother of Representative Richard Mentor Johnson, a war hero who had supposedly killed Tecumseh at the Battle of the Thames and was a friend of Monroe's. James Johnson had been a contractor to the army during the war. He was given the Yellowstone contract for transportation and supply on a cost-plus-fee basis without submitting a bid, presumably because of the difficulty of the project, but also at the urging of his fellow Kentuckian Henry Clay.[9]

The Calhoun papers document in hilarious detail what happened to the Yellowstone Expedition from 1818 to 1820. The Johnson brothers turned out to be a double version of Mark Twain's Colonel Sellers. Their trouble began when they decided to use steamboats to ascend the river. It had never before been done, and officers on the spot warned against it, but the vision of an army steaming into the wilderness for the first time in history proved irresistible. It also cost money, and Calhoun had his quartermaster send regular advances to the Johnsons, but to little effect. The contractors wrote enthusiastic letters to the Secretary, and western papers continued to boost the project, but the steamboats did not appear. By the summer of 1819 the Secretary had begun to worry, but the President, fresh from a trip to Kentucky, where enthusiasm for the project ran high, directed that more advances be sent. When the expedition finally got under way, the officers discovered that the long-awaited boats were poorly designed and underpowered, drew too much water, provided no shelter for troops, carried an inexperienced crew, and were stocked with barrels of tainted meat. The Johnson steamboats, one of them called the *Calhoun,* became the laughingstock of the West, and the quartermaster general claimed that all the Johnsons put together had less capacity than "a common quarter sergeant."[10]

Calhoun, of course, was not laughing. Caught between the overblown expectations of the President and the public, the empty coffers of the department, and the grandiose visions of the Johnsons, there was little he could do. While the officers on the river saw themselves fighting a losing a battle against the current, Richard Mentor Johnson continued to chant his anthem. "I now say that no earthly power can prevent success," he wrote Calhoun, "omnipotence alone can frustrate your plans. The devil and his angels cannot." When Calhoun replied sternly that it is "not my nature to form plans and leave them half executed," Johnson blithely urged him to be "a second Columbus" and not expect "to go in Silver Slippers."[11]

By the end of 1819 the great Yellowstone Expedition had become stalled at Council Bluffs some fourteen hundred miles short of its destination despite advances to the contractor of $229,000. The War Department was practically bankrupt, and Congress, faced with the problem of cutting government expenses during a depression, had lost its enthusiasm for exploration. Funds were cut off in March 1820. In the autobiography of 1843 Calhoun did not mention the Yellowstone Expedition.

As Secretary of War Calhoun was the President's representative in all matters dealing with the Indians. Less than two weeks after taking office he met with a group of fifteen Cherokee, Wyandot, and Seneca chiefs. This was to be a common experience over the next eight years, and one cannot help wondering, as he presided over the distribution of gifts (swords, feathered hats, pistols, blankets, etc.), if Calhoun ever recalled the image of his father's old hat, peppered with the balls of Indian muskets.

Superficially, at least, government policy toward the Indians had come a long way since Patrick Calhoun's youthful days as an Indian fighter. Then the policy had been to help settlers kill Indians; now it was to help keep Indians alive. But in the early nineteenth as in the eighteenth century, the fundamental goal was to facilitate the takeover of Indian lands by white people. To this end the official policy of the government before 1817 had been to regulate trade, monopolize land transactions enforced through the army, provide agents to negotiate with Indians, police traders, and settle disputes. Monroe intended to follow this policy, but he also wanted to move as many tribes as possible west of the Mississippi. The Secretary of War maintained general oversight over the tribes, and the superintendent of Indian trade under his direction administered a number of "factories" or trading posts designed to complement the valuable fur trade and prevent exploitation of the Indians.[12]

Although Calhoun does not seem to have invested as much of himself in administering Indian affairs as he did in his planning for the army, he was as conscientious in this regard as he was with everything else. He searched the Library of Congress to learn what he could about the fur trade and sent Jedidiah Morse on a trip that was to produce in 1822 the most thorough survey of Indians in the United States up to that time. Calhoun's own analysis of the Indian problem was made in an 1818 report to Congress which assumed that contact with white civilization was changing Indian culture for the worse. Once their knowledge had been limited, Calhoun wrote, but "commensurate with their wants and desires." Now, by "a fixed law of nature," they had become dependent on whites for guns, powder, axes, hoes, etc. which they could not provide themselves. The Indians, therefore, needed protection; they could not function in an uncontrolled marketplace, and that was the rationale for the factory system. Moreover, the time had come to stop considering Indians as belonging to separate nations and to begin thinking of them as an inferior people capable of improvement under the right conditions. "By a proper combination of force and persuasion," Calhoun said, "they ought to be brought within the poles of law and civilization. Left to themselves they will never reach that desirable condition. Before the slow operation of reason and experience can convince them of its superior advantages, they must be overwhelmed by the mighty torrent of our population." What this meant in practice was that those Indians ready and able to take up the white man's ways should be allowed to do so, and those who wanted to develop at their own pace should be allowed to do that—but not east of the Mississippi.[13]

Although Calhoun's ideas may seem hopelessly culture-bound to the modern mind, they marked him as a reformer in 1818. One of his generals, E. P. Gaines, was much closer to popular American opinion when he reminded Calhoun that wisdom and philanthropy had not yet made the Indian lay down the scalping knife. "The Savage must be taught and compelled to do that which is right," Gaines insisted, "and to abstain from doing that which is radically wrong. The poisonous cup of barbarism cannot be taken from the savage by the mild voice of reason alone."[14]

Calhoun's willingness to consider assimilating Indians into the dominant culture may have been encouraged by the highly civilized letters he received from Indian leaders soon after he took office. John Jolly, a Cherokee chief, wrote that although his people would continue to be herdsmen, farmers, spinners, and weavers, they planned to settle more compactly and sought schools, missionaries, and a government factory. "Such establishments," Jolly assured the new Secretary, "will be our rallying points." Abraham Williams, a Wyandot chief and part owner of thirteen sections of land which the government wanted in Ohio, said: "I write to my father to beg him that he would let me live among the whites, and do as they do. I want to be a Christian, to make my wigwam in one fixed place, to work as the white men do, and leave off hunting the beasts in the great woods."[15]

No matter how affecting such appeals may have been, Calhoun hewed close to the government line in administering policy. He tried to weed out corrupt Indian agents and those who trafficked in liquor, but he dismissed anyone who seemed overzealous in favoring Indians. He insisted on prosecuting marauding whites to the extent of paying for extra guards to keep a mob from rescuing white men accused of murdering an Indian family. At the same time he kept a close watch on missionaries inclined to push humanitarianism farther than the government permitted. He supported his superintendent of Indian trade, Thomas L. McKenney, an energetic and talented young Quaker, in a losing battle to keep John Jacob Astor and his friends from destroying the factory system. But in the final analysis it seems clear that his faith in an aggrandizing national mission took priority over whatever concern he may have felt for the Indians as human beings. In less than eight years Calhoun presided over forty-one cessions of Indian land, a rate almost twice that of his predecessors. His message to the chiefs was consistently paternalistic: Only by listening to the white father could they hope to survive.[16]

By the end of his tenure as Secretary of War Calhoun had come to believe that assimilation was impossible and that separation in permanent reservations held the only chance for Indian survival. In reaching this decision, he displayed, as he did on many later occasions in his career, a striking unwillingness to be informed by his own experience. In 1824, for example, Calhoun entered into protracted negotiations to buy land from the Choctaws. The Secretary offered $65,000; the Choctaws demanded $450,000. Calhoun pointed out that the tribe had not always placed such a value on the land. "Good chief, you are contradicting yourself," Calhoun said. "When we were trying to sell you those lands in 1820 you insisted that they were all rocks and hills and that the waters were only fit to overflow the crops, put out fires and float canoes. What is the meaning of this great change?" The chief replied: "I can only say good father, [i]n 1820 we wanted to buy; now we are anxious to sell." The Choctaws settled for $216,000 plus a $6,000 bill for expenses, which included $2,149 for liquor, $394 for oysters, and $75 for bootblacking. Although the Johnson brothers might have appreciated the accomplishment of the Choctaw chiefs, Calhoun never got the message. He paid the bills but held on to his unshakable belief in the natural superiority of his own culture—a myth that served him well in the years ahead.[17]

Although Calhoun may not have understood those he was entrusted to deal with very well, he understood his most famous general even less. Major General Andrew Jackson was the most celebrated man in the country. Some called him the Hero for leading untrained backwoods riflemen to victory over British redcoats at New Orleans. The

Indians called him Sharp Knife for his remarkable ability to kill them and take their lands. After the war Jackson had been feted in Washington and, like a triumphant Roman emperor, had made a national tour before returning to the Hermitage, his six-hundred-acre plantation in Nashville, which also served as headquarters for the Southern Division of the army.

Upon learning about the victory at New Orleans, Calhoun pronounced Jackson an American Wellington, little realizing that as Secretary of War he would discover to his sorrow that a hero who became a great national symbol could become an impossible subordinate. A master of controlled violence in war, Jackson was all too frequently slave to his own violence in peace. The musket balls he carried in his body came not from the battlefield but from frontier brawls, gunfights, and a murderous duel. He was a man given to towering rages and tender generosities. After directing the butchery of more than two hundred Creeks, he once found an Indian infant on the battlefield and sent him home as an adopted son. Jackson was definitely not the kind of general inclined to be deferential to a Secretary of War. A few months before Calhoun took office, the general had publicly announced that he would henceforth obey no order from the War Department that was not transmitted directly to him—in effect challenging the principles of civilian control of the army.

Jackson's latest assault on "the intermeddling pimps and spies" of the War Department had grown out of the discovery that one of his officers on reconnaissance had been ordered directly to New York and had gone there before Jackson knew about it. Calhoun must have discussed the matter with Monroe in advance, and he dealt with it on December 29, 1817, by sending Jackson a copy of a new general order specifying that all orders would be sent "in the first instance to the commanders of division" except when the "public interest" required direct notification to other officers. The accompanying letter, obviously composed by Calhoun himself, was masterfully diplomatic, but the message should have been understood. As Secretary, Calhoun would decide where orders would be sent, but he would defer to the general's wishes whenever possible because "In every effort to add greater perfection to our military establishment I must mainly rely for support on your weight of character and information." Upon receiving Calhoun's letter, Jackson decided that the new Secretary was "adopting the principles I contended for." It was the first in a long, fateful history of misunderstandings.[18]

Calhoun's professed willingness to rely on Jackson for support was put to the test almost immediately by problems festering on the southeastern frontier. After the war Florida remained in Spanish hands, but it was weakly defended and in American eyes functioned mostly as a haven for escaped slaves, smugglers, pirates, and marauding Seminole Indians. The last were particularly troublesome, and in November 1817 they had massacred a party of more than fifty American soldiers, women, and children on the Apalachicola River near the Georgia border. Although the Indians had been provoked by an earlier action of American troops, their attack gave Monroe's government the opportunity it sought to mount a full-scale campaign against the Seminoles. On December 16, 1817, Calhoun ordered General E. P. Gaines to attack and pursue the Indians across the Florida line "unless they should shelter themselves under a Spanish post," in which case he was to "immediately notify this department." Ten days later Calhoun directed Jackson to proceed to Fort Scott in Georgia, relieve General Gaines, and "adopt the necessary measures to terminate" the conflict.[19]

Believing that Jackson would be bound by the orders previously given to Gaines, Calhoun never explicitly told him to refrain from attacking Spanish posts. From the outset, however, Jackson believed that he was being asked to do something far more important than chase Indians. Ignoring the Secretary of War, he wrote directly to the President, assuring him that if he would pass the word through an intermediary (Congressman John Rhea of Tennessee), Jackson would guarantee to take all Florida in sixty days. Monroe claimed later that he was ill when the "Rhea letter" arrived and did not see it. Meanwhile, Jackson's letter had apparently crossed with an earlier letter to him from the President, in which Monroe spoke mysteriously about expecting "other services" beyond the chastising of the Seminoles. "Great interests are at issue," the President warned, "and until our course is carried through triumphantly and every species of danger to which it is exposed is settled on the most solid foundation, you ought not to withdraw your active support from it." Jackson interpreted this to mean he should be prepared to add to the American empire by conquering Florida, as he intended to do anyway. Once the general got his blood up he had no time for subtleties or indecision. Monroe and Calhoun wanted to neutralize the frontier without stirring up a war with Britain and France or disturbing their long-term goal, the acquisition of Florida through peaceful negotiation. But instead of a fox they sent a lion.

General Jackson moved his army south from Fort Scott into Florida in early March 1818. Killing Indians, capturing runaways, and destroying villages, he pushed the Seminoles into West Florida, where he took the Spanish post of St. Mark's, and burned three hundred houses. Writing on April 26, he reported that he had marched 107 miles in less than five days, had scattered the Seminoles, and cut them of "from all communication with those unprincipled Agents of Foreign nations, who have deluded them to their ruin." The "agents" were seventy-year-old Alexander Arbuthnot, a Scottish trader, and Robert Ambrister, a young British soldier of fortune. Three days later Jackson executed both men.

On May 13 Calhoun assured the governor of the Alabama Territory that General Jackson was "vested with full powers to conduct the war in the manner which he may judge best." He did not realize that Jackson was just then marching his troops toward Pensacola, where he was to turn his cannon on the Spanish governor, force him out of the city, and install a provisional government under an American officer. On June 2 Jackson announced: "The Seminole War may now be considered at a close." He had routed the Indians, executed two British citizens without authorization, and personally carried on an undeclared war against Spain—as promised in less than three months.[20]

The full story of what had happened in Florida did not become public until late spring. Expansionists and anglophobes were delighted; more sober-minded citizens were horrified, and almost everyone, including Calhoun, thought some kind of war was imminent. Monroe tried to duck the issue as long as he could but finally convened his Cabinet for five meetings in mid-July. The Calhoun papers are relatively silent on the subject, and our best guide to Calhoun's thinking comes from John Quincy Adams's diary, a source which is probably reliable since Adams thought highly of his colleague at this time. On July 13 Adams reported that Calhoun was "extremely dissatisfied" with

Jackson and thought his object was "to produce a war for the sake of commanding an expedition against Mexico." Once the Cabinet met, Adams found that he alone was willing to defend Jackson on the ground that what he did was essential to his mission. Crawford and Calhoun were outspokenly against the general, and Calhoun reportedly wanted an investigation and some kind of punishment, perhaps a court-martial. Meanwhile, public approval for Jackson's bold course continued to build. The President waffled and finally decided to do nothing about Jackson except to return his Florida conquests to Spain with the understanding that it guarantee a peaceful border. A few months later Spain ceded Florida to the United States for five million dollars.[21]

In trying to explain the Cabinet's decision, Calhoun told a friend in confidence that he knew of "no excuse except necessity that ought to exempt from punishment disobedience to orders." The principle was not applied to Jackson because of a difference of opinion in the way he interpreted his orders and because his popularity made it inexpedient "to take the high tone course." The difference of opinion involved Jackson's belief that in the absence of explicit instruction the order prohibiting Gaines from attacking Spanish posts did not bind him. Calhoun disagreed, assuring the President that it was a settled military principle that an officer's orders were binding on his replacement.

And so the matter rested for the moment, with Jackson convinced that he had acted under orders and Calhoun convinced of his insubordination. Monroe made matters worse by assuring the general that the Secretary had "very just and liberal sentiments" about the propriety of his actions, and Calhoun was content to let him think that the real opposition had been led by Crawford in the Cabinet and Clay in Congress.[22]

Jackson did not retire from the army until June 1821. Calhoun continued to try to handle him firmly but diplomatically, an almost impossible task since Jackson seemed to have little use for the general staff or the War Department. In the early stages of the Yellowstone Expedition, for example, Calhoun directed Jackson to order the military involved in the mission to "exercise the greatest caution and vigilance" in conciliating the Indians and to "treat licensed traders with kindness and justice." In passing these orders on to the officer in charge of the expedition, Jackson said a policy of conciliation "may be necessary," but "the treachery of the Indian character will never justify the reposing of confidence in their professions." The important thing was to always be ready to strike. As for the British traders, they should be hanged wherever found, "But the over cautious policy of the Executive has directed that they only be arrested."[23]

In most of his correspondence Calhoun seems to have gone out of his way to defer to Jackson. He wanted, he said, always to do what is best for the army "but in so doing to meet with the approbation of one who has so strong a regard for its propriety as yourself." This sounds like diplomatic chivalry, but one cannot escape the feeling that Calhoun was also condescending. The American public loved and admired Jackson, but Calhoun tended to dismiss the phenomenon as "mere momentary popularity." Calhoun thought of himself as an independent leader of principle. Jackson, he told John Quincy Adams, was a power grabber. He might act from the most patriotic motives, "but his disposition was to exercise to its utmost extent every particle of power given to him. He had not sufficient regard to the genius of our institutions. . . ."

Calhoun would make allowances for Jackson, but he would not be bullied. After learning that the general had refused to let the surgeons in his division send quarterly reports directly to the surgeon general, the Secretary laid down what could have been considered an ultimatum. "In my letter to you of 22 December last," Calhoun wrote, "I stated very fully my view in relation to the character and the nature of the permanent regulations . . . and I have seen no reason to change the opinion there found." He was sure, Calhoun said, that Jackson agreed with him on the necessity for order and efficiency in the service and would "relieve me from the necessity of determining whether I shall permit the orders of the Government to be habitually neglected, or resort to the proper means of enforcing them. Should the alternative be presented, I will not hesitate to do my duty."[24]

The record does not tell us how Jackson responded, but it would be foolish to think he was intimidated, even if he did begin to follow the regulations in question. A confrontation was avoided, but only temporarily. The truth of the matter is that despite differences in age, education, experience, and temperament, the two men were very much alike and very much in competition. On one level they were power players on a national stage—patriotic, supremely self-confident, fearless, uneasy with compromise. On another level they were southern gentlemen, with an exaggerated sense of personal honor, splendid representatives of an American baronry which had supplied republican leadership for two generations. For the moment each stood tall in the American eye. An open quarrel would hurt them both. In the short run they would need each other to help crush a common enemy. In the long run each would feel compelled to test his power against the other.

5

The Election of 1824

IN DISTINGUISHING himself from Henry Clay, Calhoun wrote to a friend in 1820 that he considered politics not "as a scramble between eminent men but as a science by which the lasting interest of the country may be advanced. Considered as a scramble it is beneath my prysuit [*sic*]." A few weeks later he wrote more fully on the subject in response to a question about his own political future:

The prosperity of our country has never perhaps depended much on the conduct of any single individual. Those rise whose principles and conduct are congenial to a majority of the people. Without this congeniality, be their conduct as it may, they cease to have control. Be this as it may as far as I am concerned, I feel conscious that I can never be swayed to any considerable extent by motives of ambition. My politics I think I may say with perfect truth has been founded on certain fixed principles, and to carry them into effect has been my highest ambition. I would despise myself if I were to change this noble object to the mean one of personal aggrandizement. Provided our country be free, powerful and moderate in her councils I care not whether I have the principal say or not.[1]

In these and other letters Calhoun showed that the future was very much on his mind as he moved into the second half of Monroe's administration. Although not yet forty, he had climbed so rapidly that he was already beginning to feel the limited opportunities at the top. The Senate at this time lacked the prestige it was to have a decade later, and Calhoun had neither the training nor the interest to be considered for the Court. The obvious alternatives were a promotion within the Cabinet (State or possibly Treasury) or the presidency itself. The difficulty lay in the fact that the aspirants for the top job already in line were all senior to the Secretary of War in age and experience. Crawford was considered the front-runner because of his strength with the congressional caucus and a strong showing against Monroe in 1816. Adams was a contender by virtue of experience and position. Clay, who had expected to be Secretary of State, was sure to run, while Jackson, a living monument, could count on substantial popular support for anything he wanted. The election of 1824 would be a scramble, and the problem for Calhoun would be to find a way in and out of it without yielding the high ground he demanded for himself.

No American of his generation was to have a more intensely political life than Calhoun, and no one was to denounce political ambition more vehemently. The apparent contradictions in his political posture impressed, baffled, infuriated, and amused Calhoun's contemporaries depending on the circumstances. Although many thought they were looking at an actor overplaying his role, Calhoun was not pretending when he insisted that he sought "just renown" but abhorred personal ambition and "mere popularity." The republican credo learned from his father had taught him that the purpose of elections was to represent virtue, talent, and property. The ideal republican candidate would be recognized for ability, probity, and "disinterested civic service." He would not seek out high office but make himself available should the people call him. There had always been a gap between this kind of republican idealism and the way politics actually worked, but as parties, managers, and journalists became increasingly involved in the process, nineteenth-century politicians like Calhoun who continued to avow republican principles were forced to reaffirm their vows with increasing urgency.[2]

Every leading actor in public life in 1820 loudly proclaimed his fealty to the republican ideal of statesmanship and accused his opponents of departing from it, but in South Carolina, where every important political leader owned slaves, the ritual was supported by a special resonance. There slaveholding was equated with personal honor and civic virtue. The ideal master, who in theory possessed absolute power over his slaves, was expected to exercise that power with restraint in the interest of an organic community in which the slave made the most humble part. Unlike the grasping businessmen in free society, the ideal master would instinctively sacrifice profit to honor. This, at least, is what most politically active citizens in South Carolina believed and why they refused to extend full political privileges to the backcountry until it had been heavily penetrated by slavery. The result was a political culture with a built-in ambivalence to power. The politician who shifted his ground to hold on to power was suspect; the statesman who independently held to course at whatever cost was admired. Thus, when Calhoun bucked the popular tide in Congress on the salary bill because "the public wish and expect us to act on the convictions of our mind and will," his state supported him.[3]

Calhoun realized that in the United States public opinion would always be important to political success. The difference between a mere politician and a statesman was that the former tended to act like a puppet while the latter resisted momentary public opinion for the long-range public good and waited for the good sense and virtue of the people to catch up with him. Therefore, public life became a duty for men of talent and character. "I deem it . . . the duty of any man of education and leisure to bring himself forward in publick business," Calhoun wrote his brother-in-law in 1820. "It is thus dignity will be given to publick affairs and the state usefully served." The following year, when his War Department projects were under fire by a Congress suddenly consumed with a desire to eliminate government programs, he advised his friend Micah Sterling that Congress needed "elevation" through "an accessing of talents and reputation."[4]

As usual in matters of this sort Calhoun was inclined to take a more moderate position against the emerging American democracy than many other South Carolina planters. William Grayson, who later served three terms as a South Carolina Congressman, remembered how in 1818 a fellow planter "thought it would become impossible for a man of any self-respect to enter the arena of political strife. Its contentions wold be intolerable." Grayson, who was to know his greatest fame as author of the proslavery poem "The Hireling and the Slave" demurred, arguing for the need of the gentleman to lead. "He must rule or be ruled," Grayson insisted. "It is a battle of life and death."[5]

When Calhoun said he would hate himself for making "personal aggrandizement" a goal of his public life, he was speaking not only as a republican and a cultural representative of South Carolina but also as Patrick Calhoun's chosen son. In agreeing twenty years earlier to let his brothers support him through seven years of education and professional preparation, John Calhoun had agreed to assume the mantle of a man who had achieved the "just renown" of his countrymen almost entirely through his own efforts, talent, and character. Unconsciously, at least,

the son was sworn to build on the father's achievement and to protect
the family honor. To fail in either vow was to compromise his identity.
Culture and psychodynamics reinforced each other in Calhoun's character to fuse his own driving energy to the public good. Thus he could
write in perfect honesty to his friend Micah Sterling on December 25,
1820: "I have thus far found it practicable to pursue what I deem right
on all great points without impairing my standing with any considerable portion of this community. I hope and believe it will so continue.
Should such not be the fact the period of our political prosperity must
soon terminate." The candor in this statement is quite remarkable.
What was good for Calhoun had to be good for the country, and for the
next thirty years he never ceased striving for that good despite protests
that his behavior often seemed to give the lie to the "fixed principles"
by which he claimed to live.[6]

There were good reasons for Calhoun to consider himself a plausible candidate for President in 1824. His legislative record during the
war was impeccable, and he had become one of the administration's
most forceful and articulate spokesmen for the nationally expansive
policies which seemed to address the spirit of the age. Finally, at a time
when party lines were becoming blurred, Calhoun had always been
known for his generally cordial and respectful attitude toward Federalists.

Certainly there were individuals in the War Department who believed their new leader had a golden future and wanted to be a part of
it. In April 1818, only a few months after Calhoun had taken office,
Christopher Vandeventer wrote a memorandum which reads very
much as if it were prepared for future political campaign purposes.
According to Vandeventer:

The career of this young man has been active and elevated. He has aimed to
advance the true interest of his country untrammeled by party and unbiased by
sectional prejudices. . . . The loss of this statesman from the halls of Congress
will be severely felt, but in the new duties in which he is called we predict the
nation will reap a higher benefit from his intelligence and his services. In the
Cabinet he will give weight and to the army reputation; the former will receive
the full benefits of an intellect which analyzes the future almost with the spirit
of prophesy. . . .

Vandeventer attached a postscript which he apparently intended to
integrate into the full eulogy: "At times he opposed each party in some

antiquated and favorite creed and he came off victorious in every conflict. The highest eulogium which can be paid to his political career is the circumstance that all parties have adopted his leading opinions as settled axioms of national policy and have awarded his talents and virtues unanimous approbation."[7]

What Vandeventer wrote may be bad history, but it comes uncannily close in substance and style to the account of his career that Calhoun authorized in 1843. Although there is no way of knowing what part the Secretary played in preparing this statement by his assistant, he must have known about it and approved it. Once a formal candidate for President, he would rely heavily on Vandeventer and high-ranking army officers for support.

As Secretary of War, Calhoun was expected to visit military institutions around the country, a practice which considerably enhanced his visibility. He made his first tour with the President in the spring of 1818, visiting facilities at Annapolis, Norfolk, and Old Point Comfort and reaching as far south as Elizabeth City, North Carolina, before leaving Monroe for a quick trip to his plantation at Bath. The following spring he and Floride accompanied the President on a longer trip to the South, which eventually took them to Charleston, Savannah, Augusta, and finally a triumphant reception in Abbeville, where Calhoun presumably basked in the just renown he coveted.

During the winter of 1820, as Washington plunged into furious debate over the issue of slavery in Missouri, Calhoun must have realized the advantages of being out of the Congress. Although as a slaveholder he naturally took a personal interest in the question, he did not have to take a public position on it. His sentiments, however, were strongly with the compromisers, and in a letter to Andrew Jackson he said confidently that the "agitators" of the issue had "completely failed" and thus destroyed their ability for "future Mischief." Once Missouri had been admitted as a slave state, the issue would be forgotten. What Calhoun feared was reagitation of the slavery issue in the territories. If the South ever came to believe that property in slaves was seriously threatened by the free states, it would surely question the value of the Union, but he did not expect that to happen.[8]

It was probably in part to discover how northerners felt about Missouri and how they felt about the political potential of a prominent South Carolinian like himself that Calhoun decided to tour the northern states in the late summer of 1820. On September 3 the Secretary, this time with his own entourage, visited Fort Niagara. Twelve days later he was in Boston, where he saw Fort Independence and the Charlestown Navy Yard and was hosted by Daniel Webster and Jeremiah Mason, the leading Federalists in New Hampshire and Massachusetts. After stopping at several other cities, including New York, where an enterprising manufacturer somehow managed to sidetrack him into visiting a silk factory when he should have been reviewing forts in the harbor, Calhoun returned to Washington in early October. He told his friends that the North-South split over Missouri was being exaggerated and that the country would still look for leadership to men of all sections supporting "the general interest." Meanwhile, his cousin and political confidant in South Carolina had already written to Chief Clerk Vandeventer asking for a list of journals and newspapers in New York "favorable" to Calhoun's "future political rise and ascendence."[9]

Although Calhoun's work in the Congress and War Department is far more important historically than his role in the 1824 presidential election, his candidacy in that contest is extremely self-revealing. Young as he was, his years in Congress and in the Cabinet had made him feel at least the equal to anyone else in the government, including the President. When he told John Quincy Adams in 1818 "that it would be a great advantage to this country to have statesmen of a philosophical turn of mind," Calhoun was not thinking of Andrew Jackson or even of Adams. The latter, despite an almost constitutional inability to praise others, recognized the legitimacy of his younger colleague's claim to distinction and urged him to add to his experience by becoming minister to France "as I expected more from him than from any other man living, to the benefit of the public service of this nation." Although Calhoun claimed to refuse the offer for financial reasons, he must have seen the suggestion for what it probably was: a ploy by a front-runner for the succession to get him out of the way.[10]

In considering the course he should take, Calhoun was less worried about a lack of experience abroad than about finding a legitimate reason for becoming a candidate. To appear too eager at his age (he was thirty-eight in 1820) could be fatal to a man who claimed to spurn ambition, especially in a contest which promised to be as factional as did the election of 1824. Calhoun would need to claim the high ground for himself, and he discovered it in the winter of 1821 as he defended his department against the ravages of Congress.

Calhoun's problems with Congress were brought on in the first instance by the Panic of 1819. A precipitous decline in commodity prices abetted by wild overspeculation in land and a blundering national bank caused countless business failures, hardship for debtors, and an ominous decline in federal revenue. When this happens in the United States, the government in power, no matter how popular when elected, becomes an immediate target. Within the administration Calhoun was especially vulnerable because of the size of the War Department's budget and because of the allegations of waste and fraud stirred up by the Yellowstone Expedition and the Mix contract. The Secretary had begun to feel the heat in March 1820, when funds for the expedition were cut off and an unsuccessful attempt was made to gut the fortifications bill. Calhoun realized that the reprieve was only temporary, and he looked forward to future encounters with foreboding. In May he told Adams that the depression had created "a general mass of disaffection to the Government, not concentrated in any particular direction, but ready to seize upon any event and looking out anywhere for a leader."[11]

When he returned to Washington that fall, he expected a struggle over retrenchment and a modest reduction in the size of the permanent army. What he got was disaster. Disdaining to consider his carefully considered plan for an expandable army with a permanent officer corps, economy-minded Congressmen overwhelmed army supporters by voting in January 1821 to decrease the army at a single stroke, officers and all, to six thousand men, while reducing fortifications money 75 percent!

At first Calhoun perceived himself as a victim of misguided, economy-minded legislators determined to cut public expenditures in time of depression, but when the retrenchment boom fizzled out over a general salary cut for all government employers, he began to believe that he and his department were being singled out as special targets. It was no coincidence, then, to discover that William Crawford's friends had been leading the charge against the army. Everyone knew the Secretary of the Treasury wanted to be President, and now he seemed to be furthering that goal by discrediting the very government he served. If he had been able to peek into Adams's diary, Calhoun would have agreed that Crawford had become "a worm preying upon the vitals of the Administration within its own body."[12]

At about the same time that Calhoun was identifying Crawford as a personal adversary and enemy of the administration, friends were asking him about his own political plans. He told Senator Ninian Edwards of Illinois in March that he had "no views to himself for the next Presidency," The Senator passed the word on to Adams, but by late April Calhoun had become more ambiguous in handling that question. "My present position both as it regard myself and the country," he confided to his friend Virgil Maxcy, "is one which requires a good deal of reserve . . . so neither I nor my friends ought to have any appearance of solicitude except as connected with that interest." The Secretary might not be scrambling, but he was poised and waiting.[13]

Meanwhile, Calhoun remained on good terms with John Quincy Adams, who carefully revised his *Reports on Weights and Measures* according to his suggestions. He also found himself making common cause with Andrew Jackson, who had been practically legislated out of the army by the retrenchers and who agreed with Calhoun that Crawford and his henchmen were to blame. Not yet candidates themselves, the Secretary and the general took turns congratulating each other for their high republican principles, and Calhoun was carefully attentive to Jackson's nephew Andrew Jackson Donelson when he visited Washington in mid-May 1821.[14]

Shortly after the general's celebrated Florida campaign, Calhoun had dismissed the Jackson phenomenon as "mere momentary popularity." Now he found himself courting the man he had once tried to court-martial. Writing to Jackson on April 8, 1821, Calhoun distinguished between "attachment to mere popularity" and "love of just renown." The first could be acquired through intrigue; the latter required "great and magnanimous actions." No one could doubt, Calhoun assured Jackson, "which of those you have persued [*sic*]." Such honeyed praise was disingenuous at best and came back to haunt Calhoun after he became Jackson's Vice President.[15]

Calhoun began to make the moves of a candidate in August, when he met with George Dallas in Bedford Springs, Pennsylvania. Politics in Pennsylvania at this time has been described as a jungle controlled by leaders who acted more like Chinese warlords than principled republicans. Dallas was one of the warlords. A well-situated Philadelphia lawyer and Princeton graduate, whose father had been in Madison's Cabinet, Dallas headed a faction known as the Family Party which had been in and out of power in Pennsylvania since 1817. We do not know exactly what transpired at the meeting. Interested in building a possible Pennsylvania-South Carolina-Ohio coalition, Dallas found Calhoun's national visibility and nationalist program attractive. He also wanted to be the United States minister to Mexico. Calhoun, of course, knew how important a Pennsylvania nomination would be for any political candidate. On this flimsy foundation an understanding seems to have been reached that if Dallas and his friends would nominate a Calhounite for the 1823 gubernatorial election and secure a Pennsylvania endorsement for Calhoun's candidacy; the latter, if elected President, would look smilingly on Dallas and his party. Calhoun would have objected to the word "understanding," but in fact, he was throwing in with a group of scramblers willing to gamble on his promise without seriously investing in his principles.[16]

Back in Washington in the fall of 1821, Calhoun called on the debonair Martin Van Buren, newly elected Senator from New York. An odd couple these two: Calhoun, tall, handsome, intense, convinced of his own disinterestedness (he told Van Buren that he would refuse a nomination before he would be bound by a caucus); Van Buren, short, balding, urbane, genial, consciously manipulative, and a master of New York politics. The early meetings of these two rising political stars were cordial, many of them taking place over the dinner and whist tables in Calhoun's house, since Van Buren was a bachelor and lived in a nearby hotel. In searching for ways to help each other, they soon found common ground in the decision to oppose New York Congressman John Taylor in his bid for reelection as Speaker of the House. Calhoun, who suspected Taylor of packing key committees with army retrenchers, and Van Buren, who thought he was losing control over his New York colleague, easily switched enough votes to ensure his defeat. However, before Calhoun could take credit for disarming an antiarmy coalition in the House, Philip Barbour of Virginia, a staunch Crawfordite, was made Speaker in Taylor's place. To make matters worse, Van Buren, who from the outset seems to have perceived Calhoun as a dangerous competitor, would soon be leading Crawford's campaign.

This encounter of 1821, which preceded by several years the bitter estrangement between the two men during Jackson's administration, is instructive because it shows how naïve Calhoun was in the face of a new democratic politics. Van Buren had become powerful by displacing De Witt Clinton, who had made himself a national hero by creating the Erie Canal. Calhoun apparently interpreted Van Buren's ascendancy over Clinton as a triumph of republican principles over an apostate politician who had strayed into the Federalist fold. In fact, although Van Buren had his share of principles, he had become New York's most powerful political leader by building a modern political machine which was to become known as the Albany Regency, in which party discipline, patronage, and centralized control counted for more than principle. Calhoun soon disparaged this new politics as political "management," and distinguished it from "true" republicanism, but it was really the politics of the future. Van Buren had already mastered it; Calhoun would never understand it.[17]

Although by December 1821 Calhoun had privately begun to warn friends that Crawford was not qualified to be President and that a New England candidate like Adams would run poorly in the South, he continued to tiptoe around his own candidacy. "Should my friends determine that the publick interest requires that I should be brought forward," he told Lewis Cass, "my age and my position would both seem to require that I should not be *protruded* on the publick notice."[18]

Much to Calhoun's discomfort another South Carolinian was almost immediately protruded upon the public when William Lowndes was nominated by the legislature in Columbia on December 18. Far better known in the country than Lowndes, Calhoun naturally did not like being shown up in his own state. His friendship for Lowndes remained secure, but Calhoun made it clear that he thought the nomination "very rash and foolish." Meanwhile, he was forced formally to throw himself into politics with the help of friends outside South Carolina. On December 28, heeding the call of a group of Family Party Congressmen, he finally declared for the presidency.[19]

Calhoun calculated his chances on the reasonable possibility that Crawford, Adams, and Clay would neutralize one another in the election. He knew about Lowndes's failing health and considered him an honorary candidate more than anything else. Meanwhile, Jackson, the potential spoiler, had stayed out of the race. If Calhoun could run well in the South, if the Pennsylvania strategy worked, if the military establishment in New York with the help of Monroe's son-in-law Samuel Gouverneur could get a movement going there, and if New England Federalists like Webster and Mason could be enticed away from Adams, then, Calhoun believed, he had as good a chance as anyone.

However strongly he may have been motivated by such remote possibilities, he presented himself primarily as "a candidate against any Southern man." In other words, Calhoun claimed to be more interested in defending Monroe's administration by taking the southern vote away from Crawford than in being President himself. Adams, the obvious beneficiary of such a strategy, found the profession hard to believe and immediately began to count Calhoun as a serious candidate. This was the common judgment.[20]

Here it becomes necessary to try to untangle the torturous relationships between Calhoun and Crawford. They had worked closely together in a friendly way during the war, when Crawford had been Secretary of War while Calhoun chaired the Committee on Foreign Relations and although Calhoun had supported Monroe over Crawford in the congressional caucus of 1816, the two men seem to have served together without friction during Monroe's first term. After that, when it became clear that Monroe would not endorse Crawford's bid for the succession and the presidential election would become a horse race for the first time, conflict between Calhoun and Crawford became inevitable because each man needed the other as an opponent. Crawford believed that Monroe's official neutrality was a mask and that the President favored the election of Adams, to be followed by Calhoun. It made political sense for Crawford, given Monroe's opposition, to attack the administration, and the alleged irregularities in the War Department, along with the need to reduce the budget, provided an obvious opportunity. If the administration could be shown to be inefficient, wasteful, or faithless to its trust, then any administration candidate except the one sounding the alarm could be knocked out of the race.[21]

Calhoun's need to find Crawford a villain was more complex. It reached beyond political necessity and below Calhoun's consciousness. Calhoun needed to run for President while believing he was doing something else, and Crawford made this possible. Hence the "qualified" candidacy which convinced Calhoun but nobody else. This is not to say that Calhoun's attack on Crawford was contrived. He would naturally have opposed the so-called radicalism of Crawford and his friends because they sought to subvert the "progressive" or national republicanism Calhoun supported. But there was much more to it than that. Crawford was the first politician to sponsor personal attacks on Calhoun, to link his name with the kind of corruption and boondoggling associated with irregular army contracts. Crawford's paper, the *Washington City Gazette,* had become relentless in publishing these allegations by the summer of 1822. Calhoun's honor was on the line. This had happened once before, almost catapulting him into a duel with Thomas Grosvenor. This time a duel was actually fought, not between Calhoun and Crawford but between their surrogates. Calhoun had known George McDuffie ever since he was a boy, had subsidized his education, and had watched his rise to prominence as a lawyer, planter, and South Carolina Congressman. McDuffie was his protégé and devoted follower. Humorless and utterly without presence in social situations, McDuffie was a talented parliamentary debater and political polemicist and had proved an effective ally in fending off the radicals, so effective, in fact, that Colonel William Cumming, a prominent Crawford editor, challenged McDuffie to a duel for suggesting that he was a tool for Crawford's ambition. The first of the three duels, which left McDuffie partially disabled for the rest of his life, took place in June 1822. Cumming was known as a crack shot, and McDuffie as one of the least likely men in the South to protect himself in a physical encounter. Calhoun, who thought his friend's life should be "considered as publick property," was distraught. When he heard that McDuffie had taken a ball in the backbone, he lamented the termination of "a life most precious to the country. He has not left behind him one of his age of equal promise." Upon learning of his friend's survival the next day, he said, "Never have my feelings undergone so great a change in so short a time." On June 9, 1822, while McDuffie's life was still in doubt, Calhoun announced that there would soon be a new paper in Washington to counter the "torrents of filth emanating from Crawford's *City Gazette.*"[22]

Calhoun's most active efforts in the campaign of 1824 took place over a period of about eighteen months from the summer of 1822 until March 1824 and are documented in his letters and in the columns of the *Washington Republican and Congressional Examiner*. Edited by his former assistant for Indian affairs, Thomas L. McKenney, another casualty of the retrenchers, the paper was an explicitly anti-Crawford organ. Although Calhoun tried to keep his name out of it at first, his influence was all over the paper. The article in one of the early issues on the need for civic virtue in a large diverse country was either written by him directly or adapted from one of his speeches in Congress. And the recurrent attacks on Crawford for looseness with the public purse as Secretary of the Treasury, for attempts to undermine Monroe's administration, and for being a "superannuated clerk without *one single act* from which the country has derived either *honor* or *advantage*," clearly reflected the animus Calhoun felt toward his Cabinet colleague. Both the *Republican* and Calhoun professed to believe that Crawford represented a dangerous new political breed. "There has not been in the history of the Union," Calhoun assured Adams, "another man with abilities so ordinary, with service so slender, and so thoroughly corrupt, who has continued to make himself a candidate for the Presidency."[23]

Calhoun's image of Crawford was a gross distortion. Crawford came from the same kind of background as his own and had risen as high without the benefit of Calhoun's education. He had served ably in the Senate and in the Cabinets of two Presidents, had represented the nation honorably in France, and had negotiated on even terms with Talleyrand. He was probably as efficient in administering the Treasury as Calhoun was in running the War Department, which is to say that he was a good public servant.[24]

Calhoun had compared the Cumming-McDuffie duel to an attempted assassination. The journalistic assaults which he countenanced on Crawford could be described the same way, especially the anonymous letters written by Illinois Senator Ninian Edwards accusing the Secretary of the Treasury of gross negligence and implying fraud in his relationship with certain western banks. These letters, published in the *Republican*, caused a sensation, leading to demands for an official investigation. Edwards admitted writing the letters, but the ensuing congressional investigation, carried out in an atmosphere of intense political partisanship, failed to support his charges. Edwards, who had recently been appointed minister to Mexico on Calhoun's recommendation, was forced to resign. It was a messy business, and Calhoun, who must have known all along that Edwards was the anonymous author and who allowed the accusations to be printed in the *Republican,* was bound to be hurt in the fallout. Calhoun, of course, had been similarly abused by the Crawfordites, but he could hardly fight fire with fire and maintain the fiction that he remained above the political scramble.[25]

In September 1823 Crawford suffered an almost fatal stroke which did far more than hostile journalists to reduce his chances in the election. The *Republican,* however, did not let up. A few months before his stroke the paper berated Crawford for accepting supporters without distinguishing "between the gentile and the Jew" (a slap at the New York editor Mordecai Noah). Later the *Republican* reminded readers that the half-paralyzed Crawford had once favored intermarriage as a long-term solution to the problem of civilizing the Indian, thus making white fathers everywhere fearful "that the daughter of his love, and the child of his hopes, is to become nursing mother to a race of mongrels and mulattos."[26]

William Crawford never became President, and Calhoun counted his fall as a personal triumph in 1824. Although it is impossible to determine exactly how much the negative campaigning of the Calhounites had to do with his defeat, Crawford held them responsible. Crippled and embittered, but still able to call on influential friends, he lived on determined to square accounts. Eventually Calhoun was to pay the price.

Although Calhoun was careful not to let the *Republican* attack any other candidate than Crawford, he began to act more and more like a candidate in his own right. In July 1823 it became a five-man race when the Tennessee legislature added Jackson's name to those of Calhoun, Crawford, Clay, and Adams. Although the *Republican* treated everyone except Crawford with respect, Calhoun began to deprecate the candidacies of Clay and Adams in private. The West was too divided to elect Clay, he said, and Adams was too vulnerable to the charge of Federalism. "Any step which would have the appearance of yielding me up to him [Adams]," Calhoun wrote to a Pennsylvania supporter, "would be fatal to the common cause."[27]

Meanwhile, Calhoun had already paid a heavy price for joining forces with the Family Party in Pennsylvania. At a Harrisburg convention in March his supporters had hoped to pair a Family Party nominee for governor with a declaration for Calhoun. The first goal was achieved by what Dallas's biographer calls "a carefully timed doublecross," but the convention balked at supporting Calhoun, partly because of unexpected Jackson strength and partly because the delegates were tired of being manipulated by the Dallas machine.[28]

Disappointed at the results in Harrisburg, Calhoun decided to declare victory anyway. The initial goal of his campaign was virtually accomplished since Crawford and his friends had been "exposed and prostrated." The challenge now was to "ready the superstructure" for his own election. In explaining to one of his supporters how this could be accomplished. Calhoun sounded more like his own press agent than a republican statesman:

My friends must now all write, and write constantly wherever it can be done with safety. . . . In rearing the superstructure all can contribute.

My past services, my identity with the late war and with the administration, my uniform Republican course, my habits of industry and business, the distinctness of my political principles, and the openness and candour which even my enemies concede to me all furnish topics to sustain the cause.[29]

Despite these strenuous exhortations, Calhoun's campaign steadily lost ground in 1823 and 1824. He tried to compensate for the slippage by arguing that he was the second choice in every section, but that did not help.[30] Part of the trouble was in his trying to penetrate the sectional base of the other candidates. Part of it lay in the way he was perceived as a young man in a hurry to get to the top too soon. "This specialist has set up in trade for himself," one observer wrote, "to employ all his capital and credit on his own account."[31] Part of it lay in the principles Calhoun stood for. "His kindly manners and fine genius may attract a few stragglers here and there," wrote the influential Thomas Ritchie in the *Richmond Enquirer*, "but no considerate Virginian who values the constitution of his country will lend himself to the care of an ultra-politician of the federal school."[32] Finally there was the Jackson phenomenon. The general, a notorious Crawford hater and an ardent defender of the army, was bound to take some wind away from Calhoun's sails. As the Jackson momentum built, Calhoun was careful to play down his competition with the general. According to the *Republican,* Jackson and Calhoun followers were "sheep of the same tent," while Crawford and Clay were in a coalition marked by "intrigue," "management," and "political gamblers." Calhoun did what he could to keep Jackson's favorite officers in the army, and he assured the general that he found "few with whom I accord so fully in relating to political subjects as yourself."[33]

The nation did not finally choose a new President until the House of Representatives voted in February 1825, but the end for Calhoun came almost a year earlier, when the warlords in Pennsylvania unceremoniously dumped him to support an almost unanimous nomination for Jackson. As a consolation prize Calhoun was endorsed for the Vice Presidency. It was the first major defeat in his career. Although Margaret Bayard Smith reported that Calhoun looked pale and shaken at the desertion of his Pennsylvania supporters, he put a good public face on the matter and withdrew to the sidelines. Assured of the vice presidency (both the Jackson and Adams factions had nominated him), he maintained an official neutrality until the contest was finally decided.[34]

In the fall elections Jackson received 99 electoral votes, Adams 84, Crawford 41, and Clay 37. Calhoun was elected Vice President with 182 votes. The final choice for President was to be made in the House between Jackson and Adams. Calhoun told his friends that he would be happy to serve under either, that in any event, since his own position came "from the people," he would be "placed above all contingencies."[35] But not even his closest supporters knew exactly where Calhoun stood. He told General Jacob Brown that he favored Adams, but Vandeventer understood him to say that he wanted Jackson to win. The chief clerk was not convinced. "I believe he prefers the election of Adams," he confided to his diary, "not because he thinks it would make the best President"—but because a northerner in the office now might make it easier for a southerner to be elected four or eight years hence. But, Vandeventer added, Calhoun "professed to act on higher ground.[36]

6

Vice President with His Own Agenda, 1824‒1828

CALHOUN had been a fixture on the Washington scene for almost fourteen years when he took the oath as Vice President on March 4, 1825. During that period his family had grown along with the new nation and his political reputation. Floride, almost a girl when they married, had spent most of her time preparing for and recovering from childbirth. In a little more than fourteen years she had borne eight children, losing three in infancy, and had been "dangerously" ill from a miscarriage in November 1818, about a year after settling in Washington. There were three sons: Andrew, fourteen, Patrick, four, and John C., two, and two daughters: Anna Maria, eight, and the year-old Martha Cornelia, known as Cornelia. Two more sons were to follow; James Edward in 1826 and William Lowndes in 1829.

The years between 1817 and 1826, when Calhoun spent most of his time with his family in Washington, were probably the happiest in his life. They were certainly the most social. Calhoun had purchased the E Street house in the center of Washington with an eye to its suitability for entertaining. In the summer of 1822 his mother-in-law improved on that situation by purchasing the handsome mansion in Georgetown which is now called Dumbarton Oaks. Located too far from the Capitol to allow for commuting in the winter months, this estate, which Calhoun named Oakly, served as a summer residence for the Calhouns. Set on thirty acres of hilly woods and orchards, it helped satisfy Calhoun's desire to get closer to the land and relieve him of the inevitable frustrations that plagued every absentee planter. It was not a place for growing cotton, but it did allow him to experiment in a small way in the gardens and orchards, and he must have been proud to have been remembered as the man who set out the first Isabella grape in Washington.[1]

Graced with a long oval drive, a huge entry hall, and spacious parlors, Oakly was a fine place for a statesman and his wife to entertain. To most observers they made an attractive host and hostess: John, tall, handsome, dynamic, bursting with information and opinions on every issue connected with government; Floride, tiny, energetic, domestic, uninterested in politics, but apparently fortified with the social assurance of one born to wealth and social position. For guests who did not care to spend their evening discussing internal improvements, fortifications, or tariff policy, she was always ready to provide a diversion at the piano or take a place at the chessboard. George Ticknor, the Boston Brahmin who had met most of the top scholars, literary artists, and social lions in England and on the Continent, claimed that the Calhouns gave the "pleasantest of the ministerial dinners" in Washington ... and Mrs. Calhoun is a very good little woman who sometimes gives a pleasant ball."[2]

That the Calhouns were a popular young couple in Washington during his years as Secretary of War can hardly be doubted. Margaret Bayard Smith, the chronicler of Washington society during this period, remembered a ball at their house where in five crowded rooms she saw "everyone I know." She also remembered the great wave of sympathy which swept over the Washington elite when the Calhouns' five-month-old daughter Elizabeth fell mortally ill in the spring of 1820. There were calls every day from the President, his family, and the families of other Cabinet members. On one occasion the Calhouns' parlors were crowded with well-wishers, and the burial of the child was "attended by an unusually long train of carriages." All this, Mrs. Smith wrote, was "not a mere tribute to rank" but flowed from "that good will both Mr. and Mrs. C have universally excited, they are really beloved." Floride's claim on the affections of other women in the Washington social circle was not as "the good little woman" Ticknor rather condescendingly referred to who gave an occasional pleasant ball but came from the spontaneous, personal hospitality she extended to her friends. After stopping at the Calhouns' for a momentary chat one afternoon, Mrs. Smith and her two children were "firmly" swept into the house and held for dinner, at which Floride "gave Bayard calf's foot jelly, sent for oysters for him and then made him lie down on her bed where he slept for several hours. When we came away she loaded him with jelly and cakes."

However, not everyone shared Mrs. Smith's positive opinion of Floride. Charles Wilkes, the young naval officer who later led the famous United States Exploring Expedition of 1838 to 1842, recalled meeting her at a Washington banquet in the mid-1820s. "She is queer," he wrote to a friend, "small face and head, overhung large ears . . . black eyes & freckles—dressed in black velvet with lace flowers, green & orange bound round her waist—leather shoes & white stockings—wets her thimble in her mouth & now & then her finger to make it stick on—tilts her chair and draws her hand over her mouth as if she was feeling her beard. When I come back I will show you a milliner the image of her." All Wilkes could remember of Floride's conversation was that it involved her little girls who had lost their teeth.

Wilkes's description of Calhoun's wife at this point in their life together is the most detailed on record, and it is difficult to know what to make of it in view of Wilkes's reputation as an "excessively vain and conceited" young man, but it seems safe to assume that Floride probably never felt really comfortable in Washington. Later in his life Calhoun could look back with some nostalgia on the festive years they had spent on E Street and at Oakly, but Floride remembered Washington during those days as the place where she was almost constantly with child, where she failed to carry one baby to term and almost died, where her five-month-old daughter Elizabeth died after a long, painful illness, where she constantly worried that her other children would be carried away by fever in the sickly season, and where no one ever seemed to talk about anything but politics. It was the fear of his children's health more than anything else that convinced Calhoun to move his family back to South Carolina, but when he did, he found that he could never get his wife to return except under duress.[3]

Calhoun, himself was never a social lion. He had no wit and very little small talk. Unlike Webster, he could not turn every little social incident into a dramatic ceremony, nor could he imitate Clay's impudence. While the final choice of a President was still pending in the House, Louis McLane and Van Buren gave a bachelor's party for the visiting Lafayette. Calhoun attended along with Clay, Jackson, and

Adams. Seeing the two leading nominees sitting quietly by the fire separated by a vacant chair, Clay seized the opportunity to take the place himself, announcing: "Well, gentlemen, since you are both so near the chair, but neither can occupy it, I will step between you and take it myself." Everyone is supposed to have laughed at this audacity, but Calhoun could not have been amused. Politics would never be a laughing matter to him.

Never one to play to the crowd, Calhoun was realistic enough to appreciate the importance of visibility to political advancement. As a Cabinet member required to attend most of the higher-level ceremonies in Washington, he sometimes appeared with a delegation of painted Indian chiefs in tow. After his own campaign for the presidency had ended, Calhoun remained in the public eye, not just as the leading candidate for Vice President but as the administration's sole representative when Lafayette visited Yorktown, Williamsburg, Norfolk, and Richmond.

Although ceremonial roles inevitably enhanced Calhoun's reputation, he was not really a ceremonial person like Webster, called out to address the public on great historic occasions. Calhoun had a different kind of charismatic appeal. His high voice, rapid-fire delivery, and close reasoning showed to best effect in the legislative chamber, the committee room, or personal encounters. Some Washington celebrities, like Webster, could be lethargic in conversation or, like Wirt, be condescending or, like Adams, portentously solemn, but Calhoun seems to have charmed people by bringing to every social occasion the same intensity, single-mindedness, and determination to convince that characterized his public life. George Ticknor said that Calhoun was "the most agreeable person in conversation in Washington," and Ticknor's close friend Webster, who clashed with Calhoun repeatedly in the House, called him "a true man," while the journalist Ann Royall was so dazzled by his "personal beauty" and "frank and courteous manners" that she announced: "In Washington as well as elsewhere, Mr. Calhoun is held as a model of perfection." Margaret Bayard Smith agreed as she raved over "Mr. C's splendid eye" and his face "stamped with nature's aristocracy."[4]

The problem Calhoun faced after 1824 was how to maintain as Vice President the high level of visibility and approval he had acquired during fourteen years of service as one of the nation's foremost political actors. He had thought of the vice presidency as a stepping-stone to the presidency, but now that Jackson, who had lost the election at the final hour despite his plurality in popular and electoral votes, seemed almost a sure bet for 1828, the step to the presidency was longer than Calhoun had anticipated. The Vice President had almost no official responsibilities except to preside over the Senate, and historically that function had been carried out by an elected member of that body in the Vice President's absence. Some Vice Presidents rarely came to Washington; many were relatively obscure politicians, and Calhoun's predecessor, Daniel D. Tompkins from New York, was a notorious alcoholic who had been absent from the Senate for most of the preceding five years. How could Calhoun use the vice presidency in a way consistent with republican principle and also advantageous to his own future? This was the question confronting him on inauguration day, and it was almost providential that Andrew Jackson, who took the honor as the oldest Senator, should have administered the oath.

The key to understanding Calhoun's political behavior and thinking from 1825 through 1828 may be found in the peculiar conditions under which the election of 1824 had occurred. In the first place, Calhoun was elected Vice President in his own right, not as the running mate of another candidate or the choice of a party. As the editor of the Calhoun papers has observed, "Calhoun was Vice-President because of his importance, not important because he was Vice-President,"[5] having received far more electoral votes than any of the presidential candidates. This unique historical situation resulted from the demise of the first two-party system in the mid-1820s. In the second place, John Quincy Adams had been elected by a majority of states in the House of Representatives (each state casting one vote) through the influence of Henry Clay, who had been repudiated in the regular election. Since Jackson had received fifteen more electoral votes in the regular election, one could plausibly argue that a President had been chosen contrary to the will of the people. After President Adams appointed Clay Secretary of State, Jacksonites immediately claimed that the new President had stolen the election through a "corrupt bargain" with his formal rival. The charge, never proved, haunted Adams and Clay for the rest of their lives.

During the final weeks before the election was decided, Calhoun had maintained a public neutrality over the contest between Adams and Jackson and had scoffed privately to friends about reports that it might be decided by an arrangement between Adams and Clay. Close supporters like Vandeventer thought Calhoun was ambivalent about the choice, but Adams believed Calhoun was conspiring against him. When Jacob Brown, Calhoun's top general, visited Adams shortly before the final vote to assure him that Calhoun's "personal wish was for my election," Adams grumbled into his diary: "This contrasts singularly with the conduct of all his electioneering partisans." Two days after his agonizing ordeal was over, President-elect Adams was not surprised to be told that the Calhounites were threatening to organize an opposition party in coalition with Jackson unless the new President selected a Cabinet to their specifications without Henry Clay as Secretary of State. While he was still digesting this unpleasant news, General Brown called again to make a more formal plea against the Clay appointment, and Adams noted with grim satisfaction that this time the Secretary of War's emissary spoke "with some embarrassment of Mr. Calhoun's present conduct and movements." It is difficult to say how much of all this was fact, how much Calhoun supporters may have been speaking for themselves, and how much was a product of Adams's paranoid imagination, but even before the new government took office, there had developed a consensus that the new President could expect to find his own Vice President leading the ranks of the opposition.[6]

Political logic pointed clearly to a Jackson-Calhoun coalition. As an independently elected Vice President Calhoun had no obligation to support Adam's policies, and the sad truth of the matter is that the Adams presidency had begun to sink even before it was launched. The charge that Adams had stolen the office from Jackson through a "corrupt bargain" with Clay rang true to hordes of Americans almost immediately, and when Clay was actually named Secretary of State and presumably heir apparent, the charge became even more damning and the pro-Jackson sentiment more voluminous and strident. Louis McLane, the able and influential Delaware Congressman who later served in Jackson's Cabinet, echoed the sentiments of many disaffected republicans when he refused to attend Adams's inauguration and denounced the Adams-Clay coalition as "that miserable insect wrapped up in the wily toils of that poisonous snake from the western regions."[7] In this situation for Calhoun to have sided with Adams would have been both suicidal and out of character. Although his later career would show that Calhoun was not above political self-immolation, he was almost never out of character, and a week after the inauguration the new Vice President wrote confidentially to one of his former generals: "I see in the fact that Mr. Clay has made the Prest. against the voice of his constituents, and that he has been rewarded by the man elevated by him by the first office in his gift, the most dangerous stab, which the liberty of this country has ever received. I will not be on that side. I am with the people and will stay so."[8]

Clay had been corrupt because he convinced the Kentucky delegation to vote for Adams despite instructions from home to support Jackson. Calhoun's charge did not square very well with his own refusal to be instructed on the congressional salary bill vote ten years earlier, but that obviously was not the point. Calhoun could not prove, nor could anyone after him, that a bargain had been made, but that was not the point either. It was enough for Calhoun that a President had been made under circumstances which seemed to violate basic republican values. Once again he could believe that he was drawn only by principle, and once again principle and ambition would reinforce each other to take him in the same direction.

During the spring and summer of 1825 Calhoun made his longest visit to South Carolina in eight years. He enjoyed the physical activity, riding through his own fields overlooking the Savannah and visiting his mother-in-law's several properties, including Clergy Hall, the old parsonage in Pendleton, which he was soon to make famous as Fort Hill. Calhoun was a progressive planter; he considered agriculture a science, and in agriculture, as in politics, he was always trying to discover the basic principles. While running the Department of War, he had ordered the Ordnance Corps to conduct an experiment to discover the exact amount of power required for the optimum performance of different kinds of plows and had published the results in the *American Farmer.* Back on his own soil he found it refreshing to get away from politics and think about things that he could actually control, such as purchasing a new pair of mules, trying out a mechanical corn crusher, trying a different way of ditching the meadows, or monitoring the efficiency of the slave gangs.[9]

Whether he knew it or not, Calhoun was projecting a kind of Cincinnatus image—the weary warrior for the public weal, temporarily retired to the serenity of his own acres. When he was called out to address his Abbeville neighbors on May 27, he responded by telling them that throughout his advancement from state legislator to Vice President he had always been motivated by "an entire confidence in the virtue and intelligence of the American people," always sure he would be rewarded if he made "the true interest of the country" his "constant guide." He said nothing directly about the way in which the presidency had recently been decided but claimed that as a candidate he had "cared much less who should be elected than how he should be." Thus he had withdrawn from the contest when Pennsylvania declared for Jackson because he wanted to keep the election out of the House of Representatives, away "from any scheme of controlling the election by any other power than the voice of the people." There must have been many in that audience who remembered the patriarchal republican Patrick Calhoun. The son had returned to tell them that despite the changes taking place around them and in Washington, the legacy of their fathers was still intact and provided the surest guide to an uncertain future.[10]

Although Calhoun's public statements in the spring and summer of 1825 were more ritualistic than political, he was careful to keep in touch with his principal supporters outside South Carolina, urging the young men especially, like Samuel Gouverneur, to stay on for the "reformation" which lay ahead. To Gouverneur and others he urged the importance of a constitutional amendment which would return deadlocked presidential elections to the people for decision. He assured Samuel Ingham in Pennsylvania that the "entire union of the South" would stand "against the principles on which Mr. Adams has been elected" and solemnly informed his friend Joseph Swift in New York that Henry Clay had sounded his own death knell.

Mr. Clay's fate I never doubted. It is fixed. I am only surprised (considering the influence in his power to influence the public sentiment) that it should so soon be made manifest. I pity him. He is not only fallen, but has fallen under such circumstances, as will make him miserable for life. He has good and even great qualities but his character is not well balanced. He will doubtless share the lot of all, who in a great crisis permit themselves to be governed more by a regard to their own advancement than their duty to the country.[11]

However they may have felt about Henry Clay, some of Calhoun's army friends, who needed administration support and remembered Calhoun's avowed friendliness toward Adams, found his new posture puzzling. When Vandeventer brought the matter up, Calhoun was curt. "I had hardly supposed that I was an object of so much interest to a certain class of politicians with you people in New York," he replied, "or that they so badly misunderstood my character, as their specula-tions would seem to imply. He who acts honestly seems to be the greatest deceiver." Assuring his former clerk that he was following the same principles that had governed his behavior in the War Depart-ment, Calhoun closed with a statement which can be read as a mani-festo for his new role. The vice presidency, he said, "affords me an opportunity which will not be neglected, of proving my devotion to the power of the people, as against that of political leaders; and by the time I am done no one, no, not my enemies, shall doubt my character. I hold it higher than the Presidency and will never sacrifice it."[12]

The new President's first annual message to Congress in December 1825, calling for a broad national program including internal improve-ments, laws for the improvement of commerce, and the establishment of a national university, must have secretly pleased Calhoun because it went well beyond his own more limited nationalism and allowed him to criticize Adams as an extremist who threatened to undo the achieve-ments of Monroe's administration. He also grumbled about the Presi-dent's "artful" use of patronage, a criticism which was probably gov-erned less by the President's behavior than by the discovery that Calhoun had lost his own leverage to influence appointments. "There is nothing in my gift," he confessed to one supporter, "and I am so circumstanced that I can not ask."[13]

Sometime later that winter Senator Van Buren visited the Vice President at Oakly to explore the possibilities of a political alliance. The two men had worked together earlier to influence the choice of a Speaker of the House but had fallen out during the election, when Van

Buren worked for Crawford. Although Van Buren was no match for Calhoun intellectually, he was far shrewder and comprehended much more clearly where the country was headed politically. Calhoun thought of building an opposition in terms of a campaign carried on by virtuous republican leaders to alert the people to the outrage of 1825 so that they could redress it themselves in 1828. He suspected political parties and sought to restore the old consensus which had brought Monroe's government to power. Van Buren, on the other hand, could see that the old Federalist-Republican party system had disintegrated and that a new system was needed to make self-government under the Constitution work. Van Buren would be a principal architect of the "second party system" which accompanied the democratization of American politics. Calhoun was never to find a comfortable place within it.[14]

After Adams's address to Congress in the winter of 1825 Calhoun and Van Buren found temporary common ground in opposing the President's decision to send United States delegates to a conference called by the emerging Latin American republics. There were a variety of reasons for opposing the Panama Congress, including the traditional American policy of neutrality and the fact that Adams had not first sought the advice of the Senate, but the probability that American delegates would be expected to meet with black delegates from Haiti, and that slavery would be an item on the agenda, was enough to stir Calhoun's opposition. The Panama issue also provided an opportunity to organize the opposition. As Van Buren later recalled, it was part of "a general agreement of action between us."[15]

Ultimately the Senate Foreign Relations Committee reported unfavorably on sending commissioners to Panama, but the Senate approved the measure by a close vote. Southern Senators were strongly opposed, and supporters of the administration were quick to see Calhoun's hand in the matter. Webster told a friend that Calhoun "organized and arranged the opposition. He expected to defeat the measure. That would have placed the President in his power, more or less, and if the thing could be repeated, on one or two other occasions, completely so. Mr. Adams, then, would have been obliged to make terms, or he could not get on with the Govt., and those terms would have been the dismissal of Mr. Clay."[16]

Completing his first year as Vice President, Calhoun could take satisfaction in knowing that he retained considerable political leverage. Recalling to Micah Sterling how his friends had warned him away from the office because it "would not leave me sufficiently in the public eye," he now predicted with ill-disguised pride that "the whole weight of the executive will be brought to bear against me. I am proclaimed by all of the papers under its patronage, as the head of an opposition, and attacks have already commenced against me." How he could maintain this political momentum in his ceremonial office as presiding officer of the Senate remained to be seen.[17]

Why the Founding Fathers, committed to the doctrine of the separation of powers, should have made the second officer of the executive department President of the Senate has always been something of a puzzle. Calhoun's predecessors had coped with the anomaly by turning over the job for the most part to a President Pro Tempore elected by Senators from their own ranks, thus recognizing that the Senate should be a self-governing body. But this was not Calhoun's style. He had been an aggressive legislator and administrator, and it was almost inevitable that he would be an aggressive Vice President. It did not take him long to discover that he could turn the very passivity of his new position into a powerful weapon.

By the end of March 1826 the opposition to Adams, although not yet formally organized, was beginning to take shape. The *United States Telegraph,* subsidized with funds from Jackson and Calhoun supporters, was beginning to be heard in the capital and, much to Calhoun's satisfaction, would soon be under the control of Duff Green, Ninian Edwards's brother-in-law and a staunch Calhoun supporter. Green came from Missouri, where, thanks to Secretary of War Calhoun, he enjoyed the rank of brigadier general in the militia. Nine years younger than Calhoun and possessed of incredible energy and initiative, Green had already been a soldier in the War of 1812, teacher, merchant, surveyor, land speculator, stagecoach operator, lawyer, and state legislator. He began his journalism career in 1823 by purchasing the *St. Louis Enquirer,* which he immediately used to support the last gasps of Calhoun's presidential campaign before switching to Jackson. Green had been one of the first editors to exploit the "corrupt bargain" theme, and the motto of the *Telegraph,* "Power is always stealing from the many to the few," was an obvious reminder that political usurpers had triumphed in 1825.[18]

Two weeks after the Panama mission had been approved, the *Telegraph* attacked the administration with an editorial on "Intrigue, Bargain and Management," and opposition leaders in the Senate began to launch a sustained attempt to embarrass the government. John Randolph, who had almost turned obstructionism into an art form, led the charge. Hour after hour, day after day, Randolph seized the floor to denigrate Adams and Clay for their alleged attempt to get around the Constitution in connection with the Panama mission and for their perfidy in the recent election. This ranting, which Daniel Webster complained went on "for two, four and sometimes six hours at a time" with Randolph "saying whatever occurs to him in all subjects" after fortifying himself occasionally on the floor with brandy and port, eventually led to a harmless duel with Henry Clay. On April 8 the Secretary of State shot a hole in Randolph's voluminous cloak, but since nothing less than a bullet in the mouth could have shut him up, the tirades continued.[19]

Because he sat impassively in the chair and did not call Randolph to order, Adams's Senators accused Calhoun of using his position to hurt the administration, and on April 15 the Vice President claimed the privilege of the floor to argue that under Senate rules "the right to call to order, on questions touching the latitude or freedom of debate" belonged to the members of the Senate and not to the chair. Shortly thereafter Calhoun's reasoning and behavior were strongly attacked by a correspondent to the *Washington National Journal* writing under the name of "Patrick Henry." Calhoun replied a few days later under the pseudonym "Onslow" (a famous parliamentary speaker), and thus began a lengthy exchange spread over six months, in which he was able to show that what seemed to be a procedural wrangle was really an ideological conflict of fundamental importance.

There were three distinct levels to the Patrick Henry-Onslow debate. The first was technical. Henry held that Jefferson's parliamentary manual for the Senate, the history of that body, the history of Parliament, and the commonsense proposition that a presiding officer by definition is supposed to keep order all argued that the President of the Senate was duty bound to rein in people like Randolph who were only wasting the Senate's time. Calhoun held that since the rules of the Senate did not expressly give the chair the power to declare a Senator out of order except on the call of another Senator, he could not exercise the power on his own. He argued that since the Vice President was not "responsible" to the Senate (not elected by Senators as a chair), he should never exercise power not expressly given in the rules.

It is practically impossible, and not really important to our purpose, to decide who had the better of this argument. Henry had common sense on his side when he argued that to preside means to preserve order, and this is what most Senators seemed to want. The precedents which both writers cited interminably, reaching into the far recesses of parliamentary history, did not prove anything, but Calhoun probably scored points with shorter senatorial memories when he equated the arbitrary power to shut off Randolph with the "despotic Power" which had fastened the infamous sedition laws on the country in 1798.

The second level of debate was frankly partisan. In his first letter Patrick Henry asserted that the Vice President, disappointed in his own claim for the Presidency, sought "encouragement in the declamations of every enemy to the Government" and compared him with the "inconstant experimenting and reckless ambition" of Aaron Burr, an earlier Vice President of unhappy memory. The other charge against Calhoun was that he took advantage of a recently passed law heretofore used only by Presidents of the Senate Pro Tempore, to pack key Senate committees with members opposed to the administration.

The first accusation epitomized the tendency to rhetorical excess that characterized both writers. Although ambition was always a powerful engine in Calhoun, and although he wanted the government to go down, no one could ever seriously compare him with Burr. The second does not appear to be true. Calhoun's appointments, although far from giving Adams the leverage he wanted, seem to have reflected the close balance among contending factions revealed by the election, and when he refuted Henry by defending his appointees by name in laudatory terms, Calhoun may have enhanced his own standing in the Senate.

The ideological dimension to the debate is by far the most important because it shows how brilliantly Calhoun was able to rationalize his practical political position in terms of high principle. Intent from the beginning on showing that his philosophical disagreement with Henry could be reduced to the question of how power should be used, Calhoun asserted "that a public officer should construe his own powers strictly . . . particularly when those powers are invidious in their nature, and peculiarly liable to be abused." Calhoun argued that Henry, who believed in the "inherent" powers of the Vice President, showed a bias against "the democratic side of our institutions" and would always be found on the side which placed power "in the fewest and least responsible hands." He reminded his readers that a doctrine of inherent rights was really not very different from the old doctrine of "divine rights." Having placed himself squarely in the ideological tradition which had sustained Americans in their great struggles against arbitrary power in 1776, 1800, and 1812, Calhoun suggested that the issue in 1826 was the same as it had been then: whether power would be acquired fairly and used "wisely and virtuously." He was prepared to show that the attacks on the Vice President came from a government which had taken power without the consent of the people and was now trying to secure itself by consolidating that power in imitation of the British system. If Patrick Henry cared to continue the debate, he was prepared to show "that the principles on which Mr. Adams came into power and which have been attempted to be vindicated by Mr. Clay and his friends are utterly inconsistent with the Constitution, as they have been ever understood and acted on by the Republican party, and that, if not successfully resisted by the People, must, in a short time, convert our Government, first into an oligarchy, and finally at no long interval into a monarchy." Patrick Henry declined the challenge, and here the dialogue ended.[20]

It is worth asking why a Vice President of the United States would allow himself to become embroiled in a lengthy pseudonymous exchange in the national press, particularly when it became so quickly obvious that he was Onslow. The answer lies in the fact that Calhoun and most of the readers who followed the debate believed that Patrick Henry was President Adams. Although we can now show that the real Henry was Philip Fendall, a clerk in the Department of State who wrote with Adams's blessing, the popular opinion, which Calhoun shared, was that the President had disguised himself in order to chastise his most highly placed opponent. This perception added spice and drama to the encounter and thrust Calhoun to center stage. Passed over for the first office, he was demonstrating that he could transcend the normally obscure office of Vice President and play a highly visible role in shaping the political agenda.[21]

Calhoun's personal correspondence during the summer and fall of 1828 often expressed Onslow's sentiments. He advised Monroe that his administration had been correct in trying to cooperate with reformed Federalists while the new administration seemed bent in restoring the old heresy, and he told Micah Sterling, who had become a kind of alter ego, that the power of the executive was "already kingly" in the hands of Adams and Clay. But to a New England friend like Levi Woodbury he was careful to distinguish between the President and the Secretary of State. Adams was not "politically dishonest," he admitted, but too much influenced by Clay. The charge of collusion between "the Puritan and the Black Leg" which had brought Randolph and Clay to the dueling field was inaccurate. A better description would be a coalition between the Federalists of 1798 and "the bargain and sale party of the West."

Meanwhile, Calhoun moved to close ranks with Andrew Jackson. The great issue, he wrote the general on June 4, was "between power and liberty, and it must be determined in the next three years." Jackson responded by implicitly offering an alliance. "I trust that my name will always be found on the side of the people," he wrote, "and that we shall march hand in hand in their cause." It was an offer the Vice President could not refuse. "Every indication is in our favour," he replied, "or rather I should say in favour of the country's cause." By this time he had also reached out to Van Buren. An agreement was tentatively reached that Christmas, when Calhoun and Van Buren met at a friend's house in Fairfax County, Virginia, to discuss their common interest in making Jackson the next President. Through a series of subsequent meetings it was decided that Van Buren would bring New York and Virginia into Jackson's camp and try to recruit support from the Crawfordites in the South, while Calhoun encouraged the general to trust Van Buren, who had been Crawford's manager in 1824. The implicit understanding was that Calhoun would continue as Vice President under Jackson.[23]

Supporters of Clay and Adams, of course, charged that this kind of political maneuvering disclosed the real Calhoun and that the Onslow letters were no more than a high-toned rhetorical smoke screen. "You have alienated, forever, every friend of the present Administration," claimed a writer to the *Richmond Whig*, "for like Judas, you have betrayed them with a kiss. . . . You have attempted to destroy every man whose political standing obstructed your own political progress . . . and dangerous features have shown themselves in your character, such unusual distrust has been inspired, that you can never, without a miracle, attain that bright goal of your desires."[24]

Considering the political climate in Washington in the winter of 1826–1827, it was probably inevitable that Calhoun would have to cope once again with charges of fraud in the Department of War under his leadership during the previous administration. He demanded a full-scale investigation, and once again, this time in a 251-page report, the Congress found no evidence to support "the belief or even suspicion" that he had profited from the scandalous Mix contract. Commenting on the investigation, Senator William King spoke for most of Calhoun's political opponents when he claimed that he had been tried for the wrong offense. "Had the Vice President been charged with forming magnificent plans and lavishly squandering the public money in the execution of them, with political intrigue or ungovernable ambition," King wrote, "many would have yielded a ready assent to the charge; but when the accusation is peculation in office his bitterest enemies instinctively pronounce it to be false."[25][22]

Calhoun characteristically interpreted the investigation as a great personal triumph. Despite an "inquisition for forty days," he wrote to his brother-in-law, "a life of spotless political purity bore me through every difficulty, and compelled my enemies to acquit honorably." He told his old mentor Waddel that "no man is more indebted to his enemies than I am," and wrote gloatingly to Jackson, "I saw the stab that was aimed at my reputation, and that it could be effectively repelled only by the most decisive measures."[26]

Although Calhoun knew that some of Jackson's friends would oppose his reelection as Vice President, he thought he had no choice but to stand for nomination. To help Jackson win the presidency and not be identified with his administration made little sense for his own future, and because of what had happened between Adams and Clay, he could hardly be expected to accept a Cabinet position. As matters worked

Calhoun in his mid-fifties.

From the Collection of Fort Hill

out, Van Buren, who feared that his great New York adversary De Witt Clinton might get the spot by default, managed to hold off the anti-Calhoun faction led by Crawford loyalists. By January 1828 Calhoun could boast of unanimous nominations in conventions in Pennsylvania, New Jersey, Ohio, and Kentucky and a strong endorsement from Virginia. The "Jackson, Calhoun and Liberty" banner would carry the new Democratic Party to victory that fall, but the victory would be a costly one for both men.[27]

The level of personal acrimony in the election of 1828 was nicely illustrated in April, when Russell Jarvis, a partner of Duff Green's and a Jackson partisan, assaulted President Adams's son and secretary by pulling his nose in the Capitol rotunda. Adams's supporters retaliated by calling Jackson a murderous brawler, a bloodthirsty "military chieftain," a gambler, an adulterer, and the son of a prostitute mother and mulatto father. It was one of the most abusive campaigns in American history. Jackson won handily, and Calhoun, whose election as Vice President was practically uncontested, seemed to come off relatively unscathed. By his own lights he had turned a political scramble once again into a struggle over principle, and as the aging Jackson's political ally and Vice President he appeared to be the strongest contender for the presidency four years hence. There were people close to the President-elect, however, determined to preclude that possibility. "The former friends of Crawford here," wrote Alfred Balch from Nashville to Van Buren, "neither few in numbers nor weak in talents have an account to settle with Mr. Calhoun which must be settled."[28]

7

The Architect of Nullification

BY 1828 CALHOUN could congratulate himself for having successfully negotiated the shoals of Adams's unpopular presidency while attaching himself to the invincible Jackson. He was still very much alive as a national leader and prospective President, but he had come to realize that he could no longer take the support of his home state for granted. Calhoun had been away from South Carolina most of the time for more than twelve years and had developed a national focus that was necessarily larger than the view from Abbeville, Columbia, and Charleston. His aggressive nationalism during the war had been consistent with the ardent patriotism of his native state, but the consensus at home for his expansive program of national improvements after the war had been flawed from the beginning. Carolinians were willing to support a strong military establishment because they knew they could not carry their staples to world markets except under the flag of a powerful nation, but they did not expect to benefit from internal improvements, and as historic free traders they instinctively opposed tariffs.

Calhoun's support for a substantial revenue-producing tariff in 1816 had derived logically from his plan for the army and a national communications system. Building the new nation required revenue, and taxing imports was the only avenue provided by the Constitution for that purpose, which, unfortunately, introduced a sticky problem. How could one be sure that duties levied on British manufacturers to provide money to build national roads and canals were not also helping protect the people in manufacturing states from foreign competition while raising prices for people in the South and making it more difficult for them to sell in foreign markets? Indeed, if this were the case, how could such legislation be valid under a Constitution which did not expressly authorize Congress to tax imports for the purpose of encouraging domestic manufactures? Such questions came naturally to the minds of Carolinians, who lived for the most part off their exports.

Knowing how apprehensive people in his state were to any kind of tariff, Calhoun had insisted that the 1816 bill was designed solely to produce revenue for defense, but he did not hide his opinion that it might encourage a more viable manufacturing sector and thus a stronger Union. In fact, the duties in 1816 were too low to be protective, and Carolinians supported them without significant complaint. In 1820, however, when a slightly higher tariff was proposed, they stoutly opposed it. South Carolina nationalism did not go that far.

The earliest indication of strain between Calhoun and his constituents came almost unnoticed when William Smith, a wealthy planter from York, was sent to the United States Senate by the South Carolina legislature in 1816. Twenty years older than Calhoun, Smith had been a fixture in state politics for more than ten years. Overcoming a notorious early career as a boozer, philanderer, and brawler, Smith had settled down after marriage and turned himself into a capable lawyer, legislator, and judge without completely surrendering his rough manners and a tendency to resolve political differences with his fists. For the most part, however, he was willing to delegate the latter function to his associate, James Blair, a hard-drinking 350-pound giant, who once ended a dispute by riding his horse through an opponent's house.[1]

It was not likely that Calhoun would get along with a character like Smith, whom he had contemptuously dismissed in 1811 as a "weak political intriguer." Thus, as Benjamin Perry, editor of the influential *Greenville Mountaineer,* later recalled, when Smith entered the Senate, "He hated Calhoun with an intensity and cordiality seldom felt by any public man towards his opponent." Like Crawford, Smith was an old-fashioned states' rights, strict-construction republican, and his vehement denunciation of consolidation in the federal government and the ruinous effects for South Carolina planters of tariffs and extravagant expenditures for standing armies and internal improvements attracted a significant following, especially in upper country counties like York, Lancaster, and Chesterfield on the North Carolina border.[2]

For a proud man like Calhoun, who had grown accustomed to the increasingly deferential support of his native state, William Smith must have been hard to take. He did not go into the Senate to make Calhoun

President, Smith boasted, "but to do the duties of a Senator," and he interpreted these duties to mean painting the Secretary of War as an ambitious politician willing to connive with Federalists to get power. Clearly Smith had to go, and in 1822, when he stood for reelection, Calhoun and his supporters concentrated on getting the legislature to replace Smith with the handsome, well-bred Charleston lawyer Robert Hayne. The real issue was not so much the abilities of the two candidates as loyalty to Calhoun. "Let the Legislature remember," wrote the *Charleston City Gazette,* "that if Mr. Smith is elected, it will be considered as an evidence by all other states, that Carolina herself is unfavorable to Mr. Calhoun."[3]

Although Calhoun was successful in ousting Smith in 1822, the vote was reasonably close (91 to 74), and the Smith faction continued to challenge his control over the state by spreading the Crawford line about Calhoun's "impetuosity" in running for President and his recklessness in administering the War Department. When a Calhoun paper compared its candidate's decision to run for the presidency with Caesar's crossing the Rubicon, the *Yorkville Pioneer* jumped at the bait. "Caesar was a Republican too. . . . And like Mr. Calhoun to an extraordinary share of talent, he united an unconquerable thirst for distinction." Privately the combative Smith was considerably more explicit, calling Calhoun "a master spirit" of intrigue who "like the rat always quits the ship when he finds it about to sink. He has alternately abandoned and taken up Mr. Adams two or three times, and has at last taken up Adams and Jackson both." Calhoun's real goal, Smith told his friends, was to assure himself the vice presidency, force a runoff in the House for the presidency, "play that off till the 4th of March without producing a decision, and the Vice President becomes your President for the next four years. You may rely upon it that is the game he is now playing without Jackson or Adams suspecting him."[4]

Despite Calhoun's opposition, Smith proved a hard man to keep down. The Tariff of 1824, which raised duties considerably and coincided with the plunging price of cotton, was widely perceived in South Carolina as a victory for protectionists. Calhounites in Congress had been ineffectual in opposing the bill, and Smith quickly claimed that Calhoun had secretly supported it as a favor to northern friends. In the state elections that year Smith was returned to the legislature by a heavy majority, and the next year he and his faction succeeded in passing resolutions declaring protective tariffs and internal improvements unconstitutional. By 1827 Smith was back in the United States Senate boasting to cronies that Calhoun had "lost his party both at home and abroad" and could never be reelected Vice President. "He [had] no offices to exchange for patronage, no large sums of money to disburse," Smith said, and consequently had lost his friends. According to Smith, South Carolina had remained true to the old republican doctrine of states' rights while Calhoun had been juggling regional and national interests for his own political aggrandizement. It was just a matter of time, Smith predicted, before the wayward son would be forced to recant. "He has not yet made his open avowal of his errors . . . but it is said if he had a fair opportunity of doing so, he would."[5]

Although Smith probably overestimated his own importance as a political mover and shaker and underestimated Calhoun's continuing influence nationally and at home, there was considerable truth in what he said. The political agenda in South Carolina was changing, and if Calhoun expected to control it in the future, an alliance with Jackson to undo the perfidy of the Clay-Adams coalition would not be enough. He would also need to find an argument and strategy to contain and direct the new political energy welling up in his native state over the tariff.

Although Calhoun ultimately became identified with constitutional arguments against the tariff, he did not need to consult the Constitution to learn why the tariff had become an inflammatory issue. Carolinians who supported the Tariff of 1816 had sold their cotton at twenty-seven cents a pound. In 1827 they were lucky to get nine cents a pound. "Our staples can hardly return the cost of cultivation," Calhoun wrote to his brother-in-law, "and land and Negroes have fallen to the lowest prices and can hardly be sold." The common perception, which Calhoun shared, was that the tariff was responsible. Reduced to its simplest essentials, the popular reasoning held that a tariff on manufactures forced a cotton-exporting state like South Carolina to "buy high" and "sell low." We know now that Calhoun and his supporters were wrong about the causes for economic decline in their state. Low cotton prices were linked more closely to overproduction brought on by the expansion of cotton cultivation in the Southwest than by tariff policy. However, the tariff explanation was plausible enough in the mid-1820s to be politically powerful, especially when it was combined with the claim, supported by some economic historians today, that the tariff did, in fact, tend to redistribute income from cotton growers to economic producers outside the South.[6]

Calhoun made his first overt move against the tariff on February 28, 1827, when as presiding officer of the Senate he cast a tie-breaking vote to defeat a bill which would have raised the duty on woolens by 50 percent. Although he knew his action would offend supporters in the North and middle states, especially those in Pennsylvania, he really had no choice if he expected to hold on to his leadership position at home. By now antitariff sentiment had spread far beyond the Smith faction. McDuffie was denouncing tariff supporters as thunderously as he had put down the antinationalists a few years earlier, and on July 4, 1827, Thomas Cooper, the president of South Carolina College, delivered a widely publicized oration in Columbia challenging the value of a Union determined "to sacrifice the South to the North by converting us into colonies and tributaries." Cooper, whose intense commitment to Jeffersonian principles had earned him a jail sentence under the Alien and Sedition Acts, was not a man to be taken lightly, and the radical implications of his speech were spelled out in lurid detail in a series of newspaper essays by Robert J. Turnbull, a wealthy low-country planter. Tracing the crisis in 1827 to the tendency ever since the Monroe administration to extend the powers of Congress and the federal government under a loose construction of the general welfare clause of the Constitution, Turnbull warned that it would be suicidal for Carolinians to consider the protective tariff simply as a constitutional question. If Congress could pass such a tariff to promote the general welfare, what was to stop it from abolishing slavery for the same reason? Confronted by such a threat, South Carolina would have no recourse but to rely on "the undiminished sovereignty of our state—when the rights of one sovereign are invaded by another sovereign. There is no course but resistance. If resistance produced Disunion, let Disunion come." Lest any reader mistake the implications of what he meant by resistance, Turnbull provided them with a chilling metaphor: "Fellow-Citizens. We are precisely in the situation of a family who have listened to, and overheard from their windows, the conversations of robbers in the streets, and, fortunately, know that its own dwelling is to be the scene of their villainous operations. What is the course that prudence would dictate to that family? Certainly, to be prepared with blunderbuses, and to blow out their brains: so must it be with the tariff."[7]

Although Calhoun must have read Turnbull's *The Crisis* essays, he would have had little sympathy for their irresponsible rhetoric. He was sure Cooper and Turnbull did not represent the opinion of most Carolinians, but he also knew that the grievance in his state had substance. Explaining the issue to his brother-in-law, Calhoun said that wise men might differ over the question of a protective tariff, but there could be no doubt "that the power itself is dangerous and may be perverted to purposes most oppressive and unjust. Through such an exercise of it, one section of the country may really be made tributary to another." Convinced that the tariff placed an unequal burden on the South, Calhoun began to sharpen his public statements. "The Constitution of the United States intended for the protection and happiness of the whole," he said in a toast at an independence anniversary at Pendleton, "may it never be perverted into an instrument of monopoly and oppression."[8]

When the tariff advocates planned a meeting at Harrisburg, Calhoun denounced it in a letter to his Virginian friend Littleton Tazewell as an attempt on the part of "the great geographical Northern manufacturing interest in order to enforce more effectually the system of monopoly and extortion against the consuming states." If the manufacturers succeeded in electing the next President, Calhoun feared, "the simple alternative of submission or resistance will be presented." Confronted with this possibility, Turnbull had been willing to let the streets run red; Calhoun emphasized to Tazewell that he sought a more civil resolution of the problem: "a veto on the part of the local interests, or under our system on the part of the states." When Tazewell asked him how a state could void a law of Congress when that power had already been given to the Supreme Court, Calhoun admitted the difficulty and confessed: "I do not see my way clearly."[9]

What Calhoun did see clearly at this point was the connection between the election of 1824 and the potential for tariff legislation in the future. He spelled out the message in a letter to the influential Postmaster General John McLean. In 1824 a President had been made in defiance of the popular will by "using the power and the patronage of the government as the instrument of bribery." What had been done by individuals in the past now could be done by an economic interest group or section. "One section will be bribed by means flushed from another. The revenue collected from all will be partially distributed and the industry of a favorite section be promoted by the sacrifice" of one less powerful.[10]

The famous Tariff of Abominations, which forced Calhoun to systematize his case against the tariff in a hurry the following summer, resulted not from a conspiracy of one section against another but from an irresponsible bit of political chicanery in which all the sections shared. When the Twentieth Congress had met in December 1827, manufacturing lobbyists of every description, fortified by their discussions at Harrisburg that summer, showed up to get their slice of the great protective pie Congress was being pressured to bake.

The Adams-Clay coalition was clearly behind this movement, leaving the Jacksonians in a quandary. Their first priority was to elect their Hero (nobody was sure how he felt about the tariff), and that meant keeping the alliance of southern and middle state republicans intact. The ideal solution would have been to do nothing, always an appealing alternative. But there was too much of a clamor for that, so the Jackson managers decided on the next best option, which was to do so much that in the end it would come to nothing. The strategy of the Jackson men in the House was to accept the heavy duties recommended at Harrisburg, but to add a list of excessive levies on goods like hemp, iron, and molasses that would offend New Englanders. The assumption was that the bill would attract support from enough Representatives outside the South to pass the House but that New England Senators would kill it, thus laying the onus for the failed legislation on the section of the country where the administration was strongest. Artful, high-risk strategy, like fighting the devil with fire, warned George McDuffie, but Calhoun and the rest of the Carolinians went along with it to disaster. Everything proceeded according to plan in the House, where the bill passed in late April 1828 by an eleven-vote margin. In the Senate, however, the script was ignored as compensating amendments secured enough New England support to pass the law, and President Adams signed the famous Tariff of Abominations on May 19, raising duties generally from about 30 to 50 percent.[11]

Powerless to intervene, Calhoun had watched the whole ugly business take place from his presiding chair in the Senate. South Carolina, where the tariff issue had become much more than a matter of simple economic self-interest, was hurt badly. The Carolina delegation cursed, caucused, and sought to enlist other southern states to make a formal remonstrance, but without effect. Having tried to fight the devil with fire and lost, most southern politicians were content to leave the issue alone, at least until after the election. Replacing Adams with Jackson, who they hoped would be more sympathetic to southern problems, was their first priority.

Calhoun's personal reaction to the Tariff of Abominations seems to have been moderate. Two days after the bill had passed in the Senate he wrote a sanguine letter to his friend Micah Sterling in New York expressing confidence in the political future and his own role in it. In the course of the letter he made the following statement:

I certainly have had great difficulties to contend with as you state, but truth will, in the long run, prevail. I have ever relied on it as my only guide under every difficulty—lead where it may I will follow. I know not that it is, even a merit in me. I cannot do otherwise. Whether it be too great confidence in my own opinion I cannot say, but what I think I see, I see with so much appearent [*sic*] clearness as not to leave me a choice to pursue any other course, which has always given me the impression that I acted under the force of destiny.[12]

Here Calhoun is trying to explain, incompletely but with considerably more self-insight than he usually revealed, the phenomenon others were to identify as a cast-iron character. However, he was not yet prepared to play the cast-iron role over the tariff because he was still groping for an answer to South Carolina's problem. He saw the injustice of the system clearly enough, but not the solution. He spent the next six months on his plantation, surrounded by desperate planters who looked to him for deliverance, searching for the answer.

Almost everything that Calhoun was to put into the paper that became known as the *South Carolina Exposition and Protest* and provided the theoretical basis for nullification appears somewhere in his correspondence during the summer and early fall of 1828. Calhoun knew that Jackson's election and his own that fall were a foregone conclusion. Although the voters in the state did not expect him to campaign, they did expect him to provide leadership against the tariff and to help lead the new administration into the paths of righteousness in 1829 and beyond, a daunting prospect considering the divisiveness of the issue nationally, but one that appealed to Calhoun because it required rethinking the principles on which the government of the United States was based.

As Calhoun studied the question of the legitimacy of tariff legislation, he became convinced that there was "a fatal disease lurking in the system." The Founding Fathers had designed a government in which power would check power formally through the separation of the three great departments of the federal government and informally by providing for a representative form of government in a large, diverse country. James Madison had argued that the multiplicity and diversity of factions in the United States would invariably work to keep a factional majority from emerging and using the government for its own aggrandizement. But according to Calhoun, Madison's analysis did not hold up in the 1820s. "I greatly fear," he wrote to Monroe, "that the weak part of our system will be found to consist in the fact that in a country of such vast extent and diversity of interest many of the laws will be found to act unequally, and that some portions of the country may be enriched by legislation at the expense of others." In this situation parties would naturally develop to protect existing interests, and if a majority could be built around a common, favored interest, the Republic would be imperiled. Calhoun believed that the history of the mislabeled "American System" proved his point. "Mr. Adams and Mr. Clay never would have united," he wrote to Vandeventer, "but from the hope of sustaining themselves through this unequal action of the tariff system."[13]

Aware of the delicacy of his situation, Calhoun was careful to project a moderate image during the summer and fall of 1828. He was willing to agree, as he wrote to Samuel Smith in Baltimore, "that the tariff is to a certain extent constitutional, and that by a prudent exercise of the power really vested in Congress much good may result." What he meant was that the power to levy duties was always "incidental to that of raising revenue and commerce." In exercising either of these powers, Congress might also give preference to a measure calculated "to transfer manufacturing ability to our country." But, Calhoun insisted, "when Congress converts the incident into the principal [*sic*] ... it appears to be usurpation in its worst form."[14]

Although the republicanism which had informed both the Revolution and the writing of the Constitution had been born in reaction to the usurpation of power, Calhoun was trying to appeal to the reason of his friends, not to their passion. He wanted them to see that the differing economic interests of the sections were based on facts of history, geography, and population that were largely providential. Dependent on slave labor, the South probably could not turn to manufactures (thus enjoying the benefits of tariffs) even if it wanted to. And if it did, the Union would be sorely threatened. "Can we conceive a more dangerous political condition, than for free and slave labour to come into competition?" he asked McLean. "Do you think that the free laborers, the voters of the North, would permit bread to be taken out of the mouths of their wives and children by the slaves of the South?"[15]

In searching for a peaceful, constitutional way to redress the injustice done by the tariff, Calhoun rejected the idea of the Supreme Court as the ultimate arbiter of constitutionality and advised a return to the "primitive principles of our government," by which he meant a return to the principle of dual sovereignty—the separate states with their reserved powers and a United States with its delegated power. "Is not the result inevitable," he asked McLean on October 4, "that if the sovereign power be divided as between the General and State Governments neither can have the conclusive right of deciding on contested powers; and of course the acts of each is [*sic*] a negative on the other?" To expect the Supreme Court to decide the constitutionality of the tariff was inadequate because "It would not reach the danger. It presupposes that the evil to be guarded against is in those who exercise for the time the powers of the General Government, whereas it is in the *community itself*," the ability of the majority to enrich itself at the expense of the minority.

When McLean asked why the resort to state vetoes would not lead to anarchy, Calhoun reminded him that the ultimate power under the Constitution was the amending power. "Should a state abuse the power, it is in the power of Congress to call in the real creating power, that which made and that which can modify the Constitution of the General Government at pleasure, to correct the evil. I mean three-fourths of the states." By now Calhoun had arrived at the kind of certainty he needed, a certainty which he had told Sterling, made him believe he acted "with the force of destiny." When a member of the South Carolina legislature called on him early in November to justify the right of their state to nullify or veto the Tariff of 1828, he was prepared.[16]

Calhoun wrote the draft for what became the historic *South Carolina Exposition and Protest* over a two-week period in November 1828. He did so with the understanding "that all that can be done at present is an able report, fully exposing our wrongs, and unfolding our remedies," and that the state would *"abstain for the present from applying it* on grounds of respect for others and a sense of moderation." The respect for others surely included himself. Even though his pen might write with the force of destiny, Calhoun must have realized how politically dangerous it was for an incumbent Vice President of the United States, about to be reelected to the same high office, to prepare a document defending the right of a state to nullify a federal law.[17]

Calhoun's report to the special committee of the South Carolina House of Representatives appointed to prepare a protest against the tariff takes up almost ninety pages in the Calhoun papers. For the most part it is a systematic presentation of arguments Calhoun had been making in correspondence over the past year. The first part is simply a restatement of the familiar complaints made about the invidious effects of the tariff on staple-exporting states in the South. "We export to import," Calhoun wrote, pointing out that the home market could consume less than one-fourth of what southern states could sell abroad. Since southern planters could not export their crops profitably, they faced the dismal alternatives of bankruptcy or shifting to manufacturing to take advantage of the tariff, and the latter was a practical impossibility. Even if it were possible, the North would never accept an industrialized South built on slavery. "Those who now make war on our gains, would then make it on our labour. They would not tolerate that . . . their rivals take bread out of the mouths of their wives and children." Here Calhoun was appealing to the self-interest of working-class voters outside the South, and he emphasized his point by arguing that the protective system which presently was impoverishing South Carolina and other southern states would ultimately do the same for workers in the North. In Europe the war against free trade had always kept workers on the brink of starvation, and the same thing would happen in the United States. "After we are exhausted," he wrote, "the contest will be between the Capitalists and operators, for into these two classes it must ultimately divide society. . . . Under operation of the system, wages will sink more rapidly than the prices of the necessaries of life, till the operators will be reduced to the lowest point, where the portion of the products of their labour left to them, will be barely necessary to preserve existence."[18]

According to Calhoun, the tariff threatened to destroy the Republic because it was an example of unchecked majority power, and republican government could never coexist with irresponsible power. "On this great principle," Calhoun wrote, "our political system rests." If all laws worked equally on citizens in different parts of the country, a simple representative system would suffice, but a critical problem would always be to prevent a self-interested majority from passing laws contrary to the minority interest. The founders knew that "no government, based on the naked principle that the majority ought to govern . . . ever preserved its liberty even for a single generation." They therefore divided power, not just in the famous separation of the three federal (Calhoun used the word "general") departments but between the individual states and the government they created.[19]

What powers adhered to the states and what to the general government? Where did sovereignty reside in the American constitutional system? These questions have never been easy to answer, and they were not easy for Calhoun. At one point he wrote: "Our system consists of two distinct and independent 'sovereignties' or 'governments.'" He was obviously grappling with those provisions in the Constitution which delegated specific powers to the federal government and reserved all other power to "the people of the several states who created it." Calhoun finally decided that neither the individual states nor the general government were sovereign. The ultimate power lay in any combination of three-quarters of the states for the purpose of amending the Constitution. The point to be stressed was that the Constitution recognized and institutionalized a basic reality about community in American life. "Looking to facts, the Constitution has formed the states into a community only to the extent that they have common interests, leaving them distinct and independent communities, as to all other interests; drawing the line of separation as stated with consummate skill. It is manifest, that so long as this beautiful theory is adhered to in practice, the system, like the atmosphere will press substantially equally on all the parts."[20]

The question of the moment was how the beautiful theory of the Constitution would be enforced. Calhoun quickly dismissed the notion that the Supreme Court, an arm of the general government, could be the final arbiter. The Court might usefully check the abuse of power on the part of the executive or legislature or the encroachment of state power upon the general government, but it could not be expected to judge in a case where the general government (of which the Court was a part) was accused of invading the power of a state. "The right of judging in such cases is an essential attribute of sovereignty, of which the states cannot be divested without losing their sovereignty itself, and being reduced to a subordinate corporate condition." To divide power and to give to one of the parties the exclusive "right of judging of the portion allotted to each" was really "not to divide at all." Every state, then, had the right to decide on "contested points of authority" between the general government and itself.[21]

Up to this point Calhoun was not saying anything new, a point which he made himself by citing the positions of Madison and Jefferson in the Virginia and Kentucky Resolutions of 1798. He surely thought of himself as summarizing and putting in systematic form a way of thinking that had been common to South Carolina republicans ever since the Revolution and had been restated by Charles Pinckney in Congress in 1820, when he called the states "alert and faithful sentinels to disprove" unconstitutional acts of the federal government. Where Calhoun parted company with Pinckney and with the nullifiers of 1798 was in what he took to be the constitutional process through which an aggrieved state could act—not through its legislature but through a state convention chosen to determine whether or not a particular law or behavior was unconstitutional and should be vetoed.

Having rationalized more fully than anyone else the right of nullification, Calhoun was careful to end his report on a conciliatory note. This right of a state was neither revolutionary nor destabilizing and could never be exercised without cause.

The great number by whom it must be exercised of the people of a State, the solemnity of the mode, a convention especially called for the purpose, and representing the state in her highest capacity, the delay, the deliberation, are all calculated to allay excitement, to impress on the people a deep and solemn tone, highly favorable to calm investigation and decision. . . . The attitude in which the state would be placed in relation to other states, the force of public opinion. . . . The deep reverence for the General Government . . . constitute impediments to the exercise of this high protective right of the State which must render it safe.[22]

Closing with a rhetorical burst of praise for the fathers of the Constitution that Webster might have admired, Calhoun urged restraint on his fellow Carolinians. Although their case justified calling a state convention now, they should desist, hoping that "the great political revolution" about to take place would result in a "complete restoration of the pure principles of our Government."

Calhoun completed his draft of what became known as the *South Carolina Exposition* in late November and sent it to the Special Committee of the legislature, where it was reported in revised form on December 19. The legislature responded by sending a formal protest against the recent tariff to Congress and ordering four thousand copies of the *Exposition* to be printed. Although it was presented as a committee document, political insiders everywhere suspected that Calhoun had been the real author. Webster's protégé Edward Everett thought Calhoun was "working South Carolina into a frenzy on the tariff question" in order to seduce his old enemies the Crawfordites, while the well-placed Virginian William Rives thought he was ruining his political future. Calhoun himself was characteristically sanguine. "Our cause stands in principle and truth," he wrote to W. C. Preston shortly before transmitting his draft. "If well conducted on our part, it will form the greatest political era in our civil history."[23]

8

The Duel with Jackson, 1828–1831

CALHOUN was only halfway through his vice presidential term under Adams when he moved his family back to South Carolina. The E Street house was sold, Oakly was rented to Vandeventer, and in the summer of 1826, after a harrowing overland trip with their dangerously ill son John, the Calhouns settled at Clergy Hall, about three miles from the village of Pendleton. This property, which had originally served as a summer cottage for a clergyman, now belonged to Floride's mother and consisted of five hundred acres of woods, rolling hills, and rich bottomland bounded by the Seneca River with flatboat access to the Savannah. The simple frame house, which was to be transformed into the Calhoun mansion, stood on a hill with a commanding view of the river on the south and the mountains on the north.

Exactly why Calhoun decided on Clergy Hall rather than their Bath plantation on the Savannah is not clear. Before moving there permanently, the Calhouns had summered at Clergy Hall, where they found a pleasant way of life and a healthy climate. Pendleton was one attraction. Built around a common in the manner of an old New England town, the village could boast of a weekly newspaper of good quality, several stores well stocked with Charleston merchandise, and the kind of voluntary organizations endemic to an expanding democracy elsewhere but relatively hard to come by in the rural South, such as a library, a Sunday school, and an agricultural society. There was also the matter of kin and friends. The elder Floride owned other property in the neighborhood and could establish her own residence nearby, where she would be close to both her daughter's family and that of her son, John Ewing, who was building his elegant Keowee plantation west of Pendleton. Finally, there was a possible political benefit to be gained from residing in Pendleton since the village was a summer haven for some of the wealthiest and most influential families from the low country. No one who aspired to be a controlling force in South Carolina politics could isolate himself from families like the Pinckneys, Hugers, and Gaillards. Calhoun never became really intimate with the nabobs of Charleston, but the cordial relationships he maintained with most of them was probably due in part to the Pendleton connection.

It was easier for Calhoun to remove his family from Washington as Vice President than it would have been if he had continued in the Cabinet because his only official duties involved presiding over the Senate, but the most compelling reasons for making the move were the almost fatal respiratory infection of their young son John and the belief that in the long run Pendleton would be the better place for bringing up their children. Calhoun spent a significant part of the next twenty-four years of his life turning the property at Clergy Hall into a productive plantation almost three times its original size. He was to name it Fort Hill for a colonial fort which had once stood on the same site, and as Fort Hill it became known as the country seat of the most famous southern statesman to be associated in the minds of informed citizens with such celebrated residences as Jackson's Hermitage, Clay's Ashland, and Webster's Marshfield.

It is difficult to think of any major figure in American political history who worked harder or more conscientiously than Calhoun. When he was Secretary of War, his insistence on extending himself with fourteen-hour work days throughout Washington's stifling summer months so weakened him in the autumn of 1819 while returning to the capital after a brief respite in South Carolina that he was felled by a fever and almost died. As an administrator, a legislator, or an embattled politician, Calhoun always seemed to be at the center of the action in Washington. In the heat of combat he could still think more deeply about political questions than most of his contemporaries, but the systematic political thought which would endure long after his death was articulated only in fits and starts in Washington. Somehow at Fort Hill Calhoun found that the routine of a hands-on planter refreshed and reinforced his intellectual vigor. Eventually he built a separate one-room study about fifty paces directly behind his house, and there he was to spend half of each day thinking and writing while the rest of his time was spent in the details of plantation management. Despite his reputation as an abstract, metaphysical thinker, concrete detail was always important to Calhoun. As Secretary of War he had initiated experimental work on the energy efficiency of plows of different design. As a planter he insisted on getting all his plows from New England because he believed they were made with stronger stocks. The rolling meadows and fields at Fort Hill made him an expert on ditching techniques, and as he supervised the workmen putting on additions to his house in the summer of 1827 and worried about getting enough rails split to enclose his fields, he did not neglect the little amenities that eventually turned Fort Hill into a plantation of grace and self-sufficiency. "If you can conveniently bring up a few small orange plants in a small box, I would be glad of it," Calhoun wrote his mother-in-law, "as I feel confident that with a little attention and care they will succeed on the south side of our house. I would also be glad of some blue grass seed for the yard in the fall, two or three pomagranate [*sic*] plants in a box and a few real yam potatoes to obtain seed from another year."[1]

In January 1828, for the first time since his Congressman days Calhoun had returned to Washington without his wife. "I am here without family," he wrote his brother-in-law. "The inconvenience of bringing a large family so far is so great as to deter your sister from the undertaking." By this time his eldest son, Andrew, was attending an academy in Pendleton, and Anna Maria was staying with cousins and going to school in Edgefield while the rest of the children remained with their mother at Fort Hill. The following year, however, Calhoun was due to be inaugurated with President-elect Andrew Jackson. Floride swallowed her anxieties, left her children in the care of her brother, and set off once again on the long, bone-rattling ride she detested to be with her husband for what would be a truly historic spectacle.[2]

The Washington the Calhouns returned to in January 1829 was essentially the same rustic, unfinished capital that John had known as a fledgling Congressman. Foreign visitors familiar with any of the great European centers of power like London, Paris, Rome, or Madrid would have been shocked not only by the muddy, unpaved streets, the lack of pomp, and any sense of history about the place but by the fact that nothing seemed to be happening there. Keeping boardinghouses was the biggest industry in town beside the government; one incredulous foreign visitor reported that there was "not a single great mercantile house in the District of Columbia." The federal establishment itself remained incredibly small, numbering a little more than 600 civilians and uniformed personnel, including the 273 elected Representatives and Senators. When foreign ministries were added to this, the result was a society with sufficient critical mass to support an active but strikingly provincial social life among legislators, high-ranking government officials, foreign diplomats, and their families.

The apparent paradox was that the people tended to leave their capital city pretty much alone. There were few tourists, no lobbyists, and no headquarters for national or regional associations, and the sight of delegations of Indians parading in the shadow of the Capitol in war paint and feathers tended to reinforce the image of Washington as a frontier outpost among the great powers of the world. As one historian has pointed out, the citizens who did come to Washington at this time were not stout republicans of independent means and minds but "society's idle and unwanted, people sick in mind or body, imagining conspiracies against them, imploring help or bent upon revenge, pleaders for pardons and reprieves, small time confidence men, needy pamphlet writers, selling their talents for calumny for the price of a government contract."[3]

Of course, one of the things that kept people away from Washington, as Calhoun and his wife knew, was that it was not an easy place to get to. In 1826 Josiah Quincy took six hours to go to Washington from Baltimore by stage.[4] Even in a society as mobile as the United States the hardships and expense of travel would have discouraged visitation from citizens who counted their distance from the capital in hundreds of miles. But after all this is said, it remains true that Washington reflected fairly accurately the raw, unfinished character of the country at large. The new American Republic was finding its way, and citizens everywhere were much more attached to their state governments and much more likely to visit their state capitals than to make the long, arduous pilgrimage to Washington. Republican government to most people in the United States in 1829 meant local government closely watched. The people's government had not yet arrived in Washington, but it was on the way.

Although we have no record of their impressions, the Calhouns must have been astonished at what was happening to Washington in the days before the inauguration on March 4, 1829. People of all shapes, sizes, and colors, from all walks of life and from every corner of the Union, were crowding into the usually placid capital in numbers never before seen. Inflation was rampant: rents at twenty dollars a week; wood for twelve dollars a cord; eggs for almost a dollar a dozen. As the city filled, the crowd spilled into Georgetown and Alexandria, searching for decent places to stay, and some ended up sleeping on saloon floors or in brothels or in the open air.[5]

The morning broke on March 4 with a thirteen-cannon salute. Fortunately for those who had camped out the weather was clear and mild. Calhoun began the formal ceremonies by calling the United States Senate to order for the last time under the administration of John Quincy Adams. It was appropriate that a product of South Carolina's planter aristocracy and an established member of the Washington elite for sixteen years was to be inaugurated in a sedate legislative chamber attended by foreign dignitaries, Senators, Representatives, and Supreme Court Justices. This was the traditional way in which the mantle of leadership had changed hands ever since Washington. But in the streets outside the Senate chamber that tradition was being ground into the dust as Andrew Jackson, who was to witness Calhoun's inauguration, made his way to the Capitol on foot accompanied by an honor guard of veterans of the Revolution and the Battle of New Orleans. There was Jackson, bare-headed, erect, triumphant, a living relic of the most heroic moments in the American experience. There were his loyal comrades-in-arms. And there were the people, thousands of them, on foot and in carriages, carts, wagons, and every conceivable form of wheeled conveyance, flanking the presidential party as it moved slowly up Pennsylvania Avenue.

Jackson took his seat in the Senate at eleven-thirty, feigning not to notice the conspicuously empty chair of President Adams, who had chosen to boycott the inauguration on the ground that he had been earlier snubbed by Jackson. Calhoun was sworn in by the President pro Tempore of the Senate, and as the new Vice President he gave the oath to several newly elected Senators. He then proceeded with Jackson to the east portico of the Capitol, where the latter became the first Presi-

dent in the history of the country to take the oath of office and deliver
the inaugural address in the open air before an audience of thousands of
his fellow citizens.

Reversing the procedure of today, Jackson gave his address before
he received the oath. Wearing two pairs of glasses, one pushed back on
his head, the other down on his nose, he read a tidied-up version of his
own writing—a short, simple, creditable statement of the republican
creed calculated to offend no one. Seated to the left of Jackson at the
scarlet-covered table on the portico, Calhoun could have heard every
word. Most of the surging thousands below heard nothing, but what
they saw was more than enough. Their Hero had become their President, and after the ceremony was over, they broke through a restraining
cable and swarmed over the portico, shouting, whistling, and cheering,
trying their best to lay congratulatory hands on the physically fragile
President.

Although we do not know it for a fact, it is unlikely that many
boisterous strangers thumped the new Vice President on the back that
day, and he may well have been pressed into service to protect the
President from being congratulated to death. Meanwhile, the object of
the people's enthusiastic adulation, playing his role with great dignity,
mounted a splendid white horse and rode slowly down Pennsylvania
Avenue to the White House with thousands of cheering admirers in
tow.

In keeping with the democratic spirit of the day the people were
invited to meet their new leader at his residence, and they showed up in
force. The ensuing chaos has been graphically described in countless
textbooks. The White House became so jammed that enterprising citizens found their way in and out through the windows. Chairs and
crockery were broken, orange punch sloshed in the corridors, babies
cried, ladies fainted, and the President almost suffocated in the crush.

Although Calhoun later referred to Jackson's "short and noble"
inaugural address, there is nothing in his papers to reveal his impressions of the famous display of democratic enthusiasm that followed.
Perhaps he agreed with his friend Daniel Webster, who wrote: "A
monstrous crowd of people is in the City. I never saw anything like it
before. Persons have come 500 miles to see Genl Jackson & they really
seem to think that the country is rescued from some dreadful danger."

Perhaps Calhoun speculated on the implications of an increasingly American democratic political style for southern gentlemen like himself. His friend from Charleston James Hamilton described the White House mob scene as "a regular Saturnalia" in which many of the celebrants were "fit subjects for the penitentiary." No one could even imagine the like of it taking place in South Carolina.[6]

On the surface, at least, Calhoun had much to rejoice over. He had helped Jackson win a decisive popular victory, including every electoral vote south of the Potomac. The republican system, so threatened in 1824, seemed to be working again, and as Vice President a second time Calhoun could reasonably believe that he was closer to the succession than he had been four years earlier. The people had spoken, and Calhoun, chosen to replace the President should fate require, could not have failed to notice how frail Jackson looked when they dined together after the reception and how generally it was assumed he would not survive his term.

Despite the favorable indicators for his future, there was a striking irony about Calhoun's situation. His election with Jackson, widely perceived as a stunning triumph for the "power and majesty of the people," came just as he was formulating a devastating critique of the majority principle and developing a concept of sovereignty under the American Constitution that would almost inevitably thrust him into deadly conflict with the new President.

In retrospect it is easy to see that Calhoun's election as Vice President in 1828 was a recipe for disaster, perhaps the most unfortunate thing that could have happened to him. He expected that Jackson, whose belief in states' rights was well known, would take a neutral position if nullification became a hot national issue, but he hoped that the new President would move swiftly to reduce the tariff and thus avoid a confrontation between South Carolina and the federal government. If the worst came, Calhoun, as usual, had such complete confidence in his own analysis of the problem that he assumed Jackson would see things his way. If he had been more sensitive to the vagaries of the human personality, he might have recalled those extraordinary days in the War Department when the general had refused to take orders from anyone and had practically gone to war against Britain and Spain without authority. At that time Calhoun had thought of Jackson as a power grabber, an irresponsible military chieftain who would have been disciplined if Monroe and the Cabinet had not caved in under popular pressure to endorse his private war. After 1824, however, when it became clear that supporting Jackson was the only sure way to defeat the architects of the "corrupt bargain," Calhoun had fallen in at the head of the line with Van Buren, even though the only things he shared with the talented New Yorker were ambition and the desire to defeat Adams.

At the time of his inauguration no one thought Jackson would stand for reelection, but it was obvious that any potential successor would benefit enormously from his endorsement. The story of the Calhoun-Van Buren rivalry and its disastrous effects on Jackson's first administration, leading to the reorganization of the Cabinet and Calhoun's expulsion from the Jacksonian party, has been told many times, and friendly Calhoun biographers have usually emphasized the success of the Van Burenites in poisoning the President's mind against the Vice President. A more accurate way of explaining it is to say that Calhoun was victimized during the early part of Jackson's first term by being drawn into a series of confrontations that would work to his disadvantage but that he was almost powerless to control and that would provide the larger context for his ultimate confrontation with the President over nullification.

Calhoun's first setback came when the President announced his Cabinet. Although Jackson had warmly accepted the Carolinian's support before the election, had lavishly praised him in private and public, and had sought his help in drafting the inaugural address, he practically ignored the Vice President's interests in choosing the Cabinet. The two key jobs were State and Treasury. Calhoun seems to have accepted Van Buren's appointment as Secretary of State with equanimity, partly because his support in electing Jackson had been so obvious, partly because Calhoun felt Van Buren had defended him when he was attacked for the way he presided over the Senate, and partly because he underestimated the lesser-known New Yorker as a serious rival for the succession. Calhoun and other South Carolinian leaders had hoped, however, to see one of their own heading the Treasury Department, which exerted considerable leverage in shaping tariff policy. The choice of his old friend Samuel Ingham was a mixed blessing because no Pennsylvania politician, however friendly to Calhoun, could be expected to lead the country toward free trade. By appointing Ingham, the President seemed to be saying that he would chart his own course on the tariff. Most of the remaining appointments, Major John Eaton from Tennessee, Secretary of War, the North Carolinian John Branch, Secretary of Navy, and John Berrien from Georgia, Attorney General, went to men who were more open to the Crawfordites than to Calhoun's friends. John McLean, named Postmaster General, and a strong Calhoun supporter, who soon went off to the Supreme Court, was replaced by the Kentuckian William Barry, who had no particular ties to Calhoun. In fact, there was some talk that McLean's removal to the Court was really a defection caused by McLean's perception that Calhoun would have little influence in the new government, and many of Calhoun's friends suspected that Van Buren was already beginning to show his greater influence with the President. The truth seems to be that Jackson was making his own decisions without depending very much on anyone's advice, including Van Buren, who was so shocked by some of Jackson's early diplomatic appointments that he actually considered resigning.

Although keenly aware that his influence with the new President was not what he and his friends had expected, Calhoun kept most of his disappointment to himself. He was pleased to see David Henshaw get the collectorship in Boston and recommended Samuel Swartwout for the same position in New York Harbor. The latter appointment infuriated Van Buren, who predicted, correctly, as it turned out, that Swartwout would turn out to be a monumental swindler.[7]

Calhoun seems to have been most disappointed in his failure to secure decent appointments for Maxcy and Vandeventer. He approached Jackson so often on Maxcy's behalf that he finally confessed with "deep regret" and "mortification" he could do no more without losing self-respect. The case with Vandeventer was almost as bad since Major Eaton, Jackson's closest friend in the Cabinet, had gone back on his word to make Calhoun's former assistant his own chief clerk.[8]

Geography played a significant role in determining the political drift in Washington in 1829. As was his custom, Calhoun left the Capitol after the adjournment of Congress in mid-March and did not return until the Senate reconvened in December. Van Buren, who had to quit as governor of New York before joining the Cabinet, arrived in Washington shortly after Calhoun left. During the following months he was able to establish a personal rapport with Jackson that Calhoun never enjoyed. The aging President, in ill health, alone and emotionally vulnerable in the wake of his wife's death shortly before the election, began to look on his younger Secretary of State with a kind of kindred benevolence, while Calhoun, isolated from the daily management of the government by his office and physically separated from the President during the first nine months of the new administration, seemed more and more to be a troublesome rival.

During the spring and summer of 1829 Calhoun read disquieting letters from Washington friends complaining about patronage. He knew that Van Buren's great contribution to the recent election had been to bring the Crawfordites into Jackson's camp. Such an accomplishment carried a price, and he expected the Georgian's men to get a share of the spoils, but he was hurt to learn that a Crawford man had been named Treasurer, the job that Maxcy sought, especially since he knew that some of Crawford's supporters before the inauguration had been spreading stories about Calhoun's alleged disloyalty to Jackson. As the months wore on, he must have wondered if James Hamilton, Jr., was right when he said that an honorable man could no longer win the presidency. In his letters, however, Calhoun urged caution and prudence. It was too early, he said, to think about what would happen after Jackson. Meanwhile, he could take satisfaction in knowing that his friends were well placed in Congress (McDuffie headed Ways and Means in the House, where tariff revision would originate), and he could count on the influential support of friends and press in Virginia, New York, Pennsylvania, and Massachusetts when needed. By late September, however, the political danger signals he had been getting for months had become too strong to ignore, and he wrote "confidentially" to McLean about his fear "that the choice of the chief magistrate will finally be placed at the disposition of the executive power itself, through a corrupt system to be founded on the abuse of the powers and patronage of the government." He suspected that Jackson still believed in the principles "in which he was elected" but was being led astray by "some unprincipled individuals" (Van Buren and company).[9]

About the same time that Calhoun was beginning to lose confidence in Jackson, the President was recording his own disenchantment with Calhoun, not simply over matters of patronage and policy, although that was to come soon enough, but over a question of etiquette that had all Washington society atwitter. It started in January 1829, when Margaret ("Peggy") O'Neill Timberlake married John Eaton, who became Jackson's Secretary of War. Peggy, a famous Washington beauty and daughter of a well-known tavern keeper, had been married to John Timberlake, a naval purser frequently away from home. His wife's behavior while he was away had given her a reputation, the latest episode of which involved her relationship with the middle-aged widower Eaton, who boarded at her father's tavern. Shortly after Timberlake's death (presumably by suicide), Eaton married Peggy, and the good ladies of Washington who monitored social life in the capital city found themselves faced with the problem of welcoming the notorious Peggy to their drawing rooms. The stories proliferated: Peggy and Eaton had been having a "criminal" affair while she was married; she had aborted a child when it was discovered Timberlake could not possibly be the father; her humiliated husband had killed himself in despair. Eaton was Jackson's closest friend, and the President immediately saw in Peggy a younger likeness of his own beloved and recently deceased Rachel, who had also been maligned by reckless gossip. Consequently the reinstatement of Peggy O'Neill's virtue (a daunting assignment for any government) became a top priority for the new administration, and when the President found that important members among his official family, following the example of the Vice President and his wife, refused to cooperate, the question of etiquette became a critical matter of state.

We do not learn much about what Van Buren called the "Eaton malaria" from the Calhoun papers. Society was never very important to Calhoun. He knew how to behave in a drawing room and could project a certain hypnotic social presence, but he was not cut out to be a courtier, and his letters even to close friends are remarkably free of gossip. Almost everyone else in Washington followed the Eaton affair avidly, and it is clear from their accounts that whoever was to blame for the Cabinet rupture that ensued, Peggy Eaton did her best to make a bad situation worse by presuming on her friendship with the President and pretending to a kind of royal pedigree. One of her own servants pronounced the lady "the most compleat piece of deception that ever God made, and as a mistress it would be cruelty to put a dumb brute under her command."[10]

Although we may be properly suspicious of evidence volunteered by disgruntled servants and political partisans, we have Peggy Eaton's own words to vouch for the fact that she rarely presented herself as an American model of feminine deportment. In an autobiography published after her death she admitted to having driven the scion of a well-known New England family to suicide before she was seventeen. At the same time she was romantically involved with the United States adjutant general and two younger officers, the upshot of which was a failed elopement and a near duel. As a mature woman she played to perfection the leading role in a scandal which almost paralyzed Jackson's government, and as a woman of sixty, long after the "Eaton malaria" had become history, she married a young Italian aristocrat, who eventually sailed away with her fortune.[11]

Calhoun became embroiled in the Eaton controversy before leaving Washington in March, when his wife announced that since Mrs. Eaton was a woman of reputation and she had no way of verifying the truth or falsehood of the stories told about her, she could not return the social call of the Secretary of War and his wife. After the Calhouns' departure several other Cabinet members and their wives began to omit the Eatons on their invitation lists and boycott social functions where the Eatons were present. Before long social life in the White House was brought to a halt, and much to Jackson's consternation, his own niece and nephew, who lived with him, took sides against Peggy. A sorry business indeed, but Van Buren came out of it as immaculate as a saint. A widower and the principal host in the diplomatic community, he could flatter Peggy and win the President's confidence at the same time. By the fall of 1829 it was obvious that whether or not a Cabinet member and his wife accepted Peggy determined where he stood with the President, and as John Quincy Adams later observed, Calhoun was perceived as heading "the moral party, Van Buren that of the frail sisterhood." On the last day of the year, hearkening to friends who feared for his health and sought to prepare for the succession, the President wrote a letter designed to provide "a powerful lever—in raising Mr. Van Buren to the presidency." In the letter he praised Van Buren without reservation and claimed that Calhoun was responsible for "most of the troubles, vexations and difficulties I have had to encounter since my arrival in this city."[12]

Considering the perspective of most mainstream Americans today on sexuality in and out of politics, it is tempting to agree with the analysis of one observer close to the scene who wrote, "The President's Cabinet have taken their cue from a set of as unprincipled gossips as ever infested any town on the face of the earth," and to believe that Calhoun got what he deserved for allowing his prudish wife to set a standard which proscribed the free-spirited Peggy and disrupted the government.[13] But that is to ignore the real cultural issues involved. Whether Peggy and Eaton actually had an adulterous affair is not the point. We know that at the same time that Peggy Eaton was striving for acceptability in the highest social circles in Washington middle-class Americans everywhere were embracing a set of values which would consign to American wives and mothers the role of preserving moral standards in a rapidly changing, acquisitive, industrializing democracy.[14] Peggy Eaton was challenging those values; Floride and John C. Calhoun were supporting them. This is what Calhoun meant when he replied to John Eaton's public attack on him in the fall of 1831, after the entire Cabinet had been reorganized and after Calhoun had publicly broken with the President. Eaton accused Calhoun of having used the controversy over his wife to discredit Jackson. The issue, Calhoun said, had nothing to do with political ambition. The question was whether a woman of reputation, previously excluded from Washington society, should be admitted on the basis of her marriage to a man of official rank. In such questions women censored themselves, and "Happily for our country, this important censorship is too high and too pure to be influenced by any political considerations whatever," Calhoun said as he applauded "the great victory that has been achieved in favor of the morals of the country, by the high minded independence and virtue of the ladies of Washington."[15]

By the time Calhoun returned to Washington in December, his rivalry with Van Buren had become public knowledge. New York papers were already announcing that Jackson would run for reelection and that Van Buren would succeed him. Such rumors were hardly a vote of confidence in the Vice President, and neither was Jackson's message to Congress. Expressing a vigorous opposition to the Bank of the United States, the President raised an issue that Calhoun thought was extraneous to the problems of the time, while promising nothing about the tariff. Indeed, his suggestion that the government begin to plan for distributing surplus revenue among the states after the debt was retired infuriated many Carolinians because it seemed to imply a continuation of high revenues through high tariffs. At the same time Calhoun must have been aware that Van Buren had even invaded his own territory by corresponding with members of the Smith faction who were urging the Secretary of State to keep patronage away from Calhoun's friends at home.

Although the Vice President maintained his customary serene demeanor, he must have been frustrated. By nature intellectually aggressive and politically combative, he was restrained by his position from playing an active role when his own political future was at stake. Confronting the same dilemma in Adams's administration, he had managed to build a platform for himself through an extended public dialogue with "Patrick Henry." Now, without a Patrick Henry to confront directly, he was forced to rely on a surrogate in the great Senate debate which opened the new year.

On December 29 Senator Henry S. Foote of Connecticut introduced a resolution to consider limiting the sale of public lands. This brought Thomas Hart Benton from Missouri roaring onto the floor to denounce an attack on emigration to the West. To repel such dangerous sectional legislation, Benton counseled the western states to "look to the solid phalanx of the South for succor," and Senator Robert Hayne, handpicked by Calhoun to replace old Smith, supported Benton by claiming that Foote's resolution sought to impoverish the West the way tariffs impoverished the South. Hayne was speaking for Calhoun when he suggested that the South and West make common cause for lower tariffs and liberal land laws, and he closed by warning the Senate that allowing the federal government to profit by selling public lands at high prices could lead directly to the "consolidation" of centralized power in Washington. At this point Daniel Webster, representing the third great geographical interest, took the floor and cleverly diverted the direction of the debate by claiming that Hayne had raised the specter of consolidation because he believed in the "Carolina doctrine" and was against the Union. This set the stage for the famous Webster-Hayne debate in January.

By identifying nullification with disunion, Webster had forced the Senate to consider the fundamental constitutional issue raised by the *South Carolina Exposition and Protest.* His debate with Hayne took several days to complete, and Calhoun, as President of the Senate, presided over the entire encounter in excruciating silence. Hayne, who spoke first, was a better formal orator than Calhoun, but he lacked the latter's reasoning power and had not studied the question as carefully as Calhoun or Webster. His strategy was to begin by claiming that Webster and other New England Federalists had been against the Union at the time of the Hartford Convention and then to link closely the Carolina doctrine to basic principles of liberty which had sustained the Revolution and the Virginia and Kentucky Resolutions. A good speech, but no one could match Webster's rhetoric when it came to discussing the Union and the Constitution. Calhoun occasionally passed notes to reinforce Hayne, but he must have felt trapped at not being able to leap into the fray himself. Meanwhile, Webster made the most of his opportunity to show what Union had done for the country since 1787, built a strong case for a federal system "just as truly emanating from the people as from the states," and closed with the memorable peroration involving "liberty and Union, now and forever, one and inseparable" that American schoolchildren were to commit to memory for generations afterward.[16]

Although Hayne had acquitted himself well, Calhoun knew that printed copies of Webster's speech were in greater demand than any speech in congressional history. The debate with Hayne enhanced Webster's national reputation enormously, and Calhoun's adversaries in the government, including Jackson, a good friend of Hayne, were delighted to see the spokesman for his ideas so badly overshadowed. Calhoun would never admit the overshadowing, of course, any more than he would admit that he was being outmaneuvered by Van Buren. "As to my prospects I am well satisfied," he wrote Vandeventer on February 20, and he continued to urge friends not to overreact at the machinations of the Secretary of State, but to concentrate on seeing the "General through with glory." By mid-April, however, the time for a direct confrontation had arrived.[17]

On April 13 a great dinner was held at the Indian Queen Hotel to honor Jefferson's birthday. It had been organized by southern and western Democrats who backed Calhoun and sought an opportunity to put the stamp of Jefferson's authority on the kind of South-West alliance Hayne and Benton had called for in the Senate. It was an elegant affair with all the most prominent politicians in Washington attending, including the President, the Vice President, and the Secretary of State. Anticipating that the formal toasts offered at the dinner would imply an endorsement of South Carolina's position, Van Buren spent some time beforehand reminding Jackson that his own toast would point the direction he wanted the Democratic Party to take. When the time for the speeches arrived, Jackson and Calhoun were seated at the head table, framed by busts of Jefferson and a large portrait of Washington. The long litany of toasts proceeded as Van Buren had expected, with repeated emphasis on the danger of sectional legislation and the importance of states' rights. When it came time for the President to speak, the atmosphere tightened. Jackson rose, raised his glass, and, looking steadily at Calhoun, said, "Our Federal Union—it must be preserved." Van Buren, at another table, and so excited by the moment that he stood on his chair to get a better view, believed that a gauntlet had been thrown, and others thought they saw Calhoun flinch, but there was no sign of that in his immediate response: "The Union—next to our liberty the most dear; may we all remember that it can only be preserved by respecting the rights of the states and distributing equally the benefits and burdens of the Union." Van Buren followed with a toast of his own stressing "Mutual forbearance and reciprocal concessions," but that was hardly what he had in mind for the confrontation building between his President and Vice President.[18] "Van Buren glides along as smoothly as oil and as silently as a cat," wrote Jackson's adviser Amos Kendall a few days later. "He has the entire confidence of the President and all his personal friends while Calhoun is fast losing it."[19]

It was ironic that Kendall should have been predicting Calhoun's demise. As talented as he was, cadaverous Kendall had been a top Kentucky editor before breaking with Clay and had been confirmed as a

Treasury auditor only when Calhoun cast the tie-breaking vote. Kendall and Major William Lewis, an old Nashville friend of Jackson's, had become two of the President's principal advisers in the "Kitchen Cabinet" that Jackson began to consult more and more frequently during the squabble over Peggy Eaton. In Van Buren's formidable arsenal of support, they would become powerful weapons.

One month to the day after the Jefferson Day dinner the President issued a formal challenge to the Vice President in the form of a curt note demanding to know if it was true that Calhoun rather than Crawford had advised his punishment when Monroe's Cabinet was trying to decide how to deal with the invasion of Florida. Calhoun replied the same day with a short note that was equally abrupt and implied that Jackson was being misled by politicians who had been trying for years to destroy his character with "false insinuations."[20]

The facts at issue in the long, torturous controversy which ensued are simple. Calhoun, Crawford, and Monroe all had believed that Jackson had exceeded his orders by attacking the Spanish posts and executing two British subjects, and Calhoun had advised his arrest.[21] When the Cabinet, under Secretary of State Adams's goading, decided to endorse Jackson's actions, Calhoun went along with the consensus. Meanwhile, the overwhelmingly enthusiastic public response to the Florida invasion made any further discussion of the matter academic. Jackson emerged from the affair even more popular than he had been after New Orleans, thinking that his chief critics in the government had been Clay, who tried to get Congress to discredit him as a "military chieftain," and his old enemy Crawford. Jackson was told as early as 1819 that Calhoun had also opposed him but apparently rejected this report in order to concentrate his animus on Crawford. The elections of 1824, when Calhoun and Jackson both opposed Crawford, and their decision to join forces in 1828, together with Calhoun's silence about the matter, reinforced Jackson's conviction that the Secretary of War had always been on his side.

Calhoun has been criticized for not telling Jackson what had really happened in the Cabinet. "Was it proper for him as an upright man to allow the mistake to continue?" asked William Grayson many years later. "Could a man of nice sensibility permit another to be hated and himself to be held in honour with the knowledge that the disclosure of a single fact will reverse their positions?" Grayson, a South Carolina Congressman in the 1830s, believed that Calhoun's political instincts told him to stay mum unless he wanted to block his own path to the presidency. To expect him to volunteer the truth would have been "to expect a degree of self-sacrificing virtue quite beyond the limits of public life."[22]

What Grayson failed to say was that Calhoun had faced the issue long before May 1830. Sometime in the winter of 1828 Jackson was anonymously sent an old letter stolen from Calhoun's files which proved that Calhoun and Monroe had disagreed with the way Jackson had interpreted his orders in Florida. In explaining that letter to Jackson, Calhoun pointed out that it had obviously been sent to Jackson by someone who wanted to stir up a quarrel. He did not deny that as Secretary of War he had interpreted the orders in question differently from the general, but he argued that it was senseless now to revive a difference of opinion over something that had happened ten years earlier. "In fact," he wrote to Jackson, "I never did suppose that the justification of yourself or the government depended on a critical construction of them [the orders]. It is sufficient for both that they were honestly issued and honestly executed, without involving the question whether they were executed strictly in accordance with the intention that they were issued. Honest and patriotic motives are all that can be required, and I never doubted that they existed on both sides." While not exactly candid, this was a diplomatic way of closing the matter, and Jackson, with an election still ahead and Calhoun as his running mate, was willing to let the issue drop.[23]

The pretext for Jackson's raising the matter again was a new letter in which Crawford claimed that after wanting to punish the general, Calhoun had later taken credit for defending him while deliberately spreading stories that he (Crawford) had led the anti-Jackson charge in the Cabinet. Crawford's letter, addressed to a friend on April 30, 1830, was solicited by Major Lewis and given to the President with the obvious intention of creating an open rupture with Calhoun, something the Crawfordites had been trying to accomplish ever since they fell in with Jackson. The President was receptive because he was now convinced that all his earlier suspicions about the Vice President had been confirmed. Probably the most paranoid of all American Presidents, Jackson had decided that Calhoun was behind everything that was driving him crazy: the ostracism of Mrs. Eaton; the difficulty he had getting legislation and appointments through the Senate; the threat of nullification. He had convinced himself that Calhoun wanted to wreck the administration in order to become President in 1832. In this context Jackson's demand that Calhoun explain himself again makes sense as a calculated political act aimed at getting rid of his Vice President. "Thus you see," the President wrote a few days after confronting Calhoun, "he will either have to deny the truth of the statement in Mr. Crawford's letter, or be in a delicate situation if he admits the fact."[24]

The gloating on Jackson's part was premature. He did not count on Calhoun's tenacity and his absolute inability to accept defeat in any matter of principle. On May 29 the Vice President replied with a stinging letter of about nine thousand words, not including enclosures, in which he insisted that the general had obviously exceeded his orders and had no right now to complain because the Secretary of War had urged that "the usual course ought to be pursued" in his case. "My course requires no apology," he wrote, "and if it did, I have too much self-respect to make it to anyone in a case touching my official conduct."[25]

Having finally received the admission he sought, Jackson tried to dismiss Calhoun as abruptly as he had summoned him. "I had a right to believe that you were my sincere friend," he wrote, "and until now never expected to have occasion to say in the languague [sic] of Caesar, *et tu, Brute. . . .* Understanding you now, no further communication with you on this subject is necessary." But the Carolina Brutus, refusing to fall on his sword, wrote two more letters to the President in June challenging his motives and defying him to do the "impossible": to prove that he had not disobeyed his orders in Florida.[26]

At this point Jackson was reduced to ranting at anyone who would listen about the "great magician," "Cataline," "hypocrite," and "ambitious Demagogue" whose "unholy ambition" was destroying his administration. Meanwhile, Calhoun, serenely established at Fort Hill for the summer, could write to Maxcy in all seriousness: "My correspondence with the President is not yet closed, *nor is there any bitter feeling disclosed in its progress on his part.* I am determined to keep my temper but not to yield the hundredth part of an inch."[27]

Even as he wrote, a letter was in the mail from Jackson, condemning Calhoun's course as "uncandid and unmanly" and announcing his determination "to close this correspondence forever." But as usual Calhoun had the last words (more than twenty-five hundred) in an unrepentant parting statement which accused the President of deserting friends whose "open and fearless course" had put him in the White House.[28]

Meanwhile, Calhoun skirmished briefly with Crawford, who had seized upon Jackson's accusation to brand his old enemy "a degraded and disgraced man, for whom no man of honor could feel any other than the most sovereign contempt." For years Calhoun had been saying that there was nothing personal in the political animosity which separated him from Crawford. Now he simply dismissed him as a coarse "informer" unworthy of being considered a party to his dispute with the President.[29]

By the time he returned to Washington in early December 1830, Calhoun could take a certain grim satisfaction in the fact that everyone was talking about his correspondence with Jackson. The opponents of the administration wanted him to publish it, he wrote his brother, but he would not do it unless absolutely necessary. Meanwhile, "Every opening was made for me to renew my intercourse with the President, which I have declined, and will continue so to do till he retracts what he has done. His friends are much alarmed." Nevertheless, the word began to spread that despite their personal differences, Jackson and Calhoun would still be able to function together politically. "I understand that they are both willing to continue *political* friends," John Campbell, the Treasurer of the United States, wrote to his brother, "that is, Calhoun says he will continue to support Genl Jackson's administration, and the Genl will always be civil and polite to him when they meet on official business."[30]

It is interesting to discover that in late January, when his quarrel with the President was at its most critical point, Calhoun took time to write to a Mrs. J. S. Johnston who had sent him an essay on temperament and suggested that he must fall in the "nervous" category. Thanking her for the article, Calhoun wrote that he had "scarcely an ingredient of that temperament in my composition." At the same time he told Vandeventer that all his friends should "be composed. I never felt more so in my life. I stand on a rock, that of truth. At the proper time, I will move, when those, who have got up the plot will be crushed. It is proper that all my movements should be calm and defensive, and therefore, I ought to move slowly and leisurely. I do not deem it necessary to say more at present."[31]

What Calhoun said about being calm was apparently true enough. The iron in his character usually took over in moments of crisis, but the claim to be only acting on the defensive is hardly credible. Serious efforts were under way at the time to patch up the dispute. Jacksonites did not relish seeing their Hero run for reelection with a Cabinet he could not convene and a Vice President who refused to associate with him. With Calhoun's friend Swartwout acting as Calhoun's emissary a reconciliation seemed imminent. The President told Van Buren on one occasion that it had been accomplished, and Calhoun actually appeared at a dinner attended by the President and Secretary of State. Then, with no apparent warning on February 17, Duff Green printed the entire correspondence between Calhoun and Jackson along with an address to the people of the United States which clearly implied that the President was being manipulated by unscrupulous political adventurers into impeaching the character of his loyal Vice President.[32]

The reactions to this bombshell were predictable. Calhoun was triumphant, feeling that he had vindicated and at the same time liberated himself from having to support the administration. Calhounites, like Marcus Morton, speaking for Democratic officeholders everywhere, were not so sure. They saw the importance of keeping Jackson in the White House and worried that the party's health might come "to depend upon the caprice or angry feelings of any man."[33]

Calhoun had released the correspondence under the impression that the President had reviewed it in advance without objection. This was not the case since Major Eaton, for reasons of his own, had decided not to show the explosive document to his chief. Consequently Jackson had an excuse to be even more furious than he would have been ordinarily. The President, who had long suspected Duff Green as a Calhoun accomplice, now announced, "They have cut their throats and destroyed themselves in a shorter space of time than any two men I ever knew." Van Buren, who apparently had played no overt part in bringing the President and Vice President into collision but who must have known what was going on, was discreetly content in the knowledge that his rival could never be rehabilitated in Jackson's eyes. Meanwhile, the real villains in the piece, old Crawford radicals with long memories like Alfred Balch, who had sworn to get their revenge years before, felt they were closing in for the kill. Calhoun was "as restless as a guilty man's soul," Balch warned the President. "He is a spy in our camp and is worse than our open and decided enemies. The time will soon come when we shall make him wish he had never been born."[34]

The conventional wisdom holds that Calhoun made a monumentally stupid mistake when he decided to make his dispute with Jackson public. According to this interpretation, there was no way Calhoun could shake the President's enormous popularity. Instead he did irreparable damage to his own political future by giving Jackson reasonable cause to read him and his ally Green out of the party and to reorganize his Cabinet without Ingham, Branch, and Berrien, who had sided with Calhoun over the Peggy Eaton affair. In the end all that Calhoun accomplished was to give the administration a new lease on life and to isolate himself politically. Such an interpretation immediately raises the question of why he would have embarked on such a self-destructive course.

Jackson explained Calhoun's action in terms of ambition. "Mr. Calhoun will run for President," he predicted, "if his friends believe he can be got into the house." This is part of the story. By engaging Jackson directly, Calhoun was fighting as he had in Adams's administration against the obscurity of the vice presidency, and by accepting a complete separation from the President, he was positioning himself to run in opposition in 1832. How Calhoun rationalized this possibility will be discussed in the next chapter.[35]

But even if Calhoun had been able to foretell the fatal consequences, it is unlikely that he would have acted differently because his quarrel with Jackson from the beginning had involved more than a difference of opinion over facts and more than politics. It had been a matter of honor. When the President accused Calhoun of dissimulation, he meant that he had not shown him the respect one gentleman owed another. "Mr. Calhoun had a right to act in the Cabinet Council according to the dictates of his own judgment," Jackson declared, "but as long as a single spark of honor animates my own bosom I cannot concede to him the right of acting diametrically opposite to his professions." And Calhoun, in explaining to the public why he was releasing his correspondence with the President, said he felt "the most thorough conviction that the sacred obligation to vindicate my character, impeached as it has been, in one of the most important events of my life, and to prove myself not unworthy of the high station to which you have elevated me far outweights all other considerations."[36]

In 1838, while Calhoun was still coping with the political effects of his encounter with Jackson, another Carolinian, ex-Governor John Lyde Wilson, published *The Code of Honor,* in which he announced that dueling would "be persisted in as long as a manly independence and a lofty personal pride . . . shall continue to exist. If a man be smote on one cheek in public, and he turns the other, which is also smitten, and he offers no resistance, but blesses him that so despitefully used him, I am aware he is in the exercise of great Christian forbearance, highly recommended and enjoined by many very good men, but utterly repugnant to those feelings which nature and education have implanted in the human character."[37] Wilson was attempting to universalize a cultural characteristic of the South that was particularly strong in South Carolina. Both Calhoun and Jackson had grown up in a culture which demanded that a man protect his honor, if necessary, at the risk of his life. Andrew Jackson had killed one man in a duel and in addition to a clear conscience carried a bullet in the chest as his reward. As a boy Calhoun must have examined, and probably fired, one of his father's dueling pistols. As a Congressman he had committed himself to a duel which was averted by the intercession of friends at the last hour. As a presidential candidate he had watched helplessly as his protégé was shot down on the field of honor by a Crawford editor. The parallels between the traditional duel and what happened to Calhoun and Jackson are too obvious to ignore. Feeling that his own honor had been aggrieved, the President challenged Calhoun for his "unmanly" behavior. Unable to respond in the traditional way, the Vice President responded rhetorically at the risk of political death. At periodic intervals friends attempted to intercede, but he could not compromise because by definition honor cannot be compromised. Calhoun was engaged in something far more than a personal dispute; his character was at stake, and he had to act out his part in the drama all the way. The culture which he came to represent more convincingly than any other public figure demanded nothing less.

9

The Nullification Crisis, 1831–1832

FOR A MAN of presidential stature like Calhoun to break publicly with Andrew Jackson and then within a matter of months to take up the flag openly for the South Carolina nullifiers was to commit political suicide twice. This, at least, was the conventional wisdom among many shrewd men in all parties, but as usual, Calhoun thought otherwise, and he left Washington at the close of the congressional session in early March 1831 in a positive and aggressive mood. He not only had vindicated himself in a matter of personal honor with the President but had also put himself in a position where he could freely pursue his own political agenda. En route to South Carolina he stopped for two days in Richmond to meet with John Tyler, Governor John Floyd, and other influential leaders in Virginia, all of whom seemed to think that he would be that state's favorite son in 1832. Buoyed by this kind of support, which he found repeated throughout his journey, Calhoun once again convinced himself that principle could serve ambition and vault him into the presidency, and he was remarkably candid about the matter in a long interview with James Henry Hammond in Columbia two weeks later. Only twenty-four at the time, Hammond had caught Calhoun's attention as the editor of a strong states' rights paper, and his willingness to confide at length in a much younger man whom he had never met before suggests, as Hammond reported in his notes, that at this critical point in his career the customarily reserved and dignified Calhoun had become temporarily transported by a vision of himself as a potential savior of the country.

According to Hammond, Calhoun made four emphatic points: first, that Jackson's star was in decline; second, that it was possible to reconcile sectional antagonisms by maintaining the South-West alliance with the help of a constitutional amendment legalizing internal improvements; third, that the presidency was open and Calhoun was available; and fourth, that if reconciliation failed, "he looked upon disunion as inevitable and he thought it best, for the system of plunder such as it was now was the most despicable of all governments."

Hammond, intensely ambitious and committed to the Carolina cause as a way of lifting himself out of obscurity, was flattered by the great man's attention and dazzled by his long, intense, rapid-fire monologue. But the message made him uneasy. A zealous nullifier himself, Hammond found it hard to believe that anyone could realistically expect to lead both South Carolina and the nation in the immediate years ahead, and he cautioned Calhoun not to leap into the political fray until the time was ripe.[1]

Hammond had caught Calhoun in a moment of unguarded enthusiasm when anti-Jacksonism, South Carolina radicalism, and ambition for the presidency all fitted nicely together in his mind as a blueprint for utopia. In his more sober moments, however, Calhoun continued to keep a safe distance from the radicals in his own state. "Whether I am a nullifier or not," he told a North Carolina correspondent about two weeks after seeing Hammond, "will depend on the meaning to be attached to the word. If it means a disunionist, a disorganizer or an anarchist then . . . I am utterly opposed to it." Nor was he willing to admit that separating from Jackson meant leaving "the great Republican party." Despite the President's "incompetency, intellectually and morally and the wicked influence under which he acts and must continue to act," Calhoun advised Ingham that they should not separate from those in the administration but "take a position independent of them as far as it can be done without actual separation." By the end of May Calhoun seems to have convinced himself that he could take control of the party. Advising Vandeventer that he had severed "every connection personal and political" with Jackson, Calhoun insisted that in the next election he would "act second to no one. I feel that it would degrade me. I will stand on my own ground which I know to be strong in principle & the publick support. . . . I never stood stronger."[2]

One of the reasons Calhoun could speak so confidently in the spring of 1831 is that the long-expected dissolution of Jackson's Cabinet had finally taken place. It began with the voluntary resignations in early April of Van Buren and Eaton. Although the former claimed he was trying to give Jackson an opportunity to appoint a less divisive Cabinet, he was also trying to protect himself from the charge of having master-minded Calhoun's fall from grace for his own political gain. Eaton, of course, had every reason for wanting to take himself and his wife out of the spotlight. Although it took some arguing to get the President to give up Van Buren, Jackson soon saw the wisdom of it, and once the resignations of the secretaries of State and War were in hand, he forced Ingham, Branch, and Berrien, all staunch Calhounites by this time, out of the Cabinet, leaving only his old friend Postmaster General Barry in place.

Up until this point the gossip about the Peggy Eaton scandal had been confined to people familiar with Washington society and the squabble within the administration. Now the whole sordid business became a matter of public discussion. Rumors proliferated. Ingham, Branch, and Berrien gave long statements to the press denying that they had never shirked their official duties and insisting that the President had no right to interfere with the way they and their wives fulfilled their social obligations. Duff Green and the *Telegraph* took the side of the ousted Cabinet officers, and the talented, acidulous Francis ("Frank") Blair, who had replaced Green as the public printer and whose *Washington Globe* had become the leading Jackson publication, kept up the fiction that the Peggy Eaton business and everything else that had gone afoul in the government was part of a plot to make Calhoun President. When Ingham complained in public that Eaton and his friends were threatening to assassinate him, good citizens everywhere hardly knew how to react. Was this comic opera or the fall of Rome? Whatever it was, it made the government look terrible, and the President could be expected to pay a heavy price for it.

Unfortunately for Calhoun, events in South Carolina were sweeping him along so rapidly that he had little time to enjoy Jackson's discomfort. Calhoun had sent his anonymously written *South Carolina Exposition* to the legislature in the fall of 1828 with the understanding that the state would pursue a moderate course while waiting for tariff relief from the new Jackson government. Consistent with this understanding, the legislature printed and circulated a few thousand copies of the *Exposition* and published a set of resolutions embodying Calhoun's ideas but took no further action, and most of the more radical nullifiers kept their fires banked during 1829. Antitariff agitation blazed up again, however, in February 1830, when McDuffie's attempt to lower the rates of 1824 and 1828 was abruptly defeated in the House of Representatives without a vote. Convinced that there would be no redress for his state in Congress, McDuffie now became the most ferocious nullifier in the state and its most compelling orator. Singularly graceless and almost without personality in social conversation, McDuffie was transformed on the platform. Interspersing calm, lucid argument with the furious shouting, thumping, and stomping of the most desperate demagogue, he intimidated audiences he could not convince and soon had South Carolinians believing that almost half the value of their cotton crop was being stolen from them by the tariff.

By the summer of 1830 the issue in the state was not tariff reform but whether or not the legislature would authorize a convention at which the people could take direct action against it. Although most South Carolinians strongly opposed the tariff, they were deeply divided over the wisdom of calling for a convention which might decide for nullification, and the issue was creating two parties. The unionists, who had recently won the local election in Charleston, could count on some of the most talented and established men in the state like Daniel Huger, William Drayton, Joel Poinsett, and James L. Petigru, who had followed Calhoun earlier and had much in common with him intellectually and culturally, but could not stomach his sudden conversion to nullification. The nullifiers were led by staunch Calhounites like McDuffie, Hayne, William Preston, and James Hamilton. William Smith, standing for reelection to the United States Senate, and Calhoun's most tenacious and powerful enemy within the state for the past decade, lined up with the unionists. Calhoun had tried to put up with Smith because he was an old-fashioned states' rights man with reasonably popular support, but he could not afford to let South Carolina send a confirmed antinullifier back to the Senate during the impending crisis. Fortunately Smith's own friends were divided over nullification, and Calhoun, Hamilton, and others prevailed upon one of them, Stephen D. Miller, to run against him. Miller won, and Smith, who had shifted his plantation holdings to Louisiana, soon left the state in disgust.[3]

Calhoun had been trying to find some middle ground between the unionists and the nullifiers ever since 1828. He preferred "state interposition" to "nullification," stressed the consistency of all his ideas with the Constitution, and repeatedly maintained his faith in the Union. The Union was "too strong to break!" he wrote on one occasion. "Nothing can break it—but the slavery question, if that can." If South Carolina were to interpose, and a convention of the states called according to his design in the *Exposition* decided the tariff was constitutional, Calhoun believed it would be time then not for secession but to "give it up." Given such strong unionist convictions, Calhoun opposed premature action and was not displeased when the nullifiers failed in their attempts to call for a constitutional convention in the fall of 1830.[4]

There had never been much middle ground in South Carolina after 1828, and what there was practically disappeared under Calhoun's feet in the spring of 1831, after McDuffie, the virtuoso of fury, announced to a Charleston audience and to the world that democratic majorities had turned the Union into "a foul monster" and those who worshiped it were "worthy of their chains." Rhetoric like this, coming from a popular South Carolinian leader and Calhoun protégé, was bound to make headlines around the nation. Duff Green, who wanted to make Calhoun President, was almost speechless. "A curse on your dinners and your nullification," he sputtered. "The word is more odious to me than any in our language." Meanwhile, unionist papers were demanding that Calhoun put himself on record once and for all regarding the nullifiers, and James Hamilton, who was about to establish an association of states' rights clubs throughout the state, told Calhoun bluntly that the radicals would "not be diverted for one moment" by his quest for the presidency. The time had come for him to explain himself in public.[5]

Choosing as his vehicle a letter to the *Pendleton Messenger* which appeared on August 3, Calhoun, having been himself offended by the reckless rhetoric of radicals like McDuffie, struck such a conciliatory note that he managed to embrace his fellow nullifiers without using the word "nullification." Professing to be second to no one in his love of the Union, Calhoun argued that the impending crisis derived not from the tariff controversy, but because "there are those who look more to the necessity of maintaining power than guarding against its abuses." Having shifted the focus from a particular policy issue to a fundamental principle in republican ideology, he went on to assert that all successful constitutions were designed to limit not only the power of the government but the power of the major contending interests within the society as well. In England these interests were represented by three social classes, and the British constitution checked the possibility of any one class seizing power by giving to each class a separate voice in the government with a check on the other two. In the United States the different interests, represented by geographically and politically distinct states, deliberately created a federal government with specified powers and reserved all other powers to themselves. The Constitution, therefore, implicitly assumed that when a state believed the federal government was exceeding its power, the state could interpose its authority and prevent the exercise of the power in question within its borders. If efforts to negotiate the issue failed, it could be referred to a convention of the states where a vote of three-quarters of the states would be required to make the disputed power constitutional.

Calhoun quoted from Jefferson's Virginia Resolutions to show that interposition was more traditional than revolutionary, and he repeatedly played down sectionalism, arguing that the conflict was caused more by an imperfectly understood political system than by greedy northern industrialists anxious to use political power to squeeze every drop of profit out of virtuous, liberty-loving southern planters. It was natural for citizens in manufacturing states to support laws which put money in their pockets, and it was equally natural for citizens in the staple-producing states, who provided the money, to resist. Such conflicts were bound to develop, even in the most virtuous and best-regulated republics, and unless some peaceful resolution could be found, disunion and civil violence were real possibilities. The constitutional path toward peaceful resolution of such conflicts in the United States was interposition by the aggrieved state, and every sentence that Calhoun wrote in what became famous as the *Fort Hill Address* was intended to show that there was nothing to fear in the Carolina doctrine; it was profoundly conservative.[6]

Although Calhoun knew that by throwing in his lot with the nullifiers, he was hurting whatever chance he had to be a serious contender for the presidency in 1832, he would not admit that he had withdrawn from the race for another six months. Conscious that his address had evoked scattered support in the northern and western press and had even called out a nomination for him by a group of New York supporters, Calhoun proceeded to send out ambiguous signals to his friends. In one letter he advised Ingham not to wage a "desperate conflict in my favour"; in another he insisted to Maxcy, as he did to others, that only a strong southern candidate could replace Jackson. Calhoun obviously had not given up on the vision he had shared so enthusiastically with Hammond. The following paragraph, written to Francis Pickens about the same time he wrote to Maxcy, is revealing enough to be quoted in full:

As to the Presidency, it seems to me that having placed my sentiment on record, my true course is to stand still & leave it to the people without any agency on my part. I have not, nor do I intend to make any move. I could have won it, if I could have been induced even to hold general language as to my opinions; but I would not accept the office unless to insure the restoration of the Constitution. I prefer a fair reputation founded on an honest discharge of duty to any office however high. If I know myself a crown, much less the Presidency could not bend me from what I deemed right.[7]

The statement to Pickens tells us a great deal about what Calhoun needed to believe, but very little about the real political world he confronted in 1831. A significantly milder or ambiguous *Fort Hill Address* would never have healed his breach with Jackson, but it would certainly have cost him dearly in his home state and in the South. How that could have taken him to the presidency defies comprehension. Not even a man of iron can be sustained forever on reason: Sometimes, like the rest of us, he needs to be shored up by fantasy.

Calhoun's belief that he was politically strong in the South, however, was based on fact. He knew he could count on the personal support of Senators like Tazewell and Tyler of Virginia, the Mississippian George Poindexter, and Gabriel Moore of Alabama to team with South Carolina Senators and help tip the balance in any close contest with the administration. Branch and Berrien, who had come over to his side during the Cabinet battles, could be expected to use their influence on his behalf in North Carolina and Georgia. He also had friends in the border states like Felix Grundy in Tennessee and George Bibb in Kentucky, whose friendship went back to their days in Congress together. Jackson's behavior with respect to the tariff, the Kitchen Cabinet, the

Bank, and Peggy Eaton had inevitably alienated southerners of all kinds, and Calhoun profited by that as well as by their deep general suspicion of Van Buren.[8]

On the other hand, Calhoun could not escape the fact that substantial numbers of southerners even in South Carolina remained unconvinced about nullification. Some of these were old enemies connected with the Crawford faction who did not hesitate to blast the "imbecility" of his ideas in print. Others were former supporters who took a softer approach by lampooning Calhoun's ideas and reminding their readers that great minds like his frequently ran to madness. But by the fall of 1831 no amount of joking could obscure the fact that the struggle between nullifiers and unionists had become deadly serious. The nullifiers won the city elections that October in a close vote which was decided, according to James Petigru, because the nullifiers bought up every vote in sight and kept their purchases drunk and locked up until election day. Petigru, of course, was a partisan observer, but the corruption was real on both sides, so visible that the Roman Catholic bishop of Charleston published a pastoral letter warning his flock against the "seductive and debauching allurements" offered to voters.[9]

This was hardly the "spirit of '98" resurrected, and it is significant that Calhoun, whose letters at this time are filled with references to the corruption in Washington, had nothing to say about the deterioration of public virtue in Charleston. He believed in the moving force of ideas and did not bother himself with the tactics necessary to man the struggle in the streets. His mind moved easily from the principles of 1776 and 1798 to the principles of 1830. The Revolution in France, which he was following as the crisis at home came to a head, reminded him that the struggle for liberty was constant. Before he died, he complained that history was moving too rapidly, but in the early 1830s Calhoun seems to have believed, and to have made others believe, that the Carolina nullifiers for all their faults were patriots in the best sense. If confronted with evidence of corrupt electioneering, he might have said, as Jefferson had said about the earlier Revolution in France, "though we weep over the means, we must pray for the end."

If nullification and all it stood for whetted Calhoun's idealism, his struggle within two administrations had taught him how to deal with "unprincipled" politicians, and he was prepared to put that knowledge to work when he returned to Washington in November to square accounts with Martin Van Buren. Jackson had named Van Buren ambassador to England and had sent him to London several months earlier, partly as a reward for his loyalty and partly to keep him available as Calhoun's successor in 1832, and Van Buren's rejection in the Senate with Calhoun as presiding officer casting the decisive vote was just as politically inspired as his appointment. Calhoun supporters, claiming that Van Buren had plotted the destruction of Jackson's first Cabinet, teamed with Clay Senators to put the dapper little New Yorker down. Calhoun had no qualms about the matter and obviously thought of his vote as a kind of personal vindication. "I will most certainly veto him," he wrote to Ingham beforehand. "I shall never consent to give him a certificate of good behavior." After the vote, which was deliberately arranged so that Calhoun could break the tie, he is supposed to have gloated, "It will kill him, sir, kill him dead. He will never kick, sir, never kick." Although the quotation may be apocryphal, Calhoun probably did think that he was meting out justice and getting a political rival out of the way at the same time. He was wrong. The manipulated rejection of the well-known and obviously qualified former Senator, governor, and Secretary of State not only reinforced Jackson's determination to have Van Buren as President but also resulted in widespread public indignation as well as a suspicion that Calhoun had deserted his party to join hands with Clay and Webster.[10]

Shortly after killing Van Buren's nomination, Calhoun finally admitted that he was out of the presidential race. "I voluntarily retired," he wrote Bolling Hall on February 13, "and have & will continue to follow the most conciliatory course." By "conciliatory" he meant to refer to the tariff then being drafted in Congress, but he must have known that the time had passed when his constituents could find common ground with American System enthusiasts on that issue, and when a bill retaining the protective principle was finally reported and passed, every southern Senator except those from Louisiana voted against it. There was no more talk of conciliation. Since the "general government" had shown it could not do the job, Calhoun said he had "not the least apprehension of calling in the action of the state." Nullification was on the way in South Carolina, but he assured his friend that it would be peaceful and constructive. "The crisis is one of deep interest," he urged Ingham shortly before the hateful bill was passed. "You must not look on an unconcerned spectator." To his northern friends Calhoun was still presenting himself as a law-abiding moderate, but when he wrote to his countryman Waddy Thompson the next day, his words took on a harder edge. "The question is no longer one of free trade," he announced, "but liberty and despotism. The hope of the country now rests in our gallant little state. Let every Carolinian do his duty. Those who do not join us now intend unqualified submission."[11]

Chafing under their submissionist label, some of the unionists found it hard to believe that Calhoun would really stay the course. Remembering how easily he had shed his nationalist ideas, Petigru said, "It would be just like Calhoun if he were to come forward to save the Constitution at its last gasp. I should not be surprised if he were to astonish the natives with another somersault."[12]

But Calhoun, back at Fort Hill where he could feel the pulse of the state without getting involved in the heat and violence of party politics in Charleston, knew there was no turning back. The nullifiers, led by the extraordinary efforts of Governor James Hamilton, were clearly ahead in the struggle to win the fall elections. Almost a stereotype of the dashing cavalier, Hamilton was a wellborn, wealthy Charleston planter four years younger than Calhoun. He had served in Congress for several years in the 1820s as an enthusiastic nationalist, joining Calhoun in opposition to Adams and support of Jackson in 1828. The Tariff of Abominations and a growing revulsion at the increasing popular style of Jacksonian politics transformed Hamilton into a states' rights activist. Feisty, flamboyant, and successful (he survived fourteen duels), Hamilton combined the highly prized qualities of honor and gentility with a remarkable organizational ability. He was a brilliant choice to lead the nullifiers in the field and had rallied thousands of Carolinians to his banner through state conventions, mass meetings, barbecues, a well-disciplined newspaper network, and a multitude of states' rights clubs spread throughout the state. As governor in 1831 and 1832 Hamilton traveled around the state in a military carriage, resplendent in full uniform, presiding over parades, musters, and political rallies in a style that made Carolinians feel they were witnessing a reincarnation of the "spirit of '76."[13]

For all his efforts, however, Hamilton had more sail than rudder, and to the extent that nullification was a movement based on ideas as well as popular enthusiasm, he needed help from Calhoun. On July 31, knowing that he would be leading in the action when nullification came, the governor asked the latter for an expanded statement of the "principles and consequences of nullification."

Calhoun replied four weeks later in an essay that was considerably longer and more detailed than the *Fort Hill Address* and in which he made three main points. The first was the importance of getting citizens to understand the historical situation out of which the United States had emerged. It had been a creation of the states, not of the people. According to Calhoun, the "American people collectively" never existed and "never performed a single political act." Nevertheless, "a large portion" of Americans believed otherwise and instinctively thought of themselves as part of a nation. In principle they claimed to be against the consolidation of government power, but in practice they "infused into their conception of our Constitution almost all the ingredients which enter into that form of government." Calhoun knew something about the strength of national sentiment because he had helped create and exploit it during the War of 1812. Now he was trying to reason it away against almost impossible odds.

Knowing that action was frequently a more powerful lever than reason in moving the mind, Calhoun stressed to Hamilton the importance of orderly nullification procedure. Once the legislation in question was nullified in convention, all residents of the state would be committed to support the state. There would be no violence against the federal government, but officers of the state, judges, and jurymen would respect the nullification ordinance, and duties imposed by the nullified tariff would not be collected. It would be "a legal and constitutional contest, a conflict of moral and not physical force," and the federal government could not resort to force without exposing itself as a military despotism.

Finally, Calhoun told Hamilton that despite all the clamor from the opposition, nullification was not a violation of the majority principle. There were two requirements, he said, to the preservation of "free states." The first was the institution of suffrage to keep rulers responsible to their constituents. Although the numerical or "absolute majority" could work effectively here, it was also necessary to have "a power

to COMPEL THE PARTS OF SOCIETY TO BE JUST TO ONE ANOTHER BY
COMPELLING THEM TO CONSULT THE INTEREST OF EACH OTHER." This
could be done by institutionalizing the majority of the most important
parts (classes, interests, communities) of the society in a concurrent
majority. It had been this majority which ratified the Constitution, and
it was this majority (the three-quarters of the states required to amend
the Constitution) to which the nullifiers would appeal. As Calhoun put
it, the only way to preserve the American system of government was
"by maintaining the ascendancy of the CONSTITUTION—MAKING AU-
THORITY OVER THE LAW-MAKING—THE CONCURRING OVER THE ABSO-
LUTE MAJORITY."[14]

Even though the ordinary Carolina voter would have had a hard
time following Calhoun's reasoning and rhetoric, the appearance of his
statement shortly before the election must have been decisive in bringing some doubters among the elite over to the nullifiers. To others
among the rank and file the simple knowledge that the great Calhoun
had once again given his blessing to the act would have been sufficient.
Unionist leaders, of course, scoffed at the effort, but Daniel Webster
called it by far the "ablest & most plausible and therefore the most
dangerous vindication of that particular *form of Revolution* which has
yet appeared."[15]

A few days after his essay had appeared in papers across the state
Calhoun claimed that it would "forever settle the question at least as
far as reason has anything to do with settling political questions," but as
the bishop of Charleston had pointed out, there was a lot more at work
in the contest than the exercise of reason. The nullifiers would win, not
because they had the best arguments but because they represented a
new power group in South Carolina which appealed to Carolinians shut
out of the tight planter elite that had always controlled politics and
society in the state.[16] Nonslaveholders, white mechanics, and young
planters on the make, like James Henry Hammond, all believed they
could boost their prospects by swelling the ranks. Calhoun's great contribution was to legitimize nullification by showing that it was constitutional, rational, and consistent with traditional American political ideology, but in the heat of battle in 1831 and 1832 many of his supporters
resorted to intimidation, violence, fraud, and every kind of demagoguery to get the votes they needed. Hamilton advised his editors to spare

no malice in chastising the unionists, and as a result, one of his favorites was killed in a duel. Armed bands roamed the streets of Charleston at night. Unionists of the highest social standing, like Poinsett and Drayton, were assaulted. Paupers were bribed with liquor and money, and wise men went to the polls armed. It was a republican nightmare, but it worked.[17]

The elections were held on October 8 and 9, and the nullifiers won the two-thirds majorities they needed in the House and Senate to begin the formal process of nullification. Governor Hamilton then called for an extraordinary session of the legislature, which met on October 22 and passed a bill calling for a constitutional convention. Nullification was assured. Calhoun watched it all in uncorrupted seclusion at Fort Hill and was content. He had earlier prophesied that the Carolina doctrine would spread rapidly and in a few years would be "the established political faith of the country."[18]

10

The Compromise of 1833

CALHOUN was in his fiftieth year in 1832, no longer the "Young Hercules" who had helped take his country into war and urge his fellow citizens to "conquer space" and build a great nation. The struggle for political survival and personal honor over the past eight years had begun to take a toll on his appearance. The stock of bushy hair rising straight up from his head had begun to gray and grow out of control. It looked "about the size of an ordinary hat," to one observer and suggested that "like the Jews of old," Calhoun "had sworn not that he would not eat but that his head should not be trimmed until he had slain Paul." That May he went to a wedding party for his friend George Bibb, and in the midst of the celebration reports came in that New York papers had begun to support Van Buren for Vice President. Clay and Webster continued their convivial ways, but Calhoun received the news looking "sour, lean and lank." William Cullen Bryant, who saw Calhoun in Washington sometime that same year, described his "thick shock of hair, dull complexion and . . . anxious expression. . . . He looks as if the fever of political ambition had dried up all the juiciness and freshness of his constitution."[1]

In ordinary years Calhoun would have escaped from Washington to Fort Hill in the early spring, but 1832 was not an ordinary year, and the congressional session dragged on until July. By the time he did get home Jackson's massive reelection victory with Van Buren as his running mate was assured, but Calhoun's confidence in his own analysis of political history never wavered. An obvious way of interpreting Jackson's popularity was to say that people supported his policies, including the strong sense of nationalism he had seemed to evoke when he had traded toasts with Calhoun at the Jefferson Day dinner. But Calhoun explained Jackson's victory as "the legitimate fruits of consolidation," tracing the downward spiral of the Republic to the persistent efforts of

Presidents and presidential hopefuls ever since 1816 to turn the government into a partisan, moneymaking power. Crawford had tried to do this with the caucus and failed. Adams and Clay had succeeded for one term, and now Jackson was following their example. The remedy was the restoration of the rights of the states, which could be effected only "by the separate action of some one state in the first instance."

It was appropriate that the presidential election and the South Carolina Constitutional Convention should have been held at about the same time. Jackson had repudiated Calhoun, and South Carolina repaid the favor by casting its eleven electoral votes for John Floyd of Virginia as President and the Massachusetts free trader Henry Lee as Vice President. The convention would add to this insult by challenging Jackson's authority and that of the Congress with a specific act of nullification. It was as if Calhoun and his loyal, little state were determined to flout the will of the people and their Hero not once but twice.

When delegates to the convention finally assembled at Columbia on November 19, however, Calhoun was not there. A document in the Calhoun papers strongly suggests that he was either in or on his way to Georgia on that date to witness the transfer of a mining property owned by his son Andrew. By the time the convention acted on November 24 to nullify the tariffs of 1824 and 1828, Calhoun was back at Fort Hill. Without any specific information about the action taken, he wrote Ingham that it was "the last great effort to save the liberty of this country."[2]

Calhoun could not escape being known as the mastermind of nullification. He would take great pride in that, but he did not want to be known as the man who had managed the process, not only because he looked down on political "managers" of all kinds but because he had to recognize the delicacy of his situation as both a nullifier and the Vice President of the United States. However, the latter had become a burden he was soon to discard.

Events moved swiftly over the two weeks following the convention, and the American people turned their attention away from Columbia and Charleston to Washington, where President Jackson was preparing to respond to South Carolina's challenge. No one really knew what to expect because Jackson's attitude toward state and federal power reflected a basic ambiguity in the country at large. On the one hand,

Jackson claimed, "The state governments hold in check the federal and must ever hold it in check," and he had made no effort to enforce a Supreme Court decision affecting the Cherokee tribes which was being openly defied by the state of Georgia. On the other hand, he believed passionately in majority rule and the permanence of the Union, and he had made it clear on several occasions to the Carolina nullifiers in private and in public that he thought nullification in theory was a constitutional heresy and in practice would be tantamount to treason. Jackson did not have to worry about the consistency of the ideas that composed this strange blend of nationalism and localism, and neither did most of his countrymen. Their political connections were almost always local, and their most familiar political ideas held that surrendering power to people in distant places was always dangerous. On the other hand, they had expanded with patriotic pride after the war against Britain and took satisfaction in knowing that whether they lived in states like Virginia or Connecticut where they were born or had moved to one of the new western territories, they were still Americans, still protected by the same flag which had flown triumphantly at New Orleans. Most Americans, whether they could articulate it or not, were for states' rights *and* nationalism—and so was Jackson.[3]

The President's first public statement after the South Carolina nullification ordinance came in the form of his annual message to Congress on December 4, in which he astounded everyone by a conciliatory tone calling for tariff reform and a return to the simple government envisioned in the republican ethos. This message horrified strong nationalists like John Quincy Adams and Webster, but not for long. Six days later Jackson issued his famous proclamation declaring nullification *"incompatible with the existence of the Union, contradicted expressly by the letter of the Constitution, unauthorized by its spirit, inconsistent with every principle on which it was founded, and destructive of the great object for which it was formed."* Closely following the arguments that Webster had used against Hayne, Jackson asserted that the people of the United States had formed a nation when they ratified the Constitution and were thus obliged to obey the laws of the government they had created. Each state in entering the Union had surrendered "essential parts of sovereignty." Therefore, neither nullification nor secession was constitutionally justified. Noting that the governor of South Carolina had already called for troops to support nullification, Jackson claimed that the nullifiers "are deluded by men who are either deceived themselves or wish to deceive you . . . the laws of the United States must be executed. . . . Disunion by armed force is treason."[4]

Two days after the President's proclamation, the South Carolina General Assembly elected Calhoun to the United States Senate, replacing Robert Hayne, who had been made governor. Calhoun left Fort Hill for Washington on December 22, pausing in Columbia to confer with Governor Hayne and other state leaders and to write to Secretary of State Edward Livingston, resigning his office as Vice President. Proceeding though Raleigh and Richmond, where he talked briefly with anxious state leaders, he arrived in Washington a few days after New Year.

By this time it had become a matter of common gossip that the President was threatening to hang him along with assorted other nullifier chiefs. Some people laughed at the possibility of a President of the United States punishing his Vice President for treason, but having presided over the War Department during one of Jackson's earlier hanging fits, Calhoun would have seen the point in Benton's remark that "when Jackson begins to talk about hanging, they can begin to look out for ropes."[5]

Calhoun knew, however, that he was not as isolated as the President thought. The proclamation with its unqualified nationalism, rejection of the right of secession, and threat of force had alarmed political leaders through the South, and Calhoun set out to exploit these fears on his way north by haranguing everyone who would listen about the dangers of Jackson's turning the government into a military despotism. Arriving in Washington on January 4, he was cordially received by his many friends in Congress and quickly learned that despite all the presidential bombast, the House Ways and Means Committee under Representative G. C. Verplanck of New York was proceeding with a bill that would generously reduce tariff rates. After a week in the capital Calhoun told his brother that a "satisfactory adjustment" seemed attainable.[6]

Sitting in the Senate a few days later while the clerk read the President's request for authority, including the use of federal troops, to enforce the collection of duties in Charleston, Calhoun must have felt that the despotism he had warned about was beginning to close around him. It was hard for anyone to take a moderate position on the force bill, as Jackson's request was called. Former Tennessee comrades were ecstatic, and James Wyley spoke for them when he boasted that their "Old Chief could rally force enough if necessary, upon two weeks' notice . . . to stand in the Saluda Mountains and piss enough . . . to float the whole nullifying crew of South Carolina into the Atlantic Ocean." But there was plenty of evidence that the task of disciplining South Carolina would not be quite that easy, and editors from nearby Richmond warned the President that if he wanted to march troops to Charleston, they might have to fight their way through Virginia. Meanwhile, the reaction in South Carolina was mixed. Unionists like Poinsett, who was in regular personal contact with the President, were vastly relieved. Fire-eaters like James Hamilton and Robert Barnwell Rhett breathed more fire, but some of the nullifiers, like twenty-four-year-old Isaac Hayne, clerk of the nullification convention, were visibly intimidated. "I trust we are not to fight as *rebels* with halters about our necks," Hayne wrote to a friend, "but as independent people with our own natural banner floating above us. The clouds thicken and blacken with each new day. There is but one doubt that is *appalling* to my mind—a doubt of the spirit *within our own borders among our own mess.*"[7]

Perhaps Calhoun had the Isaac Haynes of South Carolina in mind when in a violation of parliamentary rule he immediately seized the floor in the Senate to denounce the President for acting like a petulant Roman emperor eager to draw the sword on citizens attempting to assert their constitutional rights. He spoke in such haste and heat about being "threatened to have our throats cut, and those of our wives and children" that he found himself at the end apologizing "for the warmth with which he had expressed himself." Some of his listeners in the chamber thought he had been too excited to make a good impression, but Calhoun as usual felt otherwise, and much of his excitement may have been calculated. Writing to friends immediately after his speech, he predicted that Jackson's latest message would help Carolina by uniting the South. Dismissing the possibility of his own arrest, Calhoun called it a foolhardy act that could only "immortalize" the Carolina cause.[8]

Calhoun seems to have sensed correctly that Jackson had begun to overplay his hand. The issue now was not so much the constitutionality of nullification as whether or not a President should be allowed to chastise freely citizens of a state that disagreed with him. Predicting that Congress would not give Jackson the power he sought unless some rash action on the part of South Carolina supplied a pretext, Calhoun continually urged moderation on leading nullifiers like Hayne, Preston, and Hamilton. Heeding his advice, they managed to postpone the date on which nullification would take effect from February 1 until after Congress adjourned in early March, thereby giving the House and Senate more time to find their way out of the crisis.

During the following weeks Calhoun's strategy was to yield nothing in principle while leaving himself open to compromise in practice. "Be firm, and be prudent," he advised Hamilton. "Give no pretext for force and all will end as we desire. I never felt more confident." This was his advice on January 16, but he also knew that prudence was not an outstanding Carolina virtue. The chance that armed conflict could break out between nullifiers and unionists was very real. Calhoun was convinced that this was what Jackson wanted, and there were people close to the President who believed that civil war was "inevitable." By early February even Calhoun's vaunted confidence had begun to falter. The force bill would probably pass, he told Preston, while the compromise on the tariff failed. In that case the South Carolina convention should resume its deliberations and be prepared to justify nullification to the rest of the states. Although their cause was "greater than that of the Revolution," Carolinians should "only think of secession in the last extremity."[9]

Like everyone else involved, Calhoun knew that ultimately the fate of the nullifiers would depend not just on themselves or on what the President and Congress did but on how the other states responded to the crisis. Here the verdict was mixed. In Georgia, which was fighting a decision of the Supreme Court designed to make Georgians respect the treaty rights of the Cherokees, there was a vociferous nullifier faction, but it remained a minority. Governor Wilson Lumpkin, a strong Calhounite on most issues, made it clear that he could not support nullification, and the leaders of what was left of the Crawford party continued to denigrate their old adversary. The Virginia legislature, a traditional champion of states' rights, passed a resolution which in effect said to Jackson and Calhoun, "A plague on both your houses." Virginia supported the Virginia and Kentucky Resolutions but opposed nullification along with the protective tariff and the force bill. Calhoun could take some satisfaction from the fact that although the South generally was cool to nullification, it was decidedly against any attempt on the part of federal authorities to force the issue. If there was any consensus among the states, it was on the need for compromise, and after Van Buren had persuaded the New York legislature to support this position, even the bellicose Jackson began to understand that this was how the confrontation must end.[10]

Meanwhile, the political brokers were at work. Clay, the acknowledged master at this sort of thing, had leaped into the breach, and at some point soon after his return to Washington Calhoun had met with Clay to assure him that Carolina would accept a reasonable compromise on the tariff. Clay on February 12 submitted a bill calling for a gradual reduction of duties over a period of several years, and Calhoun endorsed it in principle in a brief, generous speech which evoked thunderous applause from Senators and gallery spectators. When Duff Green was elected printer of the Senate a few days later, it became obvious to everyone that a bargain had been reached. There were still important details to be worked out concerning the tariff, and Calhoun served on a select committee with Clay to keep Webster and other protectionists at bay while a bill was fashioned. It passed the Senate during the last week in February and was reported to the House to substitute for the stalled Verplanck bill.[11]

Calhoun could vote for Clay's tariff because it seemed implicitly to give up the principle of protection (Webster vehemently opposed it for that very reason) and because the level of duties for any given year were of far less importance to him than the right of a state to defend itself against unjust, unconstitutional federal legislation. In his view the President's request for special powers to enforce the collection of duties in South Carolina fell in the latter category, and he had no intention of compromising with it. When the Judiciary Committee reported the force bill granting the President wide powers, including the use of troops and the establishment of special jails, Calhoun responded with a set of resolutions designed to affirm state sovereignty and test the constitutional principles on which the bill was based. This paved the way for a momentous debate with Webster.

Although Webster had become the point man for the administration on the force bill, he was slow to take up the challenge of Calhoun's resolution. Webster's reputation had grown enormously since his debate with Hayne. He was not sure he could equal that performance a second time and would have preferred to avoid clashing with Calhoun, a much tougher opponent in parliamentary debate than Hayne. He also suspected that Calhoun was conspiring with Clay to destroy the tariff. If Webster stood to gain anything from the furious politicking which convulsed Washington in the winter of 1833, it would have to come by slaying the nullification dragon a second time—but he would not hurry. Convinced that Calhoun was too distraught by the force bill to deliver an effective speech against it, Webster wanted him to make the first move. Calhoun had introduced his resolutions on January 22, but Webster, who had already begun to chastise southern Democrats for not supporting the force bill, refused to take the bait.[12] On February 5, three days after having endorsed Clay's tariff compromise, which put Senators in a more receptive mood to hear what he had to say about the force bill, Calhoun gave his first major political speech in seventeen years.

Except for the brief, impassioned outburst in the Senate upon first hearing Jackson's request for authority to enforce revenue collections in Charleston, all of Calhoun's public statements about nullification had been more like philosophical treatises than partisan political pamphlets. Now he was free once again to join in the rough-and-tumble of political debate, and for the better part of two days he held the attention of the Senate in a long, loosely organized old-fashioned political speech. He talked about his own political history, why he and his state had supported the Tariff of 1816 out of patriotic motives, and how they had turned against it later when it became a vehicle to enrich special interests in the North. He mentioned the early hopes he and other Carolinians had had for Jackson's administration and how they had been dashed by Van Buren's "mischievous influence over the President" and other "circumstances too disreputable to be mentioned"—an obvious reference to Peggy Eaton.

Here was a side of Calhoun that most Senators had never seen before—not the abstract political philosopher, painstakingly lecturing his audience about the meaning of the Constitution, but the embattled politician, gaunt, gray, glaring, striding impatiently back and forth, and speaking in such rapid and abrupt phrases that his "ideas appeared to outrun his words and leave them limping in the rear." Following the argument in detail was like trying to study the individual railroad cars as a train sped by, but everyone knew what was happening.[13] The man who had been a power in Congress and the Cabinet and had twice served as Vice President was angry. He had been accused of lying, conniving, and plotting treason, and he would not release the Senate until he set the record straight. Of course, the straightened record was not always the real record. Those Senators who remembered South Carolina's complicity in the Tariff of 1828 were no doubt surprised to hear him say now that he had abominated it from the beginning and as Vice President would have voted against it in case of a tie. And anyone privy to the mauling, brawling, and bribing that had preceded the nullification convention might have smiled at hearing Calhoun's recollection of the event: "Never was there a political discussion carried on with greater activity and which appealed more directly to the intelligence of the community. Throughout the whole no address had been made to the low and vulgar passions, but on the contrary the discussion has turned upon the higher principles of political economy."[14]

Although most of what Calhoun told the Senate on February 15 took the form of political self-justification, he made one statement toward the close of his remarks that was extraordinarily self-revealing. Replying to Delaware Senator John G. Clayton's derisive remark that the arguments for nullification were "metaphysical" and incomprehensible, Calhoun spoke in defense of the powers of reason. Rejecting the metaphysics of scholasticism, he vigorously defended the "power of analysis and combination—that power which reduces the most complex idea into its elements, which traces causes to their first principle and . . . unites the whole in one harmonious system." This was the highest power of the human mind—the genius of Newton and Laplace and as appropriate to the study of "politics and legislation" as to the physical universe. "I hold them to be subject to laws as fixed as matter itself," Calhoun said, likening himself to Galileo and predicting that "the time will come when truth will prevail in spite of prejudice and denunciation, and when politics and legislation will be considered as much a science as astronomy and chemistry." For Calhoun nullification would always be more than a political act or a constitutional right because it was based on principles like the concurrent majority, as immutable as the laws of physics.[15]

After continuing for two more hours on February 16 and contrasting the tyrannical use of majority rule with the "perfect majority" that had been expressed in the conventions which ratified the Constitution, Calhoun surrendered the floor. Webster, who privately belittled the Carolinian's effort as "too inconsiderable for an answer," nevertheless succeeded him and, in a lengthy panegyric to the Union which essentially repeated his celebrated reply to Hayne, spoke against the resolutions Calhoun had introduced some days earlier. For Webster every speech was a ceremonial spectacle. Deliberate, stately, sonorous, he played well to Senators after the intense, staccato, sometimes threatening performance of Calhoun, and his argument that nullification would lead to disunion made sense to most of them. Jackson was obviously repeating what he wanted to hear when he told a friend that Calhoun was acting like a demented man and that Webster "handled him like a child," but it was apparent that the Senate believed with Webster that the constitutional compact was intended to give the federal government the power to enforce its laws. As one Senator after another began to line up behind the administration bill, Calhoun's isolation became so apparent that it reminded one sympathetic observer of "a parcel of dogs baying a bull—as he throws off one, another is ready to attack him." Four days after Calhoun's speech the Senate passed the force bill 32 to 1, with Calhoun and his supporters refusing to vote. As usual, however, the Carolinian claimed the last word when he answered Webster's speech on February 26 with a long, learned disquisition on the history and meaning of the Constitution. A few days later the reduced tariff was passed, and Jackson signed the force bill together with the compromise tariff on March 2.[16]

Washington had done its part to avert the crisis. It remained for South Carolina to agree. The South Carolina Constitutional Convention was scheduled to reconvene on March 11, and Calhoun, whose support for the tariff had been an essential part of the compromise, set off for Columbia, riding day and night through heavy weather and over nearly impassable roads in an uncovered mail cart to be present for the occasion. He was not a delegate, nor did he address the Convention, but his counsel was decisive in persuading it to repeal the Ordinance of Nullification. This effectively ended the confrontation between the state and federal governments, but not until the unrepentant Carolinians had passed a new ordinance nullifying the Force Act. The latter action against what Calhoun called the "bloody bill" was essentially meaningless since South Carolina would now obey the law and there would be nothing for federal officers to enforce, but it was symbolically important as a reaffirmation of the nullification principle.[17]

Confident that his principles put to the test had proved to be both worthy and workable, Calhoun returned to his family and plantation. It was nullification, he assured his friends, that had brought the tariff down, and although a despotic force bill had been rammed through Congress, neither he nor South Carolina would recognize its legitimacy. "While the bloody bill stands among our laws," Calhoun assured the former Georgia Congressman Bolling Hall, "I hold myself not to be a free man; and while I have life, I shall resist it till it is repealed with disgrace to its authors."[18]

Naturally South Carolina unionists disagreed with Calhoun's judgment about nullification. Some like Poinsett, resigned for the moment to their minority position in the state, took comfort in the Force Act and in Webster's "triumphant refutation" of Calhoun's "wild and dangerous speculations," while others blamed the entire crisis on his failed ambitions as Vice President. If he had remained "the friend and favorite of General Jackson," with the prospect "of being able to dole out the loaves and fishes of the General Government among his Partizans," asked one scoffer, "who can believe that we should ever have heard of the . . . remedy of nullification from him or any of his tribe?"[19]

Here was a clear case of sour grapes. Calhoun had begun to develop his ideas about nullification long before his trouble with Jackson, and he was surely correct in assuming that South Carolina's willingness to act on those ideas had brought the tariff down. Although Calhoun would always insist that nullification had worked in practice because it was right in principle, the truth was rather different. The same southern Representatives and Senators who had voted overwhelmingly to reduce the tariff also gave heavy majorities for the force bill which expressed

Webster's and Jackson's ideas about the Constitution, not Calhoun's.

The real gains for Calhoun were not in principle but in politics. In the short run all the major political players gained something. Jackson showed that he could hold his temper and keep the country together. Clay, who brokered the compromise, breathed new life into a reputation mortally stricken by the election of 1832. Webster, for a while, became a favorite of both parties and a plausible successor to Jackson. But Calhoun had profited the most. Expelled from the party by the administration, he had stood up to an enormously popular President and forced him not only to forgo his hanging party but to lose much of the momentum built up by his massive electoral victory. Meanwhile, Calhoun had built a solid base of support in his home state, had helped raise the consciousness of voters in other southern states about the dangers of increasing federal power, and was to emerge in Congress as an independent leader with a loyal following capable of playing a decisive role in the critical party contests which lay ahead.[20]

Of course, one lesson of the Compromise of 1833 was that the system could work without formally instituting the concurrent majority, but Calhoun could never accept that. For him the recourse to nullification would always be essential to good government in a republic because it was based on natural laws of human behavior. "Lying at the base of our political system and resting on truth and justice," he wrote to a friend shortly before returning to Washington, "it is I trust and believe destined under Providence to arrest the alarming growth of political corruption and to save the Constitution, the Union and Liberty of these states."[21]

11

Assaulting the President, 1833–1836

A FEW MONTHS after the nullification crisis was resolved, Calhoun was toasted at a banquet in Marion, South Carolina: "John C. Calhoun: He has proved himself the champion of liberty; he that is opposed to him, may it fall to his lot to have a scolding wife, crying children and a smoked house, small potatoes, corns on his toes and a mule to ride on that will throw him bridle and saddle." About the same time diners at a Jackson meeting in Virginia raised their glasses to "John C. Calhoun—traitor to his country's interest. Is there not some chosen curse, some hidden thunder in the stores of heaven, red with uncommon wrath to blast the wretch who owes his greatness to his country's ruin?"[1]

Although nullification had raised Calhoun's political visibility to new heights, he continued his practice of avoiding barbecues, banquets, and political rallies. Still, his unwillingness to bend to the new democratic style did not mean he wanted to withdraw from the fray. Believing that the relative isolation of the nullifiers from the two major parties could be a source of strength, Calhoun reminded his friends that they could hold the balance of power in Congress. "No measure can be taken without our assent," he assured Francis Pickens. The fight with the administration continued, and Calhoun devoted most of his political time during the next three years to attacking government policy and exposing the corruption he believed would inevitably flow from Jackson's assumption of unchecked presidential power.[2]

The four years of Jackson's second term mark a crucial period in the development of Calhoun's image as a kind of political monomaniac who spent every waking hour plotting to overthrow the President, to reaffirm the principles of nullification, and eventually to destroy the Union. Actually Calhoun usually spent more than half of each year between congressional sessions at Fort Hill, where he always had a lot on his mind besides politics. Despite his many years in politics and the long absences in Washington, his interest in agriculture remained strong, and like most planters who relied on overseers, he was always sure that his plantation was best attended when he was on the ground. In the spring and summer of 1833 that meant paying attention to such mundane details as inspecting the machinery in his gin and mill, making sure that shoes were ordered for the slaves in good season, that the picked cotton was kept clean and unstained, that the slave who claimed to have "lost" his overcoat had not sold it instead.[3]

During the spring and summer of 1833 he also spent about four weeks at his newly purchased mine near Dahlonega, Georgia. Dahlonega was gold-mining country, and Calhoun had paid $6,000 for a property called the Obarr Mine. Ordinarily not attracted to speculative ventures, he apparently thought the mine would provide a hedge against the uncertainties of the cotton market and employment for the twenty slaves he could spare from Fort Hill. He estimated that he could make $120 a hand every year on the venture. With his customary thoroughness he soon entered into correspondence with Nicholas Biddle and the director of the United States Mint to learn the processes and procedures for assaying ore, and in January 1834 he received a check from the mint for $612.28 for the first gold bar taken from his mine. Eventually Calhoun was able to get a branch of the Mint established in Dahlonega.[4]

Calhoun left Fort Hill for Washington on November 4, traveling by way of Charleston, where he gave his first public speech since South Carolina had reached a peaceful settlement with the federal government. Speaking on the evening of November 22, after an earlier ceremony honoring the memory of the recently deceased Robert J. Turnbull, who six years earlier had called for bloodshed to repel the tyranny of the tariff, Calhoun heated his rhetoric to suit the occasion. Reminding his audience that Washington had ordered the guns of harbor fortresses turned "against our city and our homes," he commended the local citizens for being true to their revolutionary heritage, claimed that nullification had routed the protective system, and urged unceasing resistance to the "bloody" Force Act which threatened "the very existence of the slaveholding states as political communities."[5]

Calhoun left Charleston for Washington by steamboat with the approval of the great majority of politically conscious Charlestonians ringing in his ears. It was not his oratory that had comforted his constituents as much as the absolute assurance of his demeanor. He almost always acted as if he were supremely confident and in complete control of himself and the situation at hand, an image which he both believed and cultivated. Attempting to explain this phenomenon to a friend, he claimed a disposition which "exempts me from disquiet or anxiety." Even at the height of the nullification crisis, when the outcome still hung in the balance, Calhoun said, he had never missed a meal or an hour's sleep.[6]

Calhoun's self-confidence and refusal to qualify his political judgments were never more apparent than during the congressional sessions of the second Jackson administration. Convinced that political behavior, like natural phenomena, was governed by fixed natural laws, he predicted and discovered tyranny and fraud in the government as confidently as an astronomer might predict an eclipse or announce a new planet. Unable to understand that Jackson's power lay in his historic role as symbolic leader for a rapidly expanding society caught up in the ferment of nationalism and democratization, he provided a catalyst for the opposition with the unrelenting severity of his attacks on the President.

Upon his return to Washington in December 1833, Calhoun immediately recognized the political opportunities provided by Jackson's veto of the bill to recharter the Bank of the United States and his arbitrary action in removing the federal deposits from that bank to selected state banks. Opposition to the Bank was real enough, derived partly from popular suspicion that it was a privileged monopoly, partly from business interests resentful of its restraint on credit, partly from the jealousy of New York bankers at the success of their powerful Philadelphia rival, and most important from Jackson's consuming obsession that he was ordained to slay Nicholas Biddle's bank, one of the few stabilizing institutions in a potentially runaway economy. The upshot of all this was that Jackson's irrational assaults on the Bank, although politically effective in the long run, aroused widespread opposition which carried beyond party and sectional lines. As Daniel Webster noted soon after Congress convened, many of the disaffected began to look to Calhoun for help. "Mr. Calhoun sits there perfectly happy,"

Webster grumbled on January 10, 1834. "And well may he so sit. He sees hundreds flocking to his standard in consequence of these abominable measures."[7]

Calhoun seized his opportunity to get back into the political mainstream on January 13, when he spoke in the Senate supporting Clay's resolutions to censure Jackson for removing the deposits. Arguing that the Bank had been a safe depository and "an indispensable agent" in restoring specie payments in the country, Calhoun maintained that the public funds were now endangered in "favorite and partisan banks" and that the President was guilty once again of abusing his power. The Constitution clearly gave Congress power to control the currency, but Jackson had decided to control it himself in what was really a new "Executive bank." It was all part of the inevitable tendency to consolidate power illustrated in the way he had treated South Carolina the previous spring. Calhoun and the nullifiers had resisted it then, and "standing in the front rank and manfully resisting the advance of despotic power," they would join with others to defeat it now.[8]

With Calhoun's help Clay's resolutions censuring Jackson passed the Senate. Even a confirmed Calhoun hater like Alfred Balch had to admit the "infinite ingenuity and subtlety" in Calhoun's speech, and Clay's close supporter John Sergeant believed that Calhoun had quickly become "the most confident man in either House." The confidence which Sergeant perceived came from Calhoun's conviction that southerners would recognize the link in principle between Jackson's attack on South Carolina and his assault on the Bank and would begin to act as a political unit. "You may put down the whole South as lost" to the administration, he wrote Vandeventer. "Our doctrines are spreading rapidly, and you must not be surprised to see them in the ascendant before two years." Calhoun obviously had his eye on 1836 and, fantastic as it may seem in retrospect, had not totally given up on the possibility of succeeding Jackson. "The times are propitious," he wrote Ingham, "the tariff is adjusted; the American system prostrated; consolidation deeply distrusted . . . and finally the New York system of corruption & trickery [Van Buren] grows daily the more odious." Now was the time to move. "We only want organization & impulse," he told Ingham, "and few can do more than you to both."[9]

Although presidential possibilities continued to cloud his vision on occasion, between 1833 and 1836 Calhoun's political course was largely shaped by his avowed purpose to maintain political independence and uphold the principles of the nullifiers. His support for Clay's resolutions had appeared to put him clearly as pro-Bank in company with the rest of the anti-Jacksonians who were about to regroup under the Whig banner, but when Webster introduced a bill to extend the Bank's charter an additional six years, Calhoun demurred and seized the opportunity to stake out his own ground. In a short, penetrating speech he argued that neither Democrats nor Whigs really understood the relationship among government, banking, and the currency. Jackson's response had been demagoguery at its worst; Webster's was insufficient because his vision was limited to the constitutionality of the Bank and would buy only six more years of the past while keeping the Bank at the center of a political storm. No one seemed willing to try to find a permanent solution to "the great question of the currency." Claiming the proliferation of undercapitalized state banks which flooded the country with unreliable paper money to be at the root of the trouble, Calhoun asserted that this was a problem which cried out for federal help. Here he gently took issue with ardent states' rights partisans who traditionally supported hard-money, antibank policies. Whether the framers of the Constitution had intended the government to deal in paper money or not was no longer relevant. Like the Louisiana Purchase (where constitutionality had also been an issue), banking and paper currency had become part of our history and would be part of our future. "The country has been brought into the present diseased state of the currency by banks," Calhoun said, "and must be extricated by their agency. We must, in a word, use a bank to unbank the banks . . . a new and safe system must gradually grow up under and replace the old." As an alternative to Webster's bill Calhoun proposed a twelve-year renewal period for the Bank along with policies designed to increase the value and quantity of specie by regulating the money supply. This would be accomplished by requiring the Bank gradually to decrease its issuance of small-denomination notes while the government gradually increased the instances in which it would only receive payment in specie.[10]

After it was reported in the press, Calhoun's speech attracted extravagant praise in and outside the South as an intelligent, objective analysis of a complex policy problem most Americans understood dimly, if at all. "Such a man should not be regarded as the property of party," wrote the *Philadelphia Intelligencer,* "he belongs to the country, the whole country." More recently the banking historian Bray Hammond has written that Calhoun was "distinguished among American statesmen in his realization that banking is a monetary function, that regulation of the currency is the duty of the federal government and that the duty is to be exercised through a state bank; not for more than a century would such an understanding of the subject be expressed again in Congress." No matter that his proposal was never brought to a vote, Calhoun, who always insisted that he acted in the long-range interests of the country, was satisfied. He had delivered his judgment and instructed those willing to be enlightened. At the same time he was not neglecting another agenda because his speech for the time being had helped keep him out of the Whig camp, which was just where he wanted to be. Once again sound principle appeared to reinforce good politics.[11]

Calhoun had returned to the Senate sworn to overthrow the Force Act. It was his way of keeping faith with the Carolina nullifiers, but it was an impossible mission. Although he could hardly expect to keep one-half of the compromise while destroying the other, Calhoun could have the last word, and he did. Arguing for repeal on April 9, he tried to put the recent nullification crisis in the larger perspective of American history. According to Calhoun, the election of 1824 had marked a resurgence of Federalist nationalism, resulting in the passage of the first protective tariff and the relegation of the South to permanent minority status. Unable to change the tariff in Congress, the South pinned its hopes on Jackson, a planter and "successful Military Chieftain," but a man with ambiguous principles and relatively little political experience. Then came the Tariff of 1828. Calhoun was circumspect in laying the blame for the bill but emphatic about the result. "This disastrous event opened our eyes (I mean myself and those connected with me) as to the full extent of the danger and oppression of the protective system, and the hazard of failing to effect the reform intended through the election of Gen Jackson." Calhoun was careful to separate himself and his supporters from the other Jacksonites in 1828. "We were not the mere partisans of the candidate we supported. We aimed at a far more exalted object than his election—the defence of the rights of the state, and the security of liberty and of the Constitution."

But, Calhoun went on, he and his supporters were deceived. Once in power, the new administration did nothing "to arrest the progress of consolidation and to restore the confederate principles of our Government" and soon turned itself into "a third party . . . a personal and government party made up of those who were attached to the person and the fortunes of a political chief," thus presenting Americans brought up in the republican tradition with "that most dangerous spectacle in a country like ours, a *prerogative* party, who take their creed wholly from the mandate of their chief." When this new and decidedly un-American party, bloated with revenues from the Tariff of 1828, refused to press for tariff relief in 1832, South Carolina resisted. A crisis ensued, and the compromise tariff was passed (here Calhoun gave full credit to Henry Clay). The prerogative party had been weakened, and its chief censured for his arbitrary management of public funds, but as long as the Force Act, which gave the President unlimited power over an individual state, remained law, the seeds of degeneracy would always be present to sprout again. "Reverse the scenes," Calhoun pleaded, "let the act be obliterated forever from among our laws; let the principle of consolidation be forever suppressed . . . and our country may yet realize that permanent state of liberty, prosperity and greatness, which we all once so fondly hoped was our allotted destiny."[12]

Although Calhoun did not get his way with the "bloody bill," the Whigs were delighted with his assault on the President as an Old World despot, and they chortled when he intensified his attack after Jackson formally protested the censure. Asking his fellow Senators if they wanted the President "armed" with the patronage of the federal government to become "the sole expounder of the Constitution," Calhoun finally lashed out on May 6, 1834, in a personal attack against the man whose idolization he so deeply resented: "Infatuated man! blinded by ambition—intoxicated by flattery and vanity! Who, that is the least acquainted with the human heart—who that is conversant with the page of history, does not see, under all this, the workings of a dark, lawless and insatiable ambition, which, if not arrested, will finally impel him to his own, or his country's ruin?"[13]

It was more than a partisan attack; it was a manifesto. Calhoun concluded his speech by noting the changes in party designations and character. The Jacksonians claimed to be Democrats but in fact had become the American Tories, the royal prerogative party. No wonder that men of various political backgrounds had begun to call themselves Whigs, taking their name from the English party which had tradition-ally supported legislative power. For himself, Calhoun said, he wished the Whigs well but would continue to keep company with the few real republicans who remained committed to resist "usurpation" from any quarter—whether emanating from the President or the Congress.

During this period Calhoun's control over the South Carolina dele-gation to Congress went almost unchallenged. William Grayson, then a freshman Congressman from the Sea Islands, recalled the fierce an-tagonism toward the President at that time. Only a few years earlier Jackson had been a Carolina hero and had toasted Calhoun as among "the noblest work of God." Now except for the apostate James Blair, who soon did the proper thing by committing suicide, no Carolina Representative or Senator visited the White House, and all joined in the most extravagant private and public abuse of the President. "He was compared to every tyrant that had ever disgraced humanity. Caesar was a model of patriotic control compared with Jackson, and Marius and Sulla were men of moderation and virtue."[14]

Although he insisted that friends in Congress support his harsh partisan attacks on the President, Calhoun could see the virtue of tak-ing a more conciliatory approach toward opponents at home. When the South Carolina Supreme Court declared the test oath unconstitu-tional in the spring of 1834, he counseled moderation, and from Pen-dleton that summer he worked to bring about a peaceful adjustment of that divisive issue in the state legislature. For the rest of his life Cal-houn believed that his own effectiveness in Washington depended substantially on political unity in South Carolina.[15]

When Calhoun returned to Washington at the end of 1834 after a relatively short summer recess, he must have felt reinforced not only by the unified backing of his South Carolina colleagues but also by the presence of Floride, accompanied by two of their children, Anna Maria, who was seventeen, and the five-year-old Willy. Floride's deci-sion to bring part of her family back to Washington may have been prompted by the fact that she and her husband had suffered a serious personal loss that February, when their daughter-in-law Eugenia had died shortly after giving birth to their first grandchild. Andrew Pickens Calhoun had married Eugenia, daughter of a wealthy Columbia planter, a year earlier when he was twenty-one. A good son, Andrew had already shown that he was not cut out to succeed his father, who with some misgiving had secured a West Point appointment for him. Andrew had declined that honor because he wanted to be a planter, not a soldier. After preparing at a school in Abbeville, he had gone to Yale, where he was proudly introduced to his father's old professors, and where to the amazement and infinite chagrin of his father, he was expelled for having participated in a student revolt over a geometry class. After finishing his schooling at South Carolina College, Andrew had married Eugenia Chappell and seemed poised to begin his career as a planter. The premature death of his wife, however, followed by that of his baby daughter, left him almost paralyzed with grief. The fact that Andrew had been out of state shopping for a plantation when Eugenia died was probably a factor in helping his parents decide to make the congressional session of 1835 a family affair.

Willy was too young to understand what his father was doing, and Floride had little interest in politics, but Calhoun found a real companion in Anna Maria. She sat regularly in the Senate gallery, took in every word her father said, and helped him with his correspondence in the evening. When the mail was brought to him at his desk on the Senate floor, Calhoun would stop everything, sort the letters, and immediately pass those to his daughter up to the gallery. Anna Maria's presence in Washington until her marriage in 1838, and her letters to him when they were apart, furnished one of the great joys in his life.

Not even the presence of his daughter, however, could mellow the severity with which Calhoun continued to attack Jackson and the government. As 1834 approached its end, he discovered a perfect vehicle for his offensive in a Senate committee to study executive patronage. Convinced that the President was using the surplus revenue to swell federal payrolls and extend executive power, Calhoun immediately took charge of the committee and began to collect information from Jackson's department heads. Discovering, among other things, that the Post Office Department had probably doubled the number of its employees over the past ten years, he was naturally an attentive listener to a report on corruption in the Post Office a few days later. Actually Jackson had only replaced about 6 percent of the deputy postmasters, but his Postmaster General crony William Barry had been a terrible administrator. Learning, for example, that Barry had permitted some contractors to put in ridiculously low bids with the understanding that they would increase their charges after the contract was awarded, Calhoun pointed triumphantly to the rotten fruits of unlimited power. Here was a system "more dangerous and more disgraceful than ever existed in the most corrupt ages of the Roman Republic." If the President and the people could permit such things, it was the end of "public liberty."[16]

The next day, as if to mock Calhoun's heated attack on Jackson's corrupt Post Office, Senator William R. King of Alabama presented a resolution aimed at expunging the recent censure of the President in the Senate journal. Calhoun immediately accused the Democrats of trying to reinstate "that old and worn out dogma of old and worn out nations 'The King can do no wrong,' " thus reducing the Senate to "the dumb legislation of Bonaparte's Senate." The only alternatives for the opposition were "reformation or revolution." The resolution to expunge was tabled, and Calhoun's remarks were widely printed in the Washington press.[17]

Two days later, after leaving the House of Representatives, where funeral services were held for Calhoun's deceased Carolina colleague Warren Davis, Andrew Jackson was accosted by a heavily bearded man who discharged two pistols at him at point-blank range before being subdued. Both guns misfired, and the President escaped unhurt. The potential assassin, an unemployed house painter with delusions of grandeur (he claimed to be the legitimate heir to the British throne), ultimately ended up in an asylum, but the *Washington Globe* suggested he might have had an accomplice in John C. Calhoun. Any man of unbalanced mind "if he had read and *believed*" Calhoun's wild attacks on the President, claimed the *Globe*, might have been led to think of assassination as a patriotic act.

Frank Blair, the aciduous editor of the *Globe* and Jackson's favorite journalist, had overreacted. Calhoun, who had probably slain the President a hundred times in his sleep, calmly told a hushed Senate two days later that the administration was trying to muzzle debate in the Senate by equating criticism with assassination—one more evidence that the end of liberty was approaching.[18]

Although Calhoun was sure he had won that round, he did not come away unscathed. More objective observers of the political scene than either Calhoun or Blair were disturbed by the unrelenting savage rhetorical attacks in Congress on a popularly elected President. James Fenimore Cooper spoke for them when he wrote in the *New York Evening Post* that Calhoun should expect to be "indicted before the bar of public opinion even though he is protected by law." According to Cooper, it was nonsense to call a majority leader like Jackson a king and dangerously undemocratic for a minority leader like Calhoun to show such utter contempt for the will of the majority.[19]

Even as Cooper wrote, Calhoun was putting the final touches on the report of the Senate committee to study executive patronage, a well-argued document which bore little stylistic resemblance to his shrill denunciations of the administration earlier in the session. The committee, drawn to Calhoun's specifications, included two Democrats and two Whigs plus Calhoun and one other "true republican." Although Benton and Webster were members, Calhoun took the lead in collecting statistics concerning federal revenues, disbursements, and appointments. The final report is unmistakably in his hand.

Although he wrote dispassionately for the most part and with considerable statistical backup, Calhoun obviously wanted to turn his report into another weapon against Jackson. According to the government's own figures, federal expenditures and the number of people "employed and living off the bounty of the government" had approximately doubled since 1825, with the increase accelerating during Jackson's administration. Why had this happened?

There were two big causes. The first was too much money. Despite the liquidation of the public debt, the federal surplus continued to pile up from tariff and land sale revenues. The money was being, and would continue to be, spent in ways that would inevitably help some citizens and some sections while hurting others. In other words, the country was now gripped by the corruption that Calhoun had predicted would follow the consolidation of federal power. The second reason for the crisis, according to Calhoun, was the removal of the deposits. By taking direct control of the government's money, the President was able to have a freer hand in dispensing patronage. He was also encouraging his pet banks to extend credit liberally, thus contributing to the land speculation boom that helped swell the surplus.[20]

Calhoun accompanied his report with resolutions aimed at limiting the President's authority to remove officeholders and manipulate the federal deposits. He also proposed a constitutional amendment to provide for distributing the surplus among the states. Not unexpectedly the report and the resolutions set off a furious debate in the Senate with the most acrimonious exchanges taking place between Calhoun and Benton, who, as a Democratic member of Calhoun's committee, had somehow managed to live through its hearings without having a fit. Assuming his familiar roaring ways in the ensuing debate, Benton found himself disadvantaged by the fact that in 1826 he had chaired a committee to study abuse of the patronage under John Quincy Adams, and Calhoun was able to quote copiously from Benton's earlier report to support his own. Finally Benton called Calhoun a liar and in the uproar that followed was called to order by a majority vote which overruled and practically paralyzed the presiding Van Buren, who had devoted a career to avoiding just such direct confrontations. Calhoun was usually at his best in encounters with blusterers like Benton, and although there was some talk of his challenging the Missouri Senator, it is unlikely that he even considered it. Perhaps he agreed with Philip Hone, who said challenging Benton would be like challenging a hyena.[21]

Andrew Jackson, not Benton, was Calhoun's real target. A few days after debating Benton, Calhoun was on his feet again, solemnly warning the Senate that if it did not pass a law requiring the President to show cause for removing a public officer, "in a few generations the American character will become utterly corrupt and debased." The "tyranny" of the President had become almost an obsession with Calhoun and tended to determine his position on every issue, large or small. He opposed Jackson's truculent attempts to force France to pay war claims dating from 1815 because he thought it could lead to war and increase presidential power. He even opposed regulating the attendance of women in the Senate galleries because he suspected a government design to hold on to power. "In the great struggle for liberty," Calhoun said, the galleries were always "thrown open." In such a frame of mind it was natural for Calhoun to fall into temporary despair when the Democrats scored heavily in the Virginia elections of 1835. Despite all his efforts, "King Andrew" and his minions seemed as popular as ever. "The symptom is awful," Calhoun lamented, "our condition will be worse than our slaves."[22]

It was obvious to intelligent observers at the time, and it has been obvious to historians ever since, that the image of Jackson Calhoun sought to convey had little in common with the historical personage, and the interesting question is why a man as politically experienced and intelligent as Calhoun should have been so far off the mark. Part of the answer lies in the fact that Jackson had hurt Calhoun badly by almost mortally wounding his presidential ambitions and, even more important, by impeaching his honor. For these offenses Calhoun at every level of consciousness always deeply resented the fact that the Republic had invested this man with the greatest office in its trust.

On the other hand, Calhoun can hardly be blamed for seeing in Jackson's presidency a dangerous departure from the republican tradition in which both men had been reared. In championing the power of the people and the power of the President as the representative of the people, Jackson symbolized the democratic nationalism that was transforming every aspect of American life. Jackson believed in public virtue as much as Calhoun, but he also believed that the people as the ultimate source of political power should be more involved in actually running the government and that rotation in office was consistent with democratic principles. In actual fact, Jackson removed a far smaller percentage of officeholders than Calhoun believed, and his introduction of bureaucratic regulations and procedures into the separate departments of the government was consistent with democratization. Historians have pointed out that Amos Kendall, a corrupt Jackson sycophant in Calhoun's mind, took over the Post Office from the inept Barry and turned it into a modern organization in which an employee's ability to hold a job depended not on whom he knew but on his ability to fill an office defined "impersonally, entirely by rules and regulations."[23]

Of course, Jackson judged Calhoun as harshly and incorrectly as the latter judged him, regularly denouncing him as Cataline, the demagogue who had conspired to overthrow the Roman Republic. Others less paranoid than the President dismissed Calhoun's attacks as a simple case of sour grapes, a tempting hypothesis if one recalls that the most corrupt official during the eight years of Jackson's administration was Samuel Swartwout, a thief of legendary dimension, whom Jackson had made collector of the Port of New York with Calhoun's approval over the fierce objections of Van Buren.

But we belittle Calhoun by dismissing him as a sore political loser. Whatever his limitations, Calhoun was not a petty person. He was a man of principle, and when it came to judging Jackson, his principles failed him. Believing that his political principles were as certain as the laws of physics, and watching Jackson assert federal and presidential power far greater than anything envisaged by Jefferson, Madison, or Monroe, Calhoun had to believe that the President who had abused him publicly and personally posed a fundamental threat to American liberty. Once he had accepted the premise that the Jackson presidency represented an abuse of executive power, his judgments of Jackson in office would be determined more by deduction than by evidence. Thus Calhoun would find the seeds of tyranny in the most innocent act, such as the attempt to restrict the admission of ladies to the Senate gallery to a ticket system, each Senator being allowed three tickets. Most Senators saw this as a simple attempt to rationalize the public use of a restricted space. Calhoun saw it as an attempt to keep the people from learning what the administration was doing. Every government based on power acted the same. "It goes on and on increasing and increasing, always getting what it can, and never giving up any; it must be met on the threshhold [*sic*]."

Despite Calhoun's determined and aggressive opposition, he could not often find the votes to derail Jackson's program. The result was relative political and social isolation for Calhoun himself and the South Carolina delegation. Calhoun, who usually found Washington distractingly frivolous anyway, could hardly have cared less. He was convinced that the levees at the White House, opened to "the Lowest stratum of society" were all part of Jackson's demagoguery and was happy to be left out.[24] James Henry Hammond's wife, Catherine, who had joined her husband in Washington, saw the bleak social prospects differently. Bemoaning her inability to appear at the White House Christmas Eve and New Year's parties, she admitted: "We Carolinians are in such bad odor here" that she never saw "a friendly smile."[25]

As the reign of King Andrew neared an end, Calhoun finally found himself on the winning side. On June 23, 1836, the President reluctantly signed his bill regulating the deposit banks and providing for the distribution of the federal surplus among the states. Jackson did not like the bill, but it had strong bipartisan support, and he could see just as clearly as Calhoun that money meant power and that too much of it in the hands of a republican government was always dangerous. Although the passage of this law was part of a general compromise, Calhoun rushed to take the credit for himself and for his state. Distributing the surplus among the states would "dry up the fiscal deluge out of which the spoils party arose" and gradually restore the "federative character" of the government. It was the "consummation of the Carolina doctrines, carried out in their practical consequences."[26]

Although Calhoun continued his independent course through the presidential election that fall, supporting Hugh Lawson White over more orthodox Whig nominees like Webster, Clay, and Harrison, the long struggle against Jackson was essentially over. It was just as well, for Calhoun had already discovered new dragons at the gate.[27]

12

Making the Proslavery Argument

ALTHOUGH more and more of his critics were coming to perceive Calhoun as a dangerous radical by 1835, some of his closest friends back home continued to think he did not go far enough. Unable to swallow Jackson's continued popularity, James Edward Calhoun advised his brother-in-law bluntly to "give up your attachment to the Union and cease all efforts to save it," and Francis Pickens, thoroughly alienated by the rising democratic tide in Washington, suggested that the time had come for his friend to put honor over politics and resign. Calhoun was apparently tempted but demurred because he thought his experience and influence necessary to preserve political unity in his own state and to protect "our existence as a people." By "people" he meant the white people of the South who would be "compelled to abandon the South and leave it exclusively to the black race without our most strenuous and united efforts." In 1812 he had seen almost with the "force of destiny" that the cause of liberty demanded war and national unity. In 1828 he saw that it demanded nullification and an all-out assault on Jacksonianism. By 1835 he had come to see with the same certainty that it demanded the fierce, unswerving defense of slavery.[1]

Considering Calhoun's reputation as the most celebrated defender of southern institutions before 1850, it is remarkable how little mention there is of slavery in his private and public papers before 1830. Aside from the details necessarily imposed on an absentee Carolina planter who measured his wealth largely in the ownership of other human beings, Calhoun says almost nothing about slavery during this period. Slavery was a part of his life he took for granted, like growing staple crops; it was something to be managed rather than justified.

No doubt Calhoun, like other ambitious political leaders at the national level, instinctively shied away from the divisiveness of slavery as a moral and political issue, but it is certainly true that he was never as interested in studying or discussing it as he was in analyzing political and constitutional issues. In his first session in Congress Calhoun was reported as saying "he felt ashamed" that South Carolina had supported the reopening of the slave trade. The real importance of that incident is that it marks the only negative remark of his about slavery on record. Later, when Calhoun eventually argued before the Senate that slavery was a positive good, he was simply rationalizing something he had always believed. He had grown up with slavery in the Carolina backcountry. His father's enormous prestige in Abbeville had rested in part on the fact that he was one of the largest slaveholders in the region. For Patrick Calhoun and his neighbors slavery was justified by the growing prosperity and political importance of the backcountry. If slavery in the 1830s meant barbarism to Boston abolitionists like William Lloyd Garrison and Wendell Phillips, it implied civility to Carolinians of Calhoun's generation, who recognized that as slave numbers increased in the backcountry, the shiftless, poor whites who earlier held the region back began to leave the state. Not only that, but Calhoun had spent his student years in New England when slavery was still a visible institution throughout the North—when the consensus among most educated people in the Western world was that slavery and progress were reciprocal.[2]

Unlike Jefferson, Calhoun never troubled himself over the paradox of a society which valued both slavery and freedom. He assumed that concepts like liberty and equality applied only to white people. During the furious debates in Congress preceding the Missouri Compromise, when southerners in both houses were stridently defending slavery, Calhoun remained a detached observer, assuring his friends that the sectional confrontation was largely the work of ambitious politicians, and that although some reformers "activated by notions perfectly honest" were involved, very few wanted "emancipation." In this spirit he could welcome the reelection of the eloquent antislavery Federalist Rufus King to the Senate. He could not understand why allowing slavery into a new state like Missouri caused political tension because he had not yet come to realize the critical importance of sectional balance in the Union and assumed that leaders who had appealed to the common self-interest and patriotism of Americans to win the late war could rely on their common sense to keep the slavery issue from dividing the country. Thus he could say with equanimity in the spring of 1821, "The genius of the age is equality," and predict the inevitable fall of the old order in Europe without realizing the implications of that assertion for the permanence of slavery in the South. When the Denmark Vesey insurrection plot was revealed in the summer of 1822, Calhoun as Secretary of War responded to an urgent request from the governor of South Carolina by transferring a company of federal troops from St. Augustine to Charleston. Although thirty-seven slaves were executed in that abortive uprising, Calhoun seems to have treated his role in the matter as routine. The need to defend slavery as a just and necessary social system had not yet penetrated his consciousness.[3]

There is no reason to believe that Calhoun ever studied the history of slavery in detail or that he knew much about racial differences. His thinking about slavery was shaped by the culture in which he was reared and reinforced by his own experience as a master. He assumed that black people were naturally inferior to whites and could coexist peacefully and constructively with them only as slaves. This assumption conveniently ignored the fact that the foundation of South Carolina's wealth in the beginning had been built not simply on African muscle power but on the ability of Africans to transfer the complex technology of rice cultivation from their homeland to the New World and that black slaves in South Carolina and elsewhere had mastered almost all the skills performed by white craftsmen outside the South. Evidence that blacks possessed a learning capacity similar to that of whites was even closer to home if Calhoun had been willing to open his mind to it. His neighbor Major Elam Sharpe, superintendent of a black Sunday school in Pendleton from 1819 to 1824, reported that "the coloured people under my care have behaved with distinguished propriety and been generally very attentive to their books. . . . I have found no difficulty in the capacities of negroes more than white people and think they may easily be learned to read the scriptures." Calhoun's assumption that enslavement to white people was somehow the natural condition of blacks also ignored the fact that in other societies white slaves were described as naturally inferior to black masters and that even in South Carolina some black people owned slaves. In 1830 there were about 450 black masters who owned more than 2,400 black slaves and had to cope with problems of productivity and discipline just as Calhoun did. One historian who has recently studied this subject concludes that once free blacks in South Carolina acquired slaves as investments, "There were few differences between them and white owners beyond the color of their skin."[4]

Although Calhoun always believed that racial differences justified slavery, he was without racial animus, and there is no record of his using the word "nigger." As Secretary of War he declined to honor the request for bounty land by a black man descended from a revolutionary veteran, but about the same time he issued a citation of recommendation to another black who worked in the department as a messenger. In Calhoun's mind a black could be a commendable person and a good worker without being qualified for the duties and privileges of citizenship. When Virgil Maxcy wrote lamenting the loss of a loyal servant, Calhoun replied, "We had heard of the death of your servant before I received your letter and can easily enter into your feelings at the loss of a faithful domestick raised in the family. In such a one the character of a slave is in a great measure lost in that of a friend, humble indeed, but still a friend."[5]

We will consider how Calhoun treated his own slaves in a later chapter. The point to make here is that when slavery became an unavoidable political issue, as it did in the 1830s, Calhoun entered the debate convinced that slavery was morally sound and essential to the preservation of liberty and prosperity in the South. This conviction coincided with and reinforced his discovery that southern states had become a permanent minority. "The truth can no longer be denied," he wrote to Maxcy in September 1830, "that the peculiar domestick institution of the Southern States, and the consequent direction which that and her soil and climate have given to her industry, has [sic] placed them . . . in opposite relation to the majority of the Union."[6]

"Peculiar institution" was more than a euphemism. It implied paternalistic direction of a racially different labor force and a primary commitment to staple agriculture in a rapidly changing, increasingly democratic and industrial country. If the great American experiment in self-government were to succeed in the long run, Calhoun knew that citizens outside the South would have to be convinced that what was peculiar and beneficial to the South was also good for the rest of the country. Thomas Dew's pamphlet on the abolition of slavery, which Calhoun acquired soon after it was published in 1833, was a good step in this direction. Dew, an academician in Virginia, where, unlike South Carolina, the continuance of slavery had been a matter of intense public debate, deplored southern defensiveness about the institution. Calhoun probably passed over Dew's long, elaborate arguments against the American Colonization Society not only because of the absurdity of the idea of sending the slaves back to Africa but because Calhoun had always linked the movement with the tariff as a scheme designed to rob southerners of their property. Dew's other arguments about race and the acceptance of slavery in the Bible all would have been familiar. But when Dew discussed the way slavery turned plantations into extended families and promoted equality among southern citizens by eliminating the white underclass so essential to the North, Calhoun would have paid attention because this was a point he had tried to make in a casual conversation with Josiah Quincy some years earlier. "The interests of the *gentlemen* of the North," Quincy remembered Calhoun's saying, "and those of the South are identical."[7] What he meant was that slavery helped stabilize the Union by holding down class antagonisms.

After 1830 the specter of abolitionism began to take ominous shape for many southerners, especially those sensitized by the nullification crisis. In 1831 an obscure but talented journalist in Boston began to publish the *Liberator,* a weekly paper pledged to the immediate emancipation of all slaves. Although William Lloyd Garrison's paper attracted few subscribers, it was soon being quoted in other papers throughout the country. The following year Garrison organized the New England Antislavery Society, and in 1833, the year Britain began to emancipate slavery in the West Indies, he joined with other reformers to organize the American Antislavery Society. This mobilization of abolitionist sentiment outside the South led to an avalanche of antislavery literature directed largely at southerners and to a flood of antislavery petitions to Congress.

Although Calhoun was aware of the growing abolitionist movement almost from its inception, he did not allow it to disturb his crusade against the tyrannies of Jackson. By the summer of 1835, however, the waves that Garrison had started in Boston had begun to cause ripples in southern villages as far away as Pendleton, South Carolina, and Cal-

houn was asked to participate in a public meeting organized by neighbors who agreed, among other things, to appoint a vigilance committee
to keep "incendiary publications" out of their community and "detect
and bring to justice all agents or emissaries who may be employed to
circulate them, or spread disaffection among our slaves." The Pendleton planters did not have to spell out the obvious: that they expected
Calhoun to take charge of whatever vigilance was required in Washington.[8]

Returning to Washington by steamboat to do battle with the abolitionists, Calhoun found that there were some exceptions to his vaunted
power of self-control. Once, off the North Carolina shore and approaching Cape Hatteras, the good ship *South Carolina,* on which he
and his daughter were traveling, encountered fierce headwinds, causing
a two-day delay at anchor in a heavy sea close to the bleak North
Carolina shore. "Pa was so sick the whole time," Anna wrote to a
friend, "that he could not get out of his bunk." Anna fared better by
staying on deck whenever possible, but it took the ministrations of a
gallant French passenger with better sea legs to nurse the stricken
Senator, who had boasted that he'd never lost a meal or an hour's sleep
during the darkest days of nullification.[9]

Once back in Washington for the first session of the Twenty-fourth
Congress in December 1835, he found that his vigilance against abolitionist fanaticism threatened to undo his vigilance against Jackson. The
President's message to Congress deplored the spread of antislavery agitation and called for legislation to prevent the Post Office from carrying
the very publications Calhoun's Pendleton neighbors wanted to inter-
cept. For once he could agree with Jackson's goal because he had read
papers like the *Liberator, Antislavery Record,* and *Emancipator,* which
were regularly passed around the Washington boarding house where he
stayed. On the other hand, giving government the power to censor the
mail was hardly consistent with his own goal of limiting federal power.
"It seems to me," Calhoun wrote to Ingham, "that the power is the
most odious and dangerous that can be conceived."[10]

Calhoun solved the problem by getting himself appointed to a committee and writing a report opposing congressional interference with
the mail as unconstitutional but recommending legislation requiring
the Post Office to cooperate with state laws prohibiting the distribution

of abolitionist literature. Although Congress did not pass the law, the Post Office began to follow Calhoun's recommendation in principle.[11]

The other issue forced on Congress by the abolitionists involved the reception of antislavery petitions. Calhoun, like other southern Senators, objected to petitions which caricatured him as a heartless trafficker in human flesh, a robber, kidnapper, or pirate. He argued that the Senate should refuse to accept such petitions on the grounds that they were offensive to his constituents, did not address real grievances of the petitioners, and were designed to seize the property of slaveholders in violation of the Fifth Amendment. Brushing aside the constitutional guarantee of the right of petition, Calhoun pointed out that to refuse to accept these petitions was not the same as passing a law to abridge the right of petition.[12]

The man who had refused to call John Randolph to order in the Senate, and who bridled at the merest suggestion that he himself might have defamed President Jackson, wanted to muzzle Americans who hated slavery. Free speech in a parliamentary body was to be cherished at any cost as a precious right secured by bloody struggles over the centuries to assure political liberty. Freedom to organize, write, or speak against slavery, an institution involving the investment of hundreds of millions of dollars and the ownership of millions of human beings, was too dangerous to tolerate. When James T. Austin, the attorney general of Massachusetts, sent him a copy of his speech approving the actions of the mob which killed the antislavery editor Elijah P. Lovejoy in Alton, Illinois, in September 1837, Calhoun read it with approval. Austin had likened the "orderly mob" in Illinois to the patriots in Boston who had violently resisted the Stamp and Tea acts. Calhoun found the analogy "very striking." He failed to see that thousands upon thousands of Americans outside the South who had initially distrusted the abolitionists would now turn a sympathetic ear because they were being denied their right to speak.[13]

For the rest of the session Calhoun devoted himself in the Senate to leading the charge against twin dragons: Jacksonian tyranny and abolitionist fanaticism. As usual what he said and did was based on principles he took seriously, and once again principle served politics. In assaulting the President, he was implicitly appealing to the Whigs, and in defending slavery, he was explicitly appealing to southerners of all political persuasion. For Calhoun it was simply a matter of extending his political base by standing on the truth, but in the process he managed to develop a position the South was to rely on to defend slavery for the next quarter of a century.

Calhoun began his defense of slavery by declaring that its permanence in the South should never be open to political debate because the very existence of the southern states hung in the balance. The difficulty lay in the "diversity of races," which no power on earth could overcome. Whatever Africans might be able to achieve in their own land, a "mysterious Providence" had placed them as slaves to whites in the American South, and Calhoun believed they could continue to exist in that relationship "if undisturbed for all time."

Like other Americans, Calhoun believed that God, always on the American side, had allowed republican institutions to develop in the North under a free system of labor and in the South under slavery. To attempt to tamper with the design now was to threaten a way of life, the social identity of almost half the country. Thus the question of emancipation should never be heard as part of the political dialogue. "The relation which now exists between the two races," Calhoun told the Senate on March 9, 1836, "has existed for two centuries. It has grown with our growth and strengthened with our strength. It has entered into and modified all our institutions, civil and political. None other can be substituted. We will not, cannot permit it to be destroyed . . . come what will, should it cost every drop of blood."[14]

Calhoun was quick to realize that the antislavery societies proliferating throughout the North in the early 1830s could not be dismissed as a fringe movement. Unlike the debate in 1820, which involved sectional balance and was fueled by ambitious politicians with their own agendas, the demand now for emancipation was being forced on reluctant legislators by zealous reformers with energy, talent, and the power of the printed word at their disposal. An individual abolitionist leader like Garrison might still be an obscure figure nationally, but "the incessant action of hundreds of societies and a vast printing establishment, throwing out daily, thousands of artful inflammatory publications, must make in time a deep impression." The young particularly would be vulnerable, and the inevitable tendency over the years would be to build "the basis for a powerful political party" which would act as a lever to divide the Union. Calhoun repeatedly warned his Senate colleagues that they could not let emancipation become a party issue, and it was for this reason that he insisted the Senate refuse to receive abolitionist petitions. Abolitionists should not be allowed in the door. No matter that northern Senators agreed to join with the South to table the petitions after they were received; to recognize abolitionists as legitimate political actors would be fatal in the long run. "I have no doubt of the kind feelings of our brethren from the North, on this floor," Calhoun said, "but I clearly see that while we have their feelings in our favor, their constituents, right or wrong, will have their votes however we may be affected."[15]

Calhoun failed in his attempt to keep slavery off the national legislative agenda, and he spent much of the rest of his career trying to cope with the increasingly powerful political presence of the antislavery movement, which he predicted in 1836. In the process his already towering reputation soared in the South. He became a model for southerners needing to be reassured that slavery was not only protected by the Constitution but consistent with the republican faith of their fathers.

It was a foregone conclusion that the architect of nullification would find constitutional protections for slavery in the Constitution, which, without using the word, recognized the institution in many ways, including the famous provision which allowed each state to count every slave as three-fifths of a person in determining the size of its congressional delegation. Almost no one in the 1830s seriously believed that Congress could abolish slavery in the states without a constitutional amendment, which was a practical impossibility. For this reason antislavery activists seeking to attack slavery though the political system began to petition Congress to abolish slavery in the District of Columbia. Their strategy was based on the assumption that the Constitution guaranteed the right of petition and also gave Congress power to legislate "in all cases whatsoever" over the seat of the United States government. As we have seen, Calhoun tried in vain to derail this strategy on moral and political grounds, but he also included constitutional arguments pointing out that the right of petition was qualified. The Constitution prohibited Congress from passing a law abridging the right of petition; it did not guarantee every citizen the right to petition

Congress, and Calhoun provided examples from both the British and American tradition to show that petitions once sent to the legislature did not have to be received. He pursued the same legalistic tactics with respect to the District of Columbia, arguing that the right to legislate over the District could not mean the right to violate the Fifth Amendment by taking property away from citizens without their consent.

Calhoun's most impressive constitutional argument, of course, the one the South ultimately acted on, was the argument he had developed to rationalize nullification. His solution to the problem of abolitionist publications was simply to remind Senators that each state as a sovereign community had a right to pass laws protecting itself from the circulation of dangerous newspapers and pamphlets, and the federal government was constitutionally bound to respect such laws. His repeated warnings that abolitionist agitation could break the Union was based on the assumption, widely shared in the South and elsewhere even among those who opposed nullification, that secession was the action of last resort for any oppressed state.

As we have seen on many earlier occasions, it was never enough for Calhoun to believe that the law was on his side; he had to know that he was morally right. Thus arguments about slavery as a necessary evil did not appeal to him. Even the arguments about race and Providence did not completely satisfy. When he made the case for nullification, Calhoun had insisted it was not only right for South Carolina but a positive good for the Union as well. He apparently worked out a way to make the same case for slavery during the months after he read Dew's comments about the absence of a white underclass in the South. On February 8, 1834, Calhoun wrote his brother that some northerners, frightened by Jackson's exploitation of majority rule, were beginning to suspect "that they have more to fear from their own people than we from our slaves." One of these northerners may have been Whig Congressman Horace Binney. Years later Binney remembered that one morning in 1834 Calhoun had harangued him on the esplanade of the Capitol for two hours on the blessings of slavery. The thrust of his remarks was that in the North the poor and laboring masses would use the power of the ballot to create constant turmoil. Slavery cut off this evil at its root "by the denial of all political rights," leaving the whites "to pursue without apprehension the means they think best to elevate their own condition." Slavery therefore was "indispensable to republican government."[16]

Calhoun took this argument to the floor of the Senate in February 1837. In the course of the continuing debate on the reception of antislavery petitions, Senator William Rives of Virginia admitted that although he hated the misrepresentations of slavery in the petitions, he could not approve of slavery in principle. Calhoun was immediately on his feet. Here was the crux of the matter. If slavery was wrong, "the Senator as a wise and virtuous man, was bound to exert himself to put it down." To admit it was an evil was to fan the antislavery fire. Such an admission was both counterproductive and wrong in fact. "I take higher ground," Calhoun said. "I hold then that there never has yet existed a wealthy and civilized society in which one portion of the community did not in point of fact live on the labor of the other. . . . The devices are almost innumerable, from the brute force and gross superstition of ancient times to the subtle and artful fiscal contrivances of the modern. . . . It is useless to disguise the fact. There is and always has been in an advanced stage of wealth and civilization a conflict between labor and capital. The condition of society in the South exempts us from the disorders and dangers resulting from this conflict" and explains why the South has been more stable at a time of rapid growth when the "strength and durability" of republican institutions are "about to be tested."[17] In passing the message he had given Binney on to the Senate and the country at large, Calhoun was expressing a position he had always felt but had only recently been motivated to articulate. Historians have remarked that his belief in the inevitability of class struggle makes Calhoun sound like Marx defending the master class, but this is to miss the point that when Calhoun was growing up, the conflict and disorder that had characterized life in the Carolina backcountry along with the exploitation of that region by wealthy low-country planters had diminished with the growth of slavery. What slavery had done for Carolina it could do for the Union, but only if the South was allowed to get its own way. Unlike Marx, Calhoun did not believe in the necessity for revolution, nor did he believe with Jefferson that slavery was a fire bell in the night. Like most Americans of his generation, he continued to believe in the great mission of the United States; unlike an increasing number, he believed the key to that mission—a virtuous republic offering liberty, peace, and prosperity to its citizens and a model to the world—depended on the permanence of the labor system which a "mysterious Providence" had long ago wished upon the South. Slavery was the key to the success of the American dream.[18]

13

Outfoxing the Fox, 1836–1840

LTHOUGH Calhoun had once believed that the presidential election of 1836 would provide the capstone to his own political ambitions, the break with Jackson had turned him into a relatively uninterested bystander. Dismissing Van Buren out of hand as a political saboteur and intellectual mediocrity, he could not possibly support a Whig candidate now that the Whigs had tilted increasingly toward the abolitionists. In the end Calhoun was content to have South Carolina take the "principled" but lonely course of casting its eleven electoral votes for the relatively unknown North Carolina Senator Willie Mangum, while Van Buren handily defeated the Whigs, who had compounded their own problems by running three sectional candidates, Webster from New England, the war hero William Henry Harrison from the West, and the Tennesseean Hugh White from the South.

Returning to Pendleton in July 1836, Calhoun had little to say about the coming national elections and in the few public appearances that he made that summer concentrated instead on raising the consciousness of his state and section. Attending the commencement exercises at the University of Georgia, where his old mentor Moses Waddel was president, he warned the graduates that they might one day be asked to repel the attack of northern abolitionists with their muskets as well as their talents. Ironically enough, the student speaker at that ceremony was Howell Cobb, who later became Speaker of the U.S. House of Representatives and opposed Calhoun's attempt to build a southern party.[1]

Calhoun's primary political concerns that summer of 1836 were directed to the behavior of his own state. Encouraged during the late session of Congress with the way most southerners had mobilized to fight the threat of abolitionist petitions, Calhoun had been astounded and mortified to learn that a member of his own delegation, probably with Van Buren's blessing, had pushed through a series of resolutions in the House which succeeded in tabling the petitions but yielded the vital principle that Congress had no constitutional right to abolish slavery in the District of Columbia. Although Calhoun had gone to great lengths in the Senate to demonstrate that the congressional right to legislate over the District could not include the right to confiscate property in slaves, the Charleston Representative Henry Pinckney had not been listening. Pinckney would have to go, and he did when Hugh Legaré, more poet than politician, unseated him in the fall elections. As Joel Poinsett explained the matter to a member of Jackson's administration, Pinckney had "rebelled against the supremacy and the dictation of J. C. Calhoun and must be sacrificed." The lesson here was that although Calhoun might be content to lead a minority in the Senate, he expected near-unanimous support at home, an expectation that would be sorely tried as the government passed from Andrew Jackson to Martin Van Buren.[2]

Calhoun seemed to take Pinckney's demise as a matter of course while he concentrated on matters closer at hand, like the gold mine in Dahlonega and his own harvests, which were poor even though the cotton market was strong. He could hardly escape the fact that both he and his family were getting older. Andrew had married again, this time the daughter of Calhoun's devoted friend Duff Green. The marriage had taken place in Washington before the spring recess, and Andrew and Margaret Green Calhoun were making their home at Fort Hill while Andrew continued his search for a plantation which he hoped to purchase with dowry money and the help of his father. Patrick, Calhoun's second oldest son, was recovering from being kicked by a horse and prepping for West Point. The twelve-year-old Cornelia, a semi-invalid, was busy with her needle and her books, and the three boys, James, John, and Willy, were spending most of their time hunting and fishing.

The one member of the family conspicuous by her absence was Anna, who had parted from her father in Washington to take a tour of the northern states with Senator William C. Preston and his wife. Anna had proved to be not only a great help to her father but a great hit in Washington society as well. Ever since her appearance Calhoun had shunned the reclusive ways he had favored while living alone in a temperance boardinghouse. Once Floride decided to stay in Pendleton with the rest of her family, Calhoun and Anna became a familiar sight at the ballrooms, dinners, receptions, and teas that made up the the capital's social regimen. Missing his daughter badly that summer, Calhoun eagerly awaited her enthusiastic letters from such northern tourist attractions as Niagara Falls.

Never on very good terms with the ocean, Calhoun was essentially a mountain person. The sight of the lofty Blue Ridge peaks from his own doorstep was a constant tonic to him, and he frequently studied them with a telescope. The mountains also represented a challenge with powerful political implications. Calhoun knew that no matter who claimed the White House that November, the long-term political health of the South would depend on an alliance with the West and such an alliance would be almost impossible without better physical lines of communication between the two sections. In his younger days he had seen the necessity of conquering space to make the Union strong; now he saw its importance as a way to save the South. This would mean finding a rail route through the Appalachians which would eventually link cities like Charleston with growing metropolises in the West like Louisville and Cincinnati. With Colonel James Gadsden, an old friend from War Department days, Calhoun set out to find such a route in September 1836. After nine days of "incessant activity" fording streams and clambering in and out of mountain gorges, he wrote his brother-in-law that he had found a route with tolerable grades through a hitherto-overlooked break in the mountains, which he called the Carolina Gap, near the borders of Georgia and North and South Carolina. Calhoun published a detailed account of his discovery in the *Pendleton Messenger* which helped launch the organization of the Louisville, Cincinnati & Charleston Railroad. Becoming a director of the railroad, Calhoun soon found himself in a dispute with opposing factions pushing alternate routes and was embarrassed to find himself at odds with his old friend Robert Hayne. Acting with his customary certainty, Calhoun campaigned vigorously for his route, but the project fizzled after a few years, partly because the panic of the next year dried up the federal surplus that Calhoun thought could be made available to help pay for such a road and partly because the southern leaders failed to reach an agreement. The latter was to be a familiar story for the rest of Calhoun's career.[3]

Calhoun returned to Washington in December 1836 with mixed feelings. On the one hand, Van Buren had been elected. On the other hand, he could approach the coming congressional session knowing that it would see the end of Jackson's long tenure in the White House. Determined to make the President's passage into retirement as painful as possible, Calhoun ardently opposed the administration's final initiatives. To vote Arkansas and Michigan into the Union at the last minute was wrong, he said, because it was a device to get four more electoral votes for Van Buren. To expunge the censure of Jackson from the *Senate Journal,* as Benton and the Democratic majority did on January 15, 1837, was not only a "contemptible sophistry" but an act originating in "pure, inimical personal idolatry. It is the melancholy evidence of a broken spirit ready to bow at the feet of power." Finally, on February 4, while arguing that Jackson's action in removing the federal deposits had encouraged pet banks to fund the uncontrolled speculation in public lands then sweeping the nation, Calhoun implied that the President himself was participating in the spoils. "Does any man here entertain a doubt," Calhoun asked, "that high officers of government have used those deposits as instruments of speculation in the public lands? Is not the fact notorious? Is not one in the immediate neighborhood of the Executive among those the most deeply concerned?"[4]

Outraged by the accusation, Jackson fired off a letter denying "the imputations you have cast upon me" and demanding proof or a retraction. Calhoun read the letter to the Senate on February 9 and named John McLemore, Jackson's nephew, as the person to whom he had meant to refer. He then went on to condemn the President for attempting to intimidate a Senator exercising a constitutional privilege. "I hold myself," Calhoun said, "at least equal to the Chief Magistrate himself. I as a legislator have a right to investigate and pronounce on his conduct. . . . I as a Senator may judge him; he can never judge me."[5]

It was the final act in a personal encounter that had been going on at the highest levels of government for years—between the general and the Secretary, the President and the Vice President, the President and the Senator. Calhoun as usual fired the last shot—and missed.

In reporting the event to James Henry Hammond, then traveling in Europe, Calhoun boasted: "My triumph was complete. His [Jackson's] friends in the Senate hung their heads in dumb silence." A more likely explanation for the Senators' silence was embarrassment at the display of personal rancor between two of the most esteemed men in American public life.[6]

Calhoun was obviously frustrated and angry at a turn of events which allowed Jackson to leave the White House as the most acclaimed President since Washington. That a second-rate henchman like Van Buren should be the handpicked successor made a bad situation even worse, and Calhoun could not resist lecturing the Senate about that on the eve of Van Buren's inauguration. The occasion was a bill introduced by Van Buren's lieutenant Silas Wright to reduce certain tariff duties. Calhoun's initial response was conservative and statesmanlike. Reminding his southern colleagues that they had struck a bargain on the tariff in 1833, he warned them that any lowering of duties now beyond what was called for in that agreement could lead to damaging increases in the future. Southern states constituted a permanent minority; the Compromise of 1833 was in their long-term interest, and they should do nothing to make the North and West believe they were giving it up now. In the course of his remarks Calhoun managed to blame the infamous Tariff of 1828 on Van Buren, and when Senator Rives suggested that Van Buren as a "practical politician" now sought to reduce tariffs in a way that would not injure any section, Calhoun found the opportunity he was waiting for. A practical politician, he said, was one who spurned principle to act in every instance "as expediency may require," to play other politicians off against one another or, if necessary, to curry the favor of a powerful leader by "skillfully playing" upon his vanity. The point was not lost on the Senators; Calhoun was calling the man about to be inaugurated as the eighth President of the United States an American Machiavelli. Such an indictment was music to Whig ears, but many of Calhoun's colleagues believed that he was simply acting out the role of the rejected suitor, and some of them at least could sympathize with what Senator Bedford Brown of North Carolina had earlier said when he complained about the "contemptible vanity and overweening egotism" sometimes displayed on the Senate floor.[7]

Although Calhoun did not record his impressions at Van Buren's inauguration, he could not have missed the ill omens which accompanied it. Van Buren's running mate, Richard Mentor Johnson, who had failed to get an electoral majority largely because of his notorious predilection for black mistresses, had to be elected by a voice vote in the Senate. This was the same Johnson who with his brother had practically bankrupted the War Department during the disastrous Yellowstone Expedition. The fact that this man, whose political popularity depended on his having allegedly killed the Indian chief Tecumseh, in hand-to-hand combat at the Battle of the Thames twenty-five years earlier, was now a heartbeat away from the Presidency, could only have confirmed Calhoun's darkest convictions about the growing corruption in American public life. "There is no instance on record," he wrote his friend Ingham two months later, "of so sudden a degeneracy of a people as that of ours within the last twelve years."[8]

Meanwhile, Americans everywhere who might not have understood what Calhoun meant by the degeneracy of civic virtue could see that their own prosperity was in danger. Speculation and crop shortages were driving rents and food prices sky high in eastern cities; the frenzied trading in western lands with borrowed money was building a bubble that was bound to burst, and no one had much faith in the ability of the banking system to ward off disaster. A few days after Van Buren's inauguration I. & L. Joseph, one of the biggest commercial houses in New York, failed, triggering a European rush to call in American loans and jeopardizing the solvency of countless state banks. On May 10 New York banks stopped payment in specie, threatening some fifty thousand investors, and soon banks all over the country followed suit. The Panic of 1837 was under way.

Calhoun, back in Pendleton for the congressional recess, watched the crisis develop with a certain grim satisfaction, and as he rode out into his fields from Fort Hill or tramped the nearby mountains searching for a southwestern railroad route, he pondered his own political future. Van Buren would not be another Jackson. He came into office "very weak" and might be "easily crushed with anything like a vigorous effort." In this situation what role was proper for the nullifiers? He was not tempted, as Duff Green suggested, to throw in completely with the Whigs and cast the Democrats out because, as he reminded Green, the

Whigs might be anti-Jackson, but they were also anti-states' rights. Green thought that Calhoun's route to the presidency lay through Henry Clay and that Calhoun's insistence on going his own way was based on an exaggerated estimate of his own power. Calhoun, who disapproved of his zealous friend's willingness to run with the most available candidate no matter what the principles, tried to explain his position once again. "Nothing can raise me short of saving the country from convulsions," and if this meant courting unpopularity, Calhoun would "stand alone" in his own "glory."[9]

However important it may have been for Calhoun to reaffirm his political rectitude, he had no serious intention of standing alone and was already preparing to rejoin the Democrats with the hope of restoring the party to its pre-Jackson purity. But first he would have to come to terms with Van Buren. Not only did Calhoun dislike Van Buren personally for his alleged part in turning Jackson against him, but he also deeply resented the fact that a man like Van Buren could actually sit in the White House, and his resentment had spilled over on the Senate floor on more than one occasion, most notably on February 17, 1836, when Van Buren, still Vice President, was presiding. Calhoun was delivering one of his familiar lectures on recent political history to show how Jackson had used patronage and the nullification crisis to create an executive party which split the South and made an effective opposition party impossible. However, Calhoun said, anyone expecting that the "President's nominee" could successfully play Jackson's game would be "woefully mistaken." Jackson, for all his faults, was a man of courage and boldness who had served the country "gloriously" in war, but "his nominee" (by this time every Senator must have had his eye on Van Buren) "was not of the race of the lion or the tiger; he belonged to a lower order—the fox; and it would be in vain to expect that he could command the respect or acquire the confidence of those who had so little admiration for the qualities by which he was distinguished." Van Buren, famous for his composure, never flinched, but he must have felt the sting of this studied insult and the warning which lay behind it.[10]

After such boasting less than two years earlier, how could Calhoun now think of joining ranks with Van Buren without being accused of trying to outfox the fox? In his authorized biography published in 1843

Calhoun explained his shifts in party allegiance by claiming that his "statesmanship" led him to take the "nearest practicable step toward his object, instead of refusing to do anything unless he could effect what was best in the abstract." In other words, Calhoun's goals were fixed, but the means of attaining them frequently became "questions of expediency, to be determined by the circumstances under which he is called to act." Neither Van Buren nor any other of Calhoun's Machiavellian rivals could have read these words with a straight face.[11]

By September 1837, when the President revealed his plan to cope with the panic, Calhoun had come to believe that circumstances required him to consider some kind of rapprochement with the fox. Calhoun had led the nullifiers into a temporary alliance with the Whigs to contest executive usurpation under Jackson. Now Jackson was gone, but the Whigs remained committed to a strong national government. Meanwhile, Van Buren had inherited along with the presidency a fiscal crisis which divided his own party between hard-money, no-bank radicals and soft-money conservatives who believed that some kind of tie between government and banks was essential. While this split was developing, the Whigs continued to support the old Bank of the United States. Given the three-way political split, Calhoun and the nullifiers could swing the balance toward Van Buren if they chose, and this is what lay behind Calhoun's remark to his brother-in-law, as the special session of Congress began in early September, that Van Buren had been forced "to play directly into our hands, and I am determined that he shall not escape from us."[12]

To comprehend Calhoun's political behavior from 1837 through 1840, we need to understand the difference between his ultimate purpose and his strategic short-term goals. The purpose was to protect South Carolina and the rest of the South by maintaining states' rights principles and to keep the possibility open for his own advancement to the presidency. The strategy would lead Calhoun to defend Van Buren's controversial fiscal policy, to force the Senate into taking an official antiabolitionist posture, and to demand political orthodoxy in his own state. He would accomplish it all in a masterful display of guile and power, showing that for once at least, Calhoun could be both the lion and the fox.

Calhoun believed that Jackson had caused the panic by putting the

Calhoun at the height of his campaign against Jackson, c. 1837.

Frontispiece Volume Thirteen of the Calhoun papers. National Portrait Gallery

federal deposits in favored state banks, which used them to inflate the currency and support speculation in western lands. When Jackson compounded his first mistake by issuing the specie circular which required payment for public lands in hard money, specie was drained from the East, and banks and commercial houses began to fail. Many of Jackson's critics shared the explanation which Calhoun argued so forcefully, and it became the standard historical interpretation. Historians today emphasize a more complex, international interpretation for the panic, in which foreign trade and the expansion and contraction of British investment in state transportation systems played a decisive role. According to this view, the United States, a new nation with a relatively small, developing economy, was plunged into a depression not by a blundering leader but by the capricious movement of economic forces in the larger world over which it had little control. Although Van Buren seems to have understood the actual situation better than Calhoun, he was still hard pressed to find a way of leading the country out of the depression, and he devoted his message to Congress in early September 1837 to a series of controversial recommendations designed to bring his divided party together. Calling for an issue of Treasury notes and other measures to help businesses starved for cash, the President's most innovative proposal provided for the complete separation of the government from the banks by creating what was eventually called a subtreasury system. The proposal was designed to appeal to the enemies of the Bank of the United States so effectively mobilized by Jackson.[13]

Calhoun had decided even before Van Buren's message that he would support a fiscal system in which the Treasury kept all the federal money in its own vaults and made all of its disbursements and collections without any connection to state or federal banks. He had come to believe that every federal government-bank connection was inherently opposed to the states' rights principle because it invited favoritism, bribery, and the consolidation of federal power. Although he respected the way Biddle had conducted the Bank of the United States, he had defended that bank not because it was right in principle but because Jackson was wrong in his arbitrary treatment of it.

Calhoun was willing to support Van Buren's plan for an independent Treasury, but when he did so in a speech on September 18, it was characteristically on his own terms—by offering a hard-money amendment requiring the Treasury to take nothing but specie from state banks after 1840. Although the amendment deepened the split between soft-money and hard-money Democrats, the administration supported it, and the amended bill passed the Senate in a close vote, only to fail in the House. Meanwhile, the Whigs swamped the Democrats in several state elections, including New York, where they swept the House by the astonishing margin of 121 to 27.[14]

Whig leaders divided their energies between rejoicing over the administration's reversals and gnashing their teeth at Calhoun's defection. William Henry Seward, a promising young Whig politician from New York, reported how "grieved" he was to see one of "the great names I have venerated as superior in worth and magnanimity destroy all those hopes the years had gathered round him." The prevailing view among the Whigs, however, was more cynical. One Congressman claimed that Calhoun was "less to be relied upon than any politician in modern times," and another observer, who had studied Aaron Burr's career, hypothesized that Calhoun was positioning himself to inherit the throne "should it be necessary for Mr. Van Buren to abdicate."[15]

Calhoun himself was in high spirits, cordial to the Democrats he had so recently excoriated, and, much to the amusement of some of them, acting as if *they* were the ones who should be welcomed back to the party. "Mr. Calhoun is designed to be social and communicative," wrote Joel Poinsett, the new Secretary of War. "We have, as he said, come on his ground and he shall therefore not emigrate, but abide with us. He rejoices at having left the *Nationals* and being more united with the Democracy."[16]

No doubt Calhoun was happy to find himself back in company with the party with a traditional states' rights bias, but he was even happier in the knowledge that he once again could wield real political power. "My situation was extraordinary," he confided to his daughter. "I held the fate of the country by the confession of all in my hand, and had to determine in what direction I should turn events hereafter. . . . The decision has embittered the national Republican party against me, but for that I care little." What is really extraordinary is not the situation Calhoun described but the exaggerated rhetoric he employed, which perhaps helps explain why Duff Green could accuse him of persistently overrating his political power. Calhoun's assertion about controlling the fate of the country expressed his emotional release at leaving behind the years of isolation when he had railed so futilely against the power of Jackson. Friends and foes alike, however, would have agreed that he had regained his position as a powerful political player. Thomas Ritchie, the influential Richmond editor, proclaimed that Calhoun would save Van Buren, and a Democrat in Jackson, Tennessee, spoke for the hopes of party workers everywhere when he predicted nine-tenths of the nullifiers in his district were now behind the President's Treasury bill.[17]

Although the battle for an independent Treasury was not won for several months, Calhoun was able to demonstrate his considerable political influence in other ways during the winter of 1837–1838. Unlike most Democrats, he found a direct link between the administration's fiscal policy and the defense of slavery. Calhoun advocated a complete separation between the federal government and the banks because he believed that any such connection inevitably centralized economic and political power which could one day be used by an antislavery majority to destroy the South's most valuable institution. Calhoun also believed that the marriage between Whiggery and abolitionism was only a matter of time, all of which added up to the critical importance of forcing the Democrats to take an explicit position against antislavery agitation. Since Democratic party leaders instinctively recoiled from any overture which might split the party along sectional lines, they would have to be pushed. Calhoun started the pushing on December 27, 1837, when he asked the Senate to consider six resolutions designed to protect slavery in the South.

The resolutions stated: first, that the Constitution was adopted by sovereign states wanting to increase their own security; second, that these states retained exclusive rights over their own domestic institutions; third, that the federal government as the agent of the states had a duty to resist the attempts of any part of the Union to use the government as an instrument to attack the domestic institutions of another part; fourth, that "open and systematic attacks" on slavery violated the spirit of the constitutional compact; fifth, that the "intermeddling" by states or citizens or the passage of a congressional act interfering with slavery in the District of Columbia or the territories would be considered a direct attack on the slaveholding states; sixth, that any attempt to prevent the annexation of new territory or states because it might extend the area of slavery (for example, the annexation of Texas) would violate the constitutional rights of the slaveholding states.[18]

For the next two weeks Calhoun forced his obviously discomfited colleagues to debate the issues raised in these resolutions. The question was no longer whether slavery was right or wrong but what the Senate would do to protect the South. Calhoun made sure his colleagues understood what was at stake. Those who voted against the resolutions would go on record as "throwing down all constitutional barriers in the way of the abolitionists." Those who voted for them would support constitutional liberty and the Union.

Politicians are notoriously reluctant to express definite opinions about divisive, "no-win" issues, and Calhoun's colleagues were no exception, but they were up against more than the will of one man. Senator Rives of Virginia, who had been chastised by Calhoun in an earlier debate over slavery and who also opposed him on fiscal policy, complained that the Senate had become mired "in the most schoolboyish scene I have ever witnessed in a Legislative body—disputing about the *abstractions* invoked in Mr. Calhoun's resolutions. It is a most unprofitable as well as undignified mischievous discussion, and yet such is the great anxiety of the administration people to conciliate Mr. Calhoun, on whom they rely for the whole South . . . that they blindly follow his lead."[19]

By the end of the second week in January Calhoun had beaten off or watered down most amendments and defeated all attempts to commit his resolutions to committee. Raising the specter of fifteen hundred abolitionist societies in the North poised to wage war on nine hundred million dollars of southern property, Calhoun even admitted that he had been wrong in accepting the Missouri Compromise seventeen years earlier. By mid-January he could count his victory. The first four resolutions were passed with heavy majorities, the fifth passed in amended form to emphasize the undesirability rather than the unconstitutionality of legislating on slavery in the District and the territories, and the sixth was tabled. Calhoun had a right to be proud of the result. He had forced the Senate to do something it would probably never have done without his prodding, and he had gone a long way toward making the Democrats a party committed to defend slavery and the South.[20]

The Van Buren regulars had supported Calhoun's slavery resolutions because they needed and expected his continuing support for the administration's subtreasury proposal, a slightly modified version of the legislation Calhoun had helped get through the Senate in the fall of 1837. Calhoun obliged the Democrats with a long (two hours and ten minutes) speech on February 15, 1838, which argued for the subtreasury as an example of good policy based on solid republican principles. Pointing out that opponents of the administration were now favoring a system of state banks rather than a Bank of the United States, Calhoun noted how often politicians were "compelled to vary our course in order to preserve our principles." The Whigs had been forced to support state banks in the hope ultimately of reviving a great national bank. Calhoun, who had once supported an established national bank in order to fight executive tyranny, now sought to divorce banks from the federal government in order to fight the consolidation of federal power. He could see that the only possible constitutional justification for a federally sponsored system of state banks was under a "loose and dangerous" interpretation of the general welfare clause which, if admitted in principle, could quickly lead to the passage of antislavery laws. Extending his argument, Calhoun held that if sponsored banks were not constitutional, then the government could not regulate the bank notes issued by these banks. Here Calhoun distinguished between money and currency, insisting that gold and silver were "the only money known to the Constitution." He had returned to the ranks of the hard-money Democrats.

Toward the end of his speech Calhoun clarified what he had meant some weeks earlier when he told Poinsett that the administration had "come on his ground" and would be welcomed. Any alliance between government and the banks would become bloated and powerful, he said, with unlimited control over the commerce of the country. Bankers given the use of the public's money would always conspire to get more of it; taxes would increase along with patronage. "Violence and coercion are no longer the instruments of government in civilized communities," he maintained. "Everything is now done by money. It is not only the sinew of war, but of politics, over which in the form of patronage it exercises almost unlimited control." Contrasting this insatiable antirepublican monster with the frugality of a government which would transact all its business out of four federal depositories staffed by a handful of clerks, Calhoun insisted that the Treasury bill, like the principle of nullification, could restore "the Constitution and country to their primitive simplicity and purity."[21]

Calhoun obviously wanted the subtreasury speech to justify his departure from the Whigs, and he uncharacteristically spent several days revising it for publication. The published version would be more condensed than the spoken address, he told his daughter, "for I find that I can crowd more ideas together on paper." The statement is revealing and may help explain why reading Calhoun's speeches rarely seems to measure up to the actual experience reported by his auditors.[22]

Although Calhoun had found Clay and Webster to be stubborn opponents of his slavery resolutions, the heavy trouble with these parliamentary giants came after his powerful defense of the subtreasury proposal. Clay responded four days later with a scathing attack emphasizing Calhoun's inconsistencies on policy matters and his betrayal of the Whigs. Calhoun assured his daughter that Clay's speech had been "very feeble and personal," but he spent two weeks preparing a rebuttal, which he delivered on March 10. Less than a fortnight later Webster joined the debate, which became a round robin of recrimination, innuendo, and self-justification, most of which had been said before but needed repeating in order to appease the monumental egos involved. Every partisan in Washington was sure his man had won, but James Fenimore Cooper, who listened to part of the debate, deplored the pettiness and "pitiful wrangling" which diverted the Senate from more serious business.[23]

As it turned out, the battle of the titans had little effect on the legislation immediately in question, and when the Senate finally passed the subtreasury bill, Calhoun voted against it because his special clause, which would have required the government to deal only in specie, was removed. This vote, which had no effect on the outcome, was characteristic of Calhoun's scorn for party loyalty, but the Whigs continued to regard him as their chief adversary. Complaining that he had never before been "so closely occupied since I have been in publick life," Calhoun claimed that "the whole opposition seem to think that they had nothing to do but overthrow me, in order to defeat the subtreasury." Webster, meanwhile, told Biddle that the Carolinian was making a superhuman effort to line up southern votes and that his "plausibility & endless perseverance" were accomplishing "more than I thought possible."[24]

In June 1838 the House once again defeated the bill, and it was not until February 21, 1839, that the administration resolved the issue by pushing through a law under a different name legitimizing the temporary holding of government funds in the Treasury—a practice that had been in effect since the panic began. Calhoun again voted no, preferring, as he said, "to stand on my own responsibilities" rather than accept anything but a formal separation between the government and the banks.

One of the reasons Calhoun felt so hard pressed during the Van Buren administration was the inability of South Carolina to keep in step as he weaved back and forth between the Whigs and the Democrats. When, after his earlier eloquent defense of Biddle's Bank, Calhoun suddenly switched to support the administration's independent Treasury system, long-standing Calhoun stalwarts like Hayne, Hamilton, Pierce Butler, William C. Preston, and Waddy Thompson were horrified. Seven of the nine members in the South Carolina congressional delegation refused to go along, and even the doggedly loyal McDuffie wavered. Calhoun found himself facing the unthinkable: an emerging Whig Party in his own state, as members of the old Federalist elite, like the Draytons and Pringles, joined hands with unionists like Petigru and Legaré and bankers and merchants in Charleston combined with great cotton planters like the Hamptons and up-country planters interested in internal improvements, to oppose Calhoun's alliance with the Democrats. In a state in which public opinion traditionally deferred to the elite, defection on this scale could not be tolerated.[25]

In Calhoun's mind the great danger was that South Carolina politics would become a battleground for Democrats and Whigs rather than a bastion for the old republicanism which he would always identify with nullification. When a friendly Carolina editor suggested that the state might be well advised to elect its governor by popular vote rather than through the legislature, Calhoun emphatically rejected the notion because he believed a popular contest would inevitably increase the possibilities for patronage, divide the people, and lead to "violent par-

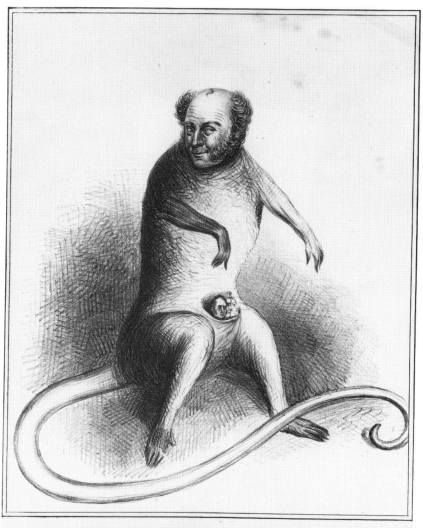

AN · INTERESTING · FAMILY.

Cartoon depicting Webster, Clay, and Calhoun in Van Buren's pocket.
Mid-1830s.

Courtesy of the Smithsonian Institution of American Art

ties," thus destroying the united front South Carolina had hitherto presented to the rest of the Union.[26]

Calhoun could count on the *Charleston Mercury* under John A. Stuart to put down the incipient Whig uprising, and he hoped that a new paper, the *Washington Reformer,* edited by Richard Crallé, would help spread the word. His old adversary, Frank Blair of the *Globe,* had recently become more friendly, but that might do more harm than good in the eyes of unforgiving nullifiers in South Carolina. Calhoun knew that if he wanted to bring the state around, he would have to rely mostly on himself, and on November 3, 1837, he published a letter of explanation in the *Edgefield Advertiser* which was really intended for all the citizens in the state. The letter is interesting stylistically for what must surely have been an intentional redundancy in the use of the words "clear" and "embarrass." Calhoun emphasized that the special congressional session had clearly demonstrated the success of the nullifiers' arguments against executive tyranny. Then it was clear that they could unite with the Whigs to crush the Democrats, clear that the time had come to restore that party to its pre-1828 purity. He also emphasized how embarrassed he was to support the Whig "nationals," embarrassed to keep company with protectionists, embarrassed to support men who wanted to reinstate the unholy government-bank alliance. When, therefore, the new Democrats offered a program to separate the banks from the government, Calhoun recognized "the only opportunity we could have of rallying anew the old States'-Rights Party of 1827." Calhoun was telling his constituents that they had been right ever since 1827 but had been forced by the apostasy of Jackson into a temporary and embarrassing alliance with the Whigs. Now they could come home. And they did; a month after his Edgefield letter the state legislature gave Calhoun an overwhelming vote of confidence.[27]

There was still some mopping up to do. Calhoun knew that Preston, just beginning his term in the Senate, would have to be tolerated, but he was determined to purge Waddy Thompson and Legaré in the 1838 elections. Thompson was a particular problem because he came from Calhoun's district. Knowing that letters to the newspaper would not dispose of Thompson, a tough, outspoken lawyer and popular militia officer in the mountain country around Greenville, Calhoun took to the stump for the first time in years. In the summer and fall of 1838 he met Thompson three times before raucous crowds of fifteen hundred or more in debates which Thompson later recalled lasted "seven hours each." Tempers ran high. Calhoun called Thompson a liar, and there was a public exchange of letters before a duel was averted. In the end Thompson won because as Calhoun sourly remarked to Duff Green, he was able to exploit his militia ties "and cried out dictation and persecution." In Charleston, however, Hugh Legaré, with none of Thompson's considerable campaigning skills, was defeated and mortified. "Who is Calhoun," he asked bitterly, "that I should be considered a cheap oblation to propitiate his offended dignity?" Later that winter the temperamental Legaré snubbed Calhoun on the Capitol steps.[28]

Although Legaré had been a unionist, he was purged because he refused to tow the line on the Treasury issue. Knowing that any revival of the unionist-nullifier struggle would be disastrous, Calhoun quietly supported the former unionist J. P. Richardson for governor in 1840. This brought him into sharp conflict with the ambitious James Henry Hammond, who wanted the job himself. Hammond asked for Calhoun's endorsement but to his disgust received instead a lecture on the importance of unity and the danger of party division in the state. Under protest Hammond sulkily accepted Richardson as governor. Unlike Legaré, Thompson, and Preston, he did not break away to the Whigs, but he never completely trusted Calhoun again.[29]

At the same time that he was forging political unity at home, Calhoun was moving to dramatize the power he and his followers could muster in Congress, and on December 16, 1839, the Calhoun faction in the House of Representatives deliberately and abruptly shifted its support from the Democrats to the Whigs to make the Virginian Robert M. T. Hunter Speaker of the House. A nominal Whig, Hunter was an outspoken states' rights man and a Calhoun supporter. By putting his own man in the Speaker's chair, Calhoun was sending more signals to Van Buren. One signal was that the President could accomplish little without Calhoun's help. The other was that Hunter could be relied on to help establish an independent Treasury. A third signal was that the time may have come for a reconciliation. Despite being perceived as a Democratic leader in the Senate, Calhoun maintained that his personal estrangement from Van Buren remained unchanged. "I have not been in the President's House," he told a friend on October

26, 1838, "nor had any intercourse with him directly or indirectly in eight years." Sometime in late December 1839 that situation changed when Calhoun responded to an invitation relayed by Senator William H. Roane of Virginia and called on the President at the White House. The interview was brief, formal, and cold. Calhoun said that he "simply intended to remove the awkwardness of defending the political measures and course of one with whom I was not on speaking terms." Van Buren said little, wondering no doubt about the vagaries of a political culture that required him, even temporarily, to identify his own political fortune with that of this stiff-necked, unforgiving visitor who detested him. Calhoun's public appearance at a White House reception on New Year's Day notified the world that the political breach with Van Buren was officially closed.[30]

A week after his White House visit Calhoun wrote a letter to the *Charleston Mercury* saying, "I am no aspirant to the Presidency, or ever expect to be. . . . All who know me know that there is not a member of Congress who takes less interest" in such matters. In fact, the Congress was loaded with men convinced that Calhoun remained as passionate an aspirant to the White House as any man alive. Webster and Clay certainly did, and began hammering away at his opportunism almost as soon as the news broke about the reconciliation with Van Buren. William C. Preston, who had watched Calhoun closely over the years, thought that the détente with the President was a very temporary thing and that he would switch to the Whig candidate William Henry Harrison at the last minute, "believing it will be easier to come in after Harrison than after Van Buren." This cynical judgment, which demonstrates how deeply Calhoun was distrusted by some of those who thought they knew him well, was certainly mistaken because Calhoun was convinced that a Whig victory would be a victory for abolitionism. "Have they lost all Southern feelings?" he asked regarding potential Harrison voters in the South. "Are they dead to their own safety, and that of family, kindred and section?" A vote for the Whigs, Calhoun repeatedly said, was not just a vote for banks and consolidation; it was a vote for antislavery fanaticism.[31]

On the other hand, Calhoun could say that "time, which tests all things, acts in my favor." By this he meant that whatever the outcome in 1840 his own prospects for the future would improve. A victorious

Van Buren would have to cooperate with the states' rights party; a victorious Harrison could create a rush of unhappy Democrats and southern Whigs to rally under a new banner. In either event Calhoun would be ready.[32]

As he watched the campaign develop, Calhoun must have been glad that he was not a candidate. How could he have competed in the "coonskin saturnalia" of 1840 in which a man's log cabin lineage and his ability to consume vast quantities of hard cider counted for more than his ability to expound the Constitution? Nevertheless, he thought Van Buren would win and was surprised when the Whigs swept both the Congress and the presidency that fall. Surprised but not despairing. Most historians have interpreted the Whig victory as a prime example of the emergence of a new democratic style in American politics. For Calhoun it was an example of "a deep principle of retributive justice"; the sins of Andrew Jackson had returned to haunt his followers. Although he had signed on again with the Democrats, he felt untouched by their defeat. "Individually I have nothing to regret," he assured his son; "their fall illustrates the truth and correctness of my course for the last 15 years."[33]

14

The Iron Man at Home

B
Y THE END of the 1830s Harriet Martineau's caricature of Calhoun as the "cast-iron man" seemed increasingly plausible to many Americans. Those who never met the man and viewed the political battles in Washington from afar, whether they looked at Calhoun through Whig or Democratic eyes, tended to see a politician who always seemed to be on his own, a Vice President who had come into open conflict with two successive Presidents, a nationalist turned nullifier, a free-lance Senator playing one party off against the other, a friend of Biddle but an enemy of the Bank. For many Americans Calhoun appeared as a kind of maverick locomotive force in American public life, who frequently failed to reach his destination but nevertheless seemed unstoppable.

Caricatures and stereotypes are usually both true and false, but they never do full justice to human beings. There are no cast-iron men, and there is overwhelming evidence in the Calhoun papers that men and women who knew Calhoun personally or met him socially respected and liked the man. However, even close associates could be put off by his single-mindedness and intensity. Dixon Lewis, for example, the states' rights Congressman from Alabama who worked closely with Calhoun in 1840, complained that he needed more congenial companionship. "Calhoun is now my principal associate," he wrote Richard Crallé, and is "too intellectual, too industrious, too intent in the struggle of politics to suit me except as an occasional companion. There is no *relaxation* with him." After living in a Washington boardinghouse with Calhoun during the nullification years Mrs. William C. Preston decided that if Calhoun had been seated next to her at the table and had asked about her family and she had reported a child on the point of death, "Mr. Calhoun would have exclaimed, 'Ah, but as I was saying, the concurrent majority, etc. etc' & neither you or yours would possess his ear or heart a minute."[1]

Although Calhoun was definitely not the one-track person suggested by Martineau and Mrs. Preston, he was, like many high achievers, remarkably focused. He was really a three-track person. One track was politics, which to Calhoun meant political science and morality rather than the art of obtaining office. A second track led to family, and a third to his life as a planter. Those who knew Calhoun primarily as a husband and father, for example, saw a side of the man the public rarely glimpsed.

Eighteen forty marked the twenty-ninth year of Calhoun's marriage to his cousin Floride. Although it had not been an idyllic marriage, Margaret Coit overstates the case when she likens Floride Bonneau Calhoun to Mary Todd Lincoln as one of the most "baffling or stormy" figures in the history of American political wives. Whatever her faults, Floride had performed her most important wifely duty heroically, bearing ten children, seven of whom survived her husband. Since Calhoun was away from home on average about five months out of every twelve, Floride spent much of her first three decades of married life alone, coping with pregnancy, child care, and the multitudinous other responsibilities attached to the role of plantation mistress.[2]

Calhoun had not planned on this kind of marriage. During the early years of his career, when he and Floride made their South Carolina home at the relatively small Bath plantation on the banks of the Savannah, he had apparently envisaged maintaining permanent residences in Washington and in Carolina, and his mother-in-law had purchased Oakly in Georgetown to provide a summer residence near the capital for her daughter and son-in-law. The years when Calhoun was Secretary of War and the two Florides had served as comistresses of Oakly, entertaining lavishly and maintaining a house that was the envy of Washington society, were probably the happiest years in his marriage. Childbearing had not yet taken the bloom of youth away from Floride, who seemed to many a suitable mate for the "young Hercules" with a seemingly limitless future.

The Washington idyll ended for the Calhouns after the election of 1824, and after moving to Fort Hill, where she was close to her mother and two brothers, Floride became increasingly reluctant to accompany her husband to Washington. The exception she made to that rule after Calhoun became Jackson's Vice President and a colleague to Peggy Eaton's husband, only reinforced her feeling that the capital city had become alien territory.

Floride had been a catalyst for the opposition to Peggy Eaton which eventually turned Jackson's Cabinet into a snake pit and helped poison her husband's relationship with the President. Although Calhoun defended his wife's role in this business, he must have wondered if the political price he would have to pay was necessary. Despite Floride's many merits as a mother and a southern lady, she was not cut out to be the kind of wife who could share in his career. That is perhaps what Webster was getting at in 1825 when he told George Ticknor that Calhoun had "talked to me among other things, of your good fortune in picking up a *companion* on the road of life." Calhoun later found this companionship in his daughter, but it was always a source of regret that Floride took so little interest in politics.[3]

Forty years ago Margaret Coit discovered that the unresolved tensions in Calhoun's marriage still held a place in family and local traditions. There were stories of Floride's tantrums, dishes flying through the air, flowers planted by the master's hand ruthlessly uprooted, the mistress of the house refusing to receive the master's guests. The actual historical record is less dramatic but not inconsistent with this tradition. Floride, like her mother, was strong-minded and independent, and it is probably significant that one of Calhoun's brothers owned a mule named Floride. Increasingly out of her depth in Washington, she was superbly prepared to take charge at Fort Hill, which had been part of her father's estate. Remembered in Pendleton as a "short, bright, brusque woman of tremendous celerity of movement and action," Floride drove her husband almost to despair by building additions to the plantation house entirely on her own while he was away. She also frequently disagreed with her husband over the management of slaves, fought bitterly with his favorite son, Andrew, and periodically produced family crises by having nervous fits which seemed to threaten imminent death without seriously impairing her health.[4]

One of the difficulties involved in reconstructing Calhoun's marriage is the lack of letters to and from Floride. Calhoun wrote regularly to his wife and children, but with rare exceptions only the letters to his children have survived. It is apparent from his complaints and her own admission that Floride was a poor correspondent. The few letters in her hand to her husband and the larger number to children and kinfolk reveal a woman given over completely to the little details and large responsibilities of running a substantial plantation household. She writes to her husband to order "immediately a large barrel of brown sugar and a bag of coffee, 5 gals. brandy" and reminds him to "see about your Negro's summer clothes sooner this year than usual." She asks her brother James Edward to purchase a variety of things for her in Charleston, including china footbaths, seventy yards of furniture calico, five gallons of molasses, and wallpaper for a sixteen-by-twenty-four-foot drawing room. "I wish it *plain* shy blue with a rich crimson border." She confesses to her daughter-in-law Margaret Calhoun, after a short stay in Washington in the spring of 1839, how glad she is to be back at Fort Hill. "I became tired of doing nothing and leading a monotonous life"—this at a critical turning point in her husband's career—"and I am sure I could not drag out a long session in Washington." She writes regularly to her son Patrick away at West Point, expressing concern about his leaky tent, advising him always to keep flannel next to his skin in the winter, reminding him to send his old clothes home "as they will come in play" for his younger brothers, and warning him about an upcoming visit to his father in Washington. "It is rather dangerous for a young man to be at Washington in the spring," she cautions, because the city is filled with "Young Ladies who go there for the purpose of marrying well," and "as they always appear to the best advantage . . . it is impossible to find them out. I hope you will be very particular in your selection of friends as it would mortify us exceedingly if you were not to marry well."[5]

Floride's letters reveal a caring, affectionate mother, tolerant enough to let one of her young sons adopt a pet deer while another brought home a live bear. She was proud of her nursing skill and even prouder of her many "improvements" at Fort Hill. Clearly she was a lady in charge. There was no patriarch at Fort Hill. It was Floride who directed the slaves in rebuilding the well, who was "up to [her] eyes in hog killing," "enjoying sausages in high style," and who helped save the house from burning down on two occasions—once when a spark ignited in the floor under the hearth and once when an angry slave left a hot coal under little Willy's pillow![6]

Floride's periodic "nervous spells" were apparently minor strokes which her family believed were brought on less by physical causes than by her tendency to undue "agitation." Her attacks may have been related to her sense of loneliness at Fort Hill; one occurred during a ten-month absence of her husband, another after her daughter Anna had moved temporarily to Georgia. She was usually packed off to a favorite spa at Glen Springs for a relatively quick recovery, only to return and complain about poor health. She was to outlive all but one of her children and died at age seventy-four.[7]

In the long run Calhoun's marriage may have survived as well as it did because he was so often away from home. As the romantic magic in their relationship dissipated, he and his wife, so different in personality and intellect, found that they shared little save family. Calhoun, constantly conflict-ridden in his public life, always treasured Fort Hill as a serene retreat, but Floride's volatility meant that he never knew what to expect when he went home. That helps explain why he allowed no one, not even his wife, to have a key to the office he had constructed as a small, separate building at the rear of the mansion. But if Floride was not a perfect wife, neither was Calhoun a perfect husband. Like other famous men, he belonged to the world at least as much as he did to his family and, with his causes and tendency to self-absorption, must have seemed almost as autonomous as a man can be. Toward the end of his life, as he reflected on more than thirty-five years of married life, he perhaps recalled the passion of his early years with Floride, the importance of her inheritance to both of them, the beauty of their children, and her competence and loyalty in holding their family together and managing their household. On balance his wife had served him well. That she was temperamental and difficult to live with he freely admitted. "I have borne with her with patience," he confessed to his son Andrew on one occasion, "because it was my duty to do so and you must do the same. It has been the only cross of my life."[8]

If Calhoun displayed little of his alleged cast-iron qualities as husband, he showed even less as a father. The man who was so combative in the Senate, who never flinched or retreated in debate, was quick to discipline wavering supporters, and always insisted on the complete

Floride Bonneau Calhoun. At the alms the age of forty.

From the Collection of Fort Hill

rectitude of his own course was a remarkably permissive parent.

By 1840 Calhoun had two grown sons, and by any objective measurement he should have been disappointed with both. The recently remarried twenty-nine-year-old Andrew seemed unable to shake off the ineffectuality of his student years. In 1836 he and his wife, Margaret, had moved into Fort Hill, living apparently on the bounty of his father and two successive dowries, and after casting about unsuccessfully for a plantation in South Carolina, he finally located one called Cane Brake in Marengo County, Alabama. At twenty thousand dollars Cane Brake was an expensive proposition. Calhoun supplied three thousand, and the rest was provided by Thomas Green Clemson, who had just become a member of the Calhoun clan by marrying Calhoun's elder daughter, Anna Maria, in 1838. Purchasing the Alabama plantation was one of the biggest mistakes Calhoun and Clemson ever made. Although Cane Brake provided a living for Andrew for fifteen years, Clemson's role in the initial transaction, as joint proprietor with Calhoun and his son or as their principal creditor, was never clarified, and the plantation was purchased at the beginning of a prolonged slump in the cotton market. Clemson kept expecting a return on his investment, which Andrew, who kept expanding the plantation and working it with slaves transferred from Fort Hill, either could not or would not pay. Soon the two brothers-in-law were at each other's throats. Clemson thought his pocket was being picked, while Andrew complained that his honor was being challenged. Finally Clemson severed all communication with Andrew and threatened legal action.

Throughout this dispute, which is documented repeatedly in his correspondence over the last ten years of his life, Calhoun showed extraordinary patience. He was the man in the middle, the fond parent anxious for his son to succeed but also devoted to his daughter, who had married Clemson. And he knew that Thomas Clemson was no ordinary son-in-law but a highly educated, talented man with friends on two continents and a reputation as a respected mining engineer. The prospect of his son and son-in-law squabbling in public over money was almost more than he could stand, and he profoundly regretted ever having involved Clemson in the Cane Brake transaction. Writing from Washington in January 1843, Calhoun poured out his heart to Clemson, who was considering legal action against Andrew Calhoun:

You must permit me, who regards your interest as deeply as my own, to speak freely. I would rather make a sacrafice [*sic*] myself than you should suffer one. I live only for my country, my family and friends. . . . You can neither doubt my solvency or attachment to you. I know you do not; and why should you think of taking such a step, so long as I stand between you and danger. I would rather lose every cent I have, and start fresh in the world even at my time of life, than that you should be a sufferer by any arrangement in which I was a party. . . . To see you & him & all my children prosperous & happy is the great object of my desire. I would not for all I am worth see them . . . embroiled in feuds & conflicts to their mutual disgrace & mine.[9]

The breach between Clemson and Andrew was not closed during Calhoun's life. When Calhoun died in 1850, the debt to Clemson was seventeen thousand dollars plus interest, and Andrew was still living off other people's money.[10]

Calhoun may have been thinking of Andrew's disastrous educational career when he sent his sixteen-year-old son Patrick to West Point in 1837. Patrick had received most of his formal education in academies at Pendleton and Willington. Although he did not show much interest in books and was frequently delinquent in writing to his father, he appeared to have mechanical talent, and Calhoun, who had a high regard for the engineering profession, may have hoped to turn his son in that direction. It was natural for a father who had been Secretary of War to take pride in seeing his son accepted at West Point, but there is every reason to believe that Calhoun was also apprehensive about his prospects. The image of Patrick which emerges from family letters is one of the spoiled son, popular but weak, immature for his age, undisciplined, and lacking in self-confidence and experience in the world. Worried that Patrick might repeat Andrew's failures at Yale or do something worse, Calhoun advised him to expect that the first quarter would be the "most severe," but "after awhile you will find all comparatively easy." The important thing was to maintain health, "be attentive to your studies, respectful to your teachers, courteous to your companions & correct in your deportment. Avoid the idle & vicious and cultivate the acquaintance of the worthy and studious." Floride overcame her reluctance for letter writing to add more moral advice: "Be careful who you associate with, and have no confidents [*sic*]; that is, be careful not to tell anything you wish kept a secret to anyone." And Anna wrote regularly, telling him how grateful the whole family was to learn of his satisfactory performance during his first months as a cadet.[11]

Patrick Calhoun needed to be reassured. Taking after his mother in size, he expected to be the shortest cadet at the Point, and his confidence was not bolstered when he found that he was only the second shortest. Bypassing his father, Patrick complained to his uncle about double-time drilling, leaking tents, guard duty, and an unremitting diet of beef and potatoes, and he admitted that when his company took part in a military funeral, some of the cadets were too frightened to load and fire their guns. The letter sounds more as if it were written by a scared young teenager than by a future warrior.[12]

Somewhat to Calhoun's surprise, Patrick survived his first year at West Point in good shape. "Your sister Anna often says," the happy father wrote, "I always told you that there was no danger of Pat and that he had too much honour & good sense to act amiss. Go on, my boy, as you have begun, take good care of your health, attend diligently to your studies, but above all shun the way of vice and scorn all that is mean and base. I look to you and the rest of the children as the solace of my declining years and I am sure I shall not be deceived." Several months later, in March 1839, learning that Patrick had been ill and was falling behind in his work, Calhoun arranged for a furlough, and that summer Patrick was back at Fort Hill with his father. He returned home with "boils or imposthumes or some such troublesome affliction" and was confined to his bed about the same time that the rest of the Calhouns were suffering malarial attacks. Already in a weakened condition, Patrick soon came down with that disease and almost died.[13]

There is no record of what happened between father and son that summer, but Calhoun's gratification over Patrick's apparent recovery must have been soured considerably by the discovery that his son's primary problem was venereal disease. Patrick returned to West Point, and when Calhoun learned that December that he was again in failing health, he wrote as follows:

I do trust your boils are not the effect of an imperfect cure of the disease that preceeded [*sic*] your fever. I will not for a moment suppose that it is a new contraction of the same disease. I have too much confidence in your prudence & good sense, not to say morals, to suppose that after what you have experienced you will again deviate from the paths of virtue. Another contraction, or the continuance of the habit, at your age, of licencious [*sic*] inter course [*sic*] would be fatal to your constitution and future prospects. It would make you old and decrepted [*sic*] before you were thirty. But I need not dwell on this. If your experience does not keep you pure, I fear that nothing which the deep solicitude of a father can say, would.

Calhoun went on from these sober and rational admonitions to describe what was happening elsewhere in the family and to offer Patrick a subscription to a Washington paper if he wanted it. "Let me hear from you often," he concluded. "Your affectionate father J. C. Calhoun." The letter, a good example of paternal love and restraint under pressure, shows how far Calhoun could separate himself in his family life from the severe, authoritarian images of his public life. Patrick Calhoun eventually graduated from West Point to an undistinguished career as an army officer, but he was never the self-reliant, self-sufficient son his father wanted.[14]

Toward the end of his life, in a long interview with the Washington journalist Oliver Dyer, Calhoun compared the southern with the New England way of education. New Englanders, Calhoun thought, pushed their sons into books too early, but in South Carolina boys were encouraged to "ride horses, leap fences and shoot squirrels" before putting their minds to work. The result, supposedly, encouraged the development of an educated elite that would never "lose their grip on matters of public and practical experience." Calhoun was perhaps generalizing on the basis of his own experience. He had begun his own formal education older than his classmates at Waddel's academy and at Yale after several years in which he had divided his time among hunting and fishing and running the family plantation. However that may be, Calhoun's educational theories, along with the capriciousness of genetics, probably helps explain why none of his five sons even remotely approached their father in educational attainments and intellectual ability.[15]

Calhoun's three youngest sons do not begin to emerge as distinct personalities in the Calhoun family record until the mid-1830s. John was seventeen in 1840, James fourteen, and Willy eleven. Brought up entirely in rural Pendleton in the shadow of the Appalachians and without the benefit of much formal schooling, they appear almost like unspoiled forest children. Calhoun doubtless enjoyed their exuberant stories about the hunting party in the mountains which "killed a panther 9 feet 8 inches long" and about James's dog Zip, which could climb trees, ride horseback and "cech a rabbit in fifteen steps. He runs so fast you cannot see his legs a going." He may not have learned about the drinking parties of the older boys in the village, but he was undoubtedly told of Johnny's ability to down ducks with a rifle, about the pigeon shoot that killed more than eight thousand in two nights, about the pair of pet snow-white rabbit hawks that followed the boys all over the plantation, and about Jimmy's bear, "the ugliest thing that you ever saw and it is not tame."[16]

Perhaps Calhoun let his boys run as wild as they did because he had been thrust into adulthood so abruptly after his father died and wanted them to enjoy a fuller, more spontaneous boyhood than his own. If he expected this pattern of child rearing to produce another statesman, however, he was to be sorely disappointed. There were repeated attempts to give them an educational base through private tutors and local academies, but their sister Anna Maria declared her three younger brothers were "growing up in ignorance." Finally Calhoun launched his sons on an undistinguished educational odyssey which included a Quaker school in Philadelphia, Erskine College (a tiny backwoods institution in the Carolina backcountry), the University of Virginia (from which James was expelled), and South Carolina College. The experiment did not validate the father's theories. Loyal and affectionate sons all, none of them achieved distinction on his own. John was to study medicine in Philadelphia but never practice; James was to practice law in California and die bankrupt; Willy was to become a high-living planter whose plantation was auctioned after his death to pay debts.[17]

Although Calhoun's affection and caring for his entire family never flagged, he reserved the softest spot in his heart for his two daughters. Cornelia, the younger, sixteen years old in 1840, suffered from a bad fall as a child which left her with a crooked back and a hearing deficiency. She was the pet of the family. Calhoun sought the help of medical specialists in Baltimore and Philadelphia to help his afflicted daughter, but to no avail. He sent her presents—the "prettiest books" he could find and a gold pencil, which she wore around her neck on a chain woven from her sister Anna's hair. Always cheerful despite her troubles, Cornelia was good company for Floride when Calhoun was away. Her favorite possession was a long silver ear trumpet which she paraded around the house in the manner of a young Harriet Martineau, and her needlework can be still admired today in the form of a handsome coverlet made for her parents' bed.[18]

The one genuine gem among Calhoun's children was his older daughter, Anna Maria. Born in 1817, Anna had spent much of her early life in Washington, and she grew up to be the most politically sensitive, intelligent, and articulate of all his children. The record of correspondence between Calhoun and his daughter dates from 1831, when she was fourteen and away at school in Columbia. Already aware that Anna was closer to him in mind and temperament than Floride or any of his other children, Calhoun insisted in his first letter that she become a regular correspondent: "You must write to me without delay and give me a full account of everything; the course of studies, the teachers, what you are learning, how many young ladies and where they are from, who are your room mates and who your particular companions. If you do not wish to write too long a letter, you may make my enquiries the subject of several."

Calhoun took every interest in Anna's education, warned her that she was still too young to "go into company," complimented her for acting "like a philosopher" in overcoming her loneliness by being first in making overtures to the other students, and encouraged her to take her lessons in posture, dance, and music seriously. He also advised her to overcome her "great aversion to early rising" because "we lose time, pleasure & health by late sleeping. Life is a journey. If we lose the morning it will require hard and fatiguing travel to reach our stage."[19]

In sending her to a girls' school which concentrated on feminine graces like learning how to walk and sit, Calhoun accepted the conventions of the day, which limited the range of a young lady's education. At the same time he was gratified to learn that Anna wanted to learn more about the political world. "I am not one of those who think your sex ought to have nothing to do with politics," he wrote. "They have as much interest in the good conditions of the country, as the other sex, and tho it would be unbecoming them to take an active part in political struggles, their opinion, when enlightened, cannot fail to have a great and salutary effect." Two years later Calhoun sent Anna a copy of his speech on the bank deposits issue and told her that he had sent another copy to Floride "tho she cares so little about politics." By 1834 Calhoun had come to depend on his seventeen-year-old daughter not only for political approval but for the kind of intimate, domestic detail he found so difficult to get from Floride. "Your Mother and Brother [Andrew] write me on grave subjects of business, or what relates to the welfare of the family," he wrote, "but you fill up the interval with those little but interesting details, which it is so agreeable to an absent father to know. Were it not for you, I would not have heard a word about the Humming birds, their familiarity, the vines, their blooms, the freshness of the spring, the green yard, the children's gardens and finally Patrick's mechanical genius & his batteaux." Anna's letters sometimes made Calhoun so homesick that he wrote: "I cannot describe my desire to see you all after so long an absence."[20]

Calhoun was fortunate to have Anna with him during the harshly partisan congressional sessions of 1835 and 1836 when they shared rooms in a comfortable boardinghouse with familiar faces from South Carolina, including James Henry Hammond and his wife and Waddy Thompson. These were the sessions in which Calhoun attacked the abolitionists on one front while continuing his perennial assault on Jackson on the other. One reason he remained serene, despite the torrents of rhetorical violence which flowed around him in the Senate, was that he knew Anna was in the gallery sharing his triumphs and frustrations and his contempt for the wicked. Calhoun later remembered that living in Washington with Anna had been "like a family party."[21]

In the summer of 1836 Anna toured the northeastern states with Senator Preston and his wife while Calhoun returned to Fort Hill. Her letters to a cousin written after she had been to Boston and down the Connecticut Valley to New Haven and New York show how completely Anna had absorbed her father's ideas. "The whole of *Yankee land* is beautiful," she wrote, "with its miles of green meadows with their stone fences, its pretty little villages lining the road—and the general air of prosperity and abundance, and I could but think when I recollected the comparatively miserable appearance of our Southern country that a good deal of this same prosperity, of not the whole, was to be traced to our money and labour unjustly taken from us." She would head south, Anna concluded, "more of a glorifier than ever" with "the determination that the South Carolinians are the finest people on earth."[22]

Calhoun enjoyed his daughter's companionship at home as well as in Washington, and the sight of the two tramping across plantation fields in earnest conversation became a familiar sight to visitors at Fort Hill. Calhoun's annual departure at the end of each summer was always a painful moment, and in late August 1837, when Floride and Anna were driving him to Pendleton, they dallied so long that he missed the stage and they were forced to "drive as hard as we could and hallo the driver for some time." Anna was probably correct in thinking that her father did not want to leave, but she may not have realized that what he regretted most was leaving without her.[23]

Finding life in Washington desolate without his daughter, Calhoun brought Anna there as much as he could. When she was absent, he rarely ventured into society, dining in solitude at a temperance boardinghouse. When she was with him, he took her to the French Ball where the dancing went on until two in the morning. Together they went to see *Madame Augusta* at the ballet and *The Barber of Seville* at the opera house. Calhoun's politics shut him out of White House society, but he took Anna to see Gulliver and Lilliput (a seven-foot-nine-inch giant and a thirty-eight-inch midget) and even to the races, where Decatur ran a four-mile course for a purse of ten thousand dollars. After watching a play called *The Kentuckian,* Anna happily reported that she never "saw father laugh or enjoy himself more." Here was a Calhoun Harriet Martineau never knew.[24]

Sometime in the early summer of 1838, while still in Washington, Anna met Thomas Green Clemson, a young multitalented mining engineer of independent means, who soon fell in love with her. The young couple became engaged in July. Except for the fact that he was not a native Carolinian, Clemson was an entirely appropriate suitor for Calhoun's spirited, intelligent, and devoted daughter. Ten years Anna's senior and son of a wealthy Quaker merchant who had left him a moderate legacy, Clemson had studied science for three years in France and was a linguist, a devotee of music and painting, and a respected engineer with strong interests in scientific agriculture.

How did Calhoun feel when he learned that his beloved daughter, friend, and companion was about to be taken away from him? Had he

Thomas Clemson as a young man in Europe before his marriage.

Anne Marina Calhoun Clemson when she was living with her husband in Brussels.

From the Collection of Fort Hill

hoped that Anna would stay by his side and brighten those long, lonely months in Washington for the rest of his life? Probably, but Calhoun was a conservative, a traditionalist who would have been hard pressed to understand how a woman could find fulfillment outside marriage and motherhood. And he must have considered it providential that Anna, gifted with a mind so attuned to his own, would marry a man of Clemson's intellectual accomplishments.

Anna, however, was explicit in reporting the ambiguity which she felt at the prospect of leaving her father. She knew how important she was to him, how her presence in the gallery on important occasions reinforced his frequently lonely battles on the Senate floor, and how eagerly he anticipated sharing with her his ideas and strategies. She also suspected that she had inherited his talents and sometimes was proud that she could help him prepare his political papers. Josiah Quincy, who met Anna in Washington in the late 1830s, always remembered the "clearness with which she represented the southern view of the situation and the ingenuity with which she parried such objections as I was able to present." There were no young ladies in Massachusetts, Quincy decided, as astute as Calhoun's daughter.[25]

It is understandable, then, that Anna should have grieved for herself and her father at the same time that she marveled at the power of her feeling for Clemson. "I do at times feel very melancholy when I think of the future," she confessed to her cousin. "You know there was no affectation in the determination I always expressed never to marry. I thought there were duties enough in life for me to perform. I felt I was useful to my father, and was not wholly without objects in life while I contributed to his pleasure in the slightest degree . . . it caused me a pang I cannot express to you to give up the cherished object of my life, and sometimes even now I sit down and take a hearty cry at the idea, either that my place cannot be altogether supplied to him or that it should be supplied by another."[26]

On November 13, 1838, John C. Calhoun gave his daughter in marriage to Thomas Clemson. For most of the family and guests at Fort Hill it was a festive celebration, but Andrew Calhoun, noticing how detached his father was from the gaiety surrounding him, remarked that he was "not as affable as usual" because "he feels that in giving up Anna he is losing his favorite, his pride, his *confident* [sic].

The glory of the house is departing with Anna."[27]

Although Calhoun was to have plenty of reason to regret involving his new son-in-law with the purchase of Cane Brake plantation, he never regretted Clemson's marriage to Anna, a marriage that was long and fruitful, leading to an extended stay abroad but eventually to a return to Pendleton after Calhoun's death. Finally his daughter would become mistress at Fort Hill. The father, long in his grave, would rest easy in that knowledge.

15

Master of Fort Hill

A S A BOY Calhoun had told his brothers that he would much rather become a planter without formal education than a "half-informed physician or lawyer." The consequence had been seven rigorous years of subsidized learning and training at Waddel's school, Yale, and Litchfield before Calhoun launched his public career with one of the best educations his country could provide. As it turned out, he became both a professionally trained politician and a planter who prided himself in doing his best in both vocations.

Calhoun chose to make his permanent plantation home in Pendleton because the house and surrounding acres of Clergy Hall (a former parsonage) which stood on a hill a few miles from the village was available as part of the estate inherited by his wife. By moving there, she would be close to her mother, who was living at Cold Harbor, on the Seneca River, and to her brother John Ewing Colhoun's showy plantation at nearby Keowee. At the same time they would remain connected with Floride's younger brother, James Edward Colhoun, and with John Calhoun's own three brothers by a direct road to Abbeville about twenty-five miles away. Moving to Fort Hill would not mean moving outside the family.

Calhoun loved what he called the tie of relationship and was never happier than when surrounded not only by his immediate family but by the extended families on both his own and Floride's side of the family. Calhoun's three brothers were all substantial planters, conscientious, sober, and generous, cut out in the image of their father. John's older brother, James, had played a decisive role in the family councils which had decided to send him off to college. Subsequently John and his brothers had launched the careers of other men outside the family, only one example of which was the celebrated George McDuffie, who had long been considered one of the Calhoun clan. John Calhoun's favorite brother was William, who frequently looked after his affairs when he was in town. Some said that he had the best mind of any of the Calhouns but was held back by poor vision. Patrick, namesake of the patriarch, had married an upper country heiress and continued to preside over the old family plantation in Abbeville. The Calhoun clan in Abbeville was very social, and there were enough nephews and nieces, christenings, weddings, and holidays to bring them together frequently. Mary Moragne, who had many friends among the Calhouns, wrote in her diary after one of their parties, "The dancing was kept up till 3 o'clock in the morning without the least abatement of good humor and conviviality." The next morning, after the Calhouns and their guests had been waked up by "the most seducing fiddle," the party continued. "Oh such a day of romping, rioting, uproarious mirth—such dancing, singing, card playing, and such laughing—it beggars all description."

John C. Calhoun did not join this celebration because he was in Washington preparing to pounce on the incoming Van Buren administration, and if he had been there, he might not have romped so freely or laughed as hard as some of the others, but he would have enjoyed the parties, because, as Mary Moragne wrote, "Who could be cold & stiff under the influence of the warm hospitality & frank courtesy of the *Calhouns?*"[1]

The gaiety of the larger Calhoun family was considerably reduced in the spring of 1838, when Patrick Calhoun, in the agony of a violent depression, tried to cut his throat with a razor. Patrick, John's younger brother, had been the only one left at home when he returned from Waddel's school after their father had died. Together they had mourned their father, consoled their bereaved mother, and, heartsick as they were, taken on the responsibilities of the plantation. Now this brother, bearing the proudest name that Abbeville had ever known, had become so dangerous to himself and those around him that his family actually considered sending him to the asylum in Columbia. At first John counseled against such a move, thinking it would kill Patrick. A few days later he changed his mind and, in reporting the matter to his brother-in-law James E. Calhoun, almost broke down as he wrote the letter. "I have written to Nancy [Patrick's wife] that unless there should be in the meantime some decided change, I think he ought to be sent to the Asylum. . . . I will write you again shortly when my mind is more at ease. I am too grieved now to touch on any other subject."

For most of the next two years Patrick Calhoun's condition remained essentially unchanged, but at one point recovery seemed possible, and in the spring of 1840 there were plans to bring him to Fort Hill to convalesce. Then came a setback, followed by Patrick's death in early September. For John Calhoun, who valued reason almost as highly as duty and practically made a fetish of his own powers of self-control, the final act came as a blessing. "His death can be considered no loss to him or family," he wrote to one of his own sons, "as there was no hope of his recovery from the depressed state of mind into which he had fallen." Two months later Calhoun's older brother, William, died after a long battle with a digestive ailment. His death was not unexpected, and Calhoun received the news serenely, having been assured by the attending physician that William had "died without a pang and met his end with great tranquillity."[2]

The deaths of his two brothers probably had the effect of drawing John Calhoun closer to his two brothers-in-law. His mother-in-law, Floride Bonneau Colhoun, had died four years earlier, and her estate had been divided up among her two sons and her daughter and son-in-law. Calhoun was doubtless happy to receive formal ownership of Fort Hill, but he had remained attentive to the elder Floride to the end. As a handsome young matron and kinswoman she had been a kind of surrogate mother to him during his student years in New England. Later she had encouraged his courtship of her daughter and put both her fortune and her influence at his disposal as he began his career. After 1830 she had become increasingly imperious and erratic, hiding herself away at Cold Harbor while entertaining various imagined grievances against her children. Calhoun, who claimed to see some of his wife's more troublesome qualities in her mother, was visibly distressed, pleaded her case to her sons, and agreed with his own Floride that her place was in Pendleton, near her mother, rather than in Washington.

The two Colhoun brothers could not have been less alike. John Ewing, who owned the great multipillared Keowee mansion which made such a magnificent display when the spring dogwoods were in bloom, was said to be so rich that his horses were shod with silver shoes. Apparently as profligate as he was wealthy, he had drunk, gambled, and mismanaged so much of his estate away by 1843 that the sheriff was sent to confiscate his slaves. Calhoun lamented his brother-in-law's indifference "both to his own and other people's business" but could do little to help. John Ewing Colhoun died in 1847, leaving his widow, several children, and the shambles of a once-great plantation behind him.[3]

Whatever limitations in friendship John Calhoun found with John Ewing were more than made up for by his relationship with James Edward Colhoun. Sixteen years Calhoun's junior, James Edward had been a lieutenant in the United States Navy, making several cruises to European and South American ports in at least five different ships and becoming a talented linguist in the process. In the early 1820s as a member of Major Stephen Long's exploring expedition, he had become a close enough observer of Indian culture to be consulted by writers on the subject and had tried unsuccessfully thereafter to get President Adams to commission him to survey the Mexican boundary and explore territory west of the Rocky Mountains. Financially self-sufficient through his inheritance, James Edward seemed satisfied to live the life of a bachelor intellectual in Washington and lease his property in South Carolina and Georgia to the care of overseers. After a forced visit to his plantations near the Savannah River in 1825, he complained, "Remaining at the North I could by this time have acquired the Hebrew and German language and improved my knowledge of Spanish. I would have also devoted much attention to the writings of the early historians and travellers on this continent, at the same time qualifying myself better as a topographer and Astronomical observer."

By 1829 James Edward Colhoun had given up his Washington life-style and settled permanently in the Abbeville district, where he developed plantations and timber holdings which eventually totaled more than sixty thousand acres. An avid nullifier, innovative planter, and first-rate scholar, he became one of John Calhoun's confidants, helping educate his boys, check up on his overseers, and provide a sounding board for his ideas. After a long bachelorhood and some notoriety as a womanizer, James Edward married Anna Maria's closest cousin and friend Maria Simkins, in 1839, an event which tied Calhoun's family in Fort Hill even closer to James Edward's vast Millwood estate on the Savannah than it had been before.[4]

Most of the major figures of Calhoun's time were associated in the

American mind with country seats. The tradition had been established by Washington at Mount Vernon and Jefferson at Monticello and continued by Jackson's handsome Hermitage, near Nashville, Clay's elaborate Ashland at Lexington, and Webster's money-draining, exotic farm at Marshfield. By the early 1830s the Calhouns' relatively modest house in Pendleton, expanded and renamed Fort Hill (there had once been a fort on the site), had become famous as Calhoun's country retreat, and the little village of Pendleton had emerged as a political locus of national significance. The village itself, though numbering not much more than forty houses when Calhoun moved there, contained a courthouse, two churches, a weekly paper—conduit for some of Calhoun's most famous public statements—and the Pendleton Farmers Society, which hosted Calhoun's first political speech. The Pendleton Fair attracted farmers and planters from all over the upper country who brought their best hogs, hay, corn, or cotton to compete for prizes. Calhoun prided himself on being part of the fair as competitor and judge, and his experience there rubbing shoulders with sturdy yeoman farmers and substantial planters like himself tended to confirm his convictions that slavery was consistent with the rough camaraderie of a society which took liberty and equality seriously.

Calhoun never liked Charleston and spent as little time there as possible, but he had plenty of occasions to meet and talk with the Charleston elite in Pendleton, where many of them kept summer homes. During the summer months the village was awash with famous low-country families like the Hugers and the Pinckneys. Francis K. Huger, who had been jailed for an abortive attempt to help Lafayette escape a French prison in 1794, was only one of the more famous residents. Thomas Pinckney, the Revolutionary War hero and former Ambassador to England, was there along with his kinsman Charles Cotesworth Pinckney, a confidant of George Washington in war and peace. The new generation of leaders was also well represented, including Governors Hamilton and Hayne and Calhoun's old friend Langdon Cheves, whose long barracks-looking plantation house baffled all visitors. Not all the Pendleton elite agreed with Calhoun's ideas on nullification. Some of his neighbors, like the eccentric and outspoken Mavericks, were blunt about their opposition, and Union sentiment in the district was always substantial, but Calhoun and his family were welcome everywhere. If the talk happened to turn to politics or political philosophy, Calhoun could be sure that the dialogue would be as stimulating as anything he could find in Washington.[5]

By and large, however, Calhoun was primarily known in the village as a planter, friend, and neighbor. People in the village remembered how the Presbyterian Calhoun dutifully accompanied Floride to the small clapboard Episcopal church which meant so much to her. They recalled the Senator picking up his voluminous mail at the tiny post office and then electing to walk the six or seven miles past tilled fields and along wooded roads to one of the three large gates leading to Fort Hill. And they remembered him not only as a member of Pendleton Farmers Society, an almost purely republican institution designed to foster agricultural enlightenment in the region, but as the man who first introduced contour ditching and Bermuda grass into the region, the man who, like his father, could run his own survey line and was once seen at the head of his slaves fighting a fire in the woods.[6]

Fort Hill was situated about seven miles west of Pendleton village along a road which ran mostly through woodlands. The main gate to Calhoun's plantation led into a drive lined with cedar trees, leading upward for several hundred yards to the transformed parsonage, which sat on the crest of the hill in a yard shaded by ancient oaks and graced by locust, wild orange, and fig trees. A vineyard and a large garden with a special patch reserved for Cornelia stood in the rear of the house with apple and peach orchards not far beyond. At Fort Hill Calhoun was master of most of what he could see. To the north of his house and about two hundred feet in elevation below it lay some of his most fertile fields along the Seneca River, where he had built his mill and boat dock. The main slave quarters, a long, rectangular stone building divided into apartments, stood about an eighth of a mile down the hill to the southwest. Between the quarters and the mansion were the carriage house, stables, and mule and sheep barns. The cook and domestic servants were housed near the mansion, and Calhoun's office, equipped with an enormous rolltop desk imported from Switzerland and lined with bookshelves, was directly behind the house. A few paces away under a large shady tree stood a double wooden step which the master used to mount his horse.

It is unfortunate that Calhoun the planter never made an impact on

FORT HILL
The Plantation of
John C. Calhoun

OLD MILL

SHEEP BARN

MULE BARN

CARRIAGE HORSES

SLAVE QUARTERS

HOME OF STABLE BOY

*Fort Hill plantation drawn by an architecture student at
Clemson University in 1958 from archival sources.*

Courtesy of the Clemson University Library

the South comparable to that made by Calhoun the political strategist and thinker, because he seems to have turned his Fort Hill property into a model of diversified farming. Census figures for 1850, the year Calhoun died, report a plantation with 9 horses, 17 milking cows, 6 working oxen, 53 cattle, 23 sheep, and 118 pigs. The plantation produced more than 25,000 pounds of cotton along with 160 bushels of wheat, 6,000 of corn, 4,000 of oats, 300 of peas and beans, and 1,200 of sweet potatoes. Calhoun also grew more than 4,000 pounds of rice, put up 1,000 pounds of honey and beeswax, harvested substantial peach orchards, and grew oranges, pomegranates, and other fruits. His plantation of about thirteen hundred acres was essentially self-sufficient with its own mills, gin, and ice pond, and there is every reason to believe that Calhoun would have died a wealthy and solvent man had he not gone heavily into debt late in life to help finance his son's Alabama plantation.[7]

Although Calhoun's absences made him rely more on overseers than he would have liked, he was a hands-on planter when he was home and rose early every morning to inspect his fields, returning to the house with a plump peach, a golden sheaf of wheat, or a particularly promising cotton plant, to display to the rest of the family around the breakfast table. Calhoun had learned most of what he knew about planting as a boy when he took over the Abbeville plantation after his father's death. In those days he had worked side by side with his slaves in the fields, and although there is no reason to believe that like his friend McDuffie, he reverted to that practice in later life, he remained engaged in supervising the plantation at every stage in the process, knowing full well that whenever his attention flagged, there would be a price to pay. On one occasion, for example, an enterprising overseer fattened thirty head of cattle at Calhoun's expense while the master was away in Washington.[8]

Every famous public person attracts visitors. Some came for immediate, practical purposes, like the South Carolina politicians who trooped to Fort Hill as the nullification crisis was building. Some came with letters of introduction from other famous people. And some came out of curiosity or on pilgrimage, as Calhoun himself had once gone to visit Jefferson. By all accounts Calhoun was a gracious host as he presided over a house of fourteen comfortable rooms built in the southern style with large pillars rising to the second-story roof on three sides. There is a simple elegance to the building, which stands today on a hill at the center of the campus of Clemson University. Much of the furniture in the house descends from the Calhouns, including a pair of drumhead tables brought to this country by Calhoun's grandparents; a Duncan Phyfe mahogany banquet table, at which the Calhouns held formal dinners; and a sideboard made out of a mahogany panel taken from the historic American frigate *Constitution* (a gift from Henry Clay). Compared with Jackson's Hermitage with its spacious interiors and ostentations guitar-shaped garden, Clay's fussily Victorian Ashland, and the elaborate peacocks and llamas on the luxurious lawns surrounding Marshfield, Fort Hill gives today, and must have given in Calhoun's time, the impression of substantial simplicity.

The rambling two-story house, which lacked the symmetry of the classic plantation mansion, in part, no doubt, because of Floride's many "innovations," suited Calhoun's style. When the young and sophisticated Paul Hamilton Hayne visited Pendleton, he found the village dull and ugly but was charmed by his Fort Hill host. "I was impressed at the simplicity of Mr. Calhoun's manners," Hayne reported to his sister. "There is no assumption of that *chilling dignity* which the Great so frequently exercise towards *inferiors,* but with an *intuitive perception* of courtesy grounded in real benevolence of heart, Mr. Calhoun adopts his conversation to the peculiar pursuits of the individual with whom he speaks & always leaves in the mind of his hearer a favorable opinion of his character—as a gentleman of tact & discernment."[9]

There is universal testimony that Calhoun was a gracious, generous host, that he invited into his house not only the well-connected, like Hayne, but much humbler guests, like the obscure itinerant Methodist minister who happened to be passing by and ended up at Calhoun's handsome table seated next to the Senator himself. On at least one occasion Anna complained about her father's tolerance for boorish visitors who overstayed their welcome.[10]

Dixon Lewis said there was no "recreation" in Calhoun, and although the images of Calhoun at play are few and far between in the historical record, it is hard not to believe that simply being at Fort Hill was recreational for Calhoun. During the summer months there was a lively social life in and around Pendleton village. There was dancing in

the ballrooms of the summer hotels or on the broad verandas of neighboring plantation houses, and Calhoun, who insisted that his boys learn
to dance, must have taken his turn with Floride and Anna. There were
always the mountains which Calhoun could see from the doorway at
Fort Hill outlined against the horizon, and he sometimes led expedi-
tions to the waterfalls in the nearby Jocassee Valley or to the summit of
Table Rock, a perpendicular granite wall of eleven hundred feet which
could be ascended by foot and carriage on one side. On one occasion he
whimsically organized such a party along military lines, delegating commissary, transportation, and reconnoitering duties to his various guests.
Fortunately he put himself in charge of transportation and narrowly
prevented his daughter from pitching over a precipice in her carriage.[11]

One of Calhoun's favorite diversions was to explore the more inac-
cessible mountain regions on foot or horseback with one or two friends,
pausing along the way to collect mineral specimens and take sightings
for a possible right-of-way through the mountains. Settlements in the
Carolina mountains were scattered in those days, and more often than
not Calhoun and his companions had their choice of camping out or
putting up in a rough mountaineer's cabin where they could be assured
of absolute anonymity and where the great man sometimes had to share
a bed with a passing hunter or mail carrier.[12]

In the summer of 1836 Calhoun, who had been fascinated by the
natural sciences ever since his studies under Professor Silliman at Yale,
joined the British geologist G. W. Featherstonhaugh, at Dahlonega,
Georgia, and spent four days riding with him through the Georgia and
Carolina hills, studying the way gold veins were being worked there,
and collecting mineral specimens. Among other things Calhoun was
delighted to find a perfectly preserved pine log under layers of sand and
gravel which presumably went back to prehistoric times. Later Featherstonhaugh made a memorable visit to Fort Hill, which reminded him of
a Tuscany villa in the Apennines and left him with romantic memories
of a delightful guest room and an agreeable dinner after which the
diners adjourned to the portico, "where with the aid of a guitar accompanied by a pleasing voice, and some capital curds and cream, we prolonged a most agreeable conversazione until a late hour."[13]

Although Featherstonhaugh does not tell us the color of the musi-
cians who enhanced his visit, we do know that Calhoun had sent two

slaves with a horse and a mule cart to bring him to Pendleton from Pickens Courthouse about twelve miles away, and it could hardly have escaped the visitor's notice that the gracious life-style and hospitality at Fort Hill were built on the forced labor of slaves. There were seventy-seven slaves at Fort Hill in 1840 and an equal number at Cane Brake, many of whom had previously belonged at Fort Hill. By 1850 there were almost two hundred slaves on the two plantations.

How did the great rationalizer of slavery treat his own slaves? This is not an easy question to answer because plantation records for Fort Hill have not survived, and we must rely on scattered references in letters by Calhoun and other family members. As we have seen, John Calhoun grew up in the Carolina backcountry at a time when slavery was becoming more and more important to the region. As a boy he was proud of the fact his father owned thirty slaves. Patrick's habit of referring to his "family black and white" was a way of expressing the paternalistic ideal which helped make slavery in the southern states distinctive. John Calhoun learned early in life that owning slaves conveyed both privilege and responsibility. The privilege came from the fact that under the law slaves were property and could be worked and traded like property. The responsibility came because masters were expected to take care of their slaves—to feed, clothe, and protect them. They were expected to be "just," and one can still find the "just master" tribute on the grave-stones of many Abbeville slaveholders who were neighbors of Patrick Calhoun.

Calhoun certainly subscribed to the paternalistic ideal. He would have approved of J. G. Clinkscales, an up-country planter who owned 110 slaves and was said to "know them all by name," and he would have agreed with the wealthy R. F. W. Allston, who deplored the absentee-ism of so many low-country planters because it weakened "that tie between master, master's family and slave, of which you know the force and which depends on much upon mutual intimate acquaintance, and occasional kindnesses shown." Calhoun's erstwhile political opponent the unionist James L. Petigru made much the same point when he said that although his plantation was not making money, he could take satisfaction "in the striking improvement in moral and physical condition of his slaves." When Calhoun spoke of the "peculiar" labor system in the South, he meant to include among other things the fact that moral considerations in slaveownership could be strong enough to defy market forces. Thus he would have understood completely what Robert Barnwell Rhett meant when he explained to a creditor that he had not taken advantage of an enormous increase in demand to sell part of his slaves and cancel his debt because "I am not one of those who regard slaves merely as property to be sold at any time upon the principle of pecuniary loss or gain. . . . I knew that in selling those slaves to me you had in view their welfare and believed their welfare temporal and spiritual was taken care of in making me their master."[14]

Although Calhoun had no aversion to buying and selling slaves and always kept a careful eye on slave prices, the increase in the slave population at Fort Hill seems to have been more a natural phenomenon than the result of commercial transactions. A visitor to the plantation in 1849 noted the large number of older slaves, some of whom had been born in Africa and purchased by Patrick Calhoun. One old woman, treated with regal respect by the other slaves, claimed to be one hundred and twelve years old and have more than sixty-three descendants living on the plantation. Every slave family was allowed an acre or two to cultivate for its own use. A favorite like Calhoun's boyhood companion Sawney might have a larger garden and clear forty or fifty dollars a year from his cotton. Calhoun recognized the importance of slave holidays and ceremonies; the four-day Christmas holiday and the festivities that went with it were fairly customary on the larger plantations. Like other masters, Calhoun could not recognize the marriage of a slave as a sacrament, but he did encourage slaves to hold their own marriage celebrations and on at least one occasion arranged for one of his domestic servants to be "married" in the mansion, where one of the older slaves acted as an unfrocked parson.[15]

Family letters show that what Allston meant by the "mutual intimate acquaintance" between slaves and the master's family and the "occasional kindnesses shown" were part of Fort Hill routine. "Alec was quite sick," Anna wrote, "and father knowing how difficult it is to make him take medicine, requested me to go out and administer it." In her haste to play the nurse Anna stepped on a loose board, hurt her foot, and was laid up herself for three days. In their letters to Patrick, one of the Calhoun boys wrote, "Mom Caty always tells me to tell you howdy for her." Anna describes herself as busy making clothes for the blacks and about her success in teaching one slave to sew. "Leah has arrived at the heel of her stocking & seems quite elated for I asked her this morning what she was laughing at & she replied with her usual effort, 'I laugh at a dis here stocking.' " The close ties which the family at Fort Hill maintained with the plantations of John and Floride's brothers seem to have been copied by their slaves. "Polly & Chloe have both been brought to bed of your plough boys and are doing very well," Anna informed Maria, her favorite cousin and the recent bride of James Edward Colhoun, "tho Chloe was very ill at the time & old mama Sarah told me she had to fight mightily with Polly." We do not learn whether Polly and Chloe were ever married to the "plough boys," but the uncertain paternity of some slave children seems to have been accepted as a matter of course. After reporting a delivery of one of her slaves, Anna wrote Maria, "She has called it *Ben* whether after Jeter's coachman or not I am unable to inform you." One sobering possibility that Anna and Maria, like everyone else in the master's immediate family, had to contemplate was that they might very easily become the owners of children with white fathers. Gossip about the carousing of white men in the quarters was so common that when Clemson reported "as an item of news" the case of a notorious planter in Abbeville who was dissipated and always "among the negro women," Anna was amused at her husband's naïveté.[16]

Floride appears to have been much more ambivalent than Anna about Fort Hill slaves and with good reason. When she was six years old, slaves on the family plantation on Twelve Mile River in Pendleton tried to poison her father. The court record of this incident describes the confession of several slaves who apparently planned to run away after the poisoning. The court sentenced Will, the young black who put the poison in her father's food, to be hanged; Sue and Sukey were to have their ears cropped in public, to be branded on their foreheads, and to receive one hundred lashes. The other conspirator, "Old Hazard," was to be branded, have both ears cropped, and get twenty-five lashes.[17]

Although we find no mention of this event in Floride's letters, it must have been a traumatic occasion for the whole family, and the memory of it consciously or unconsciously probably shaped the attitudes and behavior she extended to her own slaves at Fort Hill. On

some occasions Floride spoke highly of her slaves. She was proud of the
new cook who cost one thousand dollars and could "bone a turkey" and
of her servant Marcey, who accompanied her to Washington ("Mrs.
Pike says she never saw a servant so handsomely clothed in every respect"). Whenever she sent a wagon down to her brother's plantation
on the Savannah, she sent several slaves with it because they would be
"disappointed" at not seeing their own kin. And on one occasion she
chided her daughter-in-law because "you did not say one word about
the Negroes, yours, or ours, how is Christy and Betty pleased, is Betty's
child alive?"[18]

On the other hand, Floride always preferred white helpers and,
after getting a white nurse to take care of Cornelia, bragged that she
was a model of efficiency and did everything at the house but cook.
Since the nurse arrived, "I have scarcely had black in the house," Floride wrote. Floride obviously was afraid of some slaves. One of these
was the son of "Old Sawney," who had once been Calhoun's playmate.
"Young Sawney" had run away and been apprehended in Georgia.
Calhoun wanted him returned, but Floride objected. "I think he ought
to be sold, or he will do more mischief," she wrote to one of her sons.
"He is a bad boy . . . he might set fire to the gin house, and I know he
has been wearing a dirk for some time before he left home to kill the
overseer, and took up a rock to throw at Mr. Clemson and the overseer.
I know his father, Old Sawney, is at the bottom of all he has done. I
think him a *dangerous* old Negro, but you cannot convince his master
of it." Sawney also had a daughter named Issy, who in April 1843 tried
to fire Fort Hill by putting coals under young Willy's pillow. The fire
was quickly extinguished, and Issy was banished to Alabama. Floride
wanted her sold, but was careful not to let the matter be made public
because Issy could have been hanged for arson. Issy thereupon became
the subject of a prolonged family dispute. Calhoun and Andrew refused
to sell her; Cornelia pleaded to get her back; Floride claimed she never
wanted to see her again but reversed herself within a year and demanded Issy's return to Fort Hill.[19]

One of Calhoun's nieces intimately familiar with the ways at Fort
Hill reported that he governed his slaves and his children the same way.
"He was mild, persuasive, convincing. I never heard of his using the
lash, even a slap or any species of violence." This idealized image has

some basis in reality. Calhoun was certainly an indulgent parent, and there is no record of his ever resorting to violence in his political or personal life. No doubt he did feel a strong personal bond with some of his slaves, notably Old Sawney and his children. He allowed Sawney to grow his own cotton, made special arrangements to have him treated by a doctor away from the plantation, and went to extraordinary lengths to protect his troublesome children. Sawney was his master's favorite, but Hector and Alec were not. When Hector, a "very black" slave with a feeble voice and a "dull and sleepy appearance," ran off, Calhoun pursued him assiduously and was willing to pay an agent in Philadelphia whatever was necessary to find him. Alec, a house servant, ran away after being threatened with a "severe whipping." He was caught in Abbeville, and Calhoun arranged with a relative "to have him lodged in jail for a week, to be fed on bread & water and to employ some one for me to give him 30 lashes well laid on at the end of the time." Alec, Calhoun said, "ran away for no other reason but to avoid a correction for some misconduct" and left Floride without a male servant in the house.[20]

There is no way of knowing how often Fort Hill was plagued with runaways, but the promptness with which Calhoun dealt with them suggests that he did not take the challenge to his control lightly. When he was away in Washington, Floride would sometimes report that their slaves had become "disorderly," prompting the Senator to ask one of his brothers-in-law to investigate and take the "most decided measures . . . to bring them to a sense of duty."[21]

Although Calhoun knew that the threat and use of violence were the ultimate guarantees of order on the plantation, he also knew that a good master should give proper consideration to the feelings of his slaves. When Virgil Maxcy offered to sell a particularly talented house servant, Calhoun demurred because it would "cause discontent with the other servants, particularly our cook, whose services are no less important to us than that of a good head servant." Although Calhoun had been unwilling to sell Issy even though she was apparently guilty of a capital crime, he expected his slaves to be honest and sober and would sell any slave caught stealing, "but not at a sacrifice." Calhoun, like every other planter, had most of his capital in slaves and expected a reasonable return. Thus, when Clemson reported from Fort Hill that

Quash, Moses, Mary, Tonine, Cooper, Little Sawney, and Ursula all had been sick for a week, Calhoun had much more to worry about than their personal welfare because sick slaves could neither work nor be sold. Clemson, who managed Fort Hill for a short period, understood this well when he explained about one of the sick slaves: "Ursula was confined & has a female child. It is to be hoped that now that she has gone through the spell that when her month is out she will work, for she has not done half a days work since you left." Calhoun would have agreed with his son-in-law. In the final analysis Ursula's value as a person would always have to be weighed against her value as an investment.[22]

Calhoun was confident enough in the rising market for slave property to pay upwards of $1,300 for a house servant at a time when Oakly was being sold for $8,000. He was always conscious of the value of skilled slaves and once purchased a gardener with the expectation of training other slaves and doubling their value. In 1834 he told his son Andrew that blacks were a good investment and that he expected to make at least $120 a hand on the slaves who were working his gold mine at Dahlonega.[23]

The fundamental premise of Calhoun's proslavery argument was that African Americans were naturally suited for slavery, and his experience as a master not surprisingly confirmed the assumption. He recognized that his slaves could master valuable skills. He was loyal to slaves like Sawney who had long been a part of the Calhoun property. He expected all his slaves to obey fundamental moral rules and gave them considerable independence by allowing them to move freely with plantation horses and wagons between Fort Hill and Cane Brake. But he never seems to have suspected that in a different environment his dark-skinned servants might be equal in character and intelligence to white people anywhere. When a slave reported that on his way to Abbeville he had fallen in the river and left his greatcoat behind, Calhoun immediately assumed that the story was a "fabrication" and that "he sold or gambled away the coat." On another occasion, when Clemson informed him that one of the Fort Hill slaves hired out for twenty dollars a month wanted five dollars for himself, Calhoun was stunned. "I think it entirely out of the question. I should think $2 ample & that not to be given, except a small part, in money, but in extra supply of clothing, or something else."[24]

On the night of December 26, 1838, General Bull, a neighbor of Calhoun's brothers in Abbeville, was clubbed to death by two of his slaves. Calhoun does not mention the incident, but he surely would have known about it just as he had known about the attempt to poison Floride's father many years earlier and about the slaves murdered and mutilated on those plantations where the ideal of the just master did not prevail. If he did not dwell on such matters, it was because he accepted the existence of evil everywhere in the world whatever the system of labor. If there was a dark side to slavery, so was there a dark side to the wage system of "free" labor outside the South. Calhoun insisted time after time that he was bound to do his duty in the role Providence had given him. As a man who owned slaves, he probably lived up to the just master's ideal as well as anyone. Nowhere in his letters does he use the word "nigger"; nowhere does he say anything to ridicule or degrade his slaves. And nowhere does he express the slightest guilt or regret that he lived at Fort Hill in a house of privilege built on the forced labor of black men and women. What the slaves thought about their lives there was recorded years later when Calhoun's granddaughter Floride Clemson wrote in her diary on September 2, 1865, less than four months after Appomattox, "All negroes have now asserted their freedom. At Fort Hill all have left but some fifteen hands."[25]

16

"If It Is Ever Intended, Now Is the Time," 1840–1844

A S CALHOUN prepared to return to Washington for the recon-
vening of Congress in December 1840, he must have had mixed
feelings about the country's political future and his own. Anna
Calhoun Clemson obviously spoke her father's mind when she denounced the pitiful "humbuggery" of a government which relied on log
cabins, hard cider, and coonskins to get elected. At the same time she
consoled herself with the probability of a hopeless split among the
newly elected Whigs which might ultimately work to her father's advantage.[1]

After his political reconciliation with Van Buren, Calhoun had
pulled a loyal oar for the Democrats in the reelection campaign, and he
attributed their defeat not only to humbuggery but to the President's
weak leadership in "desperate times." Nevertheless, the style and success of the Whig campaign dismayed him because they demonstrated
the corruption not simply of a party (Calhoun believed parties always
tended toward corruption) but of the culture. "We are a changed people," he wrote Charles Yancey after returning to Washington, "and no
more like what we were thirty years ago than if we were a different
people."[2]

Calhoun's two meetings with the people's choice before the inauguration confirmed his pessimistic judgment. While not openly contemp-
tuous of Harrison, as were Van Buren's cronies, who reported that "old
'Tip' " was making a spectacle of himself, "merry as a cricket" and
garrulously full of "obscene stories" about war and lechery, Calhoun
was troubled to find the sixty-nine-year-old President-elect "uncon-
scious as a child of his difficulties and those of the country" and seem-
ing to accept his triumph as a "mere affair of personal vanity." Calhoun

hardly knew Harrison and was amazed after the election to find the old gentleman come up behind him once in the Senate, tap him on the shoulder, and immediately begin "the most familiar kind of conversation as to the course he intended to take." Embarrassed by such a public display, Calhoun quickly led him outside the chamber, where others soon broke into the conversation. The only hope, Calhoun told Anna, was that the new President "may be perfectly passive and leave it to the strongest about him to take control. And as bad as it may be, it cannot be as bad as the absence of all control."[3]

Calhoun was more optimistic about his own immediate political future than he was for the new administration. Since he had proved his worth to the Democrats under Van Buren by stamping out incipient Whiggery at home (only 15 of 169 seats in the South Carolina legislature went to the Whigs in 1840), and identifying himself not only as the spokesman for slavery and the South but with issues of economic policy which cut across sectional lines, it was not unrealistic for Calhoun to believe that he might be called to lead the country in 1844. "As to myself and my principles," he told his friend Maxcy on February 19, 1841, "if they are ever to gain ascendancy, now is the time."[4]

During the lame duck session of Congress in the winter of 1840–1841, Calhoun maintained a high profile. When the Whigs tried to pass a bill which would have distributed the proceeds of public land sales to the states, he denounced it as a ploy to reduce federal revenues and prepare the way for a protective tariff. Delighting the galleries with his acerbic challenges to Webster and Clay, and bucking up the dispirited Democrats by defending the retention of his old enemy Frank Blair as government printer, Calhoun made it clear that the Whig steamroller would not intimidate him.[5]

By mid-March Calhoun was back in Fort Hill, where family concerns always seemed to overshadow politics. Anna was struggling through a difficult pregnancy that spring. Clemson was trying to get the plantation back on a firm footing with a new overseer, and both Calhoun and Clemson were worried about their substantial investment in Andrew Calhoun's Alabama plantation. Still, Calhoun managed to spend considerable time in his office hideaway, working on what he told Orestes Brownson would be "a regular and I think I may say scientifik [*sic*] development of my views of government."[6] This apparently was the genesis of the famous *Disquisition on Government* which he continued to work on for the rest of his life. As always, his renewed interest in theory was triggered by concrete political experience—in this case the election of 1840. Although the Whigs had not even deigned to write a political platform and had ignored issues altogether during the campaign, Calhoun knew that a majority within the party would interpret its victory as a mandate to turn Clay's political program into law. When Calhoun told Maxcy that "we are a changed people," he was referring to the changing culture which had made Harrison's election possible. According to Calhoun, the degradation in the culture had been a gradual but steady process. When he had entered the Congress thirty years earlier, the country had been at peril, and despite real political differences, American leaders had been able to put the public interest first and stave off the British threat. Beginning in 1824, however, politicians had discovered that they could win federal elections by appealing to majorities driven by special interests like patronage, cheap credit and public lands, protective tariffs, and lavish federal subsidies for harbors, roads, and canals. Consequently, the government, which had been designed and originally run by statesmen, had gradually been taken over by spoilsmen. Jackson, originally perceived as a republican savior sent to reform the system, had instead been corrupted by it, and Van Buren, who had defied the spoilsmen by getting the government out of the banking business, was now replaced by a new party as intent on dividing up the spoils as the Democrats had been under Jackson. A degrading story—but all of it accomplished to the drumbeat of a roaring majority.[7]

Direct, face-to-face communication with the electorate never appealed to Calhoun. He disliked electioneering of all kinds, and with rare exceptions, such as the refusal of Waddy Thompson to follow his lead on the bank issue, he declined all offers to take the stump. Such reticence in the burgeoning American democracy of the 1840s frustrated many of his warmest supporters. They admired Calhoun's formal essays and addresses on the tyranny of unchecked majorities and the need for institutionalizing the nullification principle but despaired of his ability to put his ideas in ordinary language directly before ordinary voters. Calhoun may have been brooding over this problem in early April 1841, as he began his first trip to his son's plantation in Marengo County,

Alabama. Spending two weeks at the Cane Brake, he could not avoid being treated like a celebrity both coming and going. The new democratic style was flourishing in the Southwest, and a large proportion of the people there had roots in South Carolina and other seaboard states where nullification was popular. These ardent citizens demanded to lay hands on their hero. Calhoun was able to avoid addressing the Alabama legislature, but when he visited Marion, Alabama, where he had relatives, he was carried into town by a crowd of more than a thousand, wined, dined, "tead," breakfasted, and finally compelled to give a political talk in the new, overcrowded Baptist church. This was followed by public speeches in Selma and Montgomery, the latter of which was fully reported and is an interesting example of the way in which he tried to popularize his ideas. Although Americans generally were still agog over the sudden death of President Harrison and speculating wildly about the implications of John Tyler's presidency, Calhoun began by lamenting "that the all absorbing question" among the people was "not whether great fundamental principles should be established or overthrown, but who should be President." The decisive principles at issue, he said, derived in the beginning from the opposing policies of Hamilton, modernized by the Whigs, and the policies of Jefferson favored by the opposition. As an important part of the staple-producing South, Calhoun argued, the people in Alabama had a great stake in the outcome because Whig policies would mean transferring tax dollars from citizens in staple states favoring free trade to citizens in the region primarily interested in subsidized manufactures, internal improvements, and the exclusive use of the public treasury. Calhoun explained in a very simple analogy how the American practice of majority rule together with an allegedly equal taxation system could produce this kind of injustice.

He would illustrate: let nine persons gather around a table, on which is a box of wafers. Five are banded together by a mutual interest different from that of the four. Each of the nine take out of the box five wafers—making a circulating medium of forty-five dollars, as each wafer is supposed to represent a dollar. It is agreed to lay a tax on each man of one wafer. The tax you perceive is *equal*. The annual fund raised by its nine dollars—how shall it be appropriated? The five say for "the general welfare" and having the power of a majority, they carry the point. They of course outvote the four, and appropriate this fund *to their own use*. So the tax works, say for the space of five years. At the end of that time, an account is given by each man of the state of his finances. One of the four opens his hand, and declares he had not got a dollar; the next; then the third and fourth—each having not a cent. The first of the five opens his hand, and finds not only the original five dollars, which in the course of five years he has paid as taxes, but four dollars beside—and so it appeared to be the case with the whole five. They had been equally taxed with the four, but by the "general welfare" system of disbursements or appropriations, they had absorbed the whole circulating medium. Such is the effect of even equal taxation, when the disbursements are unequal.

In Calhoun's example, obviously the five favored wafer holders represent the Whig coalition of office seekers, stockholders, speculators, and manufacturers in the North and West, plus those recreant majorities which had carried five southern states for Harrison. The coalition of spoilsmen would naturally support the reestablishment of government banks, protective tariffs, and subsidies of all kinds, leading to higher taxes, increased disbursements, bloated patronage lists, and the establishment of a "monied aristocracy." In the end, Calhoun warned, the "mass, sickened and tired of such constant, excited political whirlwinds in which their rights are trampled upon and their industry absorbed," would gladly turn to a monarch or a dictator.

A local Whig paper remarked that Calhoun seemed "out of place on the stump." No doubt, but the Montgomery speech probably came as close as Calhoun would ever come to blending the kind of crowd-pleasing appeal American voters wanted with the ideas he thought they had to comprehend.[8]

One of the few important official acts which President Harrison performed before he died was to call a special session of Congress, beginning on May 31, 1841. The extra session was Clay's idea, and he intended to use it to repeal the Independent Treasury Act, which Calhoun had helped enact, and to drive through a Whig fiscal program, including a bank, tariff, and public land policy, which would distribute federal revenues among the states. Daniel Webster as Secretary of State was the ranking Whig in the Cabinet, but it was clear to everyone that Clay intended to direct the new administration from the floor of the Senate. However, the fate which had snatched away William Henry Harrison before he could enjoy the splendors of his high office had been equally cruel to Clay by making John Tyler President. Active in politics since 1816 as a Virginia Congressman, governor, and Senator, Tyler was not a man to be pushed around; he had been the only Senator to vote against the force bill and later had resigned his seat rather than follow instructions from the Virginia legislature to expunge the resolution of censure against Jackson. The Whigs had run him for Vice President because he was anti-Jackson and would attract southern votes, not because he was a faithful party man. In his presidency his strong states' rights convictions were bound to collide with Clay's nationalist agenda.

Back in Washington that June, Calhoun apparently believed that despite Tyler's personal constitutional objections to the reestablishment of a national bank, the new President might feel committed to the Whig program, and he feared the Whigs might have the votes to run roughshod over the Democrats in Congress. With a scattering of strategically placed supporters, Calhoun would stop them in the Senate if he could. Applying the same kinds of tactics that he had employed against Jackson almost ten years earlier, Calhoun fought Clay's legislative proposals on almost a daily basis, and his personal encounters with the Kentuckian (a too familiar story by now for some veteran Senators) were frequent and sharp. Spending seven hours a day in session plus long hours reading and preparing for the battles of the next day in the heat of a Washington summer left Calhoun "completely overwhelmed with business," but he assured his daughter that "the very existence of our institution is at stake." When Clay began to up the ante by using Senate rules to shorten the time allowed for debate, Calhoun, pale-faced and more agitated than his friends had ever seen him, accused the Whig leader of assuming King Andrew's royal mantle and gagging the opposition.[9]

Nothing Calhoun could do or say prevented Clay from accomplishing the repeal of the Independent Treasury Act, thus undoing Calhoun's work of the previous year, but the attempt to incorporate a new fiscal bank of the United States met a different fate. On Monday, August 16, 1841, after having spent the previous day in church praying for enlightenment, John Tyler vetoed the bank bill, and that night Calhoun, Benton, Buchanan, and other Democrats appeared at the White House to congratulate the President. It was a convivial meeting, helped along by brandy but counterbalanced by a mob of drunken Whigs blowing horns and shooting guns to protest the action of the faithless Tyler.[10]

Calhoun, who never took spirits, would have passed up John Tyler's brandy while sharing in the gloating over Clay's defeat. He would also have taken a certain secret satisfaction in the angry Whig demonstration outside the palace gates. Clay and Tyler were threatening to chew each other up in the battle of the bank, while Calhoun's own standing continued to rise. If only 1844 were not so far away!

Later in the session, after Tyler had vetoed a second version of the bank bill and the Whigs had read him out of their party, every member of the Cabinet resigned except Webster. Calhoun cautioned his friends against a stampede for Tyler. The President might attract antibank voters, but he would support much of the rest of Whiggery, and half a victory over the Whigs was no victory at all. "I go for victory to my own cause," he wrote Maxcy in mid-September, "complete victory. My principles must triumph or be defeated."[11]

Calhoun spent most of the fall of 1841 at home in Fort Hill, tending his plantation and pondering his own and the country's future. His fundamental problem was still the one that had dogged him throughout his career: how to hold on to his principles without losing political advantage. The stump speech he had given in Alabama in the spring had been about principles, and he had already begun to turn the simple example he had used then about the tyrannical tendency of majority rule into a profound theoretical discourse on political theory; but he had been in political life too long to believe that principles in themselves could win elections. To win the presidency, a man needed organizational support and a message that transcended sectional boundaries. Never a modest person, Calhoun did not underestimate his considerable political advantages. A long career of distinguished national service in the legislative and executive branches had given him enormous visibility across the country, and Americans knew where he stood on the big issues. No one in public life was more respected for his qualities of mind and character, and no one spoke for the South with greater authority.

As so often happens in politics, what Calhoun saw as his personal advantages were easily perceived as weaknesses from other perspectives.

One could argue that like Clay and Webster, he had been around too long and fought too many losing battles, that his self-proclaimed devotion to principle made him difficult to deal with, that ordinary citizens would never understand his intellectual approach to practical problems, and that his outspoken praise of slavery by itself was enough to sink any presidential candidate in the new democratic age.

Calhoun's anomalous position in the politics of the burgeoning American democracy was never more apparent than in the fall of 1841. He and his supporters agreed that the self-destruction of the Whigs created a once-in-a-lifetime opportunity. "Now is the time for your friends to move without reserve," Pickens wrote on October 2 after receiving letters from Congressmen in a dozen states in and outside the South supporting Calhoun's potential nomination. Calhoun agreed with Pickens about the importance of timing ("if it is ever intended, now is the time," he told his brother-in-law) but worried about what he would have called the "politics of availability." By this he meant that whenever the scales turned decisively toward the advantage of one party, as they now did to the Democrats, there was an inevitable tendency to look for an "available" candidate who could be counted on to distribute the spoils of victory generously to those who put him in office. The specter of the spoilsmen had been a whipping boy for Calhoun ever since his break with Jackson, and he revived it in November 1841, when Van Buren released a public letter suggesting that he might be available for his party's nomination in 1844. Without attacking Van Buren personally, Calhoun warned of "restoration" under the wrong kind of leadership and insisted that only the South could provide the reforms needed in the government.[12]

When Calhoun spoke of the South as a source of political reform, he meant that the South depended for its continued existence on the preservation of states' rights, low tariffs, and the maintenance of a lean, relatively weak federal government. Thus southern self-interest tended inevitably to support policies consistent with the old ideology which had launched the Republic.

Because Calhoun invariably interpreted political alignments in ideological terms, his analysis of short-run political situations frequently seems confusing. For example, he wrote his Georgia ally Wilson Lumpkin on December 26, 1841, that there were now three parties vying for control in Washington: the administration (Tylerites), the rest of the Whigs (Clayites), and the "Republicans," by which he meant the party in power under Van Buren which had finally adopted Calhoun's principles on fiscal policy. Actually, however, Calhoun usually thought in terms of four competing political forces: the Tyler party, which was right on the bank but wrong about everything else; the Clay party, which had always been wrong on everything except the abuses of power by Jackson; the Van Buren party, also right on the bank but always vulnerable to takeover by spoilsmen; and the true republicans, loyal to Calhoun. The challenge for Calhoun in the forties was to keep his own party viable by maintaining its southern base while reaching out for support elsewhere in the country and not surrendering on principle.[13]

Admitting that it would require "much prudence and skill" to negotiate the treacherous political waters which were certain to surround the Tyler administration, Calhoun made an effort to tone down his usually aggressive stance in the Senate. Meanwhile, despite Calhoun's contempt for political "managers," a committee was being set up in Charleston to prepare for his campaign. Franklin Elmore, the president of the Bank of South Carolina, headed the committee, which maintained contacts with state Democratic leaders like David Henshaw in Massachusetts and Romulus Saunders in North Carolina and assigned the mercurial Rhett to coordinate Calhoun's efforts in the North and West.[14]

Although Calhoun had made it abundantly clear in letters to his friends that he was willing to run for the presidency if chosen, no one expected him to act like a candidate. There was, however, an occasional straw in the wind to suggest how keen he was about his immediate political future. He made a point of joining the Irish Immigrant Society of New York, for example, emphasizing the pride he felt in being the son of an Irish immigrant, a pride shared by many of New York's politically influential working class. On another occasion he presented the Senate with a petition from a Tennessee convention asking for an appropriation to improve navigation in the Tennessee River. Explaining that he remained in principle opposed to using federal funds for rivers and harbors, he nevertheless wanted Tennessee's request to be given the same consideration the other states were getting. A little clumsy, perhaps, but Calhoun obviously wanted growth-oriented western voters to know that he understood their priorities.[15]

In addressing the major issues before the Senate in 1842, Calhoun tended to follow a moderate course. Refusing to budge on the fiscal crisis, he declared flatly that he would never vote for a national bank under any conditions, but he was relatively quiet about slavery.[16] Naturally he expressed the outrage of his slaveholding constituents when the British seized the American ship *Creole* and freed most of the mutinous slaves in its cargo, but he did so in a way which appealed to American rights on the high seas as much as to slaveholders' rights to their property. In a later discussion about fugitive slaves, Calhoun reiterated his belief that slavery in the South was a providential and essentially benevolent institution and claimed that no laboring class outside the United States was as well compensated as American slaves, but he carefully refrained from making an analogy with free labor in the North and West. Abolitionists would have been delighted to learn that Calhoun made these remarks at about the same time that one of his own slaves was being held in jail for attempting to set fire to an overseer.[17]

Political optimism ran high among Calhoun's managers in the winter of 1842. The Charleston committee had begun to sound out northern Democrats like Levi Woodbury of New Hampshire and Silas Wright of New York as possible running mates for the Carolinian, and Pickens believed that if Calhoun "would be quiet and say but little I have no doubt he will be elected." But Calhoun could no more play a quiet role in the Senate than he could convert to abolitionism, and although his style in debate during this period seems to have been less confrontational than usual, he was as active as ever and vigorously opposed every effort of Clay to slip parts of his American System through the Senate. Calhoun's most substantial effort, which he hoped would do the most to create a favorable impression in the public eye, was the speech he delivered on February 28 attacking Clay's proposed amendment to limit the veto power. Frustrated by Tyler's bank vetoes, Clay proposed to change the Constitution so that Congress could override by simple majorities in both houses. Such an issue was tailor-made for Calhoun, who had little trouble in demonstrating that the veto power was one of several checks written into the Constitution to protect against the evils of unlimited rule by the numerical majority. The real danger of executive tyranny, Calhoun argued, was not the veto but the actions of Congress over the years to legislate Clay's American System of banks, tariffs, and internal improvements which could only lead to more bloated government at the federal level and increased patronage powers for the President.[18]

Calhoun's speech made a great impression on his followers in Congress, and the *Washington Globe,* which had denounced him savagely when he attacked majority rule back in 1832, praised it as one of the "ablest, most luminous and unanswerable" arguments "ever delivered on the nature of this Government." By mid-March there had been a distribution of more than forty thousand copies of the speech, which Calhoun saw as a vindication of his ideas. "This will surprise you, when you read it," he wrote Anna Maria, "for it comes up almost to nullification. It is in fact the premises from which it irresistably flows."[19]

Calhoun had a special reason to welcome the visibility his veto speech gave him because it came just as Van Buren, the most famous undeclared presidential candidate in the country and the man everyone expected Calhoun would have to beat to get the nomination, was invading his home base. Using the pretext of his son's marriage to the daughter of a wealthy South Carolina planter, Van Buren had planned a southern trip which would take him through the seaboard states down to New Orleans and then up the Mississippi to Nashville, where he could expect to receive a patriarchal blessing from Andrew Jackson. The contrast between the two rivals had never been greater. While Calhoun showered the country with earnest, tightly constructed arguments about the Constitution, Van Buren sauntered through the South, banqueting and sharing cigars and Madeira with such ornaments among the Carolina elite as Joel Poinsett, James Henry Hammond, Francis Pickens, and even that old Calhoun war-horse George McDuffie. Calhoun did not expect many defections in his own state, but it must have rankled him to read the reports of Van Buren's gracious passage through the South while he exhausted himself in the Senate defending principles essential to the South's existence.[20]

Meanwhile, the presidential campaign grew closer. On March 31, 1842 Clay resigned his Senate seat, freeing himself to become a full-time candidate. After a moving valedictory to the Senate in which the Kentuckian sought to assuage personal wounds opened in the heat of political debates over the years, Calhoun was one of the first Senators in the opposition to come forward and take his hand. It was a dramatic moment, one observer remarked, because the two men "had not spoke since 1837." The sense of drama must have been heightened in Calhoun's mind by the premonition that he would probably contend against his old rival for the highest office in the country. He would soon receive a letter from a Baltimore man recounting a dream in 1837 prophesying the eclipse of Andrew Jackson, the temporary ascendence of Harrison, and the ultimate raising of Calhoun to the White House. He kept the letter.[21]

Remaining at his seat during the spring and summer of 1842, Calhoun spent most of his time fighting Whig propaganda to increase government expenditures. He opposed appropriations for an insane asylum in Washington and for a national institute for the promotion of science, not because he was hardhearted or anti-intellectual but because he feared every new federal bureaucracy would add to patronage lists, deplenish the Treasury, and hasten the day when Clay would insist on increasing government revenues by raising the tariff. A showdown over the tariff was inevitable in any case. The terms negotiated by the Compromise Tariff of 1833 expired in June 1842, and the probability of higher rates was enhanced not only by the determination of Clay's supporters to see northern manufacturers get their due but by the fact of an empty Treasury and the willingness of President Tyler, who still had enough Whig in him to accept an increase. The battle was fought in Congress over the summer. Clay was not physically on the scene, but Calhoun wrestled tenaciously with his ghost before finally admitting defeat at the end of August, when the Senate, with the help of Democratic votes from New York and Pennsylvania, passed a tariff restoring the rates of 1832.[22]

By the fall of 1842, when he was finally able to get home between sesssions of Congress, Calhoun had convinced himself that he should soon follow Clay's example and resign from the Senate. He was explicit about his reasons for leaving. Not only did he find it unseemly for a presidential candidate to embroil himself in congressional politics, but as he told Hammond, he thought he had accomplished all he could in the Senate. The next great challenges were to reform the government by cutting down on patronage and to repeal the new tariff, both of which could be met only by a decisive Democratic victory in the presidential election of 1844. Calhoun seems to have interpreted temporary defeat over the tariff as a blessing in disguise which could unite the South and force the Democrats to take his candidacy seriously. Sometime in early November Calhoun wrote to his cousin Andrew Pickens under "intense excitement," suggesting the possibility that the free trade, reform-minded republicans might be ready to break with Van Buren and go their own way. Pickens immediately replied in a long letter designed to cool off his old friend by reminding him that 1842 was not 1832, that the tariff was not the incendiary issue it had once been, and that Calhoun was not the young warrior he had been then. "Men who may rally under your standard," Pickens warned, "now cannot look forward for you to bear it 10 years from now." In retrospect Pickens's cautionary advice sounds strikingly perceptive, and Calhoun's excited aspirations appear grandiose and almost fantastic. How could a man whose claim to fame rested primarily on his uncompromising position on the two most divisive issues of the period, slavery and free trade, persist in thinking that he might become President in the burgeoning democracy of the 1840s? Congressman Robert M. T. Hunter, Calhoun's faithful friend in Virginia, believed that Calhoun realized he had no "real chance for the presidency" but was convinced that in order to maintain his position before the country, he had to appear as a presidential contender. Although there is some plausibility in this theory, it clashes sharply with the letter to Pickens in the autumn of 1842 and with what we know about Calhoun's character. No American of his generation was more driven, and no one identified political ambition more closely with moral imperatives and the conviction that he alone knew what was best for the country. Given the crisis in Washington in 1842, the vulnerability of southern institutions, and the relatively wide open contest among Democratic hopefuls for the presidential nomination, Calhoun had no choice. He could no more stay out of the race than he could deny his own nature.[23]

The active campaign for Calhoun, which lasted little more than a year, was based on the assumption that Van Buren, the front-runner in the party, could not win without the southern support which was expected to be more or less solidly for Calhoun. The candidacies of Lewis Cass in Michigan and James Buchanan in Pennsylvania were discounted, and the Calhoun managers assumed that in the showdown with Van Buren, Calhoun would get enough votes at the convention from Democrats outside the South to be nominated. They knew that Tyler was also in the running but assumed that with little support in either party he would fail and throw his strength, including the patronage of his office to Calhoun, who had effectively supported him against the fierce onslaughts of Henry Clay.

Everyone in the Calhoun camp agreed that convention timing and procedures would be crucial. Calhoun wanted the Democratic convention at Baltimore to be held in 1844 as close to the election as possible so that his policies could get maximum exposure, and he insisted that delegates to the convention be elected by congressional districts and vote as individuals. The second stipulation was intended to take advantage of Calhoun's minority strength to split delegations in states outside the South, like New York, Massachusetts, Connecticut, New Hampshire, and Ohio.

The winter session of Congress passed quickly and relatively quietly for Calhoun. Clay, whom everyone expected to be the Whig standard-bearer in 1844, was gone, while Webster was still holding on at the State Department, putting the finishing touch on negotiations with Lord Ashburton to settle the long-standing Maine boundary dispute. The absence of his traditional adversaries and a desire to appear more presidential than partisan seemed to put Calhoun in a rare ecumenical state of mind—within limits. But when Amos Kendall suggested in late February 1843 that he might bring about a reconciliation with Jackson, Calhoun declined. He would let that part of his record speak for itself.[24]

By the third week in March 1843 Calhoun's retirement from the Senate was in effect, and he was back at Fort Hill, where he was to remain for a full year, his longest continuous residence in South Carolina in thirty years. His satisfaction at this turn of events can hardly be overemphasized. Despite the consternation of many of his most zealous supporters, whatever campaigning he would do over the next several months would be done surrounded by family and slaves within the refuge of his own plantation.

Whether or not Calhoun would make a strong showing at the Baltimore convention depended heavily on what happened in Virginia and

New York, and the early news out of Virginia was not hopeful. Calhoun had hardly settled in at Fort Hill when he heard that a Democratic convention in Richmond, while agreeing to postpone the national convention, as the Calhounites demanded, insisted on one in which delegates would vote under the unit rule. Such a rule would practically assure Van Buren of victory since it would preclude counting the votes of individual Calhoun supporters in states outside the South. From Calhoun's point of view, the action of the Virginia Democrats was disastrous in principle as well as in its immediately political impact because it threatened to "transfer the control of the presidential election permanently to a few large non-slaveholding states." The party which had found room for the nullifiers during Van Buren's administration was now embracing the principle of the numerical majority in order to restore Van Buren to power. The Richmond meeting, followed by state elections in which Van Burenites again won the day, made Calhoun despair about Virginia, and especially about Thomas Ritchie, the influential editor of the *Richmond Enquirer,* who had always been Van Buren's most powerful link with the South. Now Ritchie had "stuck Virginia as a tail to N. York instead of placing her in her natural position at the head of the South."[25]

Although Virginia threatened to turn into a lost cause, Calhoun still hoped to make inroads in Van Buren's home state, and his support there, especially in New York City, was in fact encouraging. Part of it came from New York merchants, who were almost as ardent free traders as Carolinians and who resented Van Buren's lieutenant Silas Wright for voting to raise the tariffs. Part of it came from "shirtless" working-class Democrats, who were battling Tammany Hall to build a power base of their own, and part of it came from enthusiastic New York Irishmen, who saw Calhoun as a famous kinsman, "Full Blooded Irish on Both Sides as Good Game Blood as God Ever put in the Veins of Man."[26]

Calhoun's cause in New York was managed by Joseph Scoville, a zealous young journalist of great ambition and erratic inclination whose political style clashed rudely with the chivalrous ways of the gentlemen in Charleston who were allegedly in charge of Calhoun's campaign. After Scoville had helped stage several successful rallies for Calhoun in New York City, Rhett, acting as liaison between Charleston and New

York, warily informed Calhoun that a "secret organization in your favor" had been set up to take over Tammany. Although the dissimulation involved was "not consonant with our views of the fitness of things," Rhett said, it promised to be effective. Rhett hardly needed to be so fastidious about the New York campaign because Scoville was sending regular reports to Calhoun, who must have winced when he read such messages as "I have been among the Germans. They number 5000 voters in this city and follow a few leaders like a flock of sheep—by management they can be made right." Scoville did not spell out to Calhoun what he meant by "management," but he told Hunter quite bluntly what it would take in terms of customhouse patronage to build a strong Calhoun committee in New York City. *"Suppose* some of that Committee want office—*suppose* they have a Brother, Uncle or cousin (same thing) who would not mind taking a bite—and they are willing to sign, seal and deliver, in black and white their political influence to the People's candidate—we must be prepared—and ready to bargain."[27]

Calhoun understandably tried not to get too close to Scoville, but it was not easy. The man was everywhere. In addition to his organizing efforts in New York, he was managing the publication of Calhoun's speeches and edited the pro-Calhoun *Washington Spectator* for a short period before being deposed by members of the Charleston committee who accused him of failing to follow their direction and suspected him of being unreliable with "money affairs." Despite his brashness and erratic behavior, Joe Scoville remained a part of the Calhoun team because he had something that every old political leader needs: youth, loyalty, intelligence, unlimited energy, and the willingness to do whatever had to be done.[28]

Nothing distressed Calhoun supporters more than his refusal to budge from Fort Hill. He had not visited the North for twenty years and had never gone as far west as Ohio. Although party leaders hardly expected to see Calhoun rolled into town on a barrel of cider, they despaired at his reclusiveness, and even some of his Charleston advisers, knowing that the South was not as monolithic as Calhoun liked to believe, advised a tour through the South and West. Calhoun supporters in the urban centers of the Northeast, where Irish voters especially were anxious to see their hero, were eager for the candidate to show himself in the flesh, but Calhoun was adamant. He had always tried to avoid political rallies as demeaning to the kind of republican principles he represented, and refusing to change now, he patiently and courteously explained to his disappointed followers that the presidency was "too elevated . . . to be the object of personal solicitation" and that at the risk of appearing too "fastidious," he had to avoid anything that smacked of "a mere electioneering tour."[29]

Hard-nosed political operators, like Scoville, who were up to their necks in the kind of electioneering that frequently involved buying votes must have smiled at their leader's refusal even to approach the fray because he had to know, at least in a general way, what they were doing, just as he must have known what had been going on in Charleston in 1832, when the nullifiers were outbribing the unionists. On the other hand, Calhoun seems to have sincerely struggled over the issue of his own participation in the campaign. Writing candidly to Hunter, Calhoun said that quite apart from "higher considerations," he did not see how a political tour, which would probably exhaust him and alienate those supporters he could not see anyway, could help the cause. He confessed that he was tempted to travel simply to satisfy his friends, but in the final analysis he would do nothing which might "indicate a personal solicitude about an office which I do not feel." Calhoun understood himself well enough to know that he could not consciously play the role demanded by an increasingly democratic political culture. What he would never understand was the driving ambition which had forced him into an impossible contest in the first place.[30]

Believing that his long political record was the most effective campaign document he could put before the public, Calhoun arranged for the publication of an authorized biography to be paired with a selection of his speeches chosen largely by him. *The Life of John C. Calhoun, Presenting a Condensed History of Political Events from 1811 to 1843* was published by Harper and Brothers as an anonymous seventy-four-page pamphlet. Although it has been referred to frequently in these pages as Calhoun's autobiography, the actual authorship is controversial. Much of it was written by Calhoun's close friends Virgil Maxcy and Robert M. T. Hunter. How much Calhoun actually contributed to it is impossible to say, but there are parts dealing with details of his early life that could only have come from him, and it is beyond question that the *Life* presents Calhoun's career as he perceived it and as he wanted it to be perceived by the public. The *Life* was published about the time Calhoun retired from the Senate and was made widely available in an edition costing twelve and a half cents, but the publication of the speeches lagged behind, a casualty of the confusion and poor communication which dogged the entire campaign.

As a historical document the *Life* is invaluable in understanding the ways in which Calhoun rationalized the different stages in his career, and no biographer can ignore it. But as a piece of political literature designed to influence voting behavior, it was hopelessly out of date. A generation increasingly attracted to the democratic style of Davy Crockett and Jack Downing was not likely to be captivated by Calhoun's *Life* or his speeches, and it is small wonder that Harper and Brothers was soon complaining about the scarcity of orders.[31]

There was one popular issue before the American public in 1843 that might have been exploited in ways that could have helped Calhoun. In Rhode Island, where the state constitution based on a colonial charter deprived half the adult males of voting privileges, a popular party under Thomas Dorr, having revised the constitution in convention and conducted separate elections for the legislature and state offices in 1842, attempted to replace the existing government with a new government allegedly based on the power of the people. When both governments called on President Tyler for support, he authorized the use of federal troops if necessary to put down the rebellion under the provisions of the federal Constitution guaranteeing every state a republican form of government and protection against domestic violence. In the ensuing controversy, political leaders in both parties rushed to take sides. Radical Democrats, who had been trumpeting the power of the people ever since 1828, naturally lined up behind Dorr and waited to see where Calhoun would stand on the issue.

Calhoun's popularity among working-class Democrats in New York depended on his attacks on the tariff, the moneyed aristocracy, and the monopoly power of banks. He wanted to be perceived as a champion of equal rights for white men and proudly cited his support to extend the franchise to all white males in South Carolina. But Thomas Dorr caused an enormous problem for Calhoun because he had unconstitutionally overthrown a legal government and justified it in terms of the power of the people, which really was no more than the power of the numerical majority. There was no way Calhoun could support the Dorr government, and close supporters like Hunter and Dixon Lewis pleaded with him to keep quiet about it, a policy which did not sit well with pro-Calhoun editors in New York, who grumbled that their favorite's unwillingness to speak out would mean "a long farewell to the support of the Northern Democracy." Although Calhoun apparently did not feel obliged to make a public statement about Dorr, he did take advantage of an opportunity to enlighten the Rhode Island agitator personally. According to Dixon Lewis, Dorr made a midnight visit to Washington to lobby Senators. Knowing that Calhoun would be on Dorr's list, Lewis hastened to his friend's boardinghouse, arriving at 1:00 A.M. to hear Calhoun announce that Dorr had just left, "and I have given him a piece of my mind." Emboldened by this face-to-face encounter, Calhoun was prepared to make a formal announcement in the Senate the next day, but Lewis seems to have convinced him that would be unnecessarily offensive to his supporters in New York and slam the door on any lingering chance he might have for the nomination. Eventually Dorr was arrested, convicted of treason, and later pardoned, and a new constitution with liberal suffrage provisions was legally enacted in Rhode Island. The Dorr Rebellion became a part of history, and so did Calhoun's inability to speak to the democratic spirit of the new age.[32]

By the end of September 1843 the game was almost over for Calhoun. Although his New York City supporters made a surprisingly strong showing, the Van Burenites were able to nominate their man and turn back Calhoun's plan for a national convention composed according to the district system. The convention would be held late in May 1844 as the Calhounites desired, but there would not be nearly enough of them to make their candidate a serious contender. Disappointed Calhoun supporters complained of Van Buren's trickery, but that was not the real story. The simple truth was that their candidate's style and message lacked mass appeal. Various attempts were made to humanize his image by publishing stories about his frontier background, but the heavy reliance on his published biography and speeches meant that the Calhoun campaign was primarily addressed to an elite that was expected to read, understand, and approve the Calhoun record and endorse him to rank-and-file voters willing to follow the "leading men" in their communities. This was the old-fashioned politics which

Calhoun had first learned by watching his father—politics which still might work in South Carolina, but not in most of the rest of the country. Moreover, the Calhoun managers in Charleston were outgunned from the start. Their attempts to build a Calhoun press with the *Washington Spectator* and *New York Gazette* were hopelessly inadequate. The *Spectator,* for example, had less than thirty subscriptions in the entire South. New York politicians friendly to Calhoun frequently wondered who was really in charge of the campaign, and there was a general feeling among Calhoun's closest friends that Elmore and Rhett were both ineffective and unreliable.[33]

Although Calhoun seemed clearly to have lost his bid to control the National Democratic Convention, the congressional elections in the fall of 1843, which the Democrats won overwhelmingly, offered a final ray of hope. If Calhoun supporters could elect the Speaker of the House and control the key committees, they might still be able to convince party leaders that their man was the most powerful candidate. An attempt was made, halfhearted at best, but Van Buren's well-disciplined troops once again came away with the prize. In explaining this final defeat, the demoralized Rhett suggested that it might be time to forget politics and concentrate on eternity. "Let me implore you, my aged friend and political father," he wrote, "to seek God in Christ."[34]

Calhoun, who never felt the need to seek spiritual counsel from anyone, must have found this advice gratuitous. He had been telling his friends for months that who won the election was less important than what might happen afterward, and he certainly did not feel that his own political usefulness was played out. In January 1844 he published a long statement withdrawing his name from the Baltimore convention and explaining once again why the party's insistence on organizing the convention according to the majority principle would be fatal to the South in the long run. At the same time he refused to let the *Charleston Mercury* delete his name from its masthead. He was hardly ready to retire, and in a matter of weeks he suddenly found himself in the second most powerful political office in the country.[35]

17

Secretary of State, 1844–1845

RETIREMENT probably never looked sweeter to Calhoun than it did in February 1844 as he prepared to enjoy the amenities of life at Fort Hill in the bosom of his own successful acres, surrounded by a loving family and a host of admiring friends and neighbors. Moreover, his interpretation of recent political disappointments hardly encouraged a continuance in Washington as a presidential contender. "I am the last man that can be elected in the present condition of this country," he told his brother-in-law. "I am too honest and patriotick to be the choice of anything like a majority." Sounding a similar note in a letter to Duff Green, who was still hatching schemes to keep his candidacy alive, Calhoun insisted that he was through with the "fraudulent game of President making" and anxious to separate himself from the degeneration of a system which forced voters to choose between the demagoguery of Whig opportunists and the corruption of Democratic spoilsmen. The future of the country might look grim, but in judging his own role, Calhoun could say confidently that he found "nothing to regret and little to correct."[1]

Actually Calhoun was not as serene as he sounded. Chagrined at the eagerness of some of his supporters to remain in the Democratic establishment, he had reluctantly taken their advice and toned down the harsh criticism of that party which dominated the first draft of his letter withdrawing from the campaign. If he had had his way, Calhoun would have held the Democrats' feet to the fire on the antislavery issue because he suspected that with Clay as the Whig nominee, Democrats outside the South would be tempted to court the abolition vote by attacking Clay as a slaveholder. "It is a dangerous game to us," he warned one of his Virginia friends, "and ought not to be played, even if our resistance to it should lose the election. No political consideration should induce the South to permit *that question* to be tampered with."[2]

Although Calhoun's uneasiness over the political will of southerners to defend the vital interests of their region would probably have drawn him back to Washington in any event, that matter was decided by a higher power on February 28, 1844, when a huge gun on the battleship *Princeton* exploded, killing several dignitaries, including Secretary of State Abel Upshur. Calhoun learned about the disaster through the eyewitness account of his son Patrick, who had been aboard as part of a presidential party and narrowly escaped death himself. President Tyler was also spared, but Calhoun's close friends Virgil Maxcy and Thomas Gilmer, Secretary of the Navy, were killed along with Upshur.

The same mail that brought him Patrick's shocking letter informed Calhoun that he would be named by the President to replace Upshur as Secretary of State. Just one week later he received two letters from John Tyler. The first formally notified him of the nomination; the second announced his immediate confirmation by the Senate.[3]

There was never any real doubt about Calhoun's willingness to become the new head of Tyler's Cabinet, and letters pouring in from leaders of both parties urging him to accept the post soon overcame any doubts he might have had. Gratified by this spontaneous burst of approval and by the remarkable alacrity with which the Senate had acted to confirm him, Calhoun quickly sent his letter of acceptance to the President and prepared to leave for Washington.

Always a firm believer in the hand of Providence, Calhoun must have been impressed by the providential nature of a catastrophe which had taken the life of his dear friend Maxcy ("I loved him like a brother"), while sparing his son and elevating himself to the second position in the government at a time when the great question before the country was the acquisition of Texas. Dixon Lewis may have given voice to Calhoun's own thoughts when he wrote, "The beauty of the thing is that Providence rather than Tyler has put Calhoun at the head of this great question, to direct its force and control its fury."[4]

When Calhoun took over as Secretary of State on April 1, 1844, the Texas issue had been dividing Americans for years. An independent republic since 1836, when American immigrants in Texas had seized their freedom from Mexico, Texas was bound to the United States by ties of history, language, geography, and, perhaps most important, slavery. A major reason for the Texans' war for independence had been the abolition of slavery in Mexico. Once they had established their own government, the people of Texas repeatedly expressed their wish to join the Union. Congress refused the request partly because it wanted to avoid a war with Mexico, partly because Texas was a slave state and might upset the delicate balance of free and slave states that had been in place since 1820, and partly because annexation of Texas was opposed by European powers like Britain and France, seeking an independent Texas to act as a buffer against U.S. expansion, weaken the United States' control of the cotton trade, and provide a market for European exports. A second war between Mexico and Texas, which broke out in 1842 and terminated in a shaky truce with Mexico threatening to go to war again if Texas joined the Union, underscored the need for a permanent solution to the Texas problem. Mexico was now under increasing pressure from Britain to recognize Texas independence, and whether or not that recognition would require Texans to give up slavery had become a matter of serious concern to American slaveholders, who feared that a Texas committed to free labor might exert a domino effect on the southern states.

Calhoun had been an outspoken advocate of annexation ever since 1836, when he supported recognition of Texas and promised to receive Texans with "open arms" if they sought statehood. He believed that the white population in the United States would inevitably expand to the south and west and that an independent Texas heavily influenced by foreign powers opposed to slavery would threaten the stability of the Union. "Texas must be annexed," he had announced to a cheering crowd of Charlestonians as far back as March 1837.[5]

Although Clay and Van Buren, the leading contenders for the presidency in 1843, had tried to duck the divisive Texas issue, John Tyler, spurned by both parties, believed that annexation might bring him the political base he needed. It would not only assuage the anxieties of southerners offended by the Tariff of 1842 and the increasingly bold attacks of antislavery Congressmen but might also appeal to Americans everywhere caught up in the expansionist spirit of the time. Early in

1843 the President began to call for annexation, thus forcing Daniel Webster, the lone remaining Whig Cabinet member, to resign as Secretary of State. No Massachusetts man could be expected to take the lead in bringing another slave state into the Union. When Tyler replaced Webster with Upshur, a respected Virginia judge, nullification-ist, and Calhoun confidant, he was implicitly inviting Calhoun to become a partner in the administration's Texas enterprise, and by the summer of 1843, without relinquishing his own presidential hopes, the latter had become one of Upshur's chief advisers. By this time Calhoun had been alerted through letters from Duff Green, a special envoy of the President to England, and by the Texas chargé d'affaires in London, of an alleged plot in which Lord Aberdeen, the British foreign minister, under pressure from a powerful British antislavery movement, was considering a loan to Texas to cover the cost of emancipation there. Upshur, who was receiving similar reports, wrote Calhoun for advice on August 14, 1843. Calhoun responded by proposing a detailed diplomatic strategy. Agreeing with Upshur that Britain's posture toward Texas was part of a larger plan to destroy slavery throughout the South and thus control the world cotton trade, Calhoun maintained that "the safety of the Union and the very existence of the South" were at stake. He advised Upshur to keep a low profile on annexation while launching a vigorous propaganda campaign alerting the South to the dangers of abolition in Texas. At the same time the government should proceed through standard diplomatic channels to demand an explanation from Britain and warn its chief European commercial rivals of its monopolistic designs. Meanwhile, the American minister to Mexico would be instructed to bend every effort to keep that nation from cooperating with Britain. Formal negotiations with Texas about annexation were to be avoided until the "public mind" was prepared, but the Texas government should be secretly assured of the "hearty cooperation of the Executive towards effecting it when the proper time arrives."

During the following six months the Tyler-Upshur policy proceeded along the lines Calhoun advised. Edward Everett, United States minister to England, confronted Aberdeen about the alleged antislavery plot, while the Tyler press beat the drums for annexation, and Texas was covertly notified that the administration would officially push for annexation at the appropriate time. Secret negotiations followed until most of the main points in a treaty had been agreed upon by the time Upshur was killed.[6]

During the month intervening between the *Princeton* disaster and Calhoun's arrival in Washington, the Whig press broke the story of the secret negotiations, and four days after his arrival Calhoun met with the Texas minister, Isaac Van Zandt, for the first time. By April 12, less than two weeks after taking his oath of office, the new Secretary of State was able to sign a treaty bringing Texas into the Union as a territory. Calhoun was confident that despite the partisan and sectional division over the issue, the treaty would pass the Senate. "The voice of the country," he wrote on April 13, "is so decidedly in favor of annexation that any hesitancy on the part of the doubtful will probably give way to it."[7]

Slavery had always been the sticking point about Texas, and Calhoun made sure that the Senate would be forced to deal with that issue directly when he dispatched an extraordinary message to Richard Pakenham, the British minister to the United States. Pakenham had written a letter to Upshur two days before the latter's death enclosing a message from Aberdeen which explained the British position on Texas and slavery. The gist of the message was that although Britain desired the end of slavery everywhere, it would support Texas independence with or without slavery. Aberdeen insisted that his country would never tamper with domestic institutions in Texas and the United States. They remained free to make their own arrangements about slavery, and Britain remained free to disapprove of it while pursuing diplomatic goals that were "purely commercial."

Although Aberdeen and Pakenham may have thought their message was conciliatory, Calhoun, who was accustomed to claiming the high ground in any dispute, was offended by its tone of moral superiority. Before composing a reply, he met with Pakenham and suggested opening a formal correspondence on the relative merits of British emancipation and American slavery, but the British minister quickly declined, offering instead a three-party declaration by Britain, France, and the United States, guaranteeing Texas independence. In reply to this suggestion, Calhoun simply smiled. He had been given an opportunity to put himself on the side of American rights while at the same time defending slavery and exposing British hypocrisy before the world. He would make the most of it.

Calhoun decided to make his response to the Pakenham-Aberdeen letter the occasion for a long lecture to Britain and the world on the wisdom of annexation and the folly of British antislavery policy. The justification for annexation was essentially a restatement of arguments familiar to southern expansionists. British pressure on Mexico to make recognition of Texas contingent on emancipation threatened the "prosperity and safety" of the Union. Therefore, the United States had negotiated a treaty of annexation "in self defense."

Although Pakenham would have found little new in the first part of Calhoun's letter, he must have been startled by the vigorous proslavery argument which followed. According to Calhoun, the British policy of emancipation "within her own possessions" should never guide "other countries whose situation differs from hers." In the United States each state had to decide for itself whether or not to change the historic relationship between the races, and history proved that those states retaining slavery had acted wisely. To make his case, Calhoun drew heavily from statistics in the census of 1840 purporting to show that in states which had abolished slavery, black inhabitants had "invariably" sunk into poverty, vice, and disease, especially mental disease. For example, the census showed that 1 out of 96 blacks in the free states was deaf, mute, blind, or insane, while the ratio in the slave states was 1 in 672. In Massachusetts, where slavery had been abolished sixty years earlier, and where "the greatest zeal" on behalf of black people existed, their condition was "amongst the most wretched," with 1 out of 13 "either deaf and dumb, blind, idiot, insane or in prison." On the other hand, "the census and other authentic sources of information establish the fact that the condition of the African race throughout all the states, where the relation between the two has been retained, enjoys a degree of health which may well compare with that of any laboring population in any country in Christendom: and it may be added, that in no other condition, or in any other country has the negro race ever attained so high an elevation in morals, intelligence or civilization." The message was obvious. What Great Britain sought for the United States and elsewhere in humanitarian guise would only bring misery to the objects of their misguided zeal and chaos and destruction to the rest of the world.[8]

Historians have speculated at length about Calhoun's motives in writing the Pakenham letter, but the simplest explanation is that the aggressive defense of annexation was perfectly consistent with the plan of action he had outlined for Upshur the previous summer. Although the evidence does not support the notion that the British government was plotting with abolitionists to provide funds for the emancipation of Texas slaves, it was plausible for Calhoun to believe that something like that was in the wind. A few Texans who favored the idea did go to Britain to promote it. They were supported by influential British abolitionists and were actually received by Lord Aberdeen. Edward Everett, the American minister to Britain who had a close relationship with Aberdeen, discounted the idea of a British plot, but it was natural for Calhoun to distrust a Massachusetts Whig like Everett. Actually, Everett supported annexation and was pleased to learn that Calhoun had taken over the State Department, but Calhoun was not about to believe that. He had cut his political teeth fighting the New England–London axis in 1812, and he was fully prepared to find another one brewing in 1844.[9]

The political logic behind the Pakenham letter is obvious. Calhoun was still receiving letters from supporters lamenting his withdrawal from the upcoming Democratic National Convention and deploring the effect it would have in assuring Van Buren's nomination. He knew that Van Buren was trying to avoid taking a position on annexation in order to hold on to his northern base. The Pakenham letter would make that impossible. His own candidacy might fail, but Calhoun once again saw an opportunity to control the political agenda and seized it with an extraordinarily aggressive diplomatic paper which managed to appeal to both nationalist and sectional prejudices at the same time. Once the document was made public, any Democrat expecting southern support would have to stand up and be counted, and if he did not give a resounding yea to annexation, he was doomed.

On April 22 President Tyler sent the Texas treaty with supporting documents, including the Pakenham letter, to the Senate, where it was referred to the Foreign Relations Committee. Five days later it was leaked to the press, and the same day Van Buren issued a statement opposing immediate annexation. Calhoun must have read his statement with satisfaction about the same time that he was sending off a second dispatch to Pakenham. Although the British minister had replied to Calhoun's first letter in muted language which ignored his lengthy and gratuitous remarks on slavery, Calhoun pounced on the little he could find to keep the dialogue going. He was not defending slavery, he said, but simply pointing out that in the United States slaves were better off in mind, body, and spirit than free blacks, and the avowed global antislavery policy of Britain would necessarily be resisted by any United States government. Pakenham refused to continue the argument, citing to Aberdeen various "instances of bad faith, glaring perversion of facts" in Calhoun's letters and claiming there was nothing so hopeless as arguing with a man who was determined not to be convinced. Calhoun was disappointed; he had anticipated a long public debate along the lines of the Onslow-Patrick Henry exchange twenty years earlier, through which he would face down, before an international audience, the misguided antislavery policy of Great Britain. Although Pakenham and Aberdeen had wisely refused to play that game, Calhoun could take credit for marrying annexation to the defense of slavery at least for southern Democrats. As an almost instantaneous activist Secretary of State he continued to play a controlling role in domestic politics, and—perhaps best of all—he had mortally wounded an old adversary. Van Buren's letter opposing annexation had "completely prostrated him," Calhoun told a Georgia friend. "There is great confusion in the ranks of the Democracy. If they can be united under the flag of annexation an easy victory will be achieved over Mr. Clay and the Whigs."[10]

The real puzzle in this piece of Calhoun's career is not why he wrote the Pakenham letter or what effect it had, but why he chose to defend slavery in the United States on such flimsy grounds. The census of 1840 which Calhoun relied on to make his case had been exposed as a jumble of false statistics years earlier. In the summer of 1842 Edward Jarvis, a statistically minded Concord physician who had practiced in the South, challenged the accuracy of figures purporting to show extraordinarily higher rates of insanity for blacks in the North than in the South. This kind of discrepancy seemed to defy common sense. Upon closer study Jarvis found that the census was loaded with such bizarre errors that on some occasions insane blacks were listed for towns without black residents and that the number of insane blacks for given communities was repeatedly greater than the total black population. In the summer of 1843 George Tucker, a professor at the University of Virginia, published a book on the history of the census sharply criticizing the figures gathered for 1840, and on February 26, 1844, two days before the *Princeton* explosion, the House of Representatives passed a resolution directing the Secretary of State to review the census "as corrected at the Department of State in 1841." By the time Calhoun managed to reply to this request, the Pakenham letter had been written, and Calhoun was temporarily relieved of the necessity of replying to the congressional directive by the convenient discovery that somewhere between the House and the State Department the figure 1841 had been transposed to read 1843. It was therefore a simple matter for Calhoun to report to Congress on May 1 that there was no census corrected in the department in 1843 and that the corrections made to the census of 1841 were those "noted in errata on the last page of the work." John Quincy Adams, who had written the resolution asking for the review, called Calhoun's report "the most extraordinary communication ever made from the State Department" and confronted his former Vice President about the matter in a face-to-face encounter. Acting "like a true slavemonger," Adams recorded in his diary, Calhoun "writhed like a trodden rattlesnake on the exposure of his false report . . . and finally said that there were so many errors they balanced one another, and led to the same conclusion as if they were all correct." How much writhing Calhoun did on that occasion is open to question, but a few months later he did send another report to Congress reaffirming his belief in the superior condition of enslaved over free blacks and claiming that mechanical errors caused by the transposition of figures in the census of 1840 essentially canceled one another out.[11]

Calhoun could ignore his critics because his belief in the inferiority of black people did not depend on statistics; it was a fixed principle in his mind, based on what he perceived to be laws of nature and confirmed by reason, not open to amendment on the basis of empirical evidence. Statistics might be in error, but the principle that made it impossible for free black people to live in peace, health, and prosperity among white people could not be shaken. It is interesting to find, therefore, that even as he was defending the census, he was reading dispatches from American consuls in the Caribbean and South America which reinforced his basic assumption about racial inequality. Robert Harrison, writing from Jamaica, where slaves had been emancipated since 1833, reported regularly on the "wretched state to which this fine colony is now reduced by pseudo-philanthropists." According to Harrison, "wooly headed mulattoes" had seized positions in power, and there was near anarchy in the streets of Kingston, where blacks loitered, idly watching white property burn. Jamaican real estate was at one-third its former value, and commerce at a near standstill, proving that the emancipation of slaves in the Western Hemisphere, unlike the emancipation of serfs in Europe, "among people where no difference of color existed," would retard progress. In Jamaica, Harrison went on, race "hourly signalizes the former master to the late slave and by that means continues to nourish those deep rooted prejudices which exist between the two classes at the same time that it procludes [*sic*] the possibility of future change." Calhoun found a similar story in reports from Haiti, where only the old people who had "become habitually industrious" under slavery many years earlier were said to be willing to work. Meanwhile, the consul in Caracas claimed that black mobs were intimidating the courts, and the United States representative in Cuba told of plots for "a general slaughter of whites."[12]

Calhoun would have welcomed these eyewitness reports of chaos and violence because they confirmed his own unshakable convictions, and if it became necessary to go beyond this kind of evidence, he was prepared to call on the scientific community to support his belief in racial inequality. In May 1844 he met George Gliddon, an authority on the history of races in ancient Egypt, who introduced him to the work of Samuel Morton and other pioneers in the infant science of anthropology. Morton's work purported to show "that Negro-Races have ever been *servants* and *slaves*, always distinct from, and subject to the *Caucasian* in the remotest times." There was now "a new branch of science," Gliddon assured the Secretary of State, which could provide "any amount of facts . . . to support and confirm all those doctrines that for so long and bright a period have marked the illustrious career of John C. Calhoun."[13]

Although Calhoun felt no reason to retract anything he had written in the Pakenham letter, he must have known that the lasting value of that endeavor would be measured not in whether he won the argument over the validity of the census, but in the results of the Democratic National Convention and the Senate vote on the Texas treaty. When the Democrats met in Baltimore on May 27, South Carolina was not formally represented, but Calhoun asked Francis Pickens and Robert M. T. Hunter to attend as personal observers. He expected annexation to destroy Van Buren's candidacy and thought that Tyler, running as an independent Democrat, might be "safest for the South." If the convention deadlocked, Calhoun would consider a draft, a most unlikely possibility considering the strength of the Van Buren delegation. Calhoun had repeatedly predicted that any plausible proannexation candidate could take the nomination away from Van Buren, and that is the way it worked out when James K. Polk, a Jackson protégé, former Speaker of the House, and governor of Tennessee, was named on the ninth ballot.[14]

Polk was hardly an obscure figure, but his career before Baltimore had appeared to be in decline. He had lost two successive bids for the governorship of Tennessee and had actually been considered by Elmore and company as a possible running mate for Calhoun. Harrison, Tyler, and Polk, lesser men all, thrust into the highest position the country had to offer. If Calhoun felt slighted by Polk's surprising elevation, he chose not to show it, rejoicing rather in the fall of Van Buren and the "dangerous control" of the New York Dynasty.[15] Hunter remembered calling on Calhoun late one afternoon after the convention. His staff had long since retired for the day, and the Secretary, weary but composed, was resting on a sofa. When his friend tried to convince him that there might still be a chance for his own candidacy, he demurred. "Too late," Hunter recalled Calhoun's words, "that day can never come." He went on to speak about circumstances beyond his control and the impossibility of living up to the expectations of his followers even if he were elected. What he apparently meant by this was that history had moved the sectional conflict to a new level, precluding the possibility that an outspoken leader of the South could ever be a serious presidential possibility. For the moment there was no alternative to Polk. "Try him," Calhoun said. "I see no other chance."[16]

The most gratifying result of the convention was the strong annexation plank in the Democratic platform, and most of Calhoun's energy during the following weeks seems to have been directed at getting the Texas treaty through the Senate. In this he was severely disappointed. On June 18 Whig Senators, with the help of disgruntled Van Burenite Democrats and a massive oratorical display by Thomas Hart Benton, rejected the treaty by a heavy margin.

Convinced that if Polk moved into the White House, Texas could be brought into the Union one way or another, Calhoun took the defeat more calmly than many of his supporters in South Carolina. The increase of antislavery sentiment in Congress, symbolized by the repeal of the gag law in December, and the inability of Carolinians to win concessions on the tariff, along with the rebuff over Texas, led the easily disaffected Rhett to sound the old cry of nullification. At a well-publicized meeting in Bluffton, Rhett, seconded by radicals like Hammond and by the usually Calhounite *Charleston Mercury,* called for a state convention to consider radical action which could lead to secession.

Although there is something grimly humorous about the image of Texans filing into the Union past South Carolinians on their way out, Calhoun was not gratified by the prospect. He knew that much of the opposition to the Texas treaty had focused on the accusation that southern radicals intended to exploit its defeat by breaking up the Union. Benton's thundering on this theme had been regularly reported to the press for weeks, and the hotheaded Rhett seemed anxious to prove Benton right. Calhoun moved quickly to isolate the Blufftonite rebels by spreading the word through Elmore and others that the Carolina mission in 1844 was not to resurrect the spirit and behavior of 1832 but to elect Polk. When the latter called for a national meeting of Democrats in Nashville to iron out internal conflicts, Calhoun sent Pickens as his personal representative. After spending two days with the candidate, Pickens reported that Polk was fully in sympathy with Calhoun's views on the tariff and other matters and could be relied on to do the right thing as President. Armed with this assurance, Calhoun was able to put down the revolt of a radical minority in the South Carolina legislature, but he could not stop the grumbling that the state was paying a high price to keep his own fading hope for the presidency alive. Everyone knew that Polk's most important concession in seeking the nomination had been a pledge not to run for a second term.[17]

Calhoun had served as Secretary of State for six months before he could get back to Fort Hill for a brief vacation in early October 1844. Called to the capital on extraordinarily short notice, he had left his family at home and taken quarters at Mrs. King's boardinghouse, where his bill for one four-week period came to $319.50, including six extra dinners for guests and two dinner parties for ten guests each—a far cry from the sumptuous life-style he and his family had known at Oakly more than twenty years earlier.

Although Calhoun had not taken anyone from home to Washington with him, he was not without family. Patrick was stationed there, and he was joined by his younger brother John in May. John had begun to show signs of consumption, and it was decided that he should make a journey to the West in search of good health. The destination would be Fort Bent near the headwaters of the Arkansas River by way of New Orleans. If Calhoun had any misgivings about sending John with Patrick to New Orleans at Mardi Gras time, he did not reveal them. Somehow the brothers managed that experience without getting into trouble and, after outfitting themselves in St. Louis by purchasing "ammunition, guns, two double barrells, two brace pistols, two bowie knives, three horses and a servant," set off for the prairie. The trip did not do much for John's lungs, but it did include some memorable adventures, including a rammed steamboat, a meeting with the Mormon Prophet Joseph Smith shortly before his murder, buffalo hunts, fierce Indians, and a "true fish story" about a six-foot-long catfish. What did Calhoun think when he heard these stories? Was this the *Wanderjahr* experience he had never had?[18]

For a few days in July Calhoun enjoyed a bittersweet reunion with Anna Maria as the Clemsons passed through Washington on their way to New York to embark for Belgium, where Thomas was to serve as the chargé d'affaires in Brussels. Calhoun was proud to have secured the appointment for his son-in-law, who had traveled in Europe, knew French and was excited at the prospect, but both Anna and her father were saddened by the prospect of a long, distant separation.[19]

Meanwhile, Floride was holding the fort back in Pendleton. Those critics of Calhoun as the grim, unrelenting leader of the slavocracy, reading lectures on morality and politics to Lord Aberdeen and pulling every diplomatic string to expand the domain of slavery, would have been surprised at the letters he was getting from his wife. Floride had no end of instructions for the Secretary. He was to get a breastpin and a pair of black silk stockings for Cornelia, find out what had happened to "a twisted silk shawl I gave Patrick to have dyed black," and order bacon from Savannah while it was still three cents a pound. Floride made it clear that she was needed at home, that whenever she turned her back, disaster would likely strike. "If I had not come as soon as I did," she wrote after a brief absence, "all our hams would have been ruined . . . and as it was had to feed a great many to the Negroes. I had them all washed in soapsuds, dried and hung up again." Floride asked no questions about how her husband was doing reordering the state of the world but made it clear that she expected him home that summer. For her, running their plantation was a lot more important than changing the world. "I think you might leave the business of the Department to someone while you come on."[20]

Eventually Calhoun did just as Floride asked, putting his office under the direction of his friend and assistant Richard Cralle and arriving at Fort Hill on October 4. Remaining in the political background over the next few weeks, he also kept a close eye on the rebellious Blufftonites. He denied any understanding between Polk and himself and warned the editor of the *Mercury* that a strong antislavery vote might tip the balance to Henry Clay. Correct in predicting the importance of the antislavery vote, Calhoun was wrong about the result. As it turned out, Polk won by an eyelash when the antislavery Liberty Party took enough votes away from Clay in New York to give that state to the Democrats.[21]

Obviously buoyed by the knowledge that a slaveholder, a strong Texas man, and presumably a reliable political friend was about to take over the White House, Calhoun returned to Washington in good spirits. He was accompanied by a reluctant Floride, Cornelia, and his son James, prepared to shoulder at least some of the social responsibilities devolving on the first officer of the Cabinet. On November 26 he and Floride attended a dinner hosted by Secretary of Navy John Y. Mason, and Calhoun found himself seated next to Julia Gardiner Tyler, the youthful beauty who had married the President during the summer. Calhoun had helped the bride cut the wedding cake after the ceremony and had become an instant favorite of the radiant Julia. "He actually *repeated verses to me,*" she told her astonished husband after the Mason dinner. "We had together a pleasant flirtation."[22]

Giving full credit to Julia's many charms, we must believe that Calhoun's amiable frame of mind was also influenced by the perception that he was still a key player in shaping political events. He and Tyler had agreed that the refusal of the Senate to ratify the annexation treaty would not be final. The administration would bypass the Senate, where the Whigs were strong, by asking that Texas be admitted directly to the Union as a state by joint resolution of both Houses of Congress. Tyler moved toward this end in his annual message to Congress on December 3 by claiming that the recent election showed it to be "the will of the people and the states that Texas shall be annexed promptly and immediately." The President's interpretation of the election results was no more accurate than his assertion that annexation could be considered on its own merits, "isolated" from divisive issues like the extension of slavery. In fact, the Democrats had won the election by the narrowest of margins and could not claim a mandate for anything. Not only that, but Calhoun had consciously forced everyone to recognize that annexation and slavery were inextricably linked. Nevertheless, the new administration strategy seemed promising, and Tyler accompanied his message with a voluminous set of documents designed to show that the opponents of annexation were at least tacitly in league with Mexico and Britain. Two of the documents were dispatches written by Calhoun earlier that summer with the expectation that they would be published after the election.[23]

In the first dispatch, written to Wilson Shannon, the American minister to Mexico, Calhoun emphasized a variety of grievances on the part of United States citizens in Mexico and warned that Mexico was planning a bloody war of annihilation on the Lone Star State. "All that breathe are to be destroyed or driven out," Calhoun wrote, "and Texas left a desolate waste." Succeeding documents revealed that Shannon used Calhoun's dispatch as authority to begin a belligerent correspondence with the Mexican foreign minister which bristled with accusations, denials, and threats and ultimately linked the honor of the United States to annexation. Not unexpectedly the Whig press deplored the jingoism set off by Calhoun's instructions, while militant expansionists applauded it.[24]

Meanwhile, a letter from Calhoun to William R. King, the United States minister to France, was also made public. Calhoun was counting on King, a former Alabama Senator, to keep France from falling into line behind Britain on annexation. French opinion on the matter was divided. In one camp was Foreign Minister Adolphe Guizot, supported by an antislavery movement considerably weaker than its British counterpart and by a faction in the Chamber of Deputies anxious to cooperate with Britain. In an opposing camp were those connected to the French planter interest, intent on avoiding anything that might threaten slavery in the French West Indies, and those who on principle opposed collaborating with Britain. Calhoun was anxious to exploit the division of French opinion, and he found the opening he wanted when King reported that in an informal after-dinner conversation King Louis Philippe of France had mentioned that the French interst in Texas was "different" from that of Britain. Acknowledging the President's appreciation of the "declaration of the King" (a casual remark in social conversation was now transformed into a declaration), Calhoun pressed on his minister the importance of convincing the French government of the inevitablity of annexation and the ulterior, self-seeking motives of Britain in opposing it. Assuming a philanthropic posture, the British appeared to seek an independent Texas without slavery, but their real goal was the destruction of slavery everywhere in the United States in order to cripple agriculture in the South and assure themselves a monopoly in the world cotton market. Relying on reports in the British press and from American diplomatic representatives in the Caribbean and South America, Calhoun argued that emancipation had been a costly failure for Britain. Acting on "the principle that tropical products can be produced cheaper by free African labor and East India labor than by slave labor," Britain now found that its investment in those products stood "on the brink of ruin." The lesson for both the United States and France was that slavery deserved to be supported. "Can it be possible," Calhoun asked, "that governments so enlightened and sagacious as those of France and the other great continental powers can be so blinded by the appeal of philanthropy as not to see what must inevitably follow" if the British were to succeed? Without mentioning the census by name, Calhoun claimed that "statistical facts not to be shaken" proved that free blacks deprived of their masters' "guardian care" were in a "far worse condition" than slaves, and he warned once again that emancipation would lead to bloodshed and devastation.

When Calhoun's letter was published in late December, its effects in Europe were sensational. The British accused the French government of being two-faced about Texas; the parties in France attacked one another for being soft on slavery or subservient to Britain. Guizot's government almost fell, and the possibility of a concerted Anglo-French policy toward Texas disappeared. Calhoun could not have been happier.[25]

As the final months of the Tyler administration wore away, a weary Calhoun looked to the future with reasonable confidence. Stationed in the Cabinet rather than the Senate, he was spared the embarrassing task of debating the constitutionality of annexing Texas by joint resolution of both houses of Congress. Not only was the administration trying to accomplish by law what it had been unable to do by treaty, but the constitutional provisions covering the admission of new states into the Union said nothing about taking in an already established sovereign power. How could a strict constructionist support the Administration without stretching his principles? Fortunately Calhoun, convinced that public opinion would force Congress to carry the measure, was able to remain blissfully above that debate. As he looked back on his brief tenure, he was proud of his role in securing Texas for the country while defending slavery. Although he did not discuss the matter directly, he also looked forward to serving as Secretary of State in the new administration.[26]

As it turned out, Calhoun's days as a Cabinet leader were numbered. His final report on the much-maligned census of 1840 was probably a straw in the wind. Rather than appoint an independent investigator to examine the criticism of nationally recognized statistical experts, Calhoun asked William A. Weaver, the same man who had superintended the impeached document, to investigate. Not surprisingly, Weaver found that his work was sound, and the Secretary passed his conclusions on to Congress along with his own final judgment that "great and unusual care" had been taken to assure accuracy in the document, that it was generally consistent with the census of 1830, and that the demonstrated superiority of slaves over free blacks led to an inevitable conclusion that emancipation was "a curse instead of a blessing."[27]

There was no reason why any dispassionate observer should have been convinced by this self-justifying display, and Calhoun was probably not surprised to see it widely denounced in the North. Much to his dismay, however, it was received with "dead silence" in the South, leading him to confess his "deep grief to think how dead the South is to its most vital interests." The truth seems to be that Calhoun had taken a weak argument as far as it would go, and other southern leaders were not interested in pursuing the matter further. Perhaps there was a message in this for the President-elect, who conspicuously avoided Calhoun as he discussed Cabinet possibilities with other party leaders. On February 16 Calhoun visited Polk, but the meeting was confined to pleasantries. The next day Polk named James Buchanan his Secretary of State.[28]

In Congress, however, things were going Calhoun's way. The joint resolution for annexation passed the House and Senate by majority vote, and President Tyler was given the option of signing the resolution or passing it on to his successor. Calhoun advised him to sign, and he did, three days before Polk's inauguration.

Although Polk would have been intimately familiar with Andrew Jackson's warnings about Calhoun, the new President had good reasons of his own for not inviting him to remain in the Cabinet. Polk had no intention of making the defense of slavery the centerpiece of his administration and no desire to compete with Calhoun for the privilege of setting the national agenda. He was willing to recognize Calhoun's achievements by making him minister to Britain, an incongruous possibility in the light of the latter's repeated attacks on the integrity of British policy makers, but Calhoun declined in a "mild but decided manner." Outwardly Calhoun was gracious enough and assured the President of his support, but it obviously rankled him to have been passed over by a man who was showing all the earmarks of developing into a second-rate Jackson. "I stood in the way of the old Jackson regime," Calhoun wrote his son-in-law after leaving Washington, "both as to individuals and policy. . . . There is not a man in the cabinet who did not continue throughout a thorough Jackson man." In a long letter to Anna Maria, Calhoun tried to rationalize his departure by saying that he would not have stayed on if asked. "As it is," he assured his adoring daughter, "I retire from all responsibility with the good will of all. . . . I may say I never stood higher or firmer in the opinion of the country."[29]

From a political point of view, Calhoun's role in the acquisition of Texas was a brilliant success. As a principal adviser to Tyler and Upshur, he planned the strategy which led to the Texas negotiations and to the decline of foreign influence on the southeastern border. As Secretary of State he implemented this strategy and signed the treaty, which was eventually validated by joint resolution. At the same time he boldly proclaimed to the world the virtues of slavery as it existed in the United States. Spurned as a candidate himself, Calhoun made Texas and slavery the litmus test for southern support in the election of 1844, thus fatally damaging the aspirations of his two chief rivals. Once again he demonstrated that despite his own limitations as a candidate for a national party, he could significantly shape the political dialogue and the course of events.

Like most political successes born out of intense controversy, Calhoun's success had come at a greater price than he realized. His insistence on exploiting shoddy evidence to reinforce the racism which supported slavery and his unwillingness to consider the constitutional arguments against annexation did not speak well for a man who put himself on a moral plane above ordinary politicians and repeatedly insisted on his devotion to principle. Although it would have been out of character to admit a fall from grace of this magnitude, he did realize that the political price he paid for his recent triumphs was a growing conviction in the public mind that he had become more a sectional than a national leader. The controversy over Oregon and the war with Mexico gave him an opportunity to redress that balance.

18

The Peace Senator, 1845–1846

A FTER BRAVING the rain and chill which accompanied Polk's inauguration, Calhoun turned his head south, and this time his friends believed him when he said he had no intention of returning to Washington. Emaciated and feeble from a lingering bout of fever, he seemed conscious of his age, his increasing fragility, and the limited time he had left to enjoy the comforts of Fort Hill and complete the book he intended to serve as the intellectual culmination of his career. But eight months later he was again at his old seat in the Senate.[1]

Back in Pendleton he slipped easily into the routine of the retired statesman and gentleman planter, secluding himself for several hours each day in the small detached cottage which served as his private office, where he worked on his book, kept up an extensive correspondence, and read encouraging reports about the return of the Democrats to power, including the welcome news that his supporters had enjoyed conspicuous success in the Virginia elections and that Frank Blair, who had been abusing him for years in the *Washington Globe*, was to be replaced as government printer. In late June Calhoun went to Abbeville, where he erected monuments to the memory of his parents near the house where he was born and later visited George McDuffie, who had never really recovered from the wounds incurred on Calhoun's behalf twenty years earlier and was now trying to overcome the effects of a severe stroke. Not normally given to introspection, Calhoun must have been forced by these experiences to reflect on his own accomplishments and his own mortality. He had toiled long and hard in the public service, and others had given their best for him. Was his work really coming to an end? Was he ready for the judgments of history and the monuments to be erected to his own memory? It may have been with questions like this lingering in his mind, along with the knowledge that his father had never retired, that Calhoun began to consider returning to the Senate.[2]

Some of his friends wanted Calhoun back in harness to make sure that tariff reforms would pass the Senate; others worried about a leadership vacuum, the ascendance of Benton, and the return of the Van Buren Democrats to power. Although not insensible to these appeals, Calhoun seems to have been mostly concerned with the unfinished business he left behind when he turned the State Department over to Buchanan. He had agreed to replace Upshur for the express purpose of completing the negotiations over Texas and Oregon, but he had done only half the job and was clearly uneasy at the prospect of leaving the other half, concerning Oregon and the northwestern boundary, in the hands of a new President who had sounded unnecessarily belligerent upon the subject in his inaugural address. Oregon had been occupied jointly by Britain and the United States under a long-standing agreement that no longer sat well with land-hungry westerners who increasingly felt called by destiny to push the British out. Believing that British claims in Oregon were much more legitimate than their attempts to prevent the annexation of Texas, Calhoun warned his friends that Polk would only court trouble by agitating the question. The important thing was "to be quiet—to do nothing to excite attention." Texas had demanded aggressive action, but not Oregon.[3]

In retirement at Fort Hill, however, Calhoun could not maintain his accustomed leverage on public events. While old friends might still respect him, they had little reason to obey him. He began to worry about long-standing loyal supporters like Francis Pickens and John Barbour, who seemed starry-eyed about Polk, and about radicals like Rhett, unpredictable in the best of times, poised to create another crisis over the tariff, and capable of almost any kind of rashness without Calhoun's restraining hand in Washington. His diminishing influence in retirement at Fort Hill became embarrassingly clear when Calhoun tried to get James Henry Hammond to review a book on slavery by a Methodist clergyman. The former governor was generally recognized as the most effective proslavery spokesman in South Carolina next to Calhoun, but his reputation among the planter aristocracy had been badly compromised by a sexual scandal involving the nieces of the powerful Wade Hampton. Even though Hammond needed all the help he could get from leaders like Calhoun, he refused to honor the request, arguing that the book was not worth reading and even suggesting that if Calhoun had read it more carefully, he would realize that its primary message was critical of slavery.[4]

By mid-September 1845 Calhoun had had enough of retirement. "I am urged to return to the Senate," he wrote Clemson. "My inclination is against it, but the state of our affairs, external and internal, is so critical that I should feel it my duty to serve if the state should require me." A few weeks later, after Calhoun's successor, Daniel Huger, had graciously resigned, the legislature once again decided to send South Carolina's most famous citizen to the Senate of the United States.[5]

Francis Pickens, who had labored loyally in Calhoun's shadow for years and had hope to succeeded him in the Senate, warned that if Calhoun expected to be successful in Washington, he at least had to retire as a presidential candidate. "That matter ought to be stopped beyond all doubt. If it is not there will be division and distraction." Elmore and Hunter took a similar position, but Calhoun was offended at the prospect of making the declaration they sought. Such advice was small-minded, almost a vote of no confidence, and Calhoun did not forget it. He would return to the Senate but insist, as always, on keeping all other options open.[6]

As much as Calhoun appreciated his reputation as the champion of the South, he knew that neither he nor the South could go it alone in the Union in the long run. Political success in a large, diversified country like the United States went hand in hand with coalition building, and the obvious coalition for Calhoun and the South was with the West. His experience in Congress and in the Cabinet during and immediately after the war with England had helped him shape a vision for the country that endured. As Secretary of War he had pushed vigorously for improved communications between the East and West, and as a southern planter and legislator he had repeatedly participated in efforts to launch a railroad system which would link the South with the Mississippi Valley. Thus Calhoun had every reason to be interested when his old friend James Gadsden invited him to a conference to promote improved transportation facilities on the Mississippi River and between the Mississippi and the southeastern coastal states. The political stakes for the South in such a meeting were high. Southern support for the kinds of internal improvements the West needed might be traded for western support to lower the tariff, and the two sections might find common ground to support each other's aspirations for future growth, including the preservation of slavery. The big problem from Calhoun's point of view involved intellectual and ideological consistency. How could he find constitutional grounds for supporting lavish expenditures for internal improvements without watching those expenditures lead to higher budgets and hence to calls for more revenue and higher tariffs? And how could he make the necessary argument without alienating the restive nullifiers in his own state?[7]

Undaunted by such questions, Calhoun agreed to chair a convention to be held in Memphis on November 13. Arriving with his sons Patrick and Andrew, after a brief family reunion at the latter's Alabama plantation, Calhoun delivered the the keynote address to more than five hundred delegates from fifteen states. The thrust of his remarks emphasized the geographic and economic ties connecting the states in the Southeast, Southwest, and Middle West, the "great agricultural portion" of the country which produces "all the leading articles of food and raiment" required in the United States, and whose rapid growth would increasingly require world markets for continued prosperity. Expanded markets required expanded transportation facilities, navigable river channels, canals, and railroads. The rewards would be great, but so would the costs. Could the federal government finance such an ambitious undertaking? Here was the question Calhoun had been summoned to answer, and he did it by turning the Mississippi River system into a great "inland sea." Congress could appropriate funds to improve navigation there just as it could to improve it in coastal waters or in the Great Lakes. The issue with railroads and canals was not so clear, but Calhoun reminded the delegates that he and other strict constructionists had been willing to support land grants to support such projects when they passed through United States land. This kind of federal aid could be continued and might even be applied to the levee projects essential to the development of the Mississippi Valley.[8]

A fastidious mind doubtless would have had some difficulty absorbing the distinctions Calhoun made between the federal government's support of "internal improvements," which he opposed, and the "inland sea" improvements and land subsidies he supported. Henry Clay, whose mind was anything but fastidious, would not have been surprised to find his rival stretching principles to build a new political alliance. For Calhoun himself it was a matter of stretching but not abandoning principle, and he was careful to remind his audience that the cost of development could be significantly reduced with lower tariffs on critical materials like iron rails. By and large he gave a nonpartisan address which was notably silent about slavery.

John Quincy Adams was probably speaking Henry Clay's mind when he called Calhoun's inland sea concept a political device to herald his return to Washington. Once again the defiant Carolinian was proving to be a man of many political lives, and once again he could not resist celebrating his own accomplishment. The journey from Selma, Alabama, to Memphis had taken Calhoun to New Orleans and up the Mississippi by boat. The trip had been marked by enthusiastic receptions at river towns along the way as hordes of eager citizens jostled one another to catch a glimpse of the celebrated political leader in his first visit to the West. "All parties everywhere united without distinction," Calhoun proudly wrote Clemson, "in a demonstration of respect not exceeded by that shown to Gen Jackson in passing through the same places." In terms of the numbers of people who turned out to see him, Calhoun was probably correct, but he deceived himself if he thought the westerners were finding in him what they had found in Jackson. There was an enormous cultural gap separating a highly educated, aristocratic planter like him from the representatives of the rough-and-ready frontier democracy drawn so vividly in the stories of Mark Twain and the paintings of George Caleb Bingham, and Calhoun did little to bridge it. Throughout his career he had routinely rejected invitations to attend public political meetings, and he maintained that posture in the West, where stump speaking was the rule. In Vicksburg, for example, he was introduced by the thirty-seven-year-old Jefferson Davis, who tried to draw Calhoun out on the issues of the day. Declining to give a speech on the grounds that he was "unaccustomed to speak before a promiscuous crowd," the famous visitor managed to deliver a few banalities on civic duty in language that was reported as "plain to poverty" and in such a rapid style as to be almost unintelligible. During the rest of the evening, while the attending crowd danced and frolicked, Calhoun passed up all opportunities to shake new hands and make new friends, devoting instead all of his attention to Davis's pretty young wife, Varina. "The old man seemed quite struck with her," Davis recalled, half-proudly and half-ruefully, "walked with no one else talked with no one else, and seemed to have no use for his eyes except to look at her."[9]

Calhoun's concentrated attention on the young Varina Davis, who bore some resemblance to his own Anna Maria, may have reflected the loss he felt at this daughter's absence, but it also suggested his discomfort with the new democratic style endemic to the West. Stephen Douglas, Abraham Lincoln, or any other of the hundreds of younger politicians anxious to replace the leaders of Calhoun's generation would have behaved differently. It would take more than an effective speech about inland seas to turn Calhoun into an effective leader for the South and the West.

When Calhoun left South Carolina for Washington in December 1845, he was leaving a small but hot local fire behind him. It had been kindled in the columns of the *Charleston Mercury* and the halls of the legislature where the Blufftonites were once again getting a hearing by complaining that Calhoun's Memphis speech meant retreating from the principles on which the great crusade of 1832 had been based. As he approached Washington, however, Calhoun worried less about the sniping at home than he did about the possibility of the administration's blundering into unnecessary wars with Mexico and Britain. When Calhoun took his seat on December 20, Mexico had broken off diplomatic relations with the United States, refused to pay previously adjudicated indemnities to United States citizens, and was sworn to retake Texas. Meanwhile, President Polk supported the Texans' claim to a southern border along the Rio Grande and had already ordered General Zachary Taylor and thirty-five hundred troops (about half the United States Army) to a location close to that border. Despite the very real dangers of war with Mexico, the administration insisted on pouring fresh coals on the Oregon dispute. Although earlier American claims had gone no farther than the forty-ninth parallel, Polk had claimed a national right to the entire territory in his inaugural, prompting an immediate "all Oregon" movement. The United States could hardly be expected to take all of Oregon without war, but the prospect of war with two countries at the same time was hardly daunting to a new generation of American leaders and their followers, who seemed to believe that the expansion of American borders was written in the heavens.

Shortly before Calhoun reached Washington, Polk had sent his first annual message to Congress asking for a termination of the Anglo-American convention for joint occupancy of Oregon and calling for the extension of United States authority over British settlers in the territory. In effect, the President was repudiating the conciliatory policies of the previous administration, which Calhoun had helped formulate, and two days after arriving in Washington, Calhoun was in Polk's office to tell him that he had gotten off the track and should assume a softer posture toward the British by encouraging congressional restraint over Oregon. The closemouthed President said little but wrote in his diary that Calhoun could be expected to oppose his policy.[10]

The prospect of Calhoun's launching his return to the Senate by breaking openly with the President over an important foreign policy issue did not thrill many of Calhoun's ambitious friends. Richard Crallé was afraid that a new round of political infighting would tarnish his friend's Washington-like image. A supporter in Texas, where western expansionism was rampant, told Calhoun it would be folly to return to the Senate if he planned to fight the President on Oregon because an "immense majority" supported Polk, and Calhoun could easily find himself in the position the Federalists had occupied in 1812. "If we are to have war," he advised, "do not destroy yourself by vainly endeavoring to prevent it." And Francis Pickens, who had already fallen from grace, did nothing to improve his position in Calhoun's eyes by lavishly approving Polk's course and insisting that the President spoke for "99 in 100 of our people."[11]

Always inclined to feel better about himself when swimming against a strong tide, Calhoun frequently overestimated his own strength. In returning to the Senate, however, he knew that he could command enough votes to kill or carry administration proposals in any close encounter. He also expected his recent experience as Secretary of State to strengthen his position on foreign policy debates because he could command more information than any other Senator. As Secretary he had studied the history of Oregon; he had negotiated one on one with Pakenham and sparred through formal diplomatic exchanges

with Lord Aberdeen. Not only that, but he was also in private correspondence with Louis McLane, the new American minister to London,
who was equally anxious to avoid war and equally certain that any claim
beyond the forty-ninth parallel was doomed. Thus, when Calhoun insisted that an amicable settlement was possible, he could speak with an
authority that crossed party lines.[12]

As administration leaders moved to get Congress to implement
Polk's termination policy, Calhoun swung into action with a set of
proposals consistent with his own earlier negotiations with Pakenham
pointing toward an ultimate settlement at the forty-ninth parallel. Having blocked the administration at least temporarily, he made another
trip to the White House on January 10, 1846, to urge the President to
change his ways. Polk received him civilly, and even asked him to stay
on and make his case to the Cabinet, which was about to assemble.
Surprised and somewhat flustered by such an invitation, Calhoun accepted it and proceeded to argue that U.S. claims to Oregon above the
forty-ninth parallel were no better than Britain's and that compromise
was in the best interest of both countries. Polk said nothing, but Buchanan and the rest of the Cabinet stood by the President and blamed
the British for refusing to settle the dispute.[13]

Whatever disappointment Calhoun may have experienced by his
inability to change government policy at the top was more than compensated for by the approval he was getting from all parts of the country as the perceived peace leader. Almost all of his incoming correspondence during this period was about Oregon, and it was overwhelmingly
favorable. Fernando Wood, the former New York Congressman and
future mayor, wrote, "[A]ll eyes are turned on you," and encouraged
Calhoun to keep his presidential hopes alive. The volatile Hammond,
who had responded so sulkily to Calhoun's blandishments the year
before, now wrote that he had immensely elevated himself in the estimation of "the best men on the country," and Crallé assured him that
the break with Polk was worth its political cost because the people
would side with Calhoun. Meanwhile, the President put a dour face on
Calhoun's obstructionist role, attributing it solely to selfish ambition,
while high-ranking Whigs like Edward Everett and Abbott Lawrence
beamed their approval. More comfortable with the praise of men of
intelligence and position than with huzzas from the crowd, Calhoun

also appreciated the letters he got from ordinary, thoughtful citizens like the Virginia tobacco farmer Charles Anthony, who recalled that during the last war his father had been forced to exchange a hogshead of good tobacco for a small sack of salt "and had to give three dollars to boot. Such would be the effect of war at this time. It would enrich the northern manufacturers at the expense of the Southern States." Whenever he spoke about "the people," Calhoun was usually thinking of sturdy republicans like Anthony.[14]

After the Senate had been deadlocked for some weeks over the President's request to issue what many Senators perceived to be an ultimatum to Great Britain, Calhoun decided to seize the initiative with a major speech on March 16. He put the issue before the Senate in its simplest terms. Should the government notify Britain that it would withdraw from its long-standing convention of joint occupancy of Oregon, and, if so, on what terms? Calhoun would support only a statement of notice which invited continued negotiation, encouraged compromise, and recognized that claims as far north as the fifty-fourth parallel were unrealistic. Such a position would help build a concern for peace among the American people. The alternative would risk war, and Calhoun closed by asking Senators and the public to consider the consequences of a naval war on the oceans and the Great Lakes, the maintenance of several armies to cope with what would probably be a "Mexican and Indian" war as well as a war with Britain, a war that would cost at least fifty millions a year, flood the country with paper money, create enormous bureaucracies, and lead the United States, as it had led so many other republics, on "the straight and downward road" to military despotism. Finally, Calhoun, whom no one could ever accuse of being an anglophile, stressed that Britain and the United States were the two great modern nations in the vanguard of world progress. War now could make them enemies and do irreversible damage to the future of mankind. A peaceful resolution of important differences might lead to permanent peace which would allow the citizens of the United States to realize their true destiny by spreading republican institutions across "a vast domain" from ocean to ocean. "War may make us great," Calhoun concluded, "but let it never be forgotten that peace only can make us both great and free."[15]

The Oregon speech, which attracted large crowds in the Senate gallery and the corridors of the Capitol, was widely hailed in the press. Although Calhoun grumbled over the inaccuracies of some accounts and the tendency of Democratic papers to bury the speech, he was obviously proud of it and told his daughter that many thought it "the best I ever delivered." Those who praised it included not only the customary Calhoun puffers like Duff Green but Whigs and Democrats from all walks of life. As an example he sent Anna a clipping from Michael Walsh's *Subterranean*, a rabble-rousing sheet which Calhoun delicately referred to as "the organ of what may be called the lowest strata in the New York population." He might also have mentioned the letters from Arnold Buffum, a former member of the New England Antislavery Society, Elihu Burritt, father of the world peace movement, and the great New England textile tycoon Abbott Lawrence, who wrote that there was no one in the country "with whom I desire to have social converse more than yourself."[16]

Three months and two days after Calhoun's Oregon speech the Senate ratified a treaty dividing the territory along the forty-ninth parallel, as Calhoun had recommended. Although it is not possible to measure his influence with any precision, there is no doubt that his role in Congress went a long way toward neutralizing the war climate engendered by the policy and rhetoric of the Polk administration. Shortly before the treaty was ratified, Britain opened its markets to American agricultural exports by repealing the Corn Laws, and this made it possible for Congress to agree on a tariff more or less on free trade principles. Recognizing that these developments would have lowered the heat in the Oregon dispute no matter what Calhoun had done, there is still no reason to question Frederick Merk's judgment that "in penetration of judgment and lucidity of statement" his speech was "the intellectual climax of the debate and one of the greatest of Calhoun's career." In helping mastermind annexation, he had been a master politician, and in helping resolve the Oregon dispute a master statesman; it remained to be seen how Calhoun would perform during the war with Mexico.[17]

19

"Mexico Is to Us the Forbidden Fruit,"
1846–1848

THE SUMMER of 1846 found Calhoun more sanguine than he had been in years. The Oregon treaty was ratified by the Senate on June 15, a tariff rolling back duties to 1816 levels passed on July 30, and a new independent Treasury system consistent with Calhoun's hard-money convictions became law on August 6. Meanwhile, he had published his report on the Memphis convention establishing the constitutionality of federal power to improve navigation on the Mississippi and thus to link southern and western states more closely together. "Indeed," Calhoun wrote to his son-in-law, "it is not a little remarkable that all the great measures I have advocated are in a fair way of being consummated." The one great exception to this positive train of events was the war with Mexico, which had been sputtering ever since May. Contrary to the conventional wisdom which held that United States troops would make short work of the lowly Mexicans, Calhoun, who had directed the War Department at the beginning of what had become a long, costly campaign to subdue the Seminoles, anticipated the worst in Mexico. The war might encourage patriotism and valor, but he expected it to hang on, "disclose our financial weakness, involve us in a heavy debt, give a strong central tendency to our system, prevent reforms and greatly strengthen the spoils system."[1]

In January 1846 the President had ordered Zachary Taylor to move his troops to a position on or near the disputed boundary between Texas and Mexico on the Rio Grande. Although Calhoun immediately concluded that such a provocative action would lead to war, he held his peace, fearing that a break with Polk over the matter would jeopardize the Oregon treaty and the domestic legislation he supported. Meanwhile, the first shots of the war were exchanged at the end of April, when a detachment of Taylor's troops was ambushed. Upon learning of this encounter, Polk immediately asked Congress to recognize a state of war against Mexico and provide funds to fight it. The House quickly pushed through the requested legislation and rushed it to the Senate, where Calhoun argued in vain that the full story of the fighting on the Rio Grande was not being disclosed and that a distinction should be made between supporting troops actually engaged in military hostilities and a declaration of war as understood in the Constitution. His was a voice of reason, but reason was not the order of the day. A President who had been willing to risk war with Britain over Oregon would not waver at the prospect of forcing American demands upon the much weaker Mexicans. The war bill passed 40 to 2. Calhoun and two Whig Senators abstained.

Considering the situation he found himself in, Calhoun's response to Polk's war message showed considerable political courage. The patriotic tide rises rapidly once a democratic people feel that their honor has been impeached or their security threatened, and Calhoun knew this as well as anyone. He compared American public opinion in 1846 with the impetuous ardor of a young man "full of health and vigor & disposed for adventure of any description but without wisdom or experience to guide him." Convinced, as usual, that wisdom was on his side, Calhoun seemed at a loss to know how to get the young Americans of the forties to listen. If Senators ignored him, how could he expect to catch the ears of ordinary citizens?[2]

At the same time that he was failing to prevent Congress from rushing into war, Calhoun was being pressed by Charleston friends about his plans for 1848. He told them that the presidency should be "wholly dropt" for the moment because the immediate future looked so uncertain. As the hapless Pickens had already discovered, this did not mean that Calhoun was giving up the quest; it simply meant that he would wait and see. Indeed, the very difficulties of his situation seem to have whetted his political appetite, for as he told his brother-in-law, the problems involved in translating wisdom into effective political action always provided the greatest challenge for a public man. Admitting that the need to preserve popularity kept most politicians from doing the right thing in great emergencies, Calhoun wrote that he would allow for that "just as the mechanic does for friction in that of machinery. We must learn to take men as they are. If all were disinterested patriots there would be little difficulty in constructing or managing the political machine & very little merit in doing either."[3]

Calhoun was not prepared to sacrifice his future over an unwise, probably unjust war against Mexico. He knew that the war was popular in South Carolina and that troops were being vigorously recruited in Abbeville, Edgefield, and other towns where he had long been a household word. He also knew that his son Patrick wanted a promotion before he marched off to join Zachary Taylor's army, and he was willing to swallow his pride long enough to pass that information personally on to the President. Confident that his refusal to vote for the war would not hurt him in the long run with the "patriotic and reflecting" and taking into account the fact that troops were already in the field, Calhoun was prepared to give the war "a quiet but decided support."[4]

Returning to Fort Hill after Congress recessed in August 1846, Calhoun made a detour to visit Wytheville, Virginia, where his family had made its first settlement more than a century earlier. Riding over the fertile bottomland that had once belonged to his ancestors, he must have mused over the extraordinary changes which had overtaken the country since the Calhouns first invaded the wilderness. Upon arriving home, he found a letter from a Greenville friend who had met an old man named McKay who claimed to have fought Indians alongside his father on the Carolina frontier. According to the story, Patrick had been knocked down in hand-to-hand combat with a warrior but had recovered in time to save both himself and McKay from the tomahawk. Calhoun had heard stories like this before, but coming as it did after Wytheville, McKay's account would have made a special impact. Although he would leave behind almost no record of his interior life, Calhoun knew that he was the son of a legend and had become a legend himself. Blessed with advantages of wealth and education far beyond anything his father possessed, he had tried to carry on his father's struggle in a new and rapidly changing world. Patrick's enemies were not his enemies, and the tomahawk and rifle were not his tools, but in many ways the stakes were the same for the father and the son. With one foot always in the wilderness, the father had put his life on the line to carve civilization out of a brutal frontier. The son had made his career in the public forum, where he put his character on the line to preserve the political principles that civilization had created. Old and weary as he was at sixty-four, duty still called him to that task. Enemies and even some admirers had long grown tired of hearing Calhoun insist that every turn in his career was a call to duty. Neither they nor he would ever understand how duty and ambition could become so inter-mingled in a man's mind and behavior as to become almost indistin-guishable.[5]

During the four-month recess that he spent at Fort Hill, Calhoun was as busy as usual with plantation and family affairs. His son Patrick, who had gotten no closer to Mexican battlefields than New Orleans, was back home on sick leave. By this time the chill in his relationship with the administration had forced Calhoun to refuse help to all pa-tronage seekers, and this apparently included his sons. Young John, for example, wrote directly to the Secretary of the Navy for a commission in the Marines only to receive a formal, disappointing reply. Mean-while, the youngest boys, Willy and James, were still languishing after peripatetic educational careers which had taken them to a variety of tutors and schools with little appreciable effect. Floride's brother James Edward, who kept an eye on Fort Hill during the Senator's extended absences, put the matter bluntly when he said, "[G]reat injustice has been done you by those who have had the teaching of your children." Willy was apparently a particularly hard case, and even his uncle seemed to despair at correcting his "uncouth habits."[6]

It is instructive to compare Calhoun's indulgence toward his sons with the severity he extended to members of his political family. No one had been a more devoted disciple through good times and bad than his cousin Francis Pickens, but Pickens's admiration for Polk and lack of enthusiasm for Calhoun's continuing presidential aspirations had noticeably cooled the relationship between the two. When Calhoun learned that Pickens had allegedly endorsed an article in the *Southern Quarterly Review* criticizing his role at Memphis and at a public meet-ing in Edgefield had later spoken against his opposition to the Mexican War, he began to treat his old friend like a disobedient child. Before the congressional recess Pickens had called on the Senator in Washing-ton, where Calhoun gave him a formal reception and declared he did not want to see him again "until he explained his course." Pickens, a proud and sensitive man, obviously hurt by being so rudely dismissed by a man he had befriended in so many ways as both a kinsman and a politician, explained at length, but to no avail. Not even the ministrations of the sympathetic Anna could repair the breach. Pickens had to learn the hard way that however lax the discipline at Fort Hill, not even a suspicion of disloyalty would be tolerated among Calhoun's political lieutenants.[7]

During his stay in South Carolina Calhoun read encouraging reports from supporters both in and outside the South which led him to believe that he could still be a viable presidential candidate. He based this judgment partly on the ways in which his support for internal improvements and his leadership in the peace movement had enhanced his image as a national leader and partly on his estimate of the consequences likely to follow from the Wilmot Proviso. On August 8, the day before Calhoun left Washington, Democratic Congressman David Wilmot of Pennsylvania had introduced an amendment to an administration appropriation bill stipulating that slavery be prohibited in any territory which might be acquired from Mexico. The amendment passed the House but failed in the Senate as the congressional session ended. Although Calhoun did not participate in the first round of legislative maneuvering over the proviso, there was no question where he stood on the issue: The proviso must be resisted even at the cost of disunion. His initial appraisal, however, was that the proposal might work to his advantage by dividing northern and southern Whigs while bringing the two parties together in the South. "My own position is the most eligible of all the public men," he wrote Clemson in November, "and I intend to use it for the good of the whole Union, if it can be made available & if not for the portion where Providence has cast my lot." Admitting to Anna that his public silence about the Wilmot Proviso was calculated, Calhoun maintained that it made his position more imposing when time comes to act," and he repeated what he had earlier told Clemson about wanting "above all things to save the whole, but if that cannot be, to save the portion where Providence has cast my lot." As usual, he denied that personal ambition played any part in his thinking, and he agreed with his daughter when she said he already had been honored enough and did not need the presidency. Although that was the proud, sensible, self-respecting thing to say, his heart said something else.[8]

Almost immediately upon reaching Washington in December 1846, Calhoun was called in to see the President, who wanted to consult with him on military and diplomatic matters. Dissatisfied with his two Whig generals Winfield Scott and Zachary Taylor, Polk was anxious to create a new lieutenant generalship for Thomas Hart Benton, who had become a close adviser in the conduct of the war. The President must have known, however, that Calhoun, who had long considered Benton a personal as well as a political enemy, would refuse to support that idea. Determined to block any move that might transform his bombastic Missourian adversary into a war hero, Calhoun was more amenable to Polk's plan to take substantial territory from Mexico by negotiation and purchase. It was impossible to talk about acquiring territory from Mexico without considering the implications of the Wilmot Proviso. According to the President, Calhoun said that "he did not want to extend slavery, but that if the slavery restriction was put into a treaty, it would involve a principle, and that whatever the other provisions of the treaty were he would vote against it." The meeting ended on an amicable note, and the President, who did not really understand the symbolic importance of the proviso, reported that he was "pleased" at the outcome.[9]

After a dinner party at the White House on Christmas Eve Polk again sought Calhoun's support for his lieutenant general idea and was again rebuffed. Calhoun now believed that the government was floundering in the war effort. Despite Taylor's early border victories, the almost unopposed occupation of strategic locations in California and New Mexico and the capture of Monterrey in September, Mexico refused to quit. Arguing that an extended campaign into the interior of Mexico would be too costly and time-consuming, Calhoun proposed a defensive strategy. Let the army withdraw to a line of easily defensible posts holding enough territory to pay for the war and wait for the enemy to negotiate. Although such a plan was far too passive for the hawkish President, Calhoun went away from his sessions with Polk thinking that he had the upper hand. In the face of strong Whig opposition in the Senate the administration needed the support of Calhoun and his friends. "We hold the balance," he had written Clemson earlier in the summer, "and it is felt."[10]

Anxious to press his advantage, Calhoun gave his first formal speech on Mexico on February 9, 1847, when he joined the Senate debate on the administration's three-million-dollar appropriation bill. Repeating much of what he had said to the President in private, Calhoun argued that instead of driving Mexico to the point of surrender, the United States should "inflict the least possible amount of injury" on a neighbor and "sister republic" eager to "imitate our example." Even if the United States had the power to crush the Mexican Army quickly and occupy the country, such a victory could lead to disaster. "Mexico is to us the forbidden fruit," he told the Senate. "The penalty of eating it would be to subject our institutions to political death." The costs of conquest, including the cost of containing guerrilla warfare, would inevitably lead to the creation of a standing army and a centralized, antirepublican political system. The alternative, which Calhoun had already proposed to the President, was to set up a defensive line along the Rio Grande and westward along the thirty-second parallel to the Pacific and hold it until Mexico agreed to negotiate a treaty through which the United States could legally acquire territory it already occupied.[11]

In many ways Calhoun's Mexico speech compared favorably with the one he had made on Oregon. It was pacific and nonpartisan, and it expressed generous sentiments toward the enemy. At the same time it managed to say almost everything the President did not want to hear, causing Polk finally to give up on Calhoun, whom he now called "the most mischievous man in the Senate." Ritchie, speaking for the administration in the *Washington Union,* claimed that "the Mexicans achieved another victory" with Calhoun's speech, and this made his ostracism official. For the second time in his career Calhoun found himself thrown out of the Democratic Party.

The attack on Calhoun's loyalty marked the end of civility in the Mexican debate, as Calhoun and his allies moved successfully to ban Ritchie from the Senate floor. Meanwhile, administration Senators began to pour heavy fire on Calhoun for having repeatedly sabotaged the Democratic Party over a period of fifteen years. This played directly into Calhoun's hand by allowing him to spend hours justifying the consistency of this own career and claiming credit for having avoided war with Britain while putting blame for the messy Mexican War squarely in Polk's lap.[12]

It was one thing for the Democrats to ride the patriotic tide and put down their maverick colleague for criticizing a popular war, but quite another to silence him on the Wilmot Proviso. In the Mexico speech Calhoun had dealt gently with that explosive issue, limiting himself to a single paragraph in which he argued the futility of an all-out war effort which could only lead the country to the brink of disunion as slave and free states disputed with each other over their rights to enjoy the conquered territory. Ten days later, however, he addressed the Wilmot Proviso directly by proposing resolutions declaring the moral and constitutional right of citizens of any state to emigrate "with their property into any of the territories of the United States." In his accompanying remarks Calhoun pointed out the heavy numerical advantage enjoyed by the free states in the House of Representatives and electoral college and the inevitable shift in that direction as new states like Iowa and Wisconsin began to elect Senators. The prohibition of slavery in future territory acquired from Mexico would make the slaveholding states a permanent minority "at the entire mercy of the non-slaveholding states." Confronted with this prospect, the South should take refuge in the Constitution, which allowed every new state to organize its own government, stipulating only that it be "a republican form of government." Of course, one plausible explanation for the popularity of the proviso in the House was that increasing numbers of Americans were finding it difficult to reconcile slavery with republican institutions. Calhoun dismissed this possibility by contrasting the abolitionist's "vague, indefinite, erroneous and most dangerous conception of private, individual liberty" with the great "common liberty . . . the higher right of a community to govern themselves." Without mentioning nullification or secession, he insisted that the question of the right of slaveholders to their equal place in the territories could not be compromised. "Let us be done with compromises," he concluded. "Let us go back and stand on the Constitution."13

Forcing the Senate to confront the proviso head-on was exactly what the President was hoping to avoid. By this time Polk must have come to think of Calhoun as a kind of ominous dark presence, always hovering overhead and liable to rain on the administration's parade at any moment. Although a slaveholder himself, he could not understand why politicians from any section would let themselves get bogged down in an endless debate over the future of slavery in a part of the country naturally unsuited for it. For the President the important thing was to defend national honor, extend the country's borders, and thus expand the area of freedom secured by republican institutions. Calhoun and the antislavery Senators saw the question of honor differently. The latter believed that national honor could be preserved only by containing slavery and ultimately abolishing it, while Calhoun believed denying the right to take their property to the territories was to strike at the honor of southerners individually and collectively. Such moral imperatives were beyond the President's comprehension. He wanted to table the proviso as soon as possible and get on with the job of subduing Mexico, but first he would have to subdue Calhoun. Polk's surrogate in this formidable task was Benton, who now took the floor to convince Senators that Calhoun was trying to stop a war that he had helped start in the first place by leading the charge for the annexation of Texas. An old gunfighter, always at his blustering best when assaulting Calhoun, and smarting from the denial of his coveted lieutenant generalship, Benton tried to discredit Calhoun as a political outlaw who played the slavery game in order to break up the Union and provide a new political future for himself. Long accustomed to this line of abuse, Calhoun calmly pointed out that the extraordinary lengths to which the administration went "to trace the authorship of the war to me" simply proved how unpopular it had become. On the other hand, he was happy to claim all the credit Benton wanted to give him for having been "the author of this great measure" of annexation, a claim which so aroused John Tyler when he heard it that he denounced his former Secretary of State as "the great I am." Tyler had a right to be offended, but even he would have had to admit that Calhoun had skillfully handled the completion of the Texas negotiations and that he was handling Benton just as easily now.[14]

Shortly after the Calhoun-Benton encounter the Senate adjourned before Calhoun's resolutions could be brought to a vote. Meanwhile, the Wilmot Proviso was rejected, and the government managed to secure most of the resources it needed to carry on the war. Calhoun turned homeward with the consolation that if he had not been able to win the government or the country over to his side regarding the war, he had at least sounded an alarm over the perils of the peace to follow.

Stopping in Charleston on March 9, the same day that Winfield Scott was launching the momentous campaign against Veracruz that would speed victory in the war, Calhoun addressed a huge public meeting on the need for a new politics in the South to preserve traditional institutions. This speech is probably his most impressive address outside the Senate, partly because it reflects ideas he was trying to systematize in his formal political writing and partly because he was attempting to answer a question of burning importance to most southerners. Not all the Carolinians in his audience that day would have been slaveholders, but the overwhelming majority would have been relatively well-informed, prosperous citizens, comfortable with slavery, who paid their taxes, kept the law, and were proud of the role their fathers had played in the Revolution and of the loved ones they had sent off to fight and bleed in Mexico. Now Congress was threatening to shut them out of territory their sons were fighting to acquire. Calhoun's constituents were angry and confused. They had read enough about the wrangles in Congress; now their man in Washington had come home, and they expected him to explain what was happening face-to-face. The Senator might not be comfortable in public meetings outside the legislative chamber, but this was one meeting he could not avoid.

Reminding his audience that the South's minority position in the Union was counterbalanced to a considerable degree by protections guaranteed in the Constitution and by the economic importance of southern exports, Calhoun attempted to explain why the antislavery crusade outside the region was gaining political momentum. Dividing the public of the nonslaveholding states into four classes, he estimated that only about 5 percent were ardent abolitionists, matched in numbers but not in influence by an equal number of proslavery sympathizers. The rest of the public was divided into a large group of about 70 percent whose members disliked slavery but recognized its constitutional status and a remaining group of about 20 percent of political party activists who were "perfectly indifferent" to slavery as a moral issue but intensely aware of its political potential. Given the close balance of the two major parties outside the South, a small, zealous party like the abolitionists took on an importance disproportionate to its numbers as both Whigs and Democrats bade for its votes. The engine which kept this process going was the "rich and glittering prize" of the presidency with its control over "a vast amount of patronage." Thus the Wilmot Proviso was not a moral phenomenon but a calculated maneuver by politicians grasping for power and money, a game played by both parties as they sought to appease antislavery sentiment in the North without completely alienating the South.

Calhoun concluded his address by calling on the South to abandon the party politics of Whigs and Democrats and unite in one party committed to southern principles and institutions. "Let us profit by the example of the abolition party," he said, "who, as small as they are, have acquired so much influence by the course they have pursued. As they make the destruction of our domestic institutions the paramount question, let us regard every man as of our party who stands up in its defence, and every one as against us, who does not, until aggression ceases."[15]

In retrospect Calhoun's analysis of party politics in the 1840s seems simplistic. He failed to distinguish between politically active abolitionists and those who refused to vote or hold office, and he ignored the fact that Wilmot and other angry Van Burenites were at least as interested in exciting southern opposition to Polk's proposals as they were in attracting antislavery support. He also discounted the role of ideology in American parties and underestimated their role in shaping political values. Nevertheless, Calhoun's perception of the critical role minorities could play in American polities was valid, and his confidence in its efficacy must have been reinforced by the success of his own little band of supporters in the Senate. Although Calhoun did not live to see his vision of a southern party realized, it remained his principal objective for the next two years, and before he died, he incorporated many of the ideas of his Charleston address into a classic theoretical argument in defense of minority rights.

Back home at Fort Hill in mid-March, Calhoun must have found his satisfaction at being part of an environment he could control sharply tempered by the refusal of political events to bend to his will. Despite the Charleston speech, which had been widely distributed, stimulating several meetings on southern rights, Whig and Democratic leaders in the South showed no sign of abdication, and their establishments remained unshaken. The conventional wisdom in the parties was that since neither Democrats nor Whigs had been able to satisfy his ambition, Calhoun was once again using scare tactics to create a new party he could ride to the White House, but almost everyone agreed that was a most unlikely possibility. Calhoun's break with the administration had alienated some of his closest followers, and there had been such severe losses among the faithful in Virginia that some members of the Virginia delegation were refusing to distribute his speeches. Meanwhile, the South seemed as eager as ever to participate in the national nominating conventions Calhoun abhorred. A feeble attempt in Charleston (now in West Virginia) to establish a southern paper to support Calhoun's ideas led nowhere, and his exile from the party in power became a high priority for the Democrats as the President upgraded his estimation of Calhoun from "mischievous" to "wicked."[16]

Polk's estimation of Calhoun was shaped not only by his opposition to the war and insistence on keeping the slavery issue alive but by rumors that had begun to circulate in the spring of 1847 that South Carolina would support Taylor for President. After his victory at Buena Vista a few weeks earlier, the rugged, independent general was perceived more and more to be cast in the image of Andrew Jackson, and many of Calhoun's friends believe he would be invincible as the standard-bearer of any party. The irrepressible James Hamilton claimed that Taylor could not be beaten and advised Calhoun to put his own supporters under the general's banner. Examining the Taylor phenomenon more objectively, Calhoun decided that a basic political principle was being illustrated: "The party in power, which makes a war, will be sure to be turned out of power by it—if successful by the successful general, if not by the opposition." If Taylor were to be elected, Calhoun thought the country might never have another avoidable war. Therefore, as much as he was opposed to "military chieftains for Presidents," he would be content "to see him elected against Mr. Polk or any one who contributed to make the war." In late May Hammond saw Calhoun at McDuffie's plantation and found the old statesman apparently "resigned to his fate," but Hammond may have been reporting what he wanted to see because a few weeks later Calhoun wrote his daughter that he felt his political standing had become one of "entire independence of party & of great command." By midsummer, as he began to look forward once again to Washington, he told his son-in-law that while Taylor might be a popular favorite, he considered himself "the most eligible of all the public men of our country." At sixty-five he was still eager for the hunt.[17]

By the time Congress convened in December 1847, Mexico City had been in American hands for three months, but the government of Mexico still refused to come to terms, prompting the more rabid expansionists to call for blood and booty. "The people of Mexico must be made to feel this war" the *New York Globe* thundered. "We must SEIZE HER MINES—hold her towns. . . . There is a spirit abroad which will not long be stayed—a spirit of progress which will compel us, for the good of both nations and the world at large, to DESTROY THE NATIONALITY OF THAT BESOTTED PEOPLE." The *Globe* confidently predicted that "[l]ike the Sabine virgins," Mexico would soon "learn to love her ravisher." Dismayed by such sentiments, which could be found in papers of both parties, Calhoun wrote his daughter, "[o]ur people have undergone a great change. Their inclination is for conquest and empire, regardless of their institutions and liberty. . . . They think they hold their liberty by a divine tenure which no imprudence or folly can defeat." Meanwhile, the President vowed in his message to Congress never to give up New Mexico and California and threatened to occupy all Mexico if necessary. He explicitly rejected the possibility of withdrawing American troops to a defensive line.[18]

Anxious as he was to debate publicly the all-Mexico movement which Polk seemed to be endorsing, Calhoun found that he first had to cope with New York Senator Daniel Dickinson, who complicated the whole territorial question by combining an endorsement of annexation with the proposal that slavery in territories acquired through the war be left to the legislatures chosen by the people in those territories. Perceiving the Dickinson move as an administration ploy to strike at slavery under the cover of popular sovereignty, Calhoun maneuvered successfully to prevent a vote. Meanwhile, he prepared a formal reply to the President's message which he delivered to a crowded Senate on January 4, 1848.[19]

Distinguishing between the army, which had done "all that skill and gallantry could accomplish," and a government which had not been able to achieve peace, Calhoun warned against any policy which would lead the United States to incorporate Mexico into the Union or treat it as a captured province. In his earlier speech on the war he had

spoken generously of Mexico as a "sister republic" trying to profit by
the example of the United States. Now he reminded the Senate that
"Ours is the government of the white man," while Mexico with a heavy
population of Indian and mixed blood had made "the fatal error of
placing the colored race on an equality with the white." Repeating
arguments he had made when defending the census of 1840, Calhoun
assured Senators that "in the whole history of Man" there was no
record of any "civilized colored race" maintaining free institutions.
"Are we to overlook this great fact?" he asked. "Are we to associate
with ourselves as equals, companions and fellow citizens the Indians
and mixed races of Mexico? I would consider such association as degrading to ourselves and fatal to our institutions."

One alternative to taking Mexico into the Union might be to treat
it as a conquered province, but Calhoun argued that republicanism
could never coexist with empire, that patronage, massive bureaucracies,
and increasing centralized political power would overwhelm the federal
system. A better alternative would be the one that Calhoun had already
suggested: to withdraw the army to defensive positions while retaining
enough territory to satisfy American claims and encourage peace
negotiations.

However insulting to the people of Mexico (and to nonwhites everywhere), Calhoun's speech appealed to the racial prejudices of most
Americans and was a convincing demonstration of the political independence he claimed. Recognizing the real sacrifices Americans had
made in the war (South Carolina's Palmetto Regiment had suffered a
43 percent death rate), he refused to go along with those Whigs who
wanted no territory from Mexico. On the other hand, he rejected the
claims of expansionists who sought to justify huge chunks of Mexico on
the ground that they were extending the area of freedom. Calling it a
"sad delusion" to assume that all people were capable of self-government, Calhoun was still willing to settle the war on generous terms
which would give the United States enough territory "to cover all
proper claims" and "best suited for us to acquire and least disadvanta-
geous for Mexico to lose."[20]

Although the January 4 speech was reviewed favorable by papers of
both parties, leading Calhoun to claim that he had turned the tide
against conquest and annexation, even as he spoke in the Senate, the

President's peace commissioner Nicholas Trist, was hammering out a treaty with the Mexicans in which the United States agreed to pay fifteen million dollars for New Mexico and California. Calhoun wrote to his son Andrew on February 23 that the treaty had just been sent to the Senate, and he predicted that it would be quickly approved, as it was with his help on March 10.[21]

Once peace was achieved, Calhoun expected "deep agitation" to resume over the extension of slavery. "The South will be in the crisis of its fate," he warned. "If it yields now all will be lost." By this time any lingering illusions he may have sheltered about his own fate as an independent presidential candidate had finally evaporated. The Whigs and Democrats would hold their conventions, but the elections would be no more than a mere "struggle for the spoils." As usual, Calhoun professed entire satisfaction with his own role and attributed his unavailability as a candidate to his refusal to court popularity and play the party game. Not all his friends were so sanguine. According to Dixon Lewis, if Calhoun had chosen to go along with Polk and support a war to extend southern territory, "he could have controlled it, and all the politicians in the country could not have kept him from being President." Instead he had chosen to oppose a popular war and not only lost the presidency "but put himself in a position where not a friend he had outside of the South could support him and live."[22]

20

"Having Faithfully Done My Duty,"
1848–1850

DUFF GREEN frequently berated Calhoun for squandering his presidential possibilities by paying too much attention to South Carolina radicals. Green thought this had been especially true in the early 1840s, but Calhoun complained that he was badly misunderstood. "I am always happy to hear the opinion of my friends," he patiently pointed out to Green, "and often avail myself of their suggestions in modifying my course, but ever rarely in making it." Calhoun liked Green and appreciated his loyalty but obviously thought that his friend operated on a different political level. Green was an opportunist, always anxious to hoist sail and catch the freshest breeze. In the mid-forties that breeze had carried the drumbeat of war. In 1848 it was propelling a hero of that war, whose political innocence was so complete that he had never even bothered to vote, toward the White House. Calhoun had steered his own course during the war, and he would do the same during the campaign of 1848; that would mean doing his best to ignore it.[1]

Calhoun was sixty-six in 1848. Stooped, gray, haggard from a hacking tubercular cough, he had only two years to live, but they were among the most productive in his life. Not only did he continue to lead the fight in Washington to secure southerners access to the western territories, but he also completed the two formal political treatises which ensured his continuing influence over the way Americans thought and behaved long after he had died.

Calhoun's determination to finish *The Disquisition on Government* and *The Discourse on the Constitution and Government of the United States* was encouraged both by the sense that his time was running out and by his growing conviction that the political crisis he addressed in the United States was part of a larger movement in modern history. At least as interested in the tumultuous changes taking place in Europe as in the coming elections in his own country, he relied on his experience in Congress and the State Department as well as regular firsthand reports from the Clemsons in Brussels to keep him informed, and like thousands of other Americans, he waited eagerly for the transatlantic steamers bringing the latest news from abroad. As a revolutionary tide swept over the Continent, toppling monarchs in country after country, most of his countrymen rejoiced to see American principles finally catching up with the Old World. Calhoun was not so sure and cautioned his daughter not to "undervalue" a Europe which had contributed so much to the progress of the modern world. The great problems facing civilization were caused not by old-fashioned institutions holding the world back but by the pace of progress, which threatened to run out of control as human ability to master the physical environment raced ahead of people's ability to govern themselves. "If the present institutions of Europe and this country could be preserved for one century more without convulsion or revolution," he assured Anna, the world might look forward to almost unlimited progress.[2]

Although much of Calhoun's attention from 1848 to 1850 was focused westward on Oregon, California, and New Mexico, he repeatedly looked eastward, where events in Europe offered "an opportunity to test the truth or error of the principles" he was attempting to establish in his theoretical writing. While this work was still in rough draft in April 1848, Calhoun could confidently assure Anna that history would confirm his basic position because it was "drawn from facts in the moral world just as certain as any in the physical." What Duff Green and most of his other friends, to say nothing of his enemies, did not understand was that although Calhoun would never leave the political arena, his ultimate ambition was not to become President but to be known as the statesman who finally placed political science on the same solid foundation as physical science.[3]

The Disquisition on Government, which Calhoun finished on June 15, 1849, after working on it intermittently over a period of about six years, comes to just over one hundred pages in the standard edition of his works and is an extended exercise in deductive reasoning without specific reference to American history or institutions. Calhoun's purpose is to relate the origin and purpose of government to human nature and to expose through logical argument the danger of unlimited majority rule, something he first attempted in his essays on nullification twenty years earlier. Following Aristotle, he assumes that human beings are social creatures by nature, but since they are also ruled by individual self-interest, they need government to keep them from destroying society. In this sense government may be said to be of "Divine ordination," but since man's self-interest is stronger than his social instinct, the powers of government must always be suspect. It follows, therefore, that a human contrivance (which Calhoun refers to variously as "organism" or "constitution") becomes necessary to prevent the abuse of government power. As Calhoun puts it, "man is left to perfect what the wisdom of the Infinite ordained as necessary to preserve the race."[4]

In any political system, Calhoun argues, those who rule and those who are ruled stand in "antagonistic relations to each other." The first function of the Constitution, therefore, is to see that power is resisted by power, and this, in turn, leads to the necessity for suffrage, "the indispensable and primary principle in the *foundation* of a constitutional government." Here Calhoun repeats an argument in the *South Carolina Exposition and Protest* by showing that suffrage alone can do no more than give "control to those who elect over those they have elected." In a small community with a single interest suffrage might afford reasonable protection to the people. In a large, diverse community, however, the natural tendency of voters to pursue their own self-interest leads to struggle among the different interests, and eventually combinations are formed, resulting in a majority intent on securing its own interests. Once in power, the controlling majority pursues policies of taxation, disbursement, and patronage which feather the nests of its constituents. After the advantages of majority power are recognized, opposing interests begin to combine in opposition, thus dividing the community into two great parties that continue to compete with each other for the advantage of controlling the government and dividing the spoils.[5]

According to Calhoun, the way to make suffrage work for the whole community is to give each "interest either a concurrent voice in making and executing the laws or a veto in their execution." Since the numerical majority is never more than a portion of the people, the "delusive hope" of achieving democratic justice through majority rule must always be challenged. Only when the will of the people is counted by numbers and by interests will interest groups and individuals find it necessary not to antagonize each other.[6]

In one of his letters to Anna, Calhoun had admitted to being a "highly conservative" optimist. He explains this apparent paradox in *The Disquisition.* Progress depends on the ability of individuals to improve themselves intellectually, morally, and materially, and this requires "liberty and security." The best government is one that balances the liberty necessary to improvement against the power needed to provide security, and the ratio of liberty to power must depend on the circumstances of the community in question—its history, its geography, the education of its people, etc. Since liberty is "a reward to be earned, not a blessing to be gratuitously lavished on all alike," it is a great error to believe that "all men are born free and equal." Dismissing the "state of nature" as a fiction, Calhoun asserts that in fact, men are born "subject not only to parental authority, but to the laws and institutions of the country where born." These remarks on liberty are a digression from the main argument in *The Disquisition,* but they constitute an implicit rejection of the ideology of the Declaration of Independence, which had been so effectively appropriated by the abolitionists. Calhoun would be much more explicit about this point on the floor of the Senate. His purpose in *The Disquisition* is to show that liberty can be derived only from a government based on the will of the concurrent majority.[7]

It is hard to read Calhoun's most famous essay without being impressed. Never a great prose stylist, he is able to achieve a kind of stripped-down elegance and power in *The Disquisition* that is unexcelled in American political writing. Accept his assumptions, and it is difficult not to be swept along to his conclusions. But the assumptions are far from irresistible. Calhoun never really explains what he means by an "interest." He is obviously thinking of the conflicting interests of agrarian and manufacturing, and of slave and free labor communities, but it is not clear that he appreciated the importance of other variables such as language, religion, ethnicity, and ideology in defining and reconciling interests. Both in his formal writing and in his political speeches Calhoun found it easy to universalize on the basis of particular experiences. Observing the emergence of a two-party system in the United States, he assumed it was the expression of a general principle applicable to all republics, just as he interpreted the Zachary Taylor phenomenon to mean that after a war democratic societies would invariably look to a military hero for leadership.

Most of Calhoun's critics during and after his lifetime have emphasized the impracticability of the concurrent majority as a formal institution within the framework of the government of the United States. Calhoun believed that he had explained in documents like the *South Carolina Exposition* and *Fort Hill Address* how it could work through the process of nullification, and he assumed that his state had demonstrated the practicality of the process in 1833, when it forced the country to compromise on the tariff. In *The Disquisition* he points to the trial by jury as another example of the concurrent principle in action. Because they cannot reach a verdict without unanimous agreement, jurors labor under what Calhoun calls a "disposition to harmonize. . . . If the necessity of unanimity were dispensed with, and the finding of a jury made to depend on a bare majority," trial by jury would be an enormous evil because "all the factious feelings of the day would enter and contaminate justice at its source."[8] Although the analogy helps us understand the kind of mind-set Calhoun expected from citizens, it is faulty in many other respects. Judging and legislating are quite different matters, the latter being necessarily political, provisional, subject to emergency pressures, etc., while the judgments of a jury, supposedly above politics, are more permanent and, in some cases, irreversible when exercised.

It is worth pointing out, however, that Calhoun recognized the problems involved in turning his ideas into practice. It might be "difficult or even impossible" to make a perfect constitution, he admitted, but even if the constitution required the concurrence of only "a few great and important interests," the tendency would be to require a concurrent majority too large to use its power to enrich itself at the expense of the minority. Thus the principle of concurrence even imperfectly realized would make for less coercive and therefore more virtuous government. As Calhoun put it, "the number to be plundered would be too few and the number to be aggrandized too many."

Like other conservatives, Calhoun suspected government by design. He believed that a constitution was usually the result "not so much of wisdom and patriotism as of favorable combinations of circumstances" and to succeed must spring from the bossom of the community and be adapted to the intelligence and character of the people." Generalizing from the experience of Europe and America, Calhoun believed that constitutional government tended to follow an evolutionary pattern. Systems of centralized power (monarchy or government by the numerical majority) would either develop constitutions or degenerate into military despotisms.[9]

Toward the end of his essay Calhoun paid tribute to the material progress which characterized the nineteenth century, arguing, as he had in letters to his daughter, that the benefits of increased knowledge in science and technology would amount to little unless they were paired with improvements in government. Political progress would be slow because of a "law in the political as in the natural world that great changes cannot be made except very gradually without convulsions or revolution." Calhoun believed that governments in the civilized world were in a period of transition, one of uncertainty, "confusion, error and wild and fierce fanaticism" as old systems began to fail in Europe and America. The modern world, he wrote in closing, would do well to recall the experience of ancient Rome and feudal England, both of which had created long-standing republics. Rome had succeeded by creating the tribunate which protected the plebeians against the ravages of the patricians, while England had divided power among Crown, Lords, and Commons. Both were examples of genuine constitutional government.[10]

Calhoun intended *The Disquisition* to serve as a long introduction to *The Discourse on the Constitution and Government of the United States.* The first would be theoretical, demonstrating how fundamental principles of human nature shaped political behavior and institutions everywhere. The second would be particularistic and historical, demonstrating how and why the political crisis of 1848 had developed in the United States. *The Disquisition* was completed and copied but probably not reviewed by Calhoun before his death. *The Discourse,* according to Calhoun's editor Richard Crallé, was still in rough draft "bearing evident marks of interrupted and hurried composition." A work of about three hundred pages, it was probably written over the last eighteen months of Calhoun's life and lacks the logical rigor and relative intellectual detachment of *The Disquisition.* Calhoun must have written much of it in the heat of the great Senate debates over the Wilmot Proviso, and the warmth of these engagements is reflected in the essay. Most of what he wrote in *The Discourse* he had already said or was to say in one form or another in the Senate. It provides the fullest example we have of the image of American history and politics which propelled Calhoun through the last years of his life.[11]

He begins *The Discourse* with the familiar assertion that in ratifying the Constitution, the states "retained their separate existence as independent and sovereign communities." Lamenting the popular but false use of the word "national" to describe the government created by the Constitution, he calls it "a democratic federal republic" and "a joint supplemental government," designed to do what the states could not do as well themselves, primarily in the areas of foreign and interstate relations.

It is important for Calhoun to show that the Constitution was a product of the concurrent majority. Seven states representing less than one-third of the numerical population could have prevented the convention from meeting or reaching agreement on the document, and the four smallest states with less than one-tenth of the total population could have prevented ratification. Moreover, the Constitution incorporated the principles of the concurrent majority by providing for the separation of powers and a bicameral legislature in which both numbers and the individual interests of states were represented. According to Calhoun, the framers intended to make the Constitution "more popular" than a government of the numerical majority by requiring "more wills to put it in action."[12]

Quick to pay tribute to the constitutional fathers, Calhoun is just as quick to point out that they were not omniscient. They believed that political conflict under the Constitution would be between federal and state power, but in reality "for both states and people" it turned out to be a struggle to control federal power. This struggle led to the formation of two great parties, and each party when in power interpreted the Constitution in ways that augmented federal and diminished state power. The reasons for this lay partly in human nature and partly in the fact that in large complex societies government policies inevitably impose unequal burdens and rewards on the people. Citizens living in the neighborhood of a large government installation, for example, share more directly in the public funds expended to support it than do citizens in another part of the country. In a homogeneous society composed only of virtuous citizens this might not be the case, but in the real political world of the United States political power led to economic aggrandizement which encouraged parties to consolidate their control of government power whenever they could. The Constitution, built on the principle of the separation of powers and requiring the consent of two majorities before the government could act, together with the fact that the United States covered a large territory encompassing many diverse interests, might slow down the process of consolidating power but could not prevent it.

Calhoun believed that sectionalism like the consolidation or nationalization of power had developed as a natural tendency within the American political system. Parties in the United States had taken on a local character from the beginning, and as the nineteenth century progressed, the local emphasis became sectional as citizens began to realize that if a sectional party were to become a permanent majority, the safeguards written into the Constitution against uncontrolled majority rule would fail and the government would fail under the "absolute control" of the "mere numerical majority." This in fact was happening. In Calhoun's reconstruction of American political history the seeds of crisis and failure had been planted early. The Constitution had been flawed from the beginning, when the framers refrained from including an explicit negative of federal law among the powers reserved to the states. This flaw in the system was compounded by the First Congress, which passed the Judiciary Act of 1789 and also decided that the President could dismiss federal officeholders and that the federal government could accept bank notes rather than specie for some transactions. By providing for judicial review by federal courts, Congress ignored the fact that the Constitution had made state and federal governments coordinate powers, and by putting the power of patronage in the hands of the executive, it turned the presidency into a rich prize to be won. As if this were not damaging enough to the cause of political liberty and virtue, the First Congress went on to put the money power of the country squarely on the side of a powerful national government. In

Calhoun's version of American history the "national impulse" given to the government under the direction of Federalists like Hamilton was intensified by the War of 1812, the growth of the spoils system, and the decline of the old states' rights Jeffersonian party. The move toward consolidation reached a climax in 1833, with the passage of the Force Act, when it was openly proclaimed that the government had the right to judge the extent of its own power and to "put down all resistance by force."

Moving on to a discussion of the slavery issue, Calhoun found a direct link between the Force Act and the growth of a national antislavery movement. Abolitionists had immediately recognized that a Congress which could impose its will on a state which disagreed with its tariff policies might one day be led to strike directly at slavery. Thus a tiny group of fanatics grew into an influential movement in the North and West in the 1830s and 1840s and was courted by both major parties intent on winning national elections and controlling the spoils. The importance of the antislavery vote prevented both of the evenly matched parties from protecting the "assaulted" South and created the crisis of 1848.

How would it all end? Calhoun did not know, but he made it clear in *The Discourse*, as he did on the Senate floor, that secession and disunion were obvious possibilities. Although he continued to insist on the right of nullification, Calhoun now maintained that the federal character of the government could be restored only by the repeal of the Judiciary Act of 1789 and the Force Act of 1833 along with a reduction in congressional power to enact tariffs and the President's patronage power. Above all, sectional balance would have to be restored between the North and South. Denying the South access to new territories would soon give the free states a permanent majority and the power to "mould the Constitution" to their pleasure. Not even the right of nullification could address such a threat. Without going into detail, Calhoun suggested the possibility of a plural executive as one way of instituting an effective concurrent majority. In *The Disquisition* he had closed his essay by citing the experience of Rome and England. Now he pointed to the experience of his native state, which in 1808 had reaped "the happy fruits of a wisely constituted Republic by voluntarily amending its constitution to equalize the legislative power of its two principal sections, the Tidewater and the Backcountry." He omitted to say that compromise had been made possible by the acceptance and rapid growth of slavery in the western half of the state.[13]

Although Calhoun had intended *The Disquisition* and *The Discourse* to provide a definitive analysis and a reasonable solution to the political crises the United States faced at mid-century, he would never face up to the fact that premises in his first essay made it improbable that the solutions in his second could ever be implemented. In *The Discourse* he assumed that without institutional safeguards man's selfishness would always overpower his social instincts, and during the nullification crisis he had gone so far as to say that it was natural for one section in the country to confuse its own economic interest with the interests of the whole country and had even implied that if Carolinians were to trade places with New England manufacturers, they, too, might be protectionists.[14] In the forties sectional antagonism hinged less on the tariff and more on slavery, but the principle was the same. Citizens in the free states, opposed to the expansion of slavery for both ideological and economic reasons, were steadily increasing the political power to impose their will upon the South. Calhoun could hardly expect to convert this established majority by proslavery arguments or appeals to justice for the South. His only realistic hope was to unite the South and appeal to the self-interest of the rest of the states by threatening them with the specter of disunion and civil war, and this would mean eschewing the spirit of conciliation which played so significant a role in his theoretical writing and practicing the politics of crisis and confrontation.

From 1848 to 1850 Calhoun divided his time in Washington between long days in the Senate, in acrimonious controversy with old adversaries and new, and long nights in his boardinghouse room on Capitol Hill, laboring under lamplight to codify his ideas. Accustomed to political defeat in the short run, he could console himself with the conviction that his ideas would eventually prevail. When the Senate rushed to pass a resolution congratulating the French on their successful revolution, Calhoun refused to go along. The resolution passed on April 10, 1848, by a vote of 174 to 2 with Calhoun abstaining. "They have decreed a republic," he said, "but it remains for them to establish a republic." A cardinal lesson of *The Disquisition* was that it took more than simplistic notions of liberty and equality and a naïve faith in the will of the masses to build a lasting constitution.[15]

Two weeks later an audacious abolitionist plot was discovered in the shadow of the Capitol when the schooner *Pearl,* crewed by three white northerners, tried to slip out of the Potomac with eighty slaves. The *Pearl* was apprehended by a steamboat commandeered by angry citizens, and the slaves and their liberators put into jail, but the incident prompted riots in the streets by slaveholders and their friends and a furious debate in the Senate, in the course of which Calhoun forsook his philospher-statesman role long enough to compare the new antislavery Senator John P. Hale with a "maniac in bedlam." Encounters like this which seemed to dramatize the growing vulnerability of slave property to abolitionist agitation, reinforced Calhoun's determination to secure southern rights in the territories. Although he now claimed Congress had no right to control slavery anywhere in the territories (a clear repudiation of the Missouri Compromise), he was willing to see Oregon organized without mention of slavery and to allow federal courts to decide the status of slaves in California and New Mexico. He and Elmore met twice with Polk on this matter and helped push a bill dubbed the Clayton Compromise through the Senate after a nightlong debate on July 27, only to see it tabled the next day in the House when Southern Whigs decided that letting a Democratic administration solve the territory problem might lessen their chances of making Taylor President.[16]

With the demise of the Clayton Compromise any realistic hope of organizing Oregon on terms that Calhoun would approve disappeared, and on August 14 Polk finally signed a bill prohibiting slavery in that territory. Unable to alter the result, Calhoun concentrated on lecturing the Senate with arguments derived from *The Disquisition* and *The Discourse.* Most politicians believed that because slavery would never thrive in Oregon, it was a waste of time to argue about it, but Calhoun insisted that a profound principle was involved. By prohibiting slavery there, Congress was declaring that slavery was wrong and that Congress had a right to correct that wrong wherever it could. The history of government interference with slavery went back to 1787, he said, and was rooted in the "false and dangerous assumption" that "all men are born free and equal." This sentiment, "inserted in our Declaration of

Independence without any necessity," had done more "to retard the cause of liberty and civilization, and is doing more at present, than all other causes combined." Everyone knew, of course, who had written that document, and Calhoun did not flinch from condemning the sainted Jefferson for his "utterly false view" of the races and his belief that blacks were "as fully entitled to both liberty and equality as whites."[17]

In laying the blame for the growing momentum of the abolitionists' success, Calhoun came down hard on both Jefferson and Jackson. The first had planted the seeds of the movement with his mistaken ideas about equality, and the second had encouraged its growth by fostering the belief in a sovereign American nation. Once slavery was perceived as a national rather than a local institution, abolitionists plunged into politics and were soon able to tip the balance to either major party in several northern states. As a result, both parties catered to them, and a fanatical faction found itself with political influence disproportionate to its numbers. The upcoming presidential election offered a perfect example of the capitulation of both parties to the antislavery movement. The Democrats had nominated Lewis Cass on a platform that promised to let settlers in the territories decide for themselves about slavery. Cass was presumably sworn to veto the Wilmot Proviso, but antislavery voters knew that he had voted for it as a Senator. Meanwhile, the Whigs had nominated a national hero and slaveholder whose mystique was so overpowering that southern Whigs had not even insisted on an antiproviso commitment. They simply assumed that Taylor would do the right thing. Calhoun condemned both parties for caving in to the abolitionists. "The leaders and organs of the two parties at the South," he said, "have entered into a pitiful contest to prove their respective candidate and party at the North are less hostile to us than are our opponents. . . . [C]an degradation go further?" What Calhoun did not say was that he and his small band of loyal supporters had been playing a political game similar to that of the abolitionists for almost twenty years.[18]

Calhoun's refusal to endorse either Taylor or Cass infuriated Whigs and Democrats alike, and many thought he was simply positioning himself to make a southern party of his own. "Poor old dotard," sneered the young Georgia Whig Congressman Robert Toombs, "to suppose he could get a party now on any terms. Hereafter treachery itself will not trust him." Although events would prove that Toombs was far off the mark in trying to belittle Calhoun's influence, it was true that he hoped for a new party to save the South. Thus he was encouraged by the news that dissident New York Democrats and antislavery politicians from both parties had decided to run Van Buren as a Free Soil candidate. The great hope in a Free Soil Party, he wrote Clemson, was that it might unite the South and lead to two great sectional parties. As it turned out, however, the Whigs and Democrats survived the election in robust shape, with Taylor winning a close vote almost equally divided between the parties and the sections. Tylor won eight slave and seven free states, while Cass took eight free and seven slave states. Van Buren failed to carry a single state but nudged the verdict to Taylor by splitting the Democratic vote in New York.[19]

Even as the election returns were being tallied, Calhoun was hurrying southward to welcome his daughter and her family on leave from their Belgium post after an absence of four long years. Upon learning earlier in the year that Clemson's inability to reclaim any of his investment in the Alabama plantation might require him to return without Anna and her children, the desperate father, despite the poor cotton market, had managed to raise six hundred dollars for the passage, and he joined the Clemsons at their new plantation house near Abbeville in mid-November. He was delighted to find this portion of his family, young and old, in good health and spirits, and their proximity to Fort Hill in the winter of 1848–1849 was a constant tonic to him.

Long accustomed to being physically and psychically renewed at home, Calhoun had begun to find that his plantation was not always the safe haven it had once been. The depressed cotton market and chronic cash-flow problems which seemed to afflict his entire family were part of the problem. Hardly more than a boy when he had begun to take his father's place, Calhoun had long since become the patriarch of the clan, and in his old age, despite the debilitating effects of disease, political disappointment, and financial distress, he found the rest of the family still feeding on his depleted strength. John had become a physician but showed no indication of being able to support himself by his profession. His tuberculosis was a source of recurring anxiety to Calhoun along with Cornelia's deafness and Floride's nervous irritability.

Calhoun as he appeared one year before his death.

Patrick's career possibilities in the army were apparently no better than "Doctor John's" in medicine. Oblivious of his father's financial problems, Patrick continued on his self-indulgent course despite all paternal admonitions and frequently required emergency infusions of cash. Meanwhile, James at long last appeared to be performing well at the University of South Carolina, and Willy, the youngest and wildest of the Calhoun boys, was preparing to follow suit. Everyone loved Willy, whom the celebrated Dr. Otis F. Nott described as "a perfect child of nature," but Calhoun would surely have taken this as a dubious compliment for his nineteen-year-old son.[20] Only Andrew had shown any aptitude for planting, and he was seldom able to meet his debts without his father's help. The Calhoun brood was lovable enough, devoted to and dependent on their father, and a source of strong emotional satisfaction to him, but Calhoun would have been less than human if at some points in his increasingly stressful later years he had not longed for sons more like his father and himself.

It was the child he saw the least who continued to mean the most to Calhoun. Anna had served as his eyes and ears during the revolutions in Europe, and it was to her that he confided more than anyone else about his political plans and ideas. Her return for a stay of several months in the winter of 1848 was the emotional high point of the last two years of his life. Calhoun's relationship to Anna remained both filial and collegial. She supplied the tenderness that had disappeared long ago between Floride and him along with an understanding of his ideas and an appreciation for his public role that all the rest of the family put together could not equal.

After a painfully short visit with his family Calhoun returned to Washington in mid-December bolstered by the assurance that the Clemsons would spend time with him there on their way back to Europe the following February. Meanwhile, convinced that the election results confirmed his own analysis, Calhoun was ready to get back to work, more determined than ever to unite the South. Oregon had been lost, and the question of California, which was attracting thousands of immigrants to its goldfields, could not be put off. The increasingly aggressive antislavery politicians would see to that. On December 21 they succeeded in passing a House resolution which condemned slavery as "a reproach to our country throughout Christendom and a

serious hindrance to the progress of republican liberty among the nations of the earth" and called for the end of the slave trade in the
District of Columbia. Calhoun saw this action as part of a new pattern
of outrageous behavior toward the South. It included resolutions which
not only would prohibit slavery in California and New Mexico and in all
reservations under federal control but would put the matter of slavery
in the District to a vote of all inhabitants, including slaves and free
blacks! Here was an assault which demanded immediate retaliation by
southerners in Congress no matter what their party. Calhoun called for
a southern caucus, and this time his colleagues listened. Eighteen Senators and fifty-one Congressmen met in the Senate chamber on December 22. Every slave state except Delaware was represented, and a Committee of Fifteen was appointed to prepare and address of grievances.
Calhoun was to write the document.[21]

Although he left no record of his activities over the next few weeks,
we know that Calhoun was laboring mightily to lay the ideological
foundation for a southern party strong enough to act as a concurrent
majority. His report to the committee, which became known as the
Address of the Southern Delegates in Congress to Their Constituents,
contained nothing new. After reciting a litany of grievances beginning
with the Missouri Compromise and ending with the attacks on slavery
in the present Congress, Calhoun warned that the addition of new
states without slavery would soon make it possible for abolitionists to
amend the Constitution, emancipate the slaves, and enroll them in
their own party while keeping southern whites in subjection. "We
would, in a word, change conditions with them, a degradation greater
than has ever yet fallen to the lot of a free and enlightened people."
This horror story could become reality because southerners had preferred to play party politics rather than rally around the central question
of slavery. "If you become united and prove yourself in earnest," Calhoun concluded, "the North will be brought to a pause . . . and the
adoption of a course of policy that may quietly and peaceably terminate
this long conflict between the two sections."[22]

Although he apparently never realized it, Calhoun had stumbled
into a trap set not by northern fanatics but by southern Whigs, who
had no intention of letting his appeal for southern unity break up their
victorious national party. They had joined hands with Calhoun not to

help him but to slay him. Even as Calhoun was toiling to find language all southerners could accept, Toombs was confiding to friends that "after mature consideration" he and others like him had joined the Carolinian's movement "in order to crush it." A part of the plan had been implemented when Toombs's colleague Alexander Stephens was appointed to chair the Committee of Fifteen. Stephens, who a few years earlier had called Calhoun a "humbug" who had invented nullification to destroy the Whigs, almost succeeded in killing Calhoun's *Address* in committee. Failing that, he and the other Whigs managed to get enough revisions in Calhoun's draft to reduce it to a "weak milk and water document." The Whigs obviously did not share Calhoun's sense of desperation. Instead of turning the pending antislavery resolutions into a cause célèbre as he desired, they quietly managed to keep that obnoxious business from coming to a vote in the House, making it clear all the while that they had decided to put the future of the South in better hands than Calhoun's. "I went into the first meeting of the Southern members for the purpose of preventing mischief, and I succeeded," Stephens boasted. "I believe most of the Southern Whigs concur with me. We feel secure under General Taylor—we are determined to insist on his controlling the question."

The defection of the Whigs plus Polk's outspoken objections to continued agitation of the sectional issue left Calhoun hopelessly outgunned, and the strain on his failing energies showed. On December 19 he collapsed in the Senate and was absent for several days, in the course of which a weakened version of his address was accepted by 48 out of a total of 121 southern Congressmen and Senators, including two lonely Whigs. "We have completely foiled Calhoun in his miserable attempt to form a Southern party," chortled Toombs. "I told him that the union of the South was neither possible nor desirable until we were ready to dissolve the union."[23]

As usual, Calhoun put the best possible face on what happened when he told Anna that his *Address* had been "a decided triumph under the circumstances." The truth was that he was losing his grip among younger leaders from the slave states, who tended to agree with the New Orleans paper that suggested that Calhoun might have "outlived his time." They had begun to perceive him as an aging Cassandra figure, and they snickered in increasing numbers when they heard that

Benton had dubbed him the "nigger king" for his scare tactics on race. Calhoun never reported what it felt like to be put down so decisively in a face-to-face encounter with an upstart like Toombs, but he surely would have been offended to learn that Toombs intended to defend the sacred principles of the South by using the "cursed slave pens" in the District as a bargaining chip—or, as the Georgian put it, "to trade them off to advantage." And he certainly would not have been consoled to learn that Toombs's young Democratic colleague Howell Cobb, soon to be the Speaker of the House, had denounced him as an "old reprobate," saying, "If it could please our Heavenly Father to take Calhoun . . . home, I should look upon it as a national blessing."[24]

After it became apparent that his bid for southern unity would not achieve the unanimity he sought, Calhoun played a lesser role than usual in the Senate, where alternative proposals by the administration and the Whigs to create some kind of government for California and New Mexico continued to sputter without result. In late March 1849, after a reasonably friendly interview with the newly inaugurated President Taylor, he headed for South Carolina once again, but Fort Hill was not what it had been when the Clemsons were nearby. Doubtful that he would ever see his daughter and grandchildren again, he wrote her a long, almost poetic letter about the beauties of Carolina in the spring: the bloom of dogwood in the woods, the freshly greened fields of Fort Hill sprinkled with shocks of wheat, and the serpentine rows of cotton plants along the hill sides that he had drained and contoured years before when she was just a girl. Father and daughter had spent countless happy hours tramping and riding over that familiar landscape, and their talk had frequently turned from plantation and family matters to politics. Writing to her in June 1849, Calhoun paused in his descriptions of the physical charms of Fort Hill to announce that he had just finished *The Disquisition* ("125 pages of foolscap closely written") and was about to begin working on the longer work on the Constitution. He wished he could read them both to her.[25]

Except for his daughter's absence, the summer of 1849 seems to have agreed with Calhoun. A daily routine of outdoor supervision of the plantation, together with several hours a day in his office writing out his analysis of the American political system, improved his health, and by mid-October he was within about forty pages of finishing his book. For

the most part he left politics alone. Everyone knew where he stood on
the big issues, and although he followed his customary practice and
made no public statements outside the Senate, there was enough interest nationwide in what his next move might be to make James Gordon
Bennett, editor of the *New York Herald,* send a reporter to the South
with orders to keep a special eye on Calhoun. This move must have
gratified Calhoun, not only because the reporter in question was his old
friend and loyal supporter Joe Scoville but because the surge of interest
in his political ideas and plans had been stimulated by the lavish attention his southern *Address* had received in the national press.

The one big exception to Calhoun's public silence during the summer of 1849 was his detailed response to a long attack by Benton in the
National Intelligencer in late June. Calhoun and Benton had been
feuding ever since the gloating Missourian had forced the Senate to
expunge from its journal the censure against Jackson. Benton was a
slaveholder alert to southern interest, but he scorned Calhoun as a
disunionist who agitated the slavery issue for personal gain. He thought
it was wrong to extend slavery into the western territories and even
more wrong to crusade for slavery in territories like California and New
Mexico where it could never thrive. But there were slaveholders in
Missouri who felt otherwise, and when they managed to get a resolution through the state legislature instructing their Senators to follow
Calhoun's leadership, Benton exploded with a violent personal denunciation of the man he had been in rhetorical combat with for more than
fifteen years. Although Benton's attack was no more than a synthesis of
charges levied many times before, Calhoun sensed that his old enemy
had become suddenly vulnerable to the accusation that he was soft on
slavery and southern rights. In true republican style Calhoun published
his response to Benton in the columns of his village paper the *Pendleton Messenger,* but it was printed widely in papers around the country,
including Missouri, where Benton lost his seat in the fall elections. His
defeat was generally interpreted as a victory for Calhoun.[26]

Meanwhile, Calhoun endorsed the call of a state convention in
Mississippi for a bipartisan convention of southern states to meet in
Nashville in June 1850. At the same time he began to hear reports that
southern Whigs were already beginning to fall out of love with Taylor
as stories circulated that the new President was overlooking his south-

ern friends in choice patronage appointments. Calhoun might be old, might even be scorned in some parts of the South, but his ideas seemed to have a future; there was reason to believe that the mainstream of southern politics was moving in his direction as he returned to Washington on the last day of November 1849.

No Congress had ever tried to organized itself in the face of greater sectional antagonism. It took three weeks, sixty-three ballots, and a load of furious antislavery and disunion rhetoric before Howell Cobb was elected Speaker of the House. Cobb was surprised when southern radicals did not torpedo his candidacy, but Calhoun apparently preferred a southern Democrat outside his own camp to no southern Democrat at all. He made it clear, however, that Cobb was not his choice but had been forced on the House by the North.

The mood in the new Congress had changed radically from the previous spring, and no one expressed it better than Robert Toombs, who was now spouting disunion threats with the same careless abandon that had characterized his dismissal of Calhoun a few months earlier. The latter, of course, gauged the new mood with satisfaction, but a sense of his own physical limitations and a determination to put the finishing touches on his manuscript kept him from plunging into the Senate debates. President Taylor had set the agenda in his annual message by urging that California be admitted directly to the Union as a new state whenever it applied. Californians had already begun to draft their own constitution, and everyone expected it to prohibit slavery. New Mexico, with a sparser population, would probably follow the California example. Taylor was turning out to be an unusual slave-holder—a strong nationalist opposed to the extension of slavery and more interested in preserving the Union than in agitating for southern rights. Whether slavery was a realistic possibility in the western territory or not, most southerners, Whigs and Democrats, could not stomach the exclusion of their property from the vast area involved and supported a variety of counterproposals to save southern honor, such as the carving of a new slave state out of Texas and passage of an effective fugitive slave law.

It was at this stage of the controversy that Calhoun was felled by an attack of pneumonia which kept him bedridden for two weeks. In his absence on January 29 Henry Clay introduced the famous proposals

which finally led to compromise. To appease the South, Clay offered a
strong fugitive slave law and a pledge that Congress would not interfere
with slavery in the District of Columbia. For the North he offered
admission of California as a free state and New Mexico as a territory
without reference to slavery. Although slavery would continue in the
District without threat of federal interference, the slave trade would be
prohibited there. Additional provisions called for adjustment of the
Texas-New Mexico border and for the federal assumption of the Texas
debt.

As Clay defined his proposals, Calhoun lay prostrate in a boardinghouse across from the Capitol, trying to recoup enough energy to join
the debate. The prognosis of his case was a matter of highly visible
speculation in the press, but Calhoun had no intention of dying without being heard, and on February 6 he wrote Clemson that he was
recovering and would soon be back at work. Meanwhile, he was studying the debates as reported in the papers and listening to the firsthand
accounts of southern colleagues who called on him. Buoyed by the news
that with few exceptions southern Senators were forming a solid phalanx against compromise, Calhoun wrote Hammond about the renewed importance of the Nashville convention in June. Under no illusions about his own ability to attend, Calhoun apparently expected
Hammond to make South Carolina's case at the convention and to act
as a personal emissary. Despairing of any agreement in the Senate
acceptable to the South, he seemed to share the general impression that
"disunion is the only alternative that is left us." Decisive, unified action
would be required by the southern states at Nashville, and Hammond
not only was obligated to attend but should stop in Washington and
confer with Calhoun on the way. "Never before," Calhoun wrote
pleadingly, "has the South been placed in so trying a situation, nor can
it ever be placed in one more so. Her all is at stake."[27]

On February 18, four days after President Taylor had sent a copy of
the California constitution to the Senate, Calhoun returned to his seat,
but a spell of bad weather soon had him back in his rooms again. He
wrote his daughter expressing a confidence he probably did not feel
about his recovering health and determination to join the debate, and
on March 2 Webster called at his rooms for a two-hour conference.
Webster had known about Clay's plan in advance and generally sup-

ported it but was distraught by the militant threats being made by abolitionists and southerners alike. Word had it that there had been an angry exchange at the White House when Stephens and Toombs told the President that secession was a likely alternative to Clay's compromise and Taylor responded like Jackson by threatening to hang all traitors. Calhoun and Webster had first encountered each other in Congress when Toombs and Stephens were still in swaddling clothes. The political history of the country had become intertwined with the clashing of their ideas and ambitions. How did the two famous old adversaries relate to each other now? They may have found common ground in a desire to save the Union, but it is unlikely that they were able to agree on a common strategy. By this time Calhoun had already dictated his own speech to Joseph Scoville. The task of writing it out had been too much for him, and so was the task of delivery. It would be read by James Mason of Virginia two days after Webster's visit. It is possible that Webster read the speech in Calhoun's room, or more likely that Calhoun explained generally what he planned to say. In either event Webster could not have ended his visit in an encouraged frame of mind.[28]

On March 4, supported by James Hamilton and wrapped in a long, voluminous cloak which could not conceal the ravages of the disease which each day dragged him closer to the grave, Calhoun appeared in the Senate. Thanking the Senators for their courtesy in allowing Mason to speak for him, he slumped in his seat and proceeded to listen to his own words. Almost twenty years earlier Calhoun had found himself in a similar situation when he sat as the Senate presiding officer while Robert Hayne presented his arguments for states' rights and nullification. At that time the possibility of disunion had been an alarming but still theoretical possibility. Now it seemed an imminent reality. James Mason solemnly read off the reasons—reasons which Calhoun had repeatedly articulated in the Senate and had developed in systematic length in his recently completed treatises. The sectional equilibrium had been destroyed, not by the slow processes of time but by an aggressive federal government which had deferred to northern fanatics to shut southern states out of western territories, had burdened them with unfair economic policies, and had persistently changed the nature of the federal system "from a federal republic, as it originally came from the hands of its framers, into a great national consolidated democracy . . . as absolute as that of the Autocrat of Russia, and as despotic as any absolute government that ever existed."

How could the Union be saved? Not by pious rhetoric, appeals to patriotism or to compromise, but by restoring the old equilibrium: opening the West to slavery, silencing the abolitionists, enforcing the fugitive slave laws, providing by constitutional amendment the power the South was intended to have under the Constitution to protect itself. Disunion was not something that would happen at a given moment, but a process that took place gradually as the cords binding states and citizens together began to part. In this sense disunion had already begun, and he pointed to the recent sectional separation of American Baptists and Methodists.

Throughout his career Calhoun had repeatedly called on republican principles, the Constitution and his own political ideas to defend his state and section. Because he was willing to face up to the possibility of disunion without flinching, he had been called a demagogue and traitor—a new Benedict Arnold. Now, in what Calhoun knew might well be his last major address to the Senate and the country, he invoked the example of the immortal Washington on his own behalf. Washington had been a man of Calhoun's father's generation and had shared a similar way of life. "He was one of us—a slaveholder and a planter" who grew up and achieved distinction under the union of the colonies with Great Britain. Washington had been devoted to that union, but when he saw it become a source of oppression rather than protection, "he did not hesitate to draw his sword and head the great movement" of the Revolution. "This was the great and crowning glory of his life."

Although it was important for Calhoun to assert that he and those who stood with him had as good a claim to the great symbols of the Revolution as any other Americans, he must have dictated these words, and Mason presumably delivered them, without revolutionary fervor. He did not want to call men to the barricades but to set the record straight. His final message, composed more in the spirit of resignation than triumph, left the country, in unity or dismemberment, to the will of Providence, and Calhoun himself secure in the knowledge that "having faithfully done my duty. . . . I shall have the consolation, let what will come, that I am free of all responsibility."[29]

An ultimatum delivered under extraordinary circumstances by a dying chieftain with almost his last breath. Under the circumstances no Senator was anxious to begin rebuttal, and the Senate adjourned. Six days later Webster picked up the challenge with his famous appeal to save the Union. Considering that he came from Massachusetts, Webster took a giant's step in Calhoun's direction by concentrating more on southern than on northern grievances, by abusing the abolitionists, and by demanding a strong fugitive slave law. Although the speech soiled Webster's reputation forever in the minds of an entire generation of younger New England intellectuals, it was not strong enough for Calhoun. Webster had contributed nothing toward "a permanent settlement of the question," he wrote to Clemson. His speech might lead to a temporary patching up of the near rupture between the sections, but "[n]othing short of the terms I propose can settle it finally and permanently. Indeed it is difficult to see how two people so different can exist together in one common Union."[30]

We will never know how much Calhoun would have lent his influence to the patching-up process that Webster was proposing. He returned to the Senate only once after Webster's speech, and then but briefly. Although reports in the press during the following weeks that he had been seen at a White House reception encouraged his family to hope that his health was returning, the truth was the opposite. Some Calhoun watchers claimed that he secluded himself in order to finish his book, others that he was plotting secession strategy under cover of illness, but he was simply dying from the effects of tuberculosis and a failing heart. "Doctor John" was the only family member to be with him at the end, but Calhoun refused to alert the rest of his children or his wife. Always committed to a spartan life-style, he seemed determined to die like a Spartan.

The reports we have of Calhoun's last few weeks suggest a man enormously reduced in physical power and besieged on many fronts but determined to maintain composure. Despite his role, whether played onstage or off, in the great political drama of the day, he continued to worry about his family, and some of his final efforts were directed at getting son Patrick away from the fleshpots of New Orleans and preventing son James from rushing off to California like any other rootless adventurer.[31] When confined to his rooms, Calhoun conversed daily with members of the Congress, particularly those from his own delegation. On good days he received company on more formal terms. His old friend Maria Dallas Campbell remembered how frail he seemed except for the great masses of gray hair falling around his shoulders, but how affectionate and serene in conversation as he lamented the precariousness of the Union while insisting on the South's right to self-preservation. Joseph Henry, director of the Smithsonian and the finest scientific mind in the country, visited Calhoun about the same time and confirmed his impression that "no man in Washington" was "more interesting in conversation . . . no one so quick to catch an idea and give it back to you enlarged and improved."[32]

Like the spirits of other strong-willed individuals battling a fatal illness, Calhoun's soared and sank depending on his condition at the moment. One day toward the end he made the revealing admission that his decline might be irreversible, and "if he did live it would be like bringing up an infant," which would have been a much more intolerable prospect to him than death. This helps explain why Calhoun would not go home to die or summon his wife and family to Washington. Nothing was more important to him than his sense of autonomy. He could not face the prospect of an indefinitely extended invalidism, even at Fort Hill.[33]

On the other hand, he would not give in to death any more than he would concede to the Websters, Clays, Bentons, and abolitionists of the world. On Wednesday, March 27, Calhoun asked South Carolina's other Senator, A. P. Butler, to get a postponement in the debate on Clay's resolutions until the following Tuesday, when he expected to be well enough to speak. At the same time he was planning for a strenuous expedition to Crallé's plantation near Lynchburg, where he planned to convalesce. But the effort was beyond him. Saturday night his heart and lungs began to fail. Calhoun knew that his time had come and asked his son John to put his watch and papers in a secure place. Dr. John and Scoville sat with him through the night. He died at seven-ten on Sunday morning. There were no final tears, prayers, or confessions, and his last words were "I am very comfortable." Prepared for death without having made any of the customary arrangements for it in the form of burial instructions or a will, Calhoun might well have chosen for an epitaph the judgment of his village newspaper, which wrote that its great man had fallen as he wished, "with his harness on and his feet to the foe, in unflinching performance of duty to the last sigh."[34]

Afterword

FTER CALHOUN'S SPEECH on March 4, the sophisticated New York Whig Philip Hone wrote in his diary that it was probably Calhoun's "last kick, and if he is to be judged by the sentiments of this effort, the sooner he is done kicking the better." Upon learning of Calhoun's death a few weeks later, Hone wrote, "One of the great lights of the Western world is extinguished."[1] Northern abolitionists expressed a similar ambivalence. They hated Calhoun for his support of slavery but could barely conceal their admiration for his tenacity and refusal to compromise. A New York paper once quoted Calhoun as saying, "Duty is ours, events belong to God."[2] Garrison and Wendell Phillips had expressed the same sentiment hundreds of times, and it is little wonder that Garrison wrote a few years before Calhoun died, "He is a man who means what he says and who never blusters. He is no demagogue." Phillips, whose eloquent abuse of proslavery politicians became legendary, called Calhoun "the pure, manly and uncompromising advocate of slavery; the Hector of a Troy fated to fall." Harriet Martineau probably spoke for most of the abolitionists when she wrote that she respected Calhoun far more than Webster and Clay. "All were hugely ambitious," she admitted, "but Calhoun was honest in the main point. He lived and died for the cause of slavery; and however far such a career is from the sympathies of the English people, the openness and directness of his conduct was [sic] at least respectable."[3]

Southern unionists, on the other hand, even in South Carolina, could not conceal their relief at Calhoun's death. Benjamin Perry called it "fortunate for the country" and predicted that "the slavery question will now be settled." Joel Poinsett insisted that Calhoun had been "bent on the destruction of the Union," and William C. Preston called his death "the interposition of God to save the country."[4] Such sentiments in more muted form throughout the southern states prevented the emergence of a defiant unified South at the Nashville convention for which Calhoun had expressed such high hopes, but that did not mean that he was forsaken. When the telegraph brought the news of Calhoun's death to Charleston on March 31, the bells tolled at St. Michael's throughout the day, ships in the harbor lowered their flags, and public buildings along with private houses were draped in black. Meanwhile, in Washington Calhoun's body was brought into the Senate, and he was eulogized by his colleagues. Webster and Clay remarked on the powers of Calhoun's mind, the purity of his life, and his extraordinary devotion to duty. From Washington Calhoun's body traveled by steamer, railroad car, and horse-drawn hearse to Fredericksburg, Richmond, Petersburg, Wilmington, and on to Charleston. In North Carolina the trees were draped in mourning shrouds for miles, and thousands of people knelt by the side of the road. In Charleston the funeral procession was so long that it took two hours to pass at any one point. Rhett gave the principal oration, emphasizing, like Webster and Clay before him, the spartan qualities in his friend's personality and repeating a theme that Calhoun had himself suggested toward the end of his final speech by paying tribute to "WASHINGTON and CALHOUN— the former the founder of a great Republic—the latter as the discoverer of the true principles of free government."[5]

Although Calhoun had always scorned politicians who courted popularity, he would have been gratified by a public response to his death which appeared to recognize both his contributions to the Union and his unyielding defense of the South. In the long run, he had always believed, the leader who consistently responded to the imperatives of duty could always claim the just esteem of the people. He would not, however, have wanted his final journey to stop in Charleston.

Unlike Webster, who died a little more than two years later and was buried in a tomb of his own design on his own land at Marshfield, Massachusetts, Calhoun had not bothered himself with posthumous details and had even neglected to leave a will. The governor wanted Calhoun's tomb in Charleston, and Patrick, who never had understood his father, agreed. Floride, who had gone to Charleston for the funeral, knew better. We do not know the extent to which she may have discussed the matter with her husband before his death, but she surely understood how much Calhoun preferred the comfort and simplicity of Fort Hill to the sensuous, commercial city by the sea which he had once condemned for "the intemperance and debaucheries" of its citizens. "Every arrangement is making to receive his body here," Floride wrote Anna Maria, "to be deposited on fort hill, the highest rise on the top of the hill, which I mention that you may know precisely where he is laid and think of the spot. We will enclose an acre at least and have it walled in with either stone or brick. It is to be hereafter a resting place for us all." But in the end, despite the lamentations of the *Pendleton Messenger,* Calhoun's final resting place was handled as a matter of state, and he was interred in the burial ground across from St. Philip's Church. Webster was to lie under a stone inscribed with an epitaph he had carefully composed. Calhoun, never a man to waste words, finally rested under a simple but imposing rectangle of white marble inscribed only with his last name.[6]

During the spring of 1850 Calhoun was eulogized hundreds of times from platforms and pulpits throughout the South, but the judgment which meant the most to him in his life had been delivered three years earlier by an English journalist named Sarah Maury. In *The Statesmen of America in 1846,* which included sketches of Webster, Clay, Benton, Van Buren, Buchanan, John Quincy Adams, and others, Maury devoted her longest and most enthusiastic chapter to Calhoun. "I hold myself his avowed and admiring disciple," she wrote. "If this distinguished statesman could be prevailed upon to visit England either in a public or private capacity, he would command more admiration and attract more attention than any other man of Europe or of America." Fascinated by the many political faces of the man, Maury described Calhoun as "the champion of Free Trade; a slaveholder and Cotton Planter; the vindicator of States Rights, and yet a firm believer in the indestrucibility of the Federal Union; now the advocate of war and now of peace; now aclaimed as a Whig, now revered as a Democrat; now branded as a Traitor; now worshipped as a Patriot; now assailed as a Demon, now invoked as a Demi-god; now withstanding power, and now the people; now proudly accepting office, now as proudly spurning it; now goading the Administration, now resisting; now counselling the Executive, now defying. . . ." Where Calhoun's critics saw inconsistency, deception, and manipulation born of overweening ambition, Maury claimed to have discovered a leader "ever forgetful of self, and faithful only to the inspirations of the genius and the virtue of which his name is symbolic."[7]

This evaluation of Calhoun's career is significant not for its objectivity but for Maury's ability to comprehend the way in which Calhoun hoped he would be judged in history. When she sent him a copy of her book, he acknowledged as much by writing, "You have said all I could desire you to say and said it well. I hope aftertimes will not think you have drawn a likeness too flattering."[8]

The true Calhoun lies somewhere along the continuum of extreme images Maury presented. Although he provided a powerful rationalization for secession, Calhoun's contributions to the Union in the early years of the Republic were not surpassed by any other leader of his generation, and in his later years, he showed little sympathy to Carolina hotheads who wanted to fight the nullification battle all over again. On the other hand, it would be a mistake to take Calhoun at face value, as Maury did. He was no selfless knight in shining armor towering over lesser adversaries like Webster and Clay. Calhoun lived in an age of political giants and deserves a place as one of the great leaders and thinkers of that age. As driven as any of his adversaries, stronger in character than Webster but without Webster's gift to evoke the spirit of a burgeoning new nation, stronger in mind than Clay without Clay's ability to bridge the daunting chasms of sectional disputes, Calhoun probed more deeply into the nature and weaknesses of popular government than any of his contemporaries. Henry Cabot Lodge, who had been born in Massachusetts the year Calhoun died and personally remembered Garrison and Phillips, could say at the unveiling of Calhoun's statue in the national Capitol, "His statue is here of right. He was a really great man, one of the great figures in our history. In that history he stands out, clear, distinct, commanding. There is no trace of the demagogue about him. He was a bold as well as a deep thinker, and he had to the full that courage of his convictions. . . . He raised his mind to truths. He believed that statesmanship must move on a high plane, and he could not conceive that mere money making and money spending were the highest objects of ambition in the lives of men or nations."

But we must not forget the Honorable W. L. Mauldin of South Carolina who shared the platform with Lodge that day. The year was

Fort Hill after the Cruel War when it had become Thomas Clemson's property. Jim and Francis Fruster in the foreground may have been young slaves in the plantation before Calhoun died.

1910, a high point in racial segregation and violence across the country. Recalling, perhaps, that the man he was honoring had known how to play the race card to win a political point, Mauldin explicitly linked "Mr. Calhoun's character and life work for his country" with "the effort to preserve the purity and superiority of the white race."[9]

More than seventy years later, when the civil rights movement had become a part of history, and it had become less fashionable to engage openly in the politics of race, the United States Senate passed a resolution recognizing the two hundredth anniversary of Calhoun's birth. Senators Strom Thurmond and Ernest Hollings of South Carolina spoke, emphasizing Calhoun's "balanced federalism" and his support for "modern pluralism." Calhoun no doubt would have been happy to learn that his memory was still green in South Carolina more than a century and a half after his death. But the man who had demanded near unanimity in his own state would have had trouble with the concept of pluralism and would probably have been uncomfortable with Hollings's emphasis on his willingness to compromise.[10]

In the final analysis we must conclude that Calhoun, like the rest of us, was shaped by his culture and that most of his limitations were the limitations of that culture. He had grown up in a state where republican institutions appeared to have grown apace with African slavery. He never doubted the efficacy or the morality of slavery or the assumptions of racial inequality that helped justify it. His ideas about slavery and race and their connection with republicanism were no more than a restatement of the conventional wisdom of the Old South on those subjects. It is probably true, as some of Calhoun's critics maintained, that he paid a great price for having never gone abroad. The dominant tendencies in the nineteenth-century Western world moved toward human liberty, equality, and nationality, and Calhoun, frozen in time in tiny South Carolina, seemed to defy them all.

In some ways, however, Calhoun's culture served him well. Because he spent the larger part of his career as spokesman for a numerical as well as a cultural minority, he was not swept away by the democratic tide which engulfed the country after 1815. Thus, like Tocqueville, he could argue that the roar of a popular majority emboldened by numbers could as easily be the voice of the tyrant as the voice of God. Although the concurrent majority as he envisioned it has not been formally institutionalized in the United States, many observers have pointed to its informal application in the practice of lobbying (which Calhoun would have opposed) and in the Democratic primary system in the South. Calhoun may have been more provincial than some of his more widely traveled colleagues, but this did not keep him from concentrating in the mid-nineteenth century on what became one of the greatest problems in our century: the reconciliation of large-scale centralized political power with the demands of people in disparate communities for the right to control their own lives. In theory, at least, the application of the principle of the concurrent majority could relieve many of the agonizing conflicts now going on in various hot spots in the world such as Northern Ireland, South Africa, and the former Soviet republics. In the United States, as the realities of a multicultural, multiracial, multilingual society force us to find new ways to combine civility with cultural diversity, we may find Calhoun's ideas more relevant at home. Surely we have not outlived the wisdom of the leaders who framed the Constitution, and Calhoun was one of the last in that distinguished lineage.[11] Like Calhoun, many of them owned slaves at the same time that they crafted ideas and institutions that were to advance the cause of liberty around the world. A flawed heritage, no doubt, but if history tell us anything, it is that those ideas and institutions which later generations pronounce good do not come unalloyed from the past. Calhoun once wrote, "[T]o love the people is to promote their lasting interest and not to flatter them, and on this posterity will decide."[12] Posterity decided against Calhoun's argument for the indefinite protection of slavery more than 130 years ago. What he had to say about the need in popular governments like our own to protect the rights of minorities, about the importance of choosing leaders with character, talent, and the willingness to speak hard truths to the people, and about the enduring need, in a vast and various country like our own, for the people themselves to devolop and sustain both the civic culture and the institutional structures which contribute to their lasting interest is as fresh and significant today as it was in 1850.

ALL CORRESPONDENCE to and from John C. Calhoun can be located by date in the published volumes of the Calhoun papers unless otherwise noted. I have used the following abbreviations:

AHR   *American Historical Review*

CP   Robert L. Meriwether and Clyde N. Wilson, eds., *The Papers of John C. Calhoun,* 20 vols. to date (Columbia, S.C.: 1958–)

Crallé   Richard Crallé, ed., *The Works of John C. Calhoun,* 6 vols. (New York: 1888)

Jameson   J. Franklin Jameson, ed., *Letters of John C. Calhoun* (Washington, D.C.: 1899)

LOC   Library of Congress

JSH   *Journal of Southern History*

SCHM   *South Carolina Historical Magazine*

SCHS   *South Carolina Historical Society*

SCL   *South Caroliniana Library*

UNC   University of North Carolina

Notes

Prologue

1. Featherstonhaugh, an English gentleman and graduate of Oxford, married an American and made his residence in New York. He reported on his travels in the South and his meetings with Calhoun in two books, *Excursion through the Slave States* (New York: 1844), and a second two-volume edition, *A Canoe Voyage up the Minnay Sotor*, first published in 1847 and reprinted by the Minnesota Historical Society in 1970.

1. Casting the Iron, 1782–1800

1. J. H. Hammond, *An Oration on the Life, Character and Services of John Caldwell Calhoun* (Charleston: 1850), p. 18.
2. Harriet Martineau, *Retrospect of Western Travel* (London: 1838), p. 147. Daniel Webster, *Works* (Boston: 1881), vol. V, p. 369.
3. *Life of John C. Calhoun Presenting a Condensed History of Political Events from 1811 to 1843* (New York: 1843). Reprinted in CP, vol. XVII, pp. 3–113. References to Calhoun's autobiography refer to the reprinted document.
4. J. C. to Rev. N. Murray, March 2, 1840. See also Lucretia Ann Calhoun Townes de Graffenreid's ms., "A History of My Family," SCL.
5. J. C. to James Edward Colhoun, Jameson, p. 706.
6. CP, vol. XVII, p. 5. E. Estyn Evans, "The Scotch Irish: Their Cultural Adaptation and Heritage in the American Old West," in E. R. R. Green, *Essays in Scotch-Irish History* (London: 1969), pp. 69–87. Rachel Klein, "The Rise of the Planters in the South Carolina Backcountry," Ph.D. dissertation, Yale, 1979, p. 36.
7. Carl Bridenbaugh, *Myths and Realities: Societies of the Colonial South* (New York: 1972), p. 67.
8. John H. Logan, *History of the Upper Country of South Carolina* (Charleston: 1859), pp. 21, 69. Robert L. Meriwether, *The Expansion of South Carolina* (Kingsport, Tenn.: 1940). CP, vol. XVII, p. 6.
9. Arthur Henry Hirsch, *The Huguenots of Colonial South Carolina* (Durham: 1928), p. 38.
10. George Price to Patrick Calhoun, April 2, 1865, Duke.
11. Charles Woodmason, *The Carolina Backcountry on the Eve of the Revolution*, ed. Richard J. Hooker (Chapel Hill: 1953).
12. Klein, p. 66.
13. Richard Maxwell Brown, *The South Carolina Regulators* (Cambridge, Mass.: 1963). A. S. Salley, Jr., "Journal of William Calhoun," *Publications of the Southern Historical Association*, vol. 8 (1904).
14. J. C. to Anna Maria Calhoun, December 30, 1831.
15. Brown, pp. 18–22.
16. CP, vol. XVII, p. 6.
17. Patrick Calhoun to J. E. Colhoun, September 30, 1795, SCL.
18. Patrick Calhoun's legislative career can be pieced together from the *South Carolina Journal of the House of Representatives* beginning on December 5, 1769, when he was appointed to a committee to recommend a petition for a ferry on the Broad and Saluda rivers.
19. Klein, p. 16.
20. Patrick's activities as a surveyor are fully documented in the South Carolina Archives in Columbia and in one of his notebooks in the Clemson Library. Most of his surveys were for plots of five hundred acres

or less for new planters, but on one occasion he laid out thirty-eight lots for the proposed town of Vienna.

21. David Duncan Wallace, *South Carolina: A Short History* (Columbia, S.C.: 1951), p. 224.

22. For a good discussion of the republican mind-set in South Carolina before the Revolution, see Robert M. Weir, "The Harmony We Were Famous For," *William and Mary Quarterly* (October 1969), pp. 473–501, and *Colonial South Carolina—A History* (Millwood, N.Y.: 1983), pp. 132–39.

23. *Charleston Morning Post and Advertizer,* March 7, 1786.

24. Edwin Hemphill, ed., *Extracts from the Journals of the Provincial Congress of South Carolina 1775–1776* (Columbia, S.C.: 1960), pp. 24, 35, 135, 150. Edwin Hemphill, ed., *Journals of the General Assembly and House of Representatives 1776–1780* (Columbia, S.C.:), pp. 50, 186, 248, 253. Lark Emerson Adams, ed., *Journals of the House of Representatives 1785–1786* (Columbia, S.C.: 1979), pp. 188, 189, 237.

25. *Charleston Morning Post and Advertizer,* February 14, 1787.

26. *Charleston Post and Morning Advertizer,* February 14, 1787.

27. *Charleston Post and Morning Advertizer,* March 6, 1787.

28. The report of Patrick Calhoun's remarks about religion and Lincoln's attack on the proposed Constitution can be found in *Debates Which Arose in the House of Representatives on the Constitution of the United States* (Charleston: 1831). John Calhoun later told his brother-in-law James Edward Colhoun about his father's opposition to the taxing power and James Edward passed the story on to Andrew Pickens Calhoun by letter years later on February 27, 1864, SCL.

29. *Charleston Post and Morning Advertizer,* February 8, 1786.

30. Hammond, pp. 8–10.

31. Mary Catherine Davis, "The Feather Bed Aristocracy: Abbeville District in the 1790's," *SCHM* (April 1979), pp. 136–55.

32. The will and inventory of Patrick Calhoun's estate are in the state archives. Colonel Starke's reminiscences of Calhoun's boyhood, written after the latter's death, the product of an old man's memory and his reading of the "autobiography," are one of very few eyewitness accounts of Calhoun's childhood. They are printed in Jameson, pp. 65–91.

33. CP, vol. XVII, p. 8. Dave Sloan, *Fogy Days and Now: Or the World Has Changed* (Atlanta: 1891).

34. Jameson, p. 74.

35. The volume of Tillotson sermons, about the size of a desktop dictionary today and almost certainly the largest book owned by the Calhouns, can be found in the state archives. Patrick Calhoun's signature is on an early page.

36. Weir, "The Harmony . . .," p. 252. Michael P. Johnson, "Planters and Patriarchy: Charleston 1800–1860," *JSH* (February 1980), pp. 44–72. CP, vol. XVII, p. 7.

37. CP, vol. XVII, p. 37.

38. Voltaire, *Works* (New York: 1901), vol. XX, pp. 19–22.

39. CP, vol. XVII, p. 8.

40. For an interesting discussion of early maturity on personality development, see Robert Weiss, "Growing Up a Little Faster: Children in Single Parent Households," *Journal of Social Issues,* vol. 34, no. 4 (1979), pp. 97–112. See also J. Marvin Eisenstadt, "Parental Loss and Genius," *American Psychologist* (March 1978), pp. 211–23.

2. *Education, Marriage, and Career, 1800–1810*

1. William J. Grayson, *James Louis Petrigu* (New York: 1866), p. 34.

2. Augustus Longstreet provides a vivid impression of Waddel's academy in his novel *Master William Mitten* (Macon, Ga.: 1864).

3. CP, vol. I, p. 3.

4. Ibid., pp. 4–10. Margaret Coit's *John C. Calhoun* (Boston: 1950) has what is by far

the best account of Calhoun's Yale experience in the secondary literature.

5. John Pierpont, ms., "Notes from Disputes, November 2, 1803, Yale College," Morgan Library, New York City.

6. CP, vol. XVII, p. 9.

7. J. C. to Andrew Pickens, Jr., January 21 and May 23, 1803.

8. *SCHM* (April 1912), p. 117. Benjamin

Franklin Perry, *Reminiscences of Public Men,* second series (Greenville, S.C.: 1889), p. 59.

9. J. C. to Alexander Noble, October 15, 1804. J. C. to Mrs. Floride Colhoun, April 13, 1806.

10. J. C. to Andrew Pickens, Jr., June 25, 1805.

11. Samuel Fisher, *Litchfield Law School* (New Haven: 1946). *Catalogue of the Law School in Litchfield* (Hartford: 1849).

12. CP, vol. I, footnote, p. 51.

13. J. C. to Andrew Pickens, Jr., November 24, 1805.

14. J. C. to Mrs. Floride Colhoun, December 23, 1805. Coit, p. 40. Floride Colhoun to J. C., September 14, 1805.

15. J. C. to Mrs. Floride Colhoun, December 22, 1806.

16. George C. Rogers, Jr., *Charleston in the Age of the Pinckneys* (Norman, Okla.: 1969). David Duncan Wallace, *South Carolina: A Short History* (Columbia, S.C.: 1951), p. 346. Robert M. Weir, *Colonial South Carolina* (Milwood, N.Y.: 1983), pp. 170–80. Alice Smith, *Journeys of Welcome Arnold Greene* (Madison, Wis.: 1957), p. 35.

17. The attempted poisoning of John Ewing Colhoun will be discussed in Chapter 15. William J. Grayson, "Autobiography," *SCHM,* vol. 49, p. 30. J. C. to Mrs. Floride Colhoun, October 1, 1807.

18. J. C. to Mrs. Floride Colhoun, October 1, 1807.

19. The growth of the up-country is documented in detail in Lacy K. Ford, Jr., *Origins of Southern Radicalism* (New York: 1988) and Rachel Klein, "The Rise of the Planters in the South Carolina Backcountry," Ph.D. dissertation, Yale, 1979, for the wagoner incident, see p. 173. For Calhoun as an apprentice Abbeville lawyer, see John W. DuBose, *The Life and Times of William Loundes Yancey* (New York: 1942), vol. I, p. 29.

20. *Carolina Gazette,* July 10, 1807. CP, vol. I, p. 34.

21. Copies of the reports of these cases can be found in the archives of the Calhoun Papers Project.

22. J. C. to Mrs. Floride Colhoun, April 6, 1809. Coit, p. 52.

23. David J. McCord, *The Statutes at Large of South Carolina* (Columbia, S.C.: 1840), vol. VII, p. 403. See Committee on Claims Report, December 1808, South Carolina Archives.

24. The total number of compensation claims for slaves who were executed or died from natural causes is unknown, but records in the state archives show that the procedure was routine. The cases mentioned here can be found in the computerized index to the records on slavery under the names of the petitioners or the slaves.

25. CP, vol. I, footnote, p. 51.

26. George F. Hoar, *Autobiography of Seventy Years* (New York: 1903), p. 8.

27. Anyone who spends serious time in South Carolina studying Calhoun will probably encounter the Calhoun-Hanks-Lincoln legend. Margaret Coit does not dismiss the possibility of a romance between Calhoun and someone named Nancy Hanks at this time in his life. The version of the story I have quoted derives from a typed letter from J. C. Hemphill to W. G. Hinson, March 6, 1909, in the Hinson Papers at Duke. See also William E. Barton, *The Lineage of Lincoln* (Indianapolis: 1929).

28. *The Death and Funeral Services of John C. Calhoun* (Columbia, S.C.: 1850), p. 167. J. C. to Mrs. Floride Colhoun, August 24, and July 1810. Calhoun's response to his wayward son will be discussed in Chapter 14.

29. J. C. to Mrs. Floride Colhoun, June 25 and July 18, 1809

30. J. C. to Mrs. Floride Colhoun, August 24, 1810.

31. J. C. to Miss Floride Colhoun, September 28, 1810.

32. J. C. to Mrs. Floride Colhoun, May 8, 1811.

3. *The War Hawk, 1810–1817*

1. Irving H. Bartlett, *Daniel Webster* (New York: 1978), p. 5.

2. For evidence that Calhoun's position was consistent with the national temper as well as that of his section, see Roger H. Brown, *The Republic in Peril* (New York: 1971) and Margaret Kinard Latimer, "South Carolina—A Protagonist of the War of 1812," *AHR* (July 1956), pp. 914–29. J. C. to Patrick Calhoun, November 14, 1811.

3. Mrs. St. Julien Ravenel, *The Life and*

Times of William Lowndes (Boston: 1902). Archie Huff, *Langdon Cheves of South Carolina* (Columbia, S.C.: 1977). Joseph Howard Parks, *Felix Grundy, Champion of Democracy* (Baton Rouge: 1940). Bernard Mayo, *Henry Clay: Spokesman of the New West* (Boston: 1937).

4. J. C. to Patrick Calhoun, November 14, 1811. CP, vol. I, pp. 63–70.
5. CP, vol. I, pp. 71–75.
6. Ibid., pp. 75–86.
7. J. C. to Mrs. Floride Colhoun, December 21, 1811. J. C. to James Macbride, February 16, 1812.
8. J. C. to Patrick Noble, March 22, 1812.
9. CP, vol. I, p. 107.
10. J. C. to Patrick Noble, June 17, 1812.
11. Augustus John Foster, ms. journal entry, July 11, 1812, LOC.
12. J. C. to Floride Calhoun, March 1, 1812.
13. CP, vol. I, pp. 155–59.
14. Bartlett, pp. 56–69. CP, vol. I, pp. 175, 254.
15. J. C. to James Macbride, December 25, 1812.
16. CP, vol. I, pp. 208–38. Henry Adams, *History of the United States* (New York: 1840), vol. I, p. 233.

17. CP, vol. I, pp. 62, 201, 271.
18. Alexander Contee Hanson to unnamed correspondent, 1813, Maryland Historical Society Henry Clay to William Thornton, December 24, 1813, *Papers of Henry Clay* (Lexington, Ky.: 1959), vol. I.
19. CP, vol. XVII, p. 24 ff. Bray Hammond, whose work is authoritative on the history of the Bank, claims that Calhoun was the only member of Congress to go beyond the question of the constitutionality of the Bank and address the need for a federal monetary policy. *Banks and Politics in America from the Revolution to the Civil War* (Princeton: 1957), ch. 9.
20. J. C. to Patrick Noble, February 11, 1815. CP, vol. I, p. 282.
21. J. C. to Mrs. Floride Calhoun, April 9, 1815.
22. J. C. to Mrs. Floride Calhoun, November 29, 1815.
23. CP, vol. I, p. 288.
24. Ibid., pp. 287, 321, 313.
25. Ibid., pp. 317, 330, 322.
26. Ibid., p. 355.
27. Ibid., p. 401ff.
28. Ibid., pp. 391, 34.
29. Ibid., p. 386.

4. *Secretary of War, 1817–1824*

1. J. C. to Monroe, November 1, 1817. J. C. to Floride Colhoun, November 15, 1817. CP vol. I, p. 403.
2. J. C. to C. J. Ingersoll, December 14, 1817. Joseph Prince to J. C., January 24, 1818. The best scholarly analysis of Calhoun's administration of the War Department is Roger Joseph Spiller, "John Calhoun as Secretary of War 1817–1825," Ph.D. dissertation, Louisiana State University, 1977.
3. CP, vol. II, pp. 56–72. These examples, taken over a few days, are typical of the kind of detail brought to Calhoun's attention.
4. Russel F. Weigley, *Towards an American Army: Military Thought from Washington to Marshall* (New York: 1962), p. 15.
5. CP, vol. V, pp. 480–90. Weigley, p. 31.
6. The Mix affair can be followed in Spiller, beginning on p. 132.
7. Ibid., p. 140. Calhoun's attentiveness to the overdue bookseller's bill can be found in a letter from John Babcock to David Dagget, February 15, 1815,

among the Calhoun manuscripts at Yale.
8. Spiller, p. 161.
9. J. C. to S. Long, December 15, 1818. J. C. to Thomas A. Smith, March 16, 1818. Henry Clay to J. C., September 9, 1816.
10. Captain Wyly Martin to Colonel Talbot Chambers, January 15, 1819. Chambers to B. Bissell, May 25, 1819. T. S. Jessup to T. Cross, June 25, 1819.
11. Richard M. Johnson to J. C., July 11, 1819. J. C. to Johnson, July 20, 1819. Johnson to J. C., July 26, 1819.
12. For a good overview of Indian policy during this period, see Francis Prucha, *American Indian Policy during the Formative Years* (Cambridge, Mass.: 1962).
13. CP, vol. III, pp. 341–55.
14. E. P. Gaines to J. C., February 16, 1818.
15. John Jolly to J. C., January 28, 1818. Abraham Williams to J. C., May 1, 1818.
16. For Calhoun and McKenney, see Herman J. Viola, *Thomas L. McKenney, Architect of America's Early Indian Policy* (Chicago: 1974). Spiller, pp. 191–223.

17. Quoted in Viola, p. 127.
18. J. C. to Andrew Jackson, December 29, 1817.
19. CP, vol. II, pp. 20, 39.
20. Ibid., p. 324. For a good account of the Seminole War from Jackson's perspective, see Robert Remini, *Andrew Jackson and the Course of American Empire* (New York: 1977).
21. John Quincy Adams, *Memoirs of John Quincy Adams* (Philadelphia: 1874), vol. IV, pp. 107, 199–201.

22. J. C. to Charles Tait, September 5, 1818. J. C. to Monroe, September 12. 1818. Monroe to Andrew Jackson, October 20, 1818.
23. J. C. to Andrew Jackson, March 6, 1819. Jackson to Colonel Atkinson, May 15, 1819.
24. J. C. to Andrew Jackson, August 10, 1820, August 10, 1819. Adams, *Memoirs*, vol. V, p. 370.

5. The Election of 1824

1. J. C. to Micah Sterling, J. C. to Charles Tait, May 20, 1820.
2. For a good definition of the republican vision and how it applied to politics, see Richard McCormick, *The Presidential Game: The Origins of American Presidential Politics* (New York: 1982).
3. Kenneth Greenberg, *Masters and Statesmen: The Political Culture of Slavery* (Baltimore: 1985) is persuasive on this point.
4. J. C. to J. E. Colhoun, October 23, 1820. J. C. to Micah Sterling, April 23, 1821.
5. William J. Grayson, "Autobiography, *SCHM,*" vol. 49, p. 222.
6. J. C. to Micah Sterling, December 25, 1820.
7. Roger Joseph Spiller, "John C. Calhoun as Secretary of War 1817–1825," Ph.D. dissertation, Louisiana State University, 1977, p. 249.
8. J. C. to Andrew Jackson, June 1, 1820.
9. Spiller, p. 272.
10. John Quincy Adams, *Memoirs of John Quincy Adams* (Philadelphia: 1874), vol. IV, p. 477.
11. Ibid., May 22, 1820.
12. Ibid., March 3, 1821.
13. J. C. to Ninian Edwards, March 9, 1821. J. C. to Virgil Maxcy, April 27, 1821.
14. Adams, February 22, 1820.
15. J. C. to Andrew Jackson, April 8, 1821.
16. John M. Belohavek, *George Mifflin Dallas, Jacksonian Patrician* (1977), pp. 3–21.
17. John Niven, *Martin Van Buren and the Romantic Age of American Politics* (New York: 1983), pp. 64, 105–26.
18. J. C. to Lewis Cass, December 10, 1821.
19. J. C. to Virgil Maxcy, December 31, 1821.
20. Adams, January 3, 1822.
21. The rationale for Crawford's opposition to Monroe's administration and particularly to Calhoun's role in it is well presented in

Harry Ammon, *James Monroe: The Quest for National Identity* (New York: 1971). Chase Mooney, *William H. Crawford* (Lexington, Ky.: 1974) argues that Calhoun's perception of a Crawford conspiracy to attack Calhoun by retrenching the army was inaccurate because it was supported by followers of Clay, Jackson, and Adams as well as by Crawfordites.
22. J. C. to J. P. Kennedy, May 12, 1822. J. C. to Micah Sterling, June 17, 18, 1822. J. C. to Thomas J. Rogers, June 9, 1822.
23. *Washington Republican and Congressional Examiner*, August 28, 1822. Adams, vol. VI, p. 57.
24. Mooney emphasizes the continuity between Crawford's and Calhoun's management of the War Department and concludes that Crawford was "reasonably imaginative, practical, efficient administratively competent and ethically sound," p. 80.
25. *Washington Republican . . .*, August 20, 1822. Mooney, p. 242. CP, vol. VIII, p. 171.
26. *Washington Republican . . .*, May 14, 1823, February 14, 1824.
27. J. C. to S. D. Ingham, November 2, 1822.
28. Belohavek, p. 20.
29. J. C. to Micah Sterling, March 27, 1823.
30. *Washington Republican . . .*, April 12, 1823. J. C. to Charles Fisher, August 1, 1823.
31. Jonathan Russell to William Crawford, 1823, Duke.
32. Quoted in Charles H. Ambler, *Sectionalism in Virginia from 1776–1861* (New York: 1964), p. 128.
33. *Washington Republican . . .*, September 18, 1823. J. C. to Andrew Jackson, March 30, 1823.
34. Margaret Bayard Smith, *The First Forty*

Years of Washington Society (New York: 1960).

35. J. C. to Lewis Cass, April 24, 1824.
36. Spiller, p. 358.

6. *Vice President with His Own Agenda, 1824–1828*

1. J. C. to John E. Colhoun, November 9, 1818. Walter Muir Whitehill, *Dumbarton Oaks; The History of a Georgetown House and Garden* (Cambridge, Mass.: 1967), pp. 38–46.
2. George Ticknor, *Life, Letters and Journals of George Ticknor* (Boston: 1876), vol. I, p. 349.
3. Margaret Bayard Smith, *The First Forty Years of Washington Society* (New York: 1906), p. 152. C. Wilkes to Mrs. William Renwick, March 25, 1825, Duke. For an unflattering appraisal of Wilkes on several accounts, see William Stanton, *The Great United States Exploring Expedition* (Berkely: 1975), pp. 20, 363.
4. Ann Royall, *Sketches of History, Life and Manners in the United States* (New Haven: 1826), p. 166. Smith, p. 334.
5. Clyde Wilson, CP, vol. X, p. XIII.
6. John Quincy Adams, *Memoirs of John Quincy Adams* (Philadelphia: 1875), vol. VI, pp. 480, 498, 506, 509.
7. L. McLane to wife, February 21, 1825, LOC.
8. J. C. to J. G. Swift, March 10, 1825.
9. J. C. to John S. Skinner, February 21, 1825.
10. CP, vol. X, p. 21.
11. J. C. to S. L. Gouverneur, June 10, 1825. J. C. to S. D. Ingham, June 10, 1825. J. C. to J. G. Swift, September 2, 1825.
12. J. C. to Vandeventer, June 24, 1825.
13. J. C. to J. G. Swift, February 19, 1826.
14. Like an older generation of republicans, Calhoun tended to identify parties with the corrupt politics of England, "the only means by which an odious and wicked ministry can be embarrassed and turned out; but here it can be effected by a far more simple and desirable process; I mean the ballot box." J. C. to J. G. Swift, June 27, 1825.
15. Martin Van Buren, *Autobiography* (Annual Report of the American Historical Association, 1912), vol. II, p. 200.
16. *Papers of Daniel Webster: Correspondence* (Hanover, N.H. 1976), vol. II, p. 98.
17. J. C. to Micah Sterling, February 4, 1826.
18. Green's early career can be followed in Kenneth L. Smith, "Duff Green and the United States Telegraph," Ph.D. dissertation, William and Mary, 1981, pp. 13–36. Calhoun's recommendation for Green's generalship was made by letter to Monroe, December 21, 1818.
19. Webster, p. 107.
20. The five "Patrick Henry" and six "Onslow" letters, running from May 1 to October 12, 1826, are printed in full in CP. In his close analysis of this debate Clyde Wilson argues: "The two essayists were engaged in nothing less than the exegesis of two different styles of 'republicanism,' essentially the same two that were at stake in 1790." CP, vol x, p. xxix.
21. For proof that Fendall wrote the Henry letters with the President's approval, see Charles J. Catlett to Philip R. Fendall, October 17, 1826, Duke.
22. J. C. to M. Sterling, May 31, 1826. J. C. to Levi Woodbury, September 21, 1826. J. C. to Andrew Jackson, January 24, 1827.
23. J. C. to Andrew Jackson, June 24, 1826. Jackson to J. C., July 18, 1826. J. C. to Jackson, January 24, 1827. John Niven, *Martin Van Buren: The Romantic Age of American Politics* (New York: 1983), p. 177.
24. CP, vol. X, p. 164.
25. *Report of the Committee Appointed on the 29th Dec. 1826 on a Letter of John C. Calhoun, Vice President of the United States Asking an Investigation of His Conduct While Secretary of War* (Washington: 1827). William R. King to J. W. White, January 10, 1827, Duke. CP, vol. X, p. 261.
26. J. C. to Lieutenant James E. Colhoun, February 4, 1827. J. C. to Waddel, February 24, 1827. J. C. to Andrew Jackson, February 25, 1827.
27. Robert Remini, *Andrew Jackson and the Course of American Empire* (New York: 1981), p. 135.
28. J. C. to Micah Sterling, January 26, 1828. Niven, p. 223.

7. The Architect of Nullification

1. A good analysis of an emerging antitariff and states' rights radicalism in South Carolina can be found in Lacy K. Ford, *Origins of Southern Radicalism* (New York: 1988), pp. 99–145. Smith's career can be followed in Caroline P. Smith, "South Carolina Radical: The Political Career of William Smith to 1826," M.A. thesis, Auburn, 1971.

2. Benjamin F. Perry, *Reminiscences of Public Men* (Philadelphia: 1883), p. 80.

3. Smith's boasting about his opposition to Calhoun appeared in the pro-Smith *Yorkville Pioneer*, April 17, 1824. *Charleston City Gazette*, November 25, 1822.

4. *Yorkville Pioneer*, April 24, 1824. Caroline Smith, p. 205.

5. W. Smith to Stephen D. Miller, January 13, 1827, SCHS.

6. J. C. to James Edward Colhoun, May 4, 1828. While rejecting the notion that the tariff was as oppressive as Carolinians argued, Gavin Wright maintains "that the orthodox assumption that the tariff hurt cotton growers is appropriate." *The Political Economy of the Cotton South* (New York: 1978), footnote, p. 131. See also Bennet D. Baack and Edward J. Ray, "Tariff Policy and Income Distribution," *Explorations in Economic History* (Winter 1973–74), pp. 103–23.

7. William W. Freehling, *The Nullification Era* (New York: 1967), pp. 21, 47.

8. J. C. to James Edward Colhoun, August 26, 1827. CP, vol. X, p. 294.

9. J. C. to L. W. Tazewell, August 25, November 9, 1827.

10. J. C. to J. McLean, September 3, 1827.

11. George Dangerfield, *The Era of Good Feelings* (New York: 1952), pp. 405–09. Charles Wiltse, *John C. Calhoun Nationalist* (New York: 1944), p. 369.

12. J. C. to Micah Sterling, May 15, 1828.

13. J. C. to Monroe, July 10, 1828. J. C. to Vandeventer, September 8, 1828.

14. J. C. to Samuel Smith, July 28, 1828.

15. J. C. to J. McLean, August 4, 1828.

16. J. C. to McLean, October 4, 1828.

17. J. C. to W. C. Preston, November 6, 1828.

18. CP, vol. X, pp. 460, 480.

19. Ibid., p. 486.

20. Ibid., p. 498.

21. Ibid., p. 506.

22. Ibid., p. 516. For an interesting analysis of Pinckney's role in the intellectual tradition of South Carolina, see Mark Kaplanoff, "Charles Pinckney and the American Republican Tradition," *Intellectual Life in Antebellum Charleston*, ed. Michael O'-Brien and David Moltke-Hansen (Knoxville: 1986).

23. John Niven, *Martin Van Buren and the Romantic Age of American Politics* (New York: 1983), p. 223. J. C. to W. C. Preston, November 21, 1828.

8. The Duel with Jackson, 1828–1831

1. J. C. to Floride Colhoun, April 9, 1827.

2. J. C. to James Edward Colhoun, January 23, 1828, March 16, 1829.

3. James Sterling Young, *The Washington Community, 1800–1829* (New York: 1966), pp. 13–37.

4. Josiah Quincy, *Figures of the Past* (Boston: 1883), p. 207.

5. For a vivid description of the inauguration based on newspaper sources, see Edwin A. Miles, "The First People's Inauguration," *Tennessee Historical Quarterly* (Fall 1978), pp. 293–307. For discussions of the event from the perspectives of Calhoun and Jackson, see Charles Wiltse, *John C. Calhoun, Nullifier* (New York: 1949), pp. 5–11, and Robert Remini, *Andrew Jackson and the Course of American*

Freedom (New York: 1981), pp. 156–89.

6. Clyde Wilson, *The Essential Calhoun* (New Brunswick, N.J.: 1992), p. 330. Wiltse, pp. 11–15. Virginia L. Glenn, "James Hamilton Jr. of South Carolina," Ph.D. dissertation, University of North Carolina, 1964. Hamilton was shocked to find a "stout black wench" calmly eating a jelly with a gold spoon in one of the White House parlors.

7. Wiltse, pp. 21–25. John Niven, *Martin Van Buren and the Romantic Age of American Politics* (New York: 1983), p. 242. J. C. to S. D. Ingham, April 23, 1829. J. C. to S. L. Gouverneur, March 30, 1830.

8. J. C. to Maxcy, June 21, 1829. J. C. to Vandeventer, March 14, 1829.

9. James Hamilton, Jr., to J. C., May 10,

1829. J. C. to J. McLean, Sept. 22, 1829.

10. Remini, p. 207.

11. *The Autobiography of Peggy Eaton* (New York: 1932).

12. John Quincy Adams, *Memoirs* (Philadelphia: 1874), vol. VIII, p. 185. Remini, p. 214.

13. John Campbell to David Campbell, Duke.

14. Barbara Welter, "The Cult of True Womanhood, 1820–1860," *American Quarterly*, vol. 18 (Summer 1966), pp. 151–74.

15. CP, vol. XI, p. 477.

16. Irving H. Bartlett, *Daniel Webster* (New York: 1978), pp. 108–22.

17. J. C. to Vandeventer, February 10, 1830, typed copy, CP Archives. J. C. to S. L. Gouverneur, March 30, 1830.

18. Historians have told this story countless times. See two Washington papers, *United States Telegraph*, April 17, 1830, and *Daily National Intelligencer*, April 20, 1830, for a detailed account.

19. Quoted in Remini, p. 237.

20. Andrew Jackson to J. C., May 13, 1830. J. C. to Jackson, May 13, 1830.

21. That Calhoun had in fact advised Monroe to arrest Jackson is made explicit in Monroe to J. C., February 10, 1831.

22. William J. Grayson, "Autobiography," *SCHM*, vol. 50, p. 82.

23. J. C. to Andrew Jackson, July 10, 1828.

24. Andrew Jackson, *Correspondence of Andrew Jackson* (Washington: 1926), vol. IV, p. 137.

25. J. C. to Andrew Jackson, May 29, 1830.

26. Andrew Jackson to J. C., May 30, 1830. J. C. to Jackson, June 1, 1830.

27. J. C. to Maxcy, Aug. 6, 1830.

28. Andrew Jackson to J. C., July 19, 1830. J. C. to Jackson, August 25, 1830.

29. William H. Crawford to J. C., October 2, 1830. J. C. to Crawford, October 30, 1830.

30. J. C. to James Edward Colhoun, January 13, 1831. John Campbell to David Campbell, January 15, 1831, Duke.

31. J. C. to Mrs. J. S. Johnston, January 22, 1831.

32. Remini, p. 305. CP, vol. XI, p. 334.

33. M. Morton to J. C., March 7, 1831.

34. Jackson, *Correspondence*, pp. 246, 315.

35. Remini, p. 306. Jackson, *Correspondence*, p. 246.

36. John Campbell to David Campbell, December 6, 1830.

37. John Lyde Wilson, *The Code of Honor* (Charleston: 1838). The importance of honor in the culture of slavery is dealt with in detail in Bertram Wyatt-Brown, *Southern Honor: Ethics and Behavior in the Old South* (New York: 1982). For a discussion of honor and dueling among Calhoun's neighbors, see Orville Vernon Burton's fascinating study *In My Father's House Are Many Mansions: Family and Community in Edgefield, South Carolina* (Chapel Hill: 1985).

9. *The Nullification Crisis, 1831–1832*

1. Entry of March 18, 1831, Hammond Commonplace Book, LOC. Drew Faust, *James Henry Hammond and the Old South* (Baton Rouge: 1982), p. 59.

2. J. C. to D. F. Caldwell, May 1, 1831. J. C. to S. D. Ingham, May 25, 1831. J. C. to Vandeventer, May 25, 1831.

3. The nullification story has been told many times, but the most detailed scholarly account is in William W. Freehling, *Prelude to Civil War* (New York: 1965).

4. CP, vol. XI, p. 533.

5. William W. Freehling, *The Nullification Era* (New York: 1967), p. 118. Duff Green to J. C., May 31, 1831. CP, vol. XI; p. 402. James Hamilton, Jr., to Stephen D. Miller, June 25, 1831, SCL.

6. CP, vol. XI, pp. 413–40.

7. J. C. to S. D. Ingham, July 31, 1831. J. C. to Maxcy, August 6, 1831. J. C. to F. W. Pickens, August 24, 1831.

8. Richard E. Ellis, *The Union at Risk* (New York: 1987), pp. 68–73.

9. The bishop's letter appeared in an extra supplement to the *Charleston Irishman* (a unionist paper), August 24, 1831. Petigru wrote to William Elliott, September 7, 1831, that the nullifiers "kept men drunk, locked up, broke houses and carried them off . . . their men who follow the craft of electioneering have nothing else to do." According to Petigru, the nullifiers had made a big mistake the previous night by killing one of their own men in a drunken brawl—a man said to be "good for at least fifty votes to them." LOC.

10. J. C. to S. D. Ingham, January 13, 1832. The "never kick" quotation seems out of character for Calhoun and derives from Benton, a bitter political enemy. After Van Buren's rejection the *Washington Globe* regularly linked Calhoun's name with Webster and Clay.

11. J. C. to Bolling Hall, February 13, 1832. J. C. to S. D. Ingham, July 8, 1832. J. C. to Waddy Thompson, July 8, 1832.

12. J. Petrigu to Elliott, August 7, 1832, LOC.

13. Virginia L. Glenn, "James Hamilton Jr. of South Carolina," Ph.D. dissertation, University of North Carolina.

14. CP, vol. XI, pp. 613–32. Like the Fort Hill Address, Calhoun's statement was a public letter published in the *Pendleton Messen-*

ger, September 15, 19, 1832, and later printed in part or full nationwide.

15. *Papers of Daniel Webster: Correspondence* (Hanover, N.H.: 1974), vol. III, p. 195.

16. Jane and William Pease, "The Economics and Politics of Charleston's Nullification Crisis," *JSH* (August 1981), pp. 335–62.

17. J. C. to P. Noble, September 10, 1832. J. Hamilton to Waddy Thompson, August 31, 1832, SCL. John M. Barillon to John T. Seibels, August 29, 1832, SCL. J. Petrigu to Wm. Elliott, September 4, 28, 1832, LOC. Petrigu to Hugh Legaré, October 29, 1832, LOC.

18. J. C. to W. M. Murray, July 30, 1832.

10. *The Compromise of 1833*

1. I. Hill to R. H. Ayer, February 18, 1832, New Hampshire Historical Society. John Campbell to David Campbell, May 23, 1832, Duke. Parke Godwin, *A Biography of William Cullen Bryant* (New York: 1883), p. 267.

2. CP, vol. XII, p. 683. J. C. to S. D. Ingham, November 1832, typed copy, CP Archives.

3. Richard E. Ellis, *The Union at Risk* (New York: 1987), pp. 41–60.

4. William W. Freehling, *The Nullification Era* (New York: 1967), pp. 155, 161, 163.

5. Ellis, p. 78.

6. J. C. to James Edward Colhoun, June 10, 1833.

7. *Correspondence of James Polk* (Nashville: 1927), vol. II, p. 16. Ellis, ch. 6. Isaac Hayne to Waddy Thompson, January 1833, SCL.

8. CP, vol. X, pp. 10–15. J. C. to James Hamilton, January 16, 1832.

9. J. C. to James Hamilton, January 16, 1832. J. C. to W. C. Preston, February 3, 1833.

10. Ellis, ch. 5–7.

11. Merrill D. Peterson, *Olive Branch and*

Sword: The Compromise of 1833 (Baton Rouge: 1982) is authoritative on the politics of the compromise.

12. *Papers of Daniel Webster, Correspondence*, vol. III, p. 211.

13. The observations on Calhoun's oratorical style are taken from William J. Grayson, "Autobiography," *SCHM*, vol. 49, p. 136, and from a letter in the *United States Gazette*, January 25, 1841.

14. CP, vol. XII, p. 58.

15. Ibid., p. 71.

16. Webster, p. 214. Irving H. Bartlett, *Daniel Webster* (New York: 1978), p. 137. S. H. Witherspoon to Stephen D. Miller, February 17, 1833, LOC. CP, vol. XII, pp. 101–37.

17. Charles Wiltse, *John C. Calhoun, Nullifier* (New York: 1949), p. 196.

18. J. C. to Bolling Hall, March 25, 1833.

19. Webster, p. 227. Mitchell King to H. Legaré, May 5, 1833, SCL.

20. Ellis, p. 180.

21. J. C. to Edward North, November 22, 1833.

11. *Assaulting the President, 1833–1836*

1. The toasts at Marion, July 4, 1833, and at Lewisburg, Virginia, August 29, 1833, are among the scores preserved in the archives of the Calhoun Papers Project. Most of them occurred in the South or in the border states.

2. J. C. to F. W. Pickens, December 12, 1833.

3. J. C. to P. Noble, April 21, 1833. J. C. to James Edward Colhoun, November 17, 1833.

4. CP, vol. XII, pp. XI–XIII. N. Biddle to J. C., September 11, 1833. Samuel Moore to J. C., January 17, 1834.

5. CP, vol. XII, pp. 180–83.

6. J. C. to John D. Gardner, March 25, 1833.

7. Bray Hammond, *Banks and Politics in America from the Revolution to the Civil War* (Princeton: 1967). *Papers of Daniel Webster: Correspondence* (Hanover, N.H.: 1974), vol. III, p. 306.
8. CP, vol. XII, pp. 200–25.
9. J. C. to Vandeventer, January 25, 1834. J. C. to S. D. Ingham, February 27, 1834.
10. CP, vol. XII, pp. 247–71.
11. Hammond, p. 368.
12. CP, vol. XII, pp. 277–99.
13. Ibid., p. 310.
14. William J. Grayson, "Autobiography," *SCHM*, vol. 50, p. 79.
15. The test oath, which required a primary oath of allegiance to South Carolina for every state officeholder, had been a part of the Ordinance of Nullification in 1832. It was repealed along with the ordinance as part of the compromise but replaced by the nullifiers as a way of maintaining state control. In the fall of 1833 Calhoun had taken a hard line on the oath in a letter to Waddy Thompson, October 18, 1833. After the Supreme Court decision he advised Francis Pickens to forget about the oath and concentrate instead on securing large nullifier majorities in the coming elections, June 5, 1834. Calhoun's role as "the advisor of pacification" was generally recognized by the unionists, Mitchell King to Hugh Legaré, December 15, 1834, SCL.

16. CP, vol. XII, p. 399.
17. Ibid., p. 403.
18. Robert Remini, *Andrew Jackson and the Course of American Democracy* (New York: 1984), p. 226. *Washington Globe,* January 31, 1835. CP, vol. XII, p. 410.
19. James Fenimore Cooper, *Letters and Journals* (Cambridge, Mass.: 1964), vol. III, p. 94.
20. CP, vol. XII, p. 415.
21. Ibid., pp. 458–78. Philip Hone, *Diary* (New York: 1984), vol. I, p. 150.
22. CP, vol. XII, pp. 491, 513; vol. XIII, p. 20.
23. For an objective assessment of the federal bureaucracy under Jackson which emphasizes the Jacksonians' fear of fraud and their concern for efficiency and their relatively modest use of patronage, see Matthew A. Cresson, *The Federal Machine: Beginnings of Bureauracracy in Jacksonian America* (Baltimore: 1975).
24. J. C. to S. D. Ingham, December 27, 1835. CP, vol. XIII, p. 78.
25. Drew Faust, *James Henry Hammond and the Old South* (Baton Rouge: 1982), p. 167.
26. J. C. to A. J. Burt, June 28, 1836.
27. White withdrew from the race in August, and South Carolina cast its eleven electoral votes for Willie P. Mangum, an anti-Jackson Democrat from North Carolina.

12. *Making the Proslavery Argument*

1. James Edward Colhoun to J. C., February 1, 1835. J. C. to F. W. Pickens, July 17, 1835.
2. CP, vol. I, p. 312. David Brion Davis, *Slavery and Progress* (New York: 1985).
3. J. C. to C. Tait, October 26, 1820. J. C. to Micah Sterling, January 24, 1820. CP, vol. VII, pp. 194–227. J. C. to C. Tait, April 23, 1821.
4. For slaves as an agent in the transfer of technology, see Daniel C. Littlefield, *Race and Slaves: Ethnicity and the Slave Trade in Colonial South Carolina* (Baton Rouge: 1981). Larry Kroger, *Free Black Slaveowners in South Carolina* (Jefferson, N.C.: 1985). p. 43. For white slaves to black masters, see John Blassingame, *The Slave Community* (New York: 1979), p. 228. Records of the Pendleton Sunday School Society, 1819–1821, Clemson.
5. J. C. to Maxcy, March 18, 1822.

6. J. C. to Maxcy, September 30, 1830.
7. Thomas R. Dew, *Review of the Debate in the Virginia Legislature of 1831 and 1832* (Richmond: 1832). pp. 112–15. Josiah Quincy, *Figures of the Past* (Boston: 1883), p. 263.
8. CP, vol. XIII, p. 7.
9. Anna Maria Calhoun to Maria Simkins, December 18, 1835, SCL.
10. J. C. to S. D. Ingham, December 24, 1835.
11. C. P. vol. XIII, p. 3.
12. Ibid., pp. 22, 42, 53.
13. J. C. to James Austin, December 28, 1837. See also Irving H. Bartlett, *Wendell Phillips Brahmin Radical* (Boston: 1961), p. 49.
14. CP, vol. XIII, p. 108.
15. Ibid., pp. 65, 106.
16. J. C. to James Edward Colhoun, February 8, 1834. Charles C. Binney, *The Life of*

Horace Binney with Selections from His Letters (Philadelphia: 1903), p. 313.

17. CP, vol. XIII, p. 390.

18. On February 6, 1837, Calhoun corrected Rives for his defensiveness about slavery after having told the Senate earlier: "A mysterious Providence had brought the black and the white people together from different parts of the globe, and no human power could now separate them. The Whites are an European race being masters, and the blacks are the inferior race and slaves. He believed that they could exist among us peacably [sic] enough, if undisturbed, for all time." Thus Calhoun opposed African colonizationists as well as abolitionists. CP, vol. XIII, pp. 371, 395.

13. *Outfoxing the Fox, 1836–1840*

1. CP, vol. XIII, p. 261.

2. John Niven, *John C. Calhoun and the Price of Union* (Baton Rouge: 1988), p. 204. Samuel Gaillard Stoney, "Poinsett-Campbell Correspondence," *SCHM* (October 1941), p. 150.

3. Charles Wiltse, *John C. Calhoun Nullifier* (New York: 1949), pp. 624–43. J. C. to James Edward Colhoun, September 19, 1836. CP, vol. XIII, pp. 286–94.

4. CP, vol. XIII, pp. 339, 363, 378.

5. Robert Remini, *Andrew Jackson and the Course of American Democracy* (New York: 1984), p. 411. CP, vol. XIII, pp. 419–24.

6. J. C. to J. H. Hammond, February 18, 1837.

7. CP, vol. XIII, pp. 472–76.

8. J. C. to S. D. Ingham, May 25, 1837.

9. J. C. to James Edward Colhoun, March 22, 1837. J. C. to Duff Green, June 26, July 7, 1837.

10. CP, vol. XIII, p. 85.

11. CP, vol. XVVI, p. 79.

12. J. C. to James Edward Colhoun, September 7, 1837.

13. Susan Prevant Lee and Peter Passell, *A New Economic View of American History* (New York: 1979), pp. 117–22, argue that the real lesson of the panic is that "small, open economies, operating with a specie based money are terribly vulnerable to economic events outside their control." See also Donald B. Cole, *Martin Van Buren and the American Political System* (Princeton: 1984), p. 292.

14. CP, vol. XIII, pp. 546–70.

15. William Henry Seward, *Autobiography* (New York: 1891), p. 338. W. B. Campbell to David Campbell, September 23, 1837, Duke. M. L. Davis to Willis Hall, September 27, 1837, New York Historical Society.

16. Stoney, p. 165.

17. J. C. to Anna Maria Calhoun, September 30, 1837. W. C. Rives to Governor Campbell, December 22, 1837, Duke. Adam Huntington to James Polk, January 1, 1838,

18. CP, vol. XIV, p. 31.

19. Ibid., pp. 127, 133, 147 p. 36. W. C. Rives to Governor Campbell, January 4, 1838, Duke.

20. CP, vol. XIV, pp. 66, 84.

21. Ibid., pp. 127, 133, 148.

22. J. C. to Anna Maria Calhoun, Feb. 24, 1838.

23. James Fenimore Cooper, ed., *Correspondence of James Fenimore Cooper* (New Haven: 1922), p. 374.

24. J. C. to Jr. Mulvaney, April 15, 1838. *Papers of Daniel Webster: Correspondence* (Hanover, N.H.: 1974), vol. III, p. 308.

25. The divisive effects within South Carolina of Calhoun's reconciliation with Van Buren through his support of the independent Treasury are discussed at length in Lacy K. Ford, *Origins of Southern Radicalism* (New York: 1988), ch. 4.

26. J. C. to A. H. Pemberton, November 19, 1838.

27. CP, vol. XIII, p. 636. Calhoun had anticipated this victory. "So much," he wrote his daughter, December 10, 1837, "for doing one's duty."

28. Waddy Thompson to Charles Lanman, October 14, 1858, SCL. J. C. to Duff Green, October 3, 1838. CP, vol. XIV, p. 405. H. Legaré to Alfred Huger, September 23, 1838, Duke. Linda Rhea, *Hugh Swinton Legaré* (Chapel Hill, N.C.: 1934), p. 162.

29. J. H. Hammond to F. W. Pickens, January 18, 1840, Duke. J. C. to Hammond, April 2, 1840.

30. J. C. to Dr. Daniell, October 26, 1838. J. C. to James Edward Colhoun, February 1, 1840. Niven, p. 236.

31. J. C. to John A. Stuart, January 17, 1840. W. C. Preston to N. B. Tucker, February

18, 1840, typed copy, CP Archives. J. C. to E. R. Calhoun, September 11, 1840.

32. J. C. to Maxcy, March 28, 1840.

33. On June 8 Calhoun told his son that conditions were "very favorable to Van Buren" and predicted one of "the most remarkable revolutions ever effected without force." On November 22 he wrote his son again, explaining Van Buren's defeat in terms of the "principle of retributive justice," CP.

14. *The Iron Man at Home*

1. Dixon Lewis to R. Crallé, March 20, 1840, LOC Mrs. W. C. Preston, Diary, typed copy, SCL.

2. Margaret Coit, *John C. Calhoun* (Boston: 1950), p. 216.

3. *Papers of Daniel Webster: Correspondence* (Hanover, N.H.: 1974), vol. II, p. 16.

4. Coit, pp. 316–25. A typed note in the archives of the Calhoun Papers Project, January 5, 1841, indicates that William Calhoun left a mule named Floride as part of his estate.

5. Floride Calhoun to J. C., February 15, 1842. Floride to James Edward Calhoun, November 8, 1840. Floride to Margaret Calhoun, April 5, 1839. Floride to Patrick Calhoun, October 10, 1840, May 26, 1841. All in SCL.

6. Floride Calhoun to James E. Colhoun, December 24, 1846, SCL. Floride to Patrick Calhoun, February 9, 1843, SCL.

7. Floride claimed her attacks were due to "termination of the blood to the brain," but her daughter wrote: "Mother continues to complain at times. She is not sick but thinks she is, which is almost as bad." Floride Calhoun to Patrick Calhoun, September 17, 1842, Anna Maria to Patrick Calhoun, September 3, 1837, SCL.

8. J. C. to Andrew Calhoun, April 12, 1847, CP Archives.

9. J. C. to Thomas Clemson, January 8, 1843.

10. The story of the ill-fated Cane Brake venture and the increasing tensions it created within Calhoun's family can be conveniently followed in the early chapters of Ernest Lander, *The Calhoun Family and Thomas Green Clemson* (Columbia, S.C.: 1983).

11. J. C. to Patrick Calhoun, July 27, 1837. Floride Calhoun to Patrick Calhoun, July 13, 1837.

12. Patrick Calhoun to Uncle James, October 22, 1837, SCL.

13. J. C. to Patrick Calhoun, August 4, 1838, March 29, 1839. J. C. to James Edward Colhoun, August 27, 1839.

14. J. C. to Patrick Calhoun, December 4, 1839.

15. Oliver Dyer, *Great Senators of the United States* (New York: 1889), p. 153.

16. James E. Calhoun to My dear Brother, July 8, 1837; to Patrick Calhoun, December 3, 1837, SCL. Sam E. Maxwell to Patrick Calhoun, December 4, 1837, SCL. James E. Calhoun to John C. Calhoun, June 3, 1838, to Patrick Calhoun, August 12, 1838, SCL. W. Lowndes Calhoun to Patrick Calhoun, September 10, 1843, SCL.

17. Anna Maria Calhoun Clemson to Patrick Calhoun, May 24, 1841, SCL.

18. Floride Calhoun to Patrick Calhoun, May 24, 1841, SCL. Cornelia's coverlet can be seen in the master bedroom of the Calhoun mansion on the Clemson campus.

19. J. C. to Anna Maria Calhoun, December 30, 1831, February 13, 1832.

20. J. C. to Anna Maria Calhoun, March 10, 1832, February 18, May 14, June 23, 1834.

21. Anna Maria Calhoun to Maria Simkins, December 18, 1835, SCL.

22. Anna Maria Calhoun to Maria Simkins, August 24, 1836, SCL.

23. Anna Maria Calhoun to Patrick Calhoun, August 27, 1836, SCL.

24. Anna Maria Calhoun to Patrick Calhoun, April 30, 1838, SCL.

25. Josiah Quincy, *Figures in the Past* (Boston: 1883), p. 264.

26. Anna Maria Calhoun to Maria Simkins, August 2, 1838.

27. Lander, p. 1.

15. Master of Fort Hill

1. "I for my part love the tie of relationship and believe those who are under its influence are usually more disposed to a virtuous life." J. C. to John Ewing Colhoun, May 27, 1823. Mary E. Moragne, *The Neglected Thread: A Journal from the Calhoun Community* (Columbia, S.C.: 1951), p. 51.

2. J. C. to A. Burt, May 18, 1838, to J. E. Colhoun, May 23, 1838, to Anna Maria Calhoun Clemson, March 24, 1840, to Patrick Calhoun, September 13, 1840, to T. G. Clemson, December 23, 1840.

3. J. C. to J. E. Colhoun, February 16, 1834.

4. Logbooks covering six different cruises for James E. Colhoun can be found at Duke. His diary is at UNC, and typed extracts from his diary are in SCL. His knowledge of Indian culture is suggested by a letter to Professor Keating, September, 3, 1824, SCL. Upon meeting him for the first time, one careful observer wrote that she had met "the eccentric & wicked but highly gifted James Edward Colhoun." Moragne, p. 111. See also Lewis Perrin, "The Hermit of Millwood," *The Press and Banner and Abbeville Medium,* June 29, 1933.

5. Charles Cotesworth Pinckney, "John C. Calhoun from a Southern Standpoint," *Lippincott's Monthly Magazine* (July 1898), pp. 81–90.

6. Dave Sloan, *Fogy Days and Now* (Atlanta: 1891).

7. CP, vol. XVI, p. XXIX.

8. Anna Maria Calhoun Clemson to Patrick Calhoun, March 1, 1841, SCL.

9. Paul Hamilton Hayne to Susan B. Hayne, September 20, 1848, Duke.

10. Anna Maria Calhoun to Patrick Calhoun, September 23, 1838, SCL.

11. "Some Letters from John Christopher Schulz 1829–1833," *SCHM,* 1955, pp. 1–6.

12. Sloan.

13. G. W. Featherstonhaugh, *A Canoe Voyage up the Minay Sotor* (London: 1847), vol. II, p. 268.

14. J. G. Clinkscales, *On the Old Plantation* (Spartanburg, S.C.: 1916). R. F. W. Alston ms., July 28, 1847, CP Archives. R. B.

Rhett to Colonel John Stapleton, January 1841, UNC.

15. The visitor writing to the *New York Herald,* July 26, 1849, was Joseph Scoville, a devout Calhoun admirer. His detailed description of Fort Hill needs to be used with caution since it is intended to make Calhoun appear as the ideal planter surrounded by beautifully ordered acres and contented slaves. The physical descriptions about the plantation layout and the anecdotes about older slaves and the slave marriage are probably reasonably accurate.

16. Anna Maria Calhoun to Patrick Calhoun, August 18, 1838, James E. Colhoun to Maria Simkins, March 28, 1840, Anna Maria Calhoun Clemson to Patrick Calhoun, January 4, 1840, to Maria Simkins Colhoun, May 14, 1843, SCL.

17. Twelve Mile River Pendleton District. Proceedings of court including Andrew Pickens, held on plantation of John E. Colhoun trying certain Negroes, SCL.

18. Floride Calhoun to J. E. Calhoun, November 12, 1848, to My Dear Brother, December 24, 1837, to Margaret Calhoun, Dec. 3, 1845, SCL.

19. Floride Calhoun to Margaret Calhoun, February 8, 1842. Ernest Lander, *The Calhoun Family and Thomas Green Clemson* (Columbia, S.C.: 1983), p. 69.

20. Lucretia Ann Calhoun Townes de Graffenreid, ms., "A History of My Family," SCL. J. C. to C. J. Ingersoll, August 9, 1815, to S. E. Colhoun, August 27, 1831.

21. J. C. to John Ewing Colhoun, January 15, 1827.

22. J. C. to Maxcy, November 10, 1822. Clemson to J. C., February 21, 1841.

23. J. C. to J. E. Colhoun, November 30, 1830. J. C. to A. P. Calhoun, December 13, 1834.

24. J. C. to P. Noble, April 21, 1833. J. C. to Clemson, January 6, 1846.

25. Moragne, p. 112. Charles M. McGee and Ernest Lander, *A Rebel Came Home* (Columbia, S.C.: 1961), p. 93.

16. "If It Is Ever Intended, Now Is the Time," 1840–1844

1. Anna Maria Calhoun Clemson to Patrick Calhoun, December 6, 1840, SCL

2. J. C. to Maxcy, February 19, 1841, to Charles Yancey, January 4, 1841.

3. John Niven, *Martin Van Buren: The Romantic Age of American Politics* (New York: 1983), p. 478. J. C. to Anna Maria Calhoun Clemson, February 17, 1841.
4. J. C. to Maxcy, February 19, 1841.
5. CP, vol. XV, pp. 476, 524.
6. J. C. to Orestes Brownson, October 31, 1841.
7. My interpretation of Calhoun's intellectual and political development at this point has been influenced by Clyde Wilson's argument that Calhoun's thinking about the concurrent majority may have been shaped more by his reactions to Whiggery after 1840 than to Jackson's administration. See CP, vol. XV. pp. xiii–xv, xvi–xv, 539.
8. CP, vol. XV, pp. xvi–xxi.
9. J. C. to Anna Maria Calhoun Clemson, June 28, 1841. CP, vol. XV, p. 611.
10. Robert Seager, *And Tyler Too* (New York: 1963), p. 156.
11. J. C. to Maxcy, September 13, 1841.
12. F. W. Pickens to J. C., October 2, 1841. J. C. to J. E. Colhoun, November 1, 1841. J. C. to A. Burt, November 28, 1841.
13. J. C. to Wilson Lumpkin, December 26, 1841.
14. J. C. to Maxcy, December 26, 1841.
15. J. C. to G. S. Rice, September 13, 1841. CP, vol. XVI, p. 35.
16. See Benjamin Tappan's journal entry, December 26, 1841, for Calhoun's statement on the bank, LOC.
17. CP, vol. XVI, pp. 12, 110. Floride Calhoun to J. C., February 15, 1842.
18. F. W. Pickens to McDuffie, March 12, 1842, typed copy, CP Archives. CP, vol. XVI, p. 135.
19. CP, vol. XVI, p. 155. J. C. to Anna Maria Calhoun Clemson, March 20, 1842.
20. Niven, p. 490.
21. W. B. Campbell to Governor David Campbell, April 21, 1842, Duke. James Robertson to J. C., April 27, 1842.

22. CP, vol. XVI, pp. 295, 342.
23. J. C. to J. H. Hammond, September 24, 1842. F. W. Pickens to J. C., November 8, 1842. Hunter's analysis of the motivations behind Calhoun's repeated attempts to keep his name alive as a presidential candidate can be found in his ms. memoir of Calhoun in the Virginia State Archives at Richmond.
24. J. C. to Amos Kendall, February 26, 1843.
25. J. C. to H. St. George Tucker, March 31, 1843.
26. John Griffin to J. C., April 29, 1843.
27. R. B. Rhett to J. C., October 3, 1842. Scoville to J. C., January 15, 1843. Scoville to R. M. T. Hunter, January 1, 1843.
28. R. M. T. Hunter to J. C., May 23, 1843.
29. The call for a political trip for Calhoun was a more or less constant refrain from his out-of-state supporters in the spring of 1843. Calhoun's disdain for "a mere electioneering tour" is taken from his letter to an unidentified northern supporter in June 1843.
30. J. C. to R. M. T. Hunter, July 10, 1843.
31. Harper and Brothers told Maxcy that sales of Calhoun's *Life* were slow even at five cents a copy in lots of one thousand. The publishers thought it should be distributed gratis to make an impression. CP, vol. XVII, p. 183.
32. The Dixon Lewis account of Calhoun's encounter with Dorr is in the Hunter memoir of Calhoun, whose formal position on the Dorr issue was made in a letter to T. W. Smith, July 3, 1843. The letter was apparently not made public. CP, vol. XVII, p. 270.
33. CP, vol. XVII, p. 580. Alexander Jones to J. C., December 7, 1843.
34. A. B. Rhett to J. C., December 2, 1843.
35. CP, vol. XVII, p. 729.

17. *Secretary of State, 1844–1845*

1. J. C. to J. E. Colhoun, February 14, 1844. J. C. to Duff Green, February 10, 1844.
2. J. C. to James Seddon, February 16, 1844.
3. Patrick Calhoun to J. C., February 28, 1844. John Tyler to J. C., March 6, 1844.
4. J. C. to Mrs. Maxcy, March 9, 1844. Dixon Lewis to R. Crallé, March 19, 1844, LOC.
5. CP, vol. XIII, pp. 198, 498.
6. For a detailed account of the Calhoun, Upshur, Tyler strategy and its implemen-

tation, see Frederick Merk, *Slavery and the Annexation of Texas* (New York: 1972), pp. 3–82.
7. J. C. to W. S. Murphy, April 13, 1844.
8. CP, vol. XVIII, pp. 53, 273–78. See also Bruno Grujer, *Free Trade and Slavery: Calhoun's Defense of Southern Interests against British Interests* (Zurich: 1971), p. 153.
9. William J. Cooper, *The South and the Politics of Slavery* (Baton Rouge: 1978), p.

375, discusses the various reasons historians give for the Pakenham letter and concludes that Calhoun's primary purpose was to force the nation to "accept his conception of the relationship between slavery and the Union and of Southern rights." For a good discussion of the Texas abolitionist effort, see Charles Shiveley, "An Option for Freedom in Texas, 1840–1844," *Journal of Negro History* (April 1965), pp. 77–96.

10. Pakenham to J. C., April 19, 1844. J. C. to Pakenham, April 27, 1844. Pakenham to J. C., April 30, 1844. Grujer, pp. 177–86. J. C. to Francis Wharton, November 20, 1844, Jameson.

11. Merk, pp. 62–69. Gerald Grob, *Edward Jarvis and the Medical World of Nineteenth Century America* (Knoxville, Tenn.: 1978), p. 72. Merk, p. 86. CP, vol. XVIII, p. 395.

12. Robert M. Harrison to J. C., March 8, 1844. T. M. Rodney to J. C., March 28, 1844. Franklin Gage to J. C., April 1, 1844. William Gooch to J. C., April 1, 1844. Allen Hall to J. C., May 25, 1844. William Miles to J. C., May 27, 1844.

13. Samuel G. Morton to J. C., May 9, 1844. George Gliddon to J. C., May 17, 1844. Although Morton and Gliddon may not seem very scientific today, they were highly respected on both sides of the Atlantic in their own time, and it was entirely reasonable for Calhoun to feel they gave authority to his own position. See William Stanton, *The Leopard's Spots: Scientific Attitudes toward Race in America 1815–1859* (Chicago: 1960).

14. J. C. to R. M. T. Hunter, May 1, 1844, May 22, 1844.

15. J. C. to Francis Wharton, July 14, 1844.

16. R. M. T. Hunter, Memoir of Calhoun, ms, Virginia State Archives, Richmond, p. 258.

17. For a detailed description of what came to be known as the Bluffton Movement, see Charles Wiltse, *John C. Calhoun Sectionalist* (New York: 1951), pp. 187–98. Wiltse called what happened at Bluffton "the first overt act of separation between North and South." See also Clyde Wilson's more recent observations in CP, vol. XIX, p. xx. Calhoun would have agreed with Elmore, who wrote that despite the "fretful temper" of some of his friends over the tariff, Calhoun could still count on the solid support of the South Carolina legislature. Elmore to J. C., July 30, 1844.

18. CP, vol. XVIII, p. 644. J. C. to Clemson, May 28, 1844. John C. Calhoun, Jr., to James E. Calhoun, July 19, 1844.

19. Ernest Lander, Jr., *The Calhoun Family and Thomas Clemson* (Columbia, S.C.: 1983), p. 80.

20. Floride Calhoun to J. C., May 22, 1844, July 4, 1844.

21. J. C. to J. A. Stuart, October 21, 1844.

22. Robert Seager, *And Tyler Too* (New York: 1963), p. 246.

23. Merk, p. 101.

24. CP, vol. XVIX, pp. 568–78. Merk, pp. 121–25.

25. CP, vol. XVIV, p. 568. Merk, pp. 105–14.

26. Merk, p. 146.

27. *Works of John C. Calhoun* (New York: 1888), vol. V, pp. 458–61.

28. J. C. to J. R. Matthews, February 10, 1845, CP Archives. Wiltse, p. 219.

29. J. C. to Anna Maria Calhoun Clemson, March 11, 1845, Jameson. J. C. to R. M. T. Hunter, March 26, 1845, typed copy, CP Archives.

18. *The Peace Senator, 1845–1846*

1. On February 18 and 20, 1845, Calhoun spoke at length with his young friend from Philadelphia Francis Wharton, who understood him to say that he was leaving Washington for good this time. Jameson, p. 644.

2. J. C. to Clemson, April 25, 1845, June 23, 1845, Jameson.

3. Duff Green to J. C., June 1, 1845, Jameson. J. S. Barbour spoke for many of Calhoun's friends when he wrote, "Your retirement is ruin and annihilation to us." Barbour to J. C., June 26, 1845, Jameson. Calhoun's remarks on Oregon were made

in a letter to John Y. Mason, May 30, 1845, Jameson.

4. J. S. Barbour to J. C., May 21, 1845, Jameson. J. C. to J. H. Hammond, August 2, 1845, J. H. Hammond to J. C., August 18, 1845, Jameson.

5. J. C. to Clemson, September 18, 1845, Jameson.

6. F. W. Pickens to J. C., September 29, 1845, typed copy, CP Archives. John B. Edmunds, *Francis W. Pickens and the Politics of Destruction* (Chapel Hill, N.C.: 1986), p. 97.

7. James Gadsden to J. C., September 30,

1845, typed copy, CP Archives. Calhoun's hesitancy to go to Memphis was probably influenced by the rigors of the trip and by the possible political perils involved. In any event Gadsden felt obliged to write him several times to make sure he would attend the convention.

8. *Works*, vol. V, pp. 246–311.
9. J. C. to Clemson, December 13, 1845, Jameson. James T. McIntosh, ed., *Papers of Jefferson Davis* (Baton Rouge: 1974), vol. 2, p. 374.
10. December 22, 1845. Milo M. Quaile, ed., *Diary of James K. Polk*, (New York: 1970), For an authoritative treatment of the Oregon dispute which does justice to Calhoun's role in it, see Frederick Merk, *The Oregon Question* (Cambridge, Mass.: 1967).
11. R. Crallé to J. C., November 16, 1845. Thomas J. Green to J. C., November 1845. F. W. Pickens to J. C., December 20, 1845, typed copies, CP Archives.
12. Charles Sellers estimated that Calhoun could carry seven of thirty-two Democratic votes in the Senate, enough to kill or carry any administration proposal in a close vote. Sellers, *James K. Polk Continentalist* (Princeton, N.J.: 1966), p. 318.
13. Polk, January 10, 1846.
14. Fernando Wood to J. C., December 26, 1845, Jameson. Hammond to J. C., January 10, 1846, Crallé to J. C., February 15, 1846, Charles Anthony to J. C., February 17, 1846, typed copies, CP Archives.
15. *Works*, vol. IV, pp. 258–90.
16. J. C. to Anna Maria Calhoun Clemson, March 23, 1846, Jameson. Arnold Buffum to J. C., March 25, 1846, Elihu Burritt to J. C., April 2, 1846. Amos Lawrence to J. C., March 30, 1846, typed copies, CP Archives.
17. Merk, p. 383.

19. *"Mexico Is to Us the Forbidden Fruit,"* 1846–1848

1. J. C. to Clemson, July 30, 1846, Jameson.
2. J. C. to Clemson, May 28, 1846, Jameson.
3. J. C. to H. W. Conner, May 15, 1846, printed copy, CP Archives. J. C. to J. E. Colhoun, May 29, 1846, Jameson.
4. Milo M. Quarfe, ed., *Diary of James K. Polk*, (New York: 1970), April 18, 1846. South Carolina's enthusiasm for the war is detailed in Ernest Lander, *Reluctant Imperialists: Calhoun, the South Carolinians and the Mexican War* (Baton Rouge: 1980), pp. 1–24.
5. J. C. to J. E. Colhoun, September 15, 1846, Jameson. A. B. Creek to J. C., September 11, 1846, typed copy, CP Archives.
6. John C. Calhoun, Jr., to John Y. Mason, October 18, 1846. Mason to John C. Calhoun, Jr., November 2, 1846, J. E. Colhoun to J. C., typed copies, CP Archives.
7. For a discussion of the Calhoun-Pickens breach sympathetic to the latter, see John B. Edmunds, *Francis W. Pickens and the Politics of Destruction* (Chapel Hill, N.C.: 1986), pp. 97–106. Pickens made the mistake of thinking he could maintain a difference of opinion "in principle" with Calhoun over issues like Oregon, Mexico, and the political virtue of President Polk and still claim Calhoun's favor, but the latter assumed that his old friend's "affinity for Mr. Polk and Mr. Buchanan was greater than his attachment to me" and spoke darkly of Pickens's "badly regulated ambition." J. C. to J. E. Colhoun, July 2, 1846, Jameson. J. C. to J. E. Colhoun, August 8, 1846, typed copy, CP Archives.
8. J. C. to Clemson, November 6, 1846, typed copy, CP Archives. J. C. to Anna Maria Calhoun Clemson, December 27, 1846, Jameson.
9. Polk, December 19, 1846.
10. J. C. to Clemson, January 30, 1847, Jameson.
11. *Works*, vol. IV, pp. 303–28.
12. Lander, p. 66. *Works*, vol. IV, pp. 328–39.
13. Ibid., vol. IV, pp. 339–49.
14. Polk dismissed Calhoun's use of the slavery issue as no more than "a political hobby to keep himself before the public." *Diary*, April 12, 1847. *Works*, Vol. IV, p. 363. Robert Seager, *And Tyler Too* (New York: 1963), p. 324.
15. *Works*, vol. IV, pp. 382–96.
16. Duff Green to J. C., March 6, 1847, typed copy, CP Archives. Polk, April 6, 1847.
17. Hamilton to J. C., April 24, 1847, typed copy, CP Archives. J. C. to Clemson, May 6, 1847, Jameson. James Hammond, Diary, May 25, 1847, LOC. J. C. to Clemson, June 15, 1847, Jameson.

18. David M. Pletcher, *The Diplomacy of Annexation* (1973), p. 57. J. C. to Anna Maria Calhoun Clemson, December 26, 1847, Jameson.
19. Charles Wiltse, *John C. Calhoun Sectionalist* (New York: 1951), p. 325.

20. *Works*, vol. IV, pp. 396–425.
21. J. C. to A. P. Calhoun, February 23, 1848, Jameson.
22. J. C. to Clemson, March 7, 1848, Jameson. Dixon Lewis to R. Crallé, May 11, 1848, LOC.

20. *"Having Faithfully Done My Duty," 1848–1850*

1. J. C. to Duff Green, April 17, 1847, Jameson.
2. J. C. to Anna Maria Calhoun Clemson, November 21, 1846, Jameson.
3. J. C. to Anna Maria Calhoun Clemson, April 28, 1848, Jameson. See Charles Wiltse, *John C. Calhoun Sectionalist* (New York: 1951), pp. 322–44, for a perceptive discussion of Calhoun's state of mind at this time.
4. *Works*, vol. I, p. 8.
5. Ibid., p. 13ff.
6. Ibid., p. 28ff.
7. Ibid., p. 58.
8. Ibid., p. 66.
9. Ibid., p. 79.
10. Ibid., p. 90.
11. Ibid., vol. VI, p. vii.
12. Ibid., p. 181.
13. Ibid., pp. 393–406.
14. CP, vol. XI, p. 428.
15. Ibid., vol. IV, pp. 450–54.
16. Wiltse, pp. 341–51.
17. *Works*, vol. IV, pp. 508–11.
18. Ibid., pp. 516–22.
19. *Annual Report of the American Historical Society* (Washington: 1913), vol. II, p. 129. J. C. to Clemson, August 11, 1848, Jameson.
20. J. C. Nott to J. C., May 2, 1847, typed copy, CP Archives.
21. Wiltse, p. 378.
22. *Works*, vol. VI, p. 311.
23. *Annual Report . . .*, pp. 58, 139, 141. Alexander Stephens to John Crittendon, January 17, 1849, Duke. William Y. Thompson, *Robert Toombs of Georgia* (Baton Rouge: 1966), p. 53. J. C. to Anna Maria Calhoun Clemson, January 24, 1849, Jameson.
24. Howell Cobb to his wife, December 2 and 4, 1849, in *Annual Report.*
25. J. C. to Anna Maria Calhoun Clemson, June 15, 1849, Jameson.
26. Elbert B. Smith, *The Magnificent Missourian* (Columbia, Mo.: 1973) pp. 243–61. Wiltse, pp. 400–04.
27. J. C. to Clemson, February 6, 1850, to Hammond, February 16, 1850, Jameson.
28. J. C. to Anna Maria Calhoun Clemson, February 24, 1850, Jameson. Wiltse, p. 459.
29. *Works*, vol. IV, pp. 542–74.
30. Irving H. Bartlett, *Daniel Webster* (New York: 1978), pp. 246–69. J. C. to Clemson, March 10, 1850, Jameson.
31. J. C. to Anna Maria Calhoun Clemson, February 24, 1850, Jameson. J. C. to James Edward Calhoun, February 24, 1850, typed copy, CP Archives.
32. John Randolph Tucker, Memorandum, Washington, 1850, typed copy, CP Archives. Joseph Henry's remarks were noted in his diary probably the day after Calhoun's death. Photocopy, CP Archives.
33. *Pendleton Messenger*, April 12, 1850.
34. R. Crallé to J. C., typed copy, CP Archives. J. Scoville to Clemson, typed copy CP Archives. *Pendleton Messenger*, April 12, 1850.

Afterword

1. Philip Hone, *The Diary of Philip Hone* (New York: 1889), vol. II, pp. 886, 890.
2. "John C. Calhoun in His Personal, Moral and Intellectual Traits of Character," *New York Daily Post*, clipping, c. 1842, SCL.
3. Wendell P. Garrison and Francis J. Garrison, *William Lloyd Garrison* (New York: 1889), vol. III, p. 217. *Liberator* (March 22, 1850). Harriet Martineau, *Autobiography* (Boston: 1885), vol. I, p. 378.
4. Quoted in Thelma Jennings, *The Nashville Convention: Southern Movement for Unity 1848–1851* (Memphis: 1980), p. 53.
5. *The Death and Funeral Ceremonies of John Caldwell Calhoun* (Columbia, S.C.: 1850).
6. Patrick Calhoun to Floride Calhoun, April

31, 1850. Floride Calhoun to Anna Maria Calhoun Clemson, April 14, 1850, typed copies, CP Archives. *Pendleton Messenger,* April 12, 1850. Irving H. Bartlett, *Daniel Webster,* (New York: 1978), p. 291.

7. Sarah Maury, *The Statesmen of America* (Philadelphia: 1847), pp. 168–70.

8. J. C. to Sarah Maury, February 18, 1847, typed copy, CP Archives.

9. *Statue of Hon. John C. Calhoun Erected in Statuary Hall of the Capitol at Washington* (Washington: 1910), pp. 45, 15.

10. *Congressional Record,* March 18, 1982.

11. For a fuller exposition of Calhoun and the Founding Fathers, see Pauline Maier, "The Road Not Taken: Nullification, John C. Calhoun and the Revolutionary Tradition in South Carolina," *SCHM,* 1981, pp. 1–19, and Lacy K. Ford, "Calhoun, South Carolina and The Constitution," *SCHM,* 1988, p. 156.

12. J. C. to Andrew Jackson, March 7, 1821.

Index

Italicized page numbers refer to illustrations.